WEAPONS AND WARFARE

*Conventional Weapons
and their Roles in Battle*

BRASSEY'S DEFENCE PUBLISHERS
Editorial Advisory Board

Group Captain D. Bolton
Director, Royal United Services Institute for Defence Studies

Lieutenant General Sir Robin Carnegie KCB, OBE

Armande Cohen CBE
International Civil Servant and formerly with the
Assembly of Western European Union

Dr Christopher Coker
London School of Economics and Political Science

Professor L. D. Freedman
Department of War Studies, King's College, London

John Keegan
Defence Correspondent, *Daily Telegraph*

The Rt Hon Lord Mulley
former Secretary of State for Defence

Henry Stanhope
Foreign Policy Correspondent, *The Times*

John Terraine
Author

Brassey's Titles of Related Interest

Brassey's Air Power: Aircraft Weapons Systems and Technology Series

Air Power: An Overview of Roles, Vol. 1
R. A. Mason

Air-to-Ground Operations, Vol. 2
J. R. Walker

Brassey's Battlefield Weapon Systems and Technology Series,
12-Vol. set

Red God of War: Soviet Artillery and Rocket Forces
C. Bellamy

Brassey's Multilingual Military Dictionary

Race to the Swift: Thoughts on 21st-Century Warfare
R. Simpkin

Mine Warfare on Land
C. Sloan

Rusi/Brassey's Defence Yearbook
Rusi

WEAPONS AND WARFARE

Conventional Weapons and their Roles in Battle

Edited by

Major General K. Perkins CB, MBE, DFC

BRASSEY'S DEFENCE PUBLISHERS
(A member of the Pergamon Group)

London · Oxford · Washington · New York · Beijing
Frankfurt · São Paulo · Sydney · Tokyo · Toronto

U.K. (Editorial)	Brassey's Defence Publishers, 24 Gray's Inn Road, London WC1X 8HR
(Orders)	Brassey's Defence Publishers, Headington Hill Hall, Oxford OX3 0BW, England
U.S.A. (Editorial)	Pergamon-Brassey's International Defense Publishers, 8000 Westpark Drive, Fourth Floor, McLean, Virginia 22102, U.S.A.
(Orders)	Pergamon Press, Maxwell House, Fairview Park, Elmsford, New York 10523, U.S.A.
PEOPLE'S REPUBLIC OF CHINA	Pergamon Press, Room 4037, Qianmen Hotel, Beijing, People's Republic of China
FEDERAL REPUBLIC OF GERMANY	Pergamon Press, Hammerweg 6, D-6242 Kronberg, Federal Republic of Germany
BRAZIL	Pergamon Editora, Rua Eça de Queiros, 346, CEP 04011, Paraiso, São Paulo, Brazil
AUSTRALIA	Pergamon-Brassey's Defence Publishers, P.O. Box 544, Potts Point, N.S.W. 2011, Australia
JAPAN	Pergamon Press, 8th Floor, Matsuoka Central Building 1-7-1 Nishishinjuku, Shinjuku-ku, Tokyo 160, Japan
CANADA	Pergamon Press Canada, Suite No. 271, 253 College Street, Toronto, Ontario, Canada M5T 1R5

Copyright © 1987 Brassey's Defence Publishers Ltd.

All Rights Reserved. No part of this publication may be reproduced, stored in a retrieval system or transmitted in any form or by any means: electronic, electrostatic, magnetic tape, mechanical, photocopying, recording or otherwise, without permission in writing from the publishers.

First edition 1987

Library of Congress Cataloging-in-Publication Data
Weapons and warfare.
Includes index.
1. Weapons systems.   2. Warfare, Conventional.
I. Perkins, K. (Ken)
UF500.W43   1987   355.8'2   87-9332

British Library Cataloguing in Publication Data
Weapons and warfare: conventional weapons
and their roles in battle.
1. Arms and armor
I. Perkins, K.
623.4   U815

ISBN 0-08-033615-9

Printed in Great Britain

Contents

List of Plates	VII
List of Figures	IX
The Authors	XIII
Preface	XVII

1. Air-to-Surface Weapons   1
Air Vice Marshal J R Walker cbe afc raf

2. Air-to-Air Weapons   57
Air Vice Marshal J R Walker cbe afc raf

3. Fixed Wing Aircraft   83
Air Vice Marshal H A Merriman cb cbe afc raf

4. Helicopters   98
Brigadier General Samuel G Cockerham

5. Land Based Air Defence   111
R F Jackson

6. Shipborne Air Defence   132
Captain W R Canning dso rn

7. Mortars, Artillery and Rocket Systems   147
B A Hill bsc MPhil

8. Tank Warfare: The Last Decades of the Dinosaurs   165
Brigadier R E Simpkin obe mc

9.	Small Arms	193
	DR EDWARD C EZELL MA PhD	
10.	Anti-submarine and Mine Warfare	207
	CAPTAIN B R LONGWORTH RN AND MAJOR GENERAL K PERKINS CB MBE DFC	
11.	Electronic Warfare: Command, Control, Communications and Intelligence	231
	AIR VICE MARSHAL P R MALLORIE CB AFC RAF	
12.	Cost Affordable Defence	269
	MAJOR GENERAL K PERKINS CB MBE DFC	

List of Plates

PLATE 1.1	BL755	22
PLATE 1.2	JP233	24
PLATE 1.3	Paveway	31
PLATE 1.4	Sea Eagle	40
PLATE 1.5	Alarm	43
PLATE 2.1	Skyflash	70
PLATE 2.2	Magic 2	72
PLATE 2.3	Skyflash	79
PLATE 3.1	Harrier	87
PLATE 3.2	Modern Conventional Cockpit	92
PLATE 3.3	Advanced Technology Cockpit	93
PLATE 3.4	The EAP	95
PLATE 4.1	AH-64 Apache Hellfire Missile	99
PLATE 4.2	OH 58D Scout	104
PLATE 4.3	UH-60A Black Hawk lifting two 105 mm Howitzers	106
PLATE 4.4	Stream of UH-60A Black Hawk engaged in troop lifting	106
PLATE 4.5	UH-60A Black Hawk in attack role	107
PLATE 5.1	SA-6 Gainful	113
PLATE 5.2	ZSU-23-4	115
PLATE 5.3	Tracked Rapier	116
PLATE 5.4	Patriot	118
PLATE 6.1	HMS *Sheffield* hit by Exocet	133
PLATE 6.2	Decoy Systems	139
PLATE 6.3	Sea Wolf	140
PLATE 6.4	Goalkeeper	142
PLATE 7.1	Merlin	151
PLATE 7.2	AS90	154

List of Plates

PLATE 7.3	FH70	156
PLATE 7.4	Multi-launch rocket system	159
PLATE 8.1	The Soviet T34/76.	166
PLATE 8.2	Leopard 2	167
PLATE 8.3	The Swedish UDES concept study for a future main battle tank has come to represent the 'Topless Tank' concept	171
PLATE 8.4	The Soviet T64	172
PLATE 8.5	The Israeli Merkava Mk 2	173
PLATE 8.6	Blazer reactive armour on an Israeli Centurion	184
PLATE 9.1	Avtomat Kalashnikova	196
PLATE 9.2	The ground version of the Soviet 12.7 × 108 mm NSV heavy machine gun	198
PLATE 9.3	The 5.56 × 45 mm NATO calibre Colt M16A2 rifle with the 40 mm M203 grenade launcher.	199
PLATE 9.4	An early version of the Heckler and Koch 4.92 mm Gewehr 11	200
PLATE 10.1	Tigerfish Torpedo	208
PLATE 10.2	Submarine showing a bow-mounted sonar	212
PLATE 10.3	Sea King Helicopter with sonar dome	216
PLATE 10.4	Lynx Helicopter with Stingray anti-submarine torpedo	224
PLATE 10.5	Limpet Mine	229
PLATE 11.1	The Fog of War	233
PLATE 11.2	Large Troposcatter dishes, Hong Kong	252
PLATE 11.3	Portable Troposcatter Aerial	252
PLATE 11.4	AWACS	254
PLATE 11.5	Satellite Reconnaissance	255

List of Figures

(Chapter 1)
Fig 1.1	Varying radius of turn at 4 'g' with change of speed.	8
Fig 1.2	Height loss in a dive recovery.	9
Fig 1.3	Minimum fire range.	10
Fig 1.4	The effect of trajectory on range estimation tolerance.	11
Fig 1.4a	Straight line trajectory similar to laser – extremely tolerant to range error.	11
Fig 1.4b	Slightly curved trajectory of a high velocity weapon – tolerant to some range error.	11
Fig 1.4c	Highly curved trajectory of a low velocity weapon – intolerant to range error.	11
Fig 1.5a	Tendency for projectiles entering a 'plastic' environment to curve towards the surface.	12
Fig 1.5b	Against shipping the effect could be used to advantage to obtain strikes in the most vulnerable part below the water-line.	12
Fig 1.6	Hollow charge weapons.	13
Fig 1.6a	Typical hollow charge head.	13
Fig 1.6b	Jet forming but yet to concentrate.	13
Fig 1.6c	Energy concentrated into small cross-section of high velocity.	13
Fig 1.7	Explosion by ERA prevents proper development of the high energy jet.	14
Fig 1.8	Bomb shapes for good ballistics and low-drag.	17
Fig 1.9a	Toss attack – The weapon is released under 'g'.	19
Fig 1.9b	Loft attack – The weapon is released in a climb but not under a 'g' pull.	19
Fig 1.10	Retarder mechanisms.	21
Fig 1.11	The conflicting P_{HIT} and P_{KILL} arguments for higher sub-munition angles.	23
Fig 1.12a	Laser Guided Bomb – Guidance Law effect on energy.	28
Fig 1.12b	'Short' bombs can result from low angle approaches using 'bang-bang' control laws.	28

List of Figures

Fig 1.13a	High Toss – LGB approaches high and picks up target returns late.	29
Fig 1.13b	Low Toss – LGB approaches low. When target is acquired, bomb tends to approach directly, losing energy and can impact short.	29
Fig 1.14	Footprint of LGB seeker head showing tendency to seek long at shallow angles.	30
Fig 1.15a	Flat, reflective target giving comprehensive signals over a wide azimuth.	31
Fig 1.15b	Targets with large vertical extent can shield the LGB from signals.	31
Fig 1.16	The Walleye Series.	32
Fig 1.17	The AGM-65 Maverick family.	35
Fig 1.18	Target area of uncertainty is a function of missile time of flight and target speed.	39
Fig 1.19	Area of uncertainty determines missile search requirement.	39
Fig 1.20	The major US ARM.	42
Fig 1.21	Defence against Stand-off missiles over a restricted arc.	46
Fig 1.22	Basic Combat Air Patrol (CAP) mathematics.	47
Fig 1.23	The radius to be covered for an intercept at 300 nm.	47
Fig 1.24	The mathematics of long distance combat on patrol.	48
Fig 1.25	Variation of aircraft required according to endurance.	50
Fig 1.26	Probability of obtaining a kill against a cruise missile target.	51

(Chapter 2)

Fig 2.1	Radiated electromagnetic energy of a body at varying temperatures.	58
Fig 2.2	IR transmission – a 1 μm path at sea level.	59
Fig 2.3	The effect of a variety of individual high probabilities on overall probability of success.	60
Fig 2.4	Typical missile firing envelope against a non-manoeuvring target.	62
Fig 2.5	Target manoeuvre negating a missile acquisition.	63
Fig 2.6	Turn Radius at low level.	63
Fig 2.7	Missile flight paths at different k-factors.	64
Fig 2.8	Skewed envelope against a manoeuvring target.	65
Fig 2.8a	Missile closure speeds	65
Fig 2.9a	All-aspect missile envelope.	67
Fig 2.9b	All-aspect envelope against a very high speed target.	67
Fig 2.9c	Degraded envelope against a very high speed target.	67
Fig 2.10	Homing methods.	69
Fig 2.10a	Passive homing.	69

List of Figures

FIG 2.10b	Semi-active homing.	69
FIG 2.10c	Active Homing.	69
FIG 2.11	Typical AAM missile profile.	74
FIG 2.12a	BVR missile engagement – missile just falls short.	75
FIG 2.12b	BVR missile engagement – missile range sufficient due to increased fighter speed.	75
FIG 2.13	BVR engagement showing effect of aircraft performance.	76
FIG 2.14	BVR engagement showing effect of missile range and speed enhancement.	77

(Chapter 3)

FIG 3.1	Air Defence Mission.	90
FIG 3.2	Interdiction Mission.	91

(Chapter 4)

FIG 4.1	UH-1 Huey. (*Bell Helicopters*)	100

(Chapter 5)

FIG 5.1	Command guidance.	122
FIG 5.2	Command to line of sight guidance.	123
FIG 5.3	Beam riding guidance.	125
FIG 5.4	Homing guidance.	127

(Chapter 6)

FIG 6.1	The threat.	134
FIG 6.2	Conceptual air defence – plan view.	136
FIG 6.3	Examples of shipborne area defence missiles.	138
FIG 6.4	Examples of shipborne local area and point defence missile systems.	138
FIG 6.5	Examples of close-in weapons systems.	141

(Chapter 7)

FIG 7.1	Field artillery fire control system. Developed by British Aerospace and Zelleeger Uster Telecommunications.	152

(Chapter 8)

FIG 8.1	Generalised weight pie of a conventional turreted tank.	175
FIG 8.2	The anti-armour threat envelope (a) horizontal – (i) classical, (ii) helicopters, aimable mines etc, (iii) top attack, (iv) combined; (b) vertical.	176
FIG 8.3	Generalised approximate distribution of the surface of a conventional tank's armoured envelope between the various aspects.	177

List of Plates

Fig 8.4	Mode of attack – (a) simple hollow charge (HEAT), (b) complex hollow charge, (c) explosively formed projective (EFP), (d) sub-calibre penetrators – (i) spin-stabilised (APDS), (ii) fin-stabilised (APFSDS).	178
Fig 8.5	Elements of armoured vehicle survivability, highlighting ballistic protection.	182
Fig 8.6	Height and exposure probability (key heights based on Chieftain), with non-tactical driving (broken line) and with good tactical handling (full line, estimated).	186
Fig 8.7	Concept schematic of an externally mounted gun with a commander's 'nacelle'.	187

(Chapter 9)

Fig 9.1	A schematic view of the Heckler and Koch 4.92 mm Gewehr 11 which illustrates the unique 'cylinder' breech mechanism designed to shoot a caseless cartridge.	202

(Chapter 10)

Fig 10.1	Sound propagation.	210
Fig 10.2	Sound propagation.	210
Fig 10.3	Towed Array	213
Fig 10.4	Acoustic minesweeping system. The Osbourne system now in service with the Royal Navy.	228

(Chapter 11)

Fig 11.1	Command and control able to exploit full capacity of forces to implement strategy.	235
Fig 11.2	Basis of command and control system.	236
Fig 11.3	The elements of a command and control system.	237
Fig 11.4	Diagram showing Headquarters processes and their interaction.	242
Fig 11.5	Command and control equipment.	243
Fig 11.6	Sensors, sensor targets and their respective vulnerabilities.	247
Fig 11.7	Air defence communications. A typical troposcatter layout.	250
Fig 11.8	Microwave. An illustration of three basic systems.	251
Fig 11.9	Command and control. Implications of electronic warfare.	261
Fig 11.10	Weapons, sensors and the command system.	264

Comprehensive and versatile response to defence needs in the air, on land, at sea and under the sea.

1. Hawk 2-seat trainer/ground attack aircraft
2. Goshawk jet trainer for US Navy
3. Tornado all-weather strike aircraft
4. Sea Harrier carrier-borne V/STOL combat aircraft
5. Harrier II advanced V/STOL combat aircraft
6. Jaguar supersonic tactical strike aircraft
7. ALARM (Air-Launched Anti-Radar Missile)
8. Swingfire long-range anti-armour weapon
9. Sea Eagle long-range sea-skimming anti-ship missile
10. Sea Skua lightweight anti-ship missile
11. Sea Urchin naval ground mine
12. Tracked Rapier mobile low-level air defence system
13. Rapier area low-level air defence system
14. Sky Flash all-weather air-to-air missile
15. Sea Dart shipborne area-defence missile
16. Seawolf shipborne anti-missile system
17. ASRAAM (Advanced Short-Range Air-to-Air Missile)
18. Hawk 200 single-seat fighter
19. Tornado Air Defence Variant
20. EFA (proposed European Fighter Aircraft)
21. EAP (Experimental Aircraft Programme)
22. Skynet military communications satellite

BRITISH AEROSPACE
...up where we belong

British Aerospace plc, 11 Strand, London.

The Authors

AIR VICE MARSHAL H A MERRIMAN CB CBE AFC FRAeS RAF

Air Vice Marshal John Walker has had very wide experience of fighter operations and in the field of tactical development of ground attack weapons and systems. He served an exchange appointment with the United States Air Force Tactical Air Command in Texas from 1966–69.

After playing a leading role in the introduction of the Jaguar, he commanded first at RAF Lossiemouth and then RAF Bruggen in Germany, where he was subsequently Group Captain Offensive Operations. As an Air Commodore he was responsible for the Central Tactics and Trials Organisation before becoming Director of Forward Policy in the Ministry of Defence.

He is now serving as Senior Air Staff Officer, Royal Air Force Strike Command with the NATO appointment of Deputy Chief of Staff (Operations and Intelligence) United Kingdom Air Forces.

AIR VICE MARSHAL H A MERRIMAN CB CBE AFC FRA RAFeS

Air Vice Marshal Merriman qualified as a test pilot at the Empire Test Pilots' School in 1957 and spent many years at the Aeroplane and Armament Experimental Establishment, Boscombe Down conducting acceptance flight tests on most of the fast jet combat aircraft to enter service with the Royal Air Force, United States Air Force, French Air Force and NATO Air Forces between 1958 and 1977. He also served at the Central Fighter Establishment as the fighter tactics specialist and finally at the Ministry of Defence as Director of Aircraft Requirements. He is now a Consultant to a number of British companies in the military aerospace industry.

BRIGADIER GENERAL SAMUEL G COCKERHAM US Army

Brigadier General Samuel Cockerham had extensive operational experience of the use of helicopters in Vietnam where he was responsible for most of the United States Army's aviation during his tour there. He was the first Manager of the Advanced Attack Helicopter Program (AH-64A) and is now Technical Advisor to the Assistant Secretary of the Army (Research, Development, Aquisition) for the light helicopter Family (LHX).

The Authors

R F JACKSON

R F Jackson, Executive Director New Projects in the Army Weapons Division of British Aerospace, has been concerned with surface to air weapon systems for thirty years. His experience covers system and design work on projects such as Thunderbird and Rapier. He is currently involved in conceptual studies on systems appropriate for the next century.

CAPTAIN W R CANNING DSO RN

Captain Bill Canning served in the Royal Navy from 1949–1983. His later sea commands included the destroyers *Cambrian* and *Norfolk* and the frigate *Broadsword* (embracing the 1982 Falklands campaign). He joined British Aerospace in 1983.

B A HILL BSC MPhil

Ben Hill is the Head of the Department of Military Technology and, for several years, has been the Senior Lecturer on Conventional Weapon Systems at the Royal Military Academy, Sandhurst.

DR EDWARD EZELL MA PHD

Edward Ezell is presently the Supervisory Curator of the Division of Armed Forces History of the Smithsonian Institution's National Museum of American History. His responsibilities include management of the National Firearms Collection, which encompasses the entire historical evolution of infantry weapons below 20 mm. He is the editor of the last two editions of *Small Arms of the World* (1977 and 1983), the author of several histories of small arms technology and is a frequent contributor to defence journals.

BRIGADIER RICHARD SIMPKIN OBE MC

Richard Simpkin was a tank soldier for thirty years. After war service in the Middle East, he served widely at regimental duty and on the staff. As an Instructor at the Army Staff College and the Royal Military College of Science, where he was later to become Military Director of Studies (Warfare and Vehicles), and as head of the Royal Armoured Corps' equipment branch, he played an important role in the development of the British Army's mechanised equipment policy.

A brilliant linguist, he retired in 1970 to establish a second career as a consultant in technical translation. At this time he also began to write a series of important military books and to lecture widely on the nature and future of mechanised warfare. His studies on Soviet tactical philosophy are of particular importance, as is his look into the next century – "Race to the Swift".

The Authors

Through his death in November 1986, the West lost one of its most forward looking military thinkers and authors.

CAPTAIN B R LONGWORTH RN

Captain B R Longworth served for over 25 years as an Underwater Specialist, including over five years in the Naval Staff, serving as Director of Naval Staff College prior to leaving the Service. Currently he is the Future Business Director of Marconi Underwater Systems Limited.

AIR VICE MARSHAL P R MALLORIE CB AFC RAF

Air Vice Marshal Paul Mallorie is a Military Command and Control Systems Consultant of international repute. After wide experience as a Flying Instructor, at Squadron duty and on the staff in many parts of the world, he became the United Kingdom Military Advisers' Representative to the South East Asia Treaty Organisation in 1963. A graduate of the Imperial Defence College, he was Assistant Chief of Staff (Information Systems) at SHAPE from 1976–79. Retiring from the Royal Air Force in 1980, he was a Research Fellow at NATO in the field of Command and Control Systems in 1981–82.

MAJOR GENERAL K PERKINS CB MBE DFC

Major General Perkins is widely experienced in the use of forces on land, sea and in the air. Commissioned into the Royal Artillery, he subsequently flew as a pilot during the Korean War and Malayan Emergency, taught at the Staff College, and commanded an air-portable Artillery Regiment and an amphibious Infantry Brigade. As Commander of the Sultan of Oman's Armed Forces with British, Jordanian and Iranian Forces also under command, he successfully concluded operations against communist guerillas in Southern Arabia. He then became Assistant Chief of Defence Staff with responsibility for Defence Crisis Management in Whitehall after which he directed British Military Assistance worldwide. He retired from the services to join British Aerospace in 1982.

Preface

Keeping abreast of developments in defence, let along understanding the implications, is increasingly difficult, given the bewildering range of technical options made possible by modern science. Moreover, choice of appropriate technology demands a grasp of strategic and tactical requirements and an understanding of the varying influences of scientists, engineers and users. It is essential, also, to recognise, at least in broad terms, the relationship between technological advance and practical improvement in actual systems. Technological progress results from innovative thinking, occurs at random and is constrained neither by international boundaries nor official perceptions. When this activity results in a significant advance which is coincident with a specific requirement, a new concept becomes possible. It will usually have tri-service application.

Any such new concept is rarely viable without the refinement of existing technology, the need for which acts as a stimulus to further ideas. The revolutionary part of this process means that technological progress and practical improvements are out of phase with one another so that enhanced capability becomes available some time after the technological progress which has led to the new concept. Recognition of this inevitable time lag is important. Where an operational need results in equipment being pressed into service earlier than is entirely comfortable from a technological viewpoint, the risks need careful assessment. Given sufficient development time, technology offers simultaneously the prospects of improved performance, lower through-life costs and greater reliability.

Just as correct decisions on technology require an understanding of strategic and technical requirements, so strategic and technical choices are influenced by the practical implications of technology. No longer can the user leave technology solely to the experts.

With so many complications, there is a need to stand back in order that a multitude of detail does not obscure the general trend. There is also a need to enlist the opinions of experts, their own views free from official constraints. This book fulfils these requirements. It is written by a number of eminent authorities, some still serving officers, each expressing a personal view rather than that of his official position. It will provide the professional strategist with food for thought. It will give the scientist and technical expert a readily accessible view across fields other than his own and it will enable the layman to make sense of an extremely complicated subject.

KEN PERKINS

Introducing Chapter 1

THE air is a ubiquitous element in all forms of war, exercising significant, and often dominating, influence at all levels of operations on land and sea. The ability of air forces to strike rapidly at long distances and to switch their attention over wide areas enables governments at home and commanders in the field to exercise an economy of force and concentration of action less characteristic of naval and land forces. Of course, no one element can triumph on its own; success depends upon co-operation between land, sea and air but the wide application of the latter makes it a suitable starting point for a study on weapons and warfare. Because it is the weapons, rather than the platforms from which they are fired, which vastly increase the scope of air force intervention, we deal with the weapons first, a frightening array. The author, drawing on his wide experience, takes us through the intricacies of weapon design and out over the battlefield on a variety of air-to-ground missions.

1

Air-to-Surface Weapons

AIR VICE MARSHAL J R WALKER CBE AFC RAF

THE first bomb was dropped from an aircraft by Lieutenant Gulio Garotti piloting an Etrieb Taube during the Italian–Turkish war in Libya on 1 November 1911. Later the Italian press published a private letter from a Guiseppe Rossi which told of his experience on an early bombing raid. Although the target was only 30 kilometres distant, he encountered fire en-route and it was soon so heavy that "*I almost abandoned our scheme*". Arriving over his target, a group of Turkish tents, the bomb was thrown from the open cockpit and Rossi paused to observe the effect. "Instantly an enormous cloud of dust whirled upward, while frightened camels and horses ran madly in all directions. It was a wonderful sight!" But then he was hit by fire which he modestly describes as heavy enough to sober even a braver man than himself. His rear crew member was hit, his motor stopped at one point and his wooden propeller was partly shattered. The vulnerability of the fragile aircraft was not lost on the *Scientific American* which, in its edition of 20 April 1920, cautioned that the vulnerable parts of the aircraft, the men, fuel tanks and propellers, should be provided with some form of protection.

Although it could be argued that this early tale is little more than an historical anecdote and that technology has moved so rapidly over the intervening years that there is little to be learned from the past, there is nonetheless a surprising similarity between the principles which emerged from those early raids and those which govern air operations today. The first and foremost is that the combat aircraft rarely, if ever, achieves the military purpose in itself; it is the weapon which does the job. Then there is the fragility of aircraft which, despite being a far cry from the early string-bags and now weighing many tons, are stressed to take high 'g' loadings and supersonic airflows, can still be severely damaged by impact with a bird. Indeed, it is not unusual for a collision with a large seagull to put an aircraft into the repair sheds for months. Fragility is relative, and aircraft remain fragile. Attrition on the way to, or on return from, the target also remains a problem. No weapon will have effect unless it arrives at the target and, even if it does, if the cost of attrition becomes too high, the commander may be forced to withdraw from his campaign on economic as much as military grounds. As the weapon itself increasingly influences the attrition picture, it becomes an important factor in the overall efficacy of air power.

That it is the weapon that achieves the task has become far more widely realised than in the past. Then weapons were the poor relations in the argument for funds and resources, probably because of the cost relationships. The change in emphasis in such relationships could explain the growing interest in weapons. A modern combat aircraft is a combination of an airframe, an engine, a sighting system, and the weapon itself. In the thirties the cost profile of a Spitfire-type aircraft would have shown the bulk of the money being spent on the airframe and the engine. The sighting system at that time was little more than a ring and bead and the guns were modifications of standard, even old-fashioned, equipment. Certainly 0.303 inch rounds did not weigh heavily on the budget.

While the trend to a higher 'avionic' content became apparent during the Second World War, with the introduction of reflector sights, more complex bombing sights and advanced navigation systems such as H2S, it was only after the war, when the radar equipped fighters and more advanced bombers appeared, that the cost profile of military aircraft started to change from virtually 50%/50% airframe/engine to something like 33%/33%/33% airframe/engine/avionics. Today these proportions can be skewed even further towards the avionic element in specialist aircraft like the TR-1, the E-3A AWACS and the EF-111. Here avionics may account for well over half the total cost of the aircraft.

More recently still, however, the fourth element in the cost profile, the weapon, has started to find its way into the total balance as the new, smarter weapons arrive in inventories – but at considerable cost. The JP-233 cratering and airfield denial weapon costs are in the order of £0.5 million. As the pilot of a Tornado releases his standard load of two weapons, he spends £1 million. The fighter pilot who takes off with four AMRAAM and four AIM 9L Sidewinders takes into the air a minimum of £1.5 million worth of weaponry. And the B-52 crew who fly with twenty AGM-86B Air Launch Cruise Missiles (ALCM) has a weapon load probably worth more than the airframe/engine combination in total. Weapons have arrived on the scene in a big way – technologically and financially.

The field of air-to-ground weapons is now very wide and any discussion needs to be structured to avoid confusion. The weapons or groups of weapons need to be typed and then examined for their individual worth, looking for both their advantages and disadvantages. Like the aircraft itself, there is as much a lack of the multi-purpose wonder weapon as there is of the multi-purpose wonder aircraft; most weapons, like most aircraft, are either highly specific and specialised for one narrow purpose or, alternatively, are heavily compromised in the search for greater flexibility.

Dumb Weapons

Dumb and *smart*, in the context of weapons, is merely a convenient shorthand for those weapons which on the one hand are not guided once released from the aircraft and, on the other, those which, to some extent or the other, influence their own flight path. The aircraft cannon-shell, as it leaves the barrel of the gun, follows only the laws of physics therefore and, notwithstanding that the shot may have been sighted by a most advanced and highly sophisticated system within the aircraft, remains 'dumb' through the time of its flight. The same applies equally to conventional unguided rockets and to bombs, regardless of their type; they may be sighted by clever systems but once fired they obey only the laws of ballistics.

Very high accuracies can be achieved by dumb weapons but they are highly dependent upon the effectiveness of the aiming system and the results are often greatly influenced by the skill of the pilot or crew. Because they are unguided following release, accuracy can be greatly influenced by environmental effects during the time of free flight, such as the wind velocity, and by unpredicted target movement. In general, the accuracy of dumb weaponry is very dependent upon time of flight; the longer the time of flight the greater the detriment to accuracy. To take an extreme case, a laser *weapon* could not be guided in flight but once laid on the target the time of flight of the beam, travelling at the speed of light, is such that the error would be negligible.

Guns

The designer of aircraft guns has a difficulty in seeking a compromise between the conflicting requirements of guns for air-to-air use and those for air-to-ground use. For air-to-ground operations, a very heavy weight of destructive power requires to be concentrated on the target and a heavy calibre weapon would tend to be the designer's choice. In terms of weight of explosive filling, the relationship is governed by volume and therefore quite small increases in weapon calibre can result in large increases in the throw weight of filling. Unfortunately, the larger the calibre of the round, the greater the propellant power needed to obtain a given muzzle velocity. Hence, heavy calibre weapons do tend to be large and heavy.

In the air-to-air case, the designer's problem is different. In weapon terms, the aircraft target is a *soft* target. When hit it is already experiencing the stresses of flight loads which, in a combat situation can already be close to the structural limit of the aircraft. The target also has within itself the seeds of its own destruction with high fuel fractions common to most combat types and turbine engines operating at tens of thousands of RPM requiring little more than an out of balance force to turn them into destructive

Weapons and Warfare

'bombs'. In modern aircraft, particularly at high level, a minor hit, even from small fragmentation, can cause the loss of canopy transparencies or decompression of the crew compartment both of which could render the machine impotent in combat. An even more modern factor is the almost total reliance upon electronic systems. Even minor damage to computers or data transfer systems can cause weapon release circuits to fail or sighting methods to prove ineffective.

Consequently, the air-to-air designer has a soft vulnerable target and does not need a heavy charge in his shell. His problem rests upon the elusiveness of his target, and even with the most modern sighting systems a successful air-to-air guns *kill* is obtained only by skill and perseverance against even a moderately competent opponent. When a shot is possible therefore the air-to-air designer requires the maximum number of shells possible, and at as high a muzzle velocity as possible, to achieve the hit he requires. This points to the need for a smaller calibre gun with a high rate of fire to ensure high burst density and a long open fire range.

Real life being what it is, most solutions are compromises although, within those compromises, there will be a move towards what is seen as the primary role of the aircraft. The F-15 and F-16, built as specialist air superiority aircraft, both utilise the 20 mm M-61 multi-barrel gun while the equally specialist ground-attack A-10A Thunderbolt II is fitted with the GAU-8/A 30 mm cannon. The Panavia Tornado, conceived as the Multi-Role-Combat-Aircraft fits 27 mm armament demonstrating the dilemma of the *multi-role* aircraft designer.

Multi-barrel aircraft guns operating on the Gatling principle have to some extent made the compromise between air-to-air and air-to-ground easier to achieve because smaller calibres are possible while still obtaining high charge weights on target through high rates of fire. A modern 20 mm aircraft may fire at anything up to 6,000 rounds per minute whereas older generation heavier calibre weapons may have been firing at only 1,200 rounds per minute. Even then comparisons must be made with care for the modern aircraft, fitted with a single multi-barrel 20 mm weapon firing at 6,000 RPM, while both effective and impressive, scarcely matches the charge weight on target of the Hunter of the 1950s. This aircraft mounted four 30 mm Aden cannon, all producing 1,200 RPM each. Those who have witnessed the Hunter firing its four cannon with HE rounds against a ground target are unlikely to have remained unimpressed.

In the past there have been some interesting approaches to the compromise problem. The Mig-15, Mig-17 and early marks of the Mig-19 had mixed gun armament comprising one 37 mm and two 23 mm cannon. This was a rather awkward arrangement because both weapons had different ballistic characteristics and the sighting problems were magnified; it is probable, for example, that the trajectories intersected at only one point within the normal firing bracket – they could only possibly have crossed at two points.

Air-to-Surface Weapons

In attempting to achieve both heavy calibre, high rate of fire and high muzzle velocity, the GAU-8/A gun on the A-10A developed into an impressive piece of machinery. Originally, the aircraft was designed for the gun to be its primary air-to-ground armament and so was effectively designed around the gun. This is a 30 mm multi-barrel weapon working on the Gatling principle. It has a variable fire rate and projects a heavy round of depleted uranium to obtain a kinetic energy kill against battlefield armour. The high muzzle velocity is obtained by *coke-bottling* the round, that is, while retaining the 30 mm calibre of the projectile, a much greater diameter is used for the propellant case to allow greater propellant charges to be employed. In consequence, the total round is very much larger than the older and more conventional 30 mm round and, as the A-10A carries 1,350 rounds, the size of the gun, plus its feed mechanism, equates to that of a Volkswagen Beetle. In order to feed the barrels of the gun with so heavy a round at firing rates which vary, the system is operated hydraulically.

An operational problem to the fore in the minds of attack pilots is that of ricochet. The need to avoid self-damage from the weapons released is common to a variety of munitions but is more problematical with forward-firing weapons because of the unpredictability of the ricochet. This is exacerbated by the higher muzzle velocities now common which are themselves designed to increase the energy at the target. In the case of weapons like the GAU-8/A, it is this high kinetic energy which is in itself the destructive mechanism. When the round ricochets, be it off the armour of a tank or off stones on rocky subsoil, it can travel very great distances while still retaining high energy levels. These are quite sufficient to do mortal damage to an aircraft. The pattern of ricochet is so unpredictable that rounds have been recorded regularly travelling at ninety degrees to the firing path. Occasionally, perhaps caused by a double ricochet off a complex target shape such as a tank, they can end up heading back towards the aircraft.

The operational effects of this can be severe, causing cease fire ranges to be opened considerably to allow the aircraft more opportunity to stay clear of the ricochet. In any forward-firing attack, the aircraft is following the rounds in to the target. Consequently, the combination of high speed attacks, unmanoeuvrable aircraft, high muzzle velocities and solid *kinetic-energy* shot can, in combination, demand a cease fire range beyond that which allows reasonably accurate attacks, notwithstanding the better, more advanced, sighting systems available today.

A major factor in the determination of the cease fire range is the probability of damage which is considered acceptable. While there is any possibility of ricochet, and even when firing into water there is some risk, there will be a chance of an aircraft strike. Even though that may be millions-to-one, it will be there. A number of air forces consider that a 1-in-10,000 chance of a ricochet causing damage which could cause the aircraft to be lost is a prudent safety measure during peacetime training and calculate their profiles with this in mind. In war a slightly higher risk is accepted and a 1-in-1,000 chance is common.

With attack aircraft costing as much as they do, and a programme cost of £1,221 million for sixty Harrier GR 5 makes this close support aircraft in excess of £20 million each[1]; risks must be considered carefully. For example, in war the purpose of the total investment is to achieve the operational aim – in this case, to kill the target. If, however, in an attempt to protect the investment, self-damage risk criteria are adopted which prevent the target being effectively engaged, then the risk has been experienced to no purpose. Equally, if the chance of a successful attack is so degraded that many more aircraft are required over the target to achieve the aim, and each one experiences a unique self-damage risk, the sum total losses may be more than sending fewer aircraft at a higher risk. Only self-damage risk is being discussed here but overall mission attrition must also be considered and this will act equally on the total numbers of aircraft sent to achieve any purpose.

Consider an example. Assume that a campaign is producing a two per cent overall attrition rate and that it has been decided to strafe using a profile which will give 1-in-1,000 chance of self-damage. If four aircraft are despatched against a target a commander would have cause to expect a *chance* of 1-in-250 of losing an aircraft to self-damage and a one-in-thirteen chance of losing an aircraft to overall mission attrition. But if the chance of a successful strafe on the 1-in-1,000 self-damage profile was considered so low that eight aircraft had to be despatched to achieve the aim then there would be a 1-in-125 of suffering self-damage but nearly a one-in-seven chance of losing an aircraft to attrition. If, however, by accepting a higher self-damage risk of, say, 1-in-100, and by doing so increase the accuracy of the attack that only four aircraft need be despatched, there would be a one-in-twenty-five chance of losing an aircraft to self-damage but only a one-in-thirteen chance of total mission attrition. Firing closer with four aircraft would risk 11.6 per cent attrition which is a better prospect than using eight aircraft flying the safer profile which results in a 15.3 per cent chance of attrition.

In peacetime training it is sometimes possible to use high explosive (HE) rounds which break into large numbers of low energy fragments with less ricochet risk than solid practice shot or operational kinetic energy rounds. Care still needs to be exercised, however, because it is not only debris from the shot which can cause damage but also debris from the range itself. Rocks can be thrown by HE rounds sufficiently high to reach aircraft on pull-out from dives.

Although normally referred to as self-*damage*, far more serious results can accrue from a ricochet strike. In 1986 a report to parliament on an aircraft accident in which a Harrier aircraft was lost while engaging in air-to-ground strafing, concluded that the most likely cause was that a round had ricocheted off the target, struck the aircraft, and had incapacitated the pilot. The result was fatal.

Environmental Conditions

In common with many other weapon deliveries, strafing is constrained by weather and by the manoeuvre limitations of the delivery aircraft. As these two factors are such over-riding constraints it is best to touch on them early in any discussion of weapons or air-to-ground operations.

Weather varies widely throughout the world and comment normally needs to be tied to scenario. This is most important because a weapon system which excels under one circumstance may not be anywhere near as impressive in another. In North-West Europe weather can range from the long spells of cloudless skies and good visibility, which characterised the period of the Battle of Britain in August and September 1940 and the two excellent summers of 1976 and 1977, through to the periods during which hardly a sortie could be flown, typified by the hard winter of heavy snow in 1947. An even more dramatic example was the grounding of the Allied fighter bomber during the bitter weather of December 1944 and January 1945, a situation which contributed much to the early German successes in the Ardennes battle.

While he may not have the technology or the funds to design to worst-case conditions, a weapon designer must seek to get as close to this ideal as possible lest his weapon loses the flexibility which is so essential to its overall cost-effectiveness. For *dumb* weapons, where there is a large measure of pilot skill involved in their successful delivery, then visibility is an important consideration affecting target acquisition. As delivery speeds increase, so the pilot needs better visibility to give him the same amount of time to conduct his attack; visibility in North-West Europe is less than 8 km for half of the time. The latitude can also affect visually laid attacks seriously; in the north of Norway there is little daylight in winter and even in the Central Region two-thirds of the *day* is *night* in the depth of winter. Cloud base too can seriously affect options, reducing the opportunity for high dive attacks and, regularly in winter, making even shallow dive attacks problematical. Precipitation can affect the transparencies of weapon sensor heads or cockpit canopies. Most weapon sighting has to be accomplished through the flat front screen and in many aircraft this becomes quite opaque in even light drizzle; the pilot can still fly the aircraft safely by looking through the curved transparencies at the side but he cannot sight the weapon through them. Overseas, sandstorms can result in much the same effect as rain except that sand is highly erosive and can pit transparencies to the point of rendering them unserviceable, particularly if aircraft are flown at high speed under such conditions. To a lesser extent, low flying over the sea can result in a build up of salt from spray off a rough surface and this too can seriously affect acquisition, particularly when combined with an attack into a low sun in some circumstances effectively reducing visibility to zero.

Weapons and Warfare

Manoeuvre

A pilot needs to manoeuvre his aircraft to place most *dumb* weapons on target and even to lay many of the 'smart' weapons. Manoeuvre requirements, visibility and cloud base are closely associated. If the weather conditions reduce the time available for manoeuvre then the pilot may need to manoeuvre proportionally harder than would have been the case had more time been available. The combination of poor weather and high speed attacks can place a heavy demand on aircraft radius of turn. The radius of turn, an important

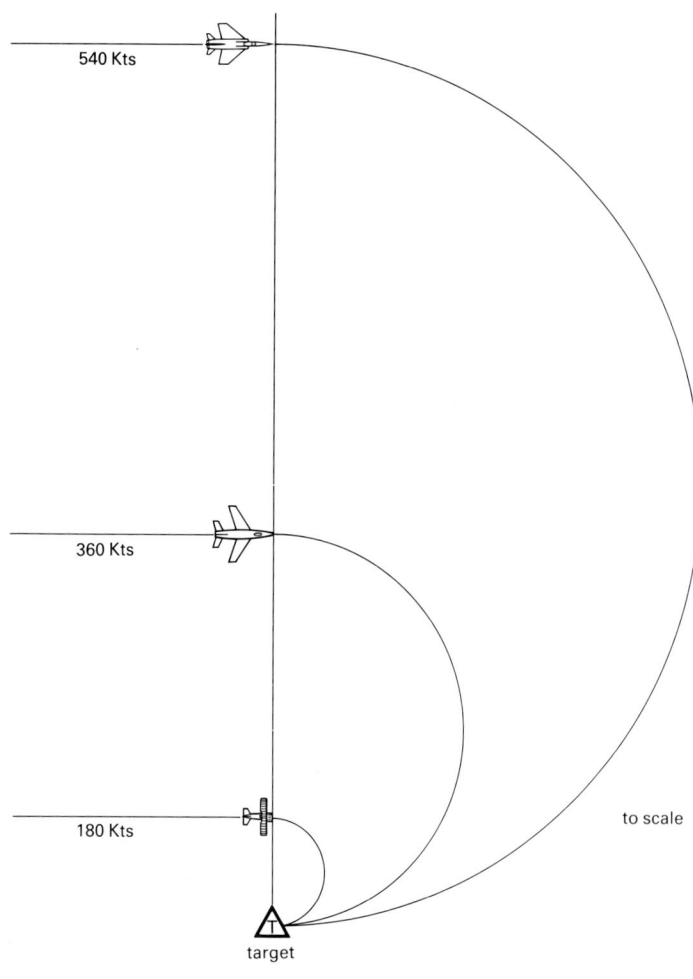

FIG 1.1 Varying radius of turn at 4 'g' with change of speed.

Air-to-Surface Weapons

factor in this context, is increased by a speed-squared function as seen in the formulae:

$$R = \frac{v^2}{g} = \frac{v^2}{g(n-1)}$$

where

R = radius of turn (ft)
v = aircraft velocity (ft/sec)
g = acceleration (32.174)
n = cockpit indicated 'g'.

To illustrate this take as an example three aircraft engaged on a search-and-destroy mission. As they patrol they see a likely target at ninety degrees to their flight path. All enter a 4 'g' turn to keep the target in sight and to attack it on the reciprocal heading. The visibility required for this particular scenario is twice the radius of turn. Fig 1.1 shows the greatly increased visibility requirements of the higher speed aircraft if the three aircraft are patrolling at 180 knots, 360 knots and 540 knots.

The greatly increased turn radius for any given 'g' is also reflected in the performance in pulling out of the dives with high speed aircraft having to initiate their recovery earlier than would slower aircraft and this, in turn, affects the range at which weapons can be fired; more correctly, it determines the minimum cease fire range. This can be seen at Figs 1.2 and 1.3.

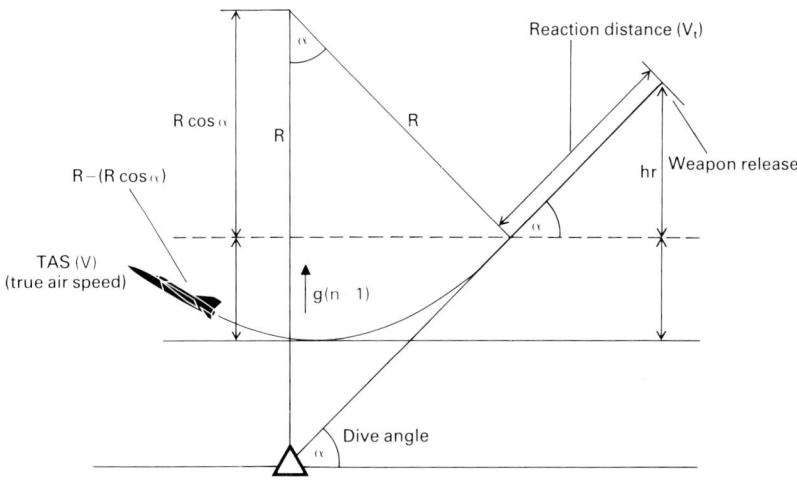

from Fig. 2 it can be seen that:- Height loss from weapons release $= \dfrac{V^2(1 - \cos \alpha)}{g(n-1)} + Vt \sin \alpha$

FIG 1.2 Height loss in a dive recovery.

Weapons and Warfare

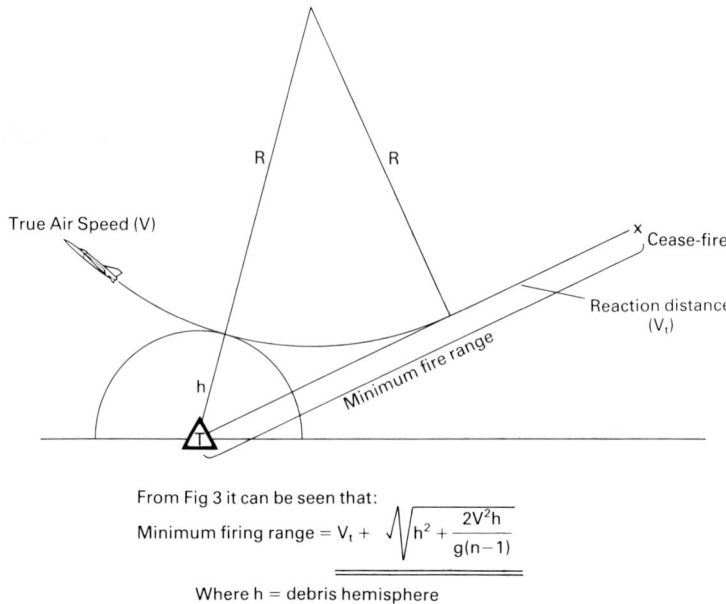

Fig 1.3 Minimum fire range.

Inherent in these two formulae is a pitfall for the unwary. The formula for minimum firing range restricts itself to determining the parameters necessary to avoid the weapon debris hemisphere. For shallow dive attacks this normally ensures ground clearance but for attacks involving steeper dives an aircraft could avoid the debris hemisphere but still impact the ground beyond the target. For this reason the prudent pilot always calculates both minimum firing range and the height loss in the dive recovery.

Rocket Projectiles (R/P)

Who first used rocket projectiles from aircraft is subject to some controversy but it is recorded that during World War Two a British officer serving in the Soviet Union alerted the War Office and the Air Ministry to the success being experienced by the Soviet Air Force using R/P against ground targets. Before the end of the war the squadrons of the Tactical Air Force were having considerable success with R/P as were the maritime attack squadrons using them against enemy shipping. The British 3-inch R/P was cheap, and by modern standards, had a crude motor. However, fitted with the heavy 60 lb HE warhead, it resulted in a good weapon-to-target match for a variety of battlefield and maritime targets. It remained in use until the 1960s and, carried in tiers, could be fitted in large numbers to tactical aircraft, even the jet aircraft, being used operationally on the Hunter force in Aden. On the Meteor

Air-to-Surface Weapons

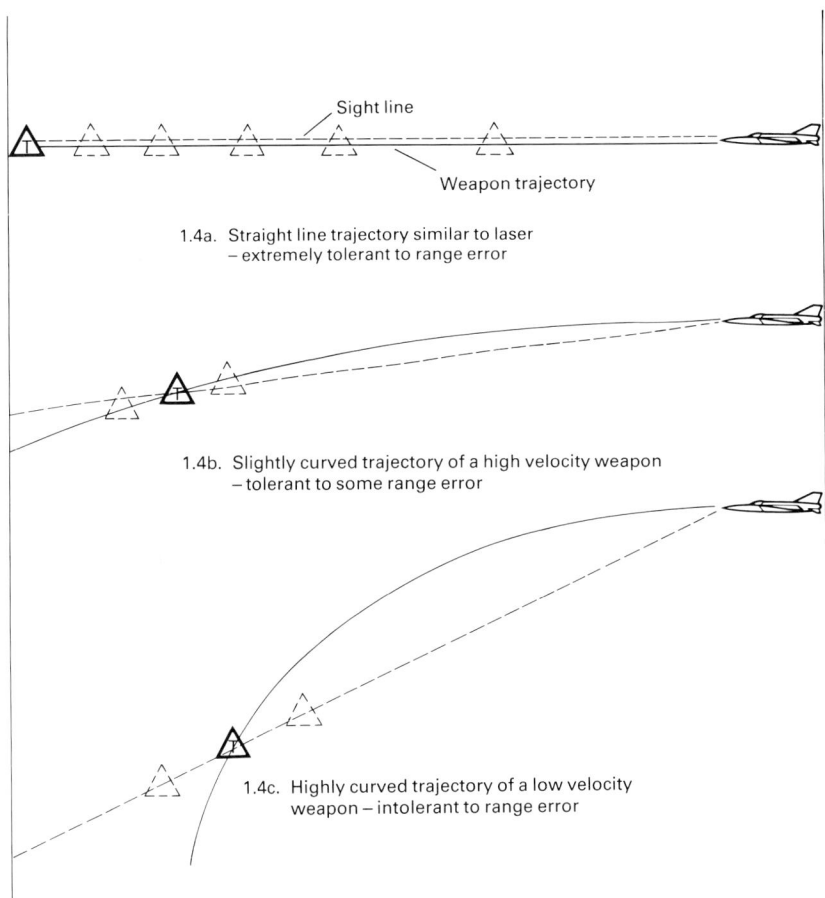

FIG 1.4 The effect of trajectory on range estimation tolerance.

twenty-four 3-inch R/P could be carried giving the aircraft the same hitting power as the broadside from a cruiser.

The 3-inch R/P, particularly with its large warhead, was neither aerodynamically or thermodynamically elegant. The motor burnt out after a very short time of flight and thereafter the weapon decelerated rapidly, resulting in a highly curved trajectory. Weapons with such curved trajectories are difficult to aim. The ideal *trajectory* is a straight line and, for this reason alone, modern weapons such as laser and some of the directed energy weapons (DEW) which operate effectively on straight line trajectories have great attractions to the weaponeer. Furthermore, curved trajectories place a premium on range estimation. This is illustrated in Fig 1.4.

But, the historian might say, the results produced by rocket firing aircraft during the Second World War were very impressive. If R/P attacks are so

Weapons and Warfare

inaccurate, how could this have been so? The answer is to be found largely in the area already discussed. Aircraft attacked at a slower speed than is the case today and could manoeuvre at quite high 'g' at those speeds. Consequently R/P could be fired at ranges which would be quite impossible to contemplate with today's front-line equipment. This meant that at such close ranges the weapon was impacting before the trajectory had started to decay markedly, hence making the aiming easier. Some of the targets were also range tolerant in that they were of large dimensions; the tank certainly was not but a column of tanks, attacked intelligently, would take out many range inaccuracies by its extended dimensions. After all, as much effect is achieved if any tank is killed, even if it is not the one aimed at. Railway targets were popular and the average locomotive presents perhaps from four to six times the target dimension of a tank. This applies even more to shipping.

In the case of shipping, the R/P had a particular quality which increased its effect and countered poor range estimation. In common with other ordnance, including bombs and shells, a rocket striking a *plastic* surface, that is a *soft* target such as water, earth or sand, will tend to be deflected back towards the surface. The degree to which this occurs will depend on many things, not least the shape of the projectile head, the characteristics of the *plastic* material, velocity of impact and, most important, the impact angle. This is shown at Fig 1.5. The advent of high speed aircraft, necessitating firing ranges outside those previously the norm, called for R/P with better range performance and flatter

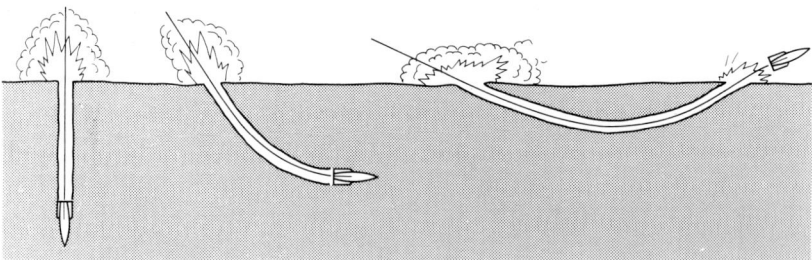

Fig 1.5a Tendency for projectiles entering a 'plastic' environment to curve towards the surface.

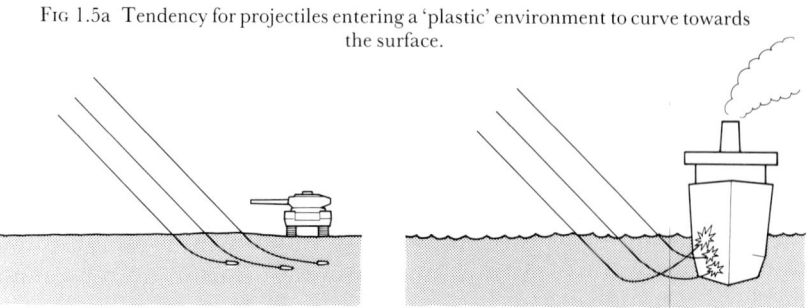

Fig 1.5b Against shipping the effect could be used to advantage to obtain strikes in the most vulnerable part below the water-line.

Air-to-Surface Weapons

trajectories. Both called for higher missile speeds, achieved to some extent by better propellants but, for a variety of reasons, there was also a trend towards smaller diameter weapons. Aerodynamic drag was reduced with smaller frontal areas and this helped range and delayed trajectory delay but equally important was the need to reduce the installed drag on the aircraft. External stores, weapons, drop-tanks, EW pods and the like, can double the drag of an aircraft and produce severe performance penalties in terms of range and speed. Aircraft capable of twice the speed of sound can be limited to speeds which are well subsonic when configured for attack missions. One answer to the external drag problem was to pod the R/P and for this purpose the smaller diameter weapon was to be preferred. Hence the advent of weapons such as the 68 mm SNEB favoured by the RAF as replacement for the 3-inch weapon, the 2.75 inch US weapon and the 57 mm Soviet weapon, all podded installations. In the case of the SNEB the R/P are carried in a pod. The 155 model, which carried 18 R/P, was retained on the aircraft when the weapons were expended. The 116 pod, however, which held 19 R/P, was jettisoned when empty to reduce drag on the aircraft.

At the time the SNEB was being introduced, in the mid-sixties as far as the RAF was concerned, the killing mechanism relied on the hollow charge principle, sometimes referred to as the shaped charge. In this the explosive charge is formed into a cone by a copper insert and this channels the explosive force into a high energy gas with a slug at its head. This can penetrate an impressive thickness of armour; typically a 68 mm weapon can penetrate some 270 mm of the type of armour used in tanks. The effect of hollow charge weapons is governed by the diameter of the charge and to some extent by the stand-off distance from the target; this latter element is needed to allow the charge to develop correctly before impacting the target. This is illustrated in Fig 1.6.

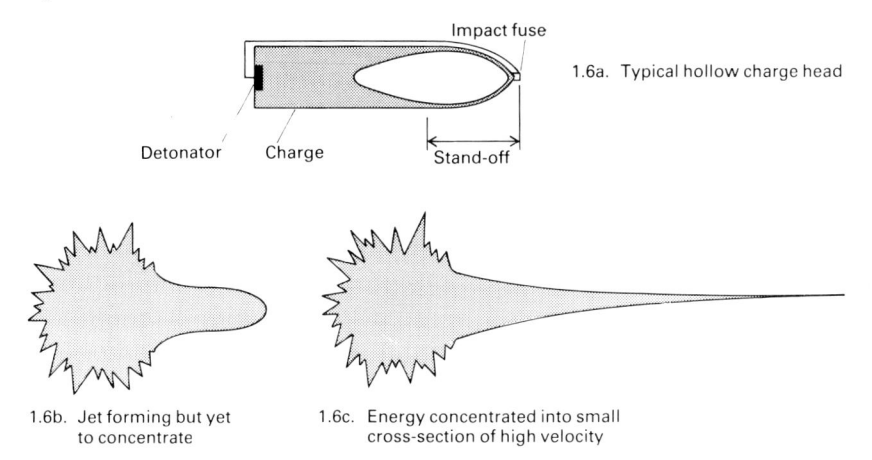

1.6a. Typical hollow charge head

1.6b. Jet forming but yet to concentrate

1.6c. Energy concentrated into small cross-section of high velocity

FIG 1.6 Hollow charge weapons.

Weapons and Warfare

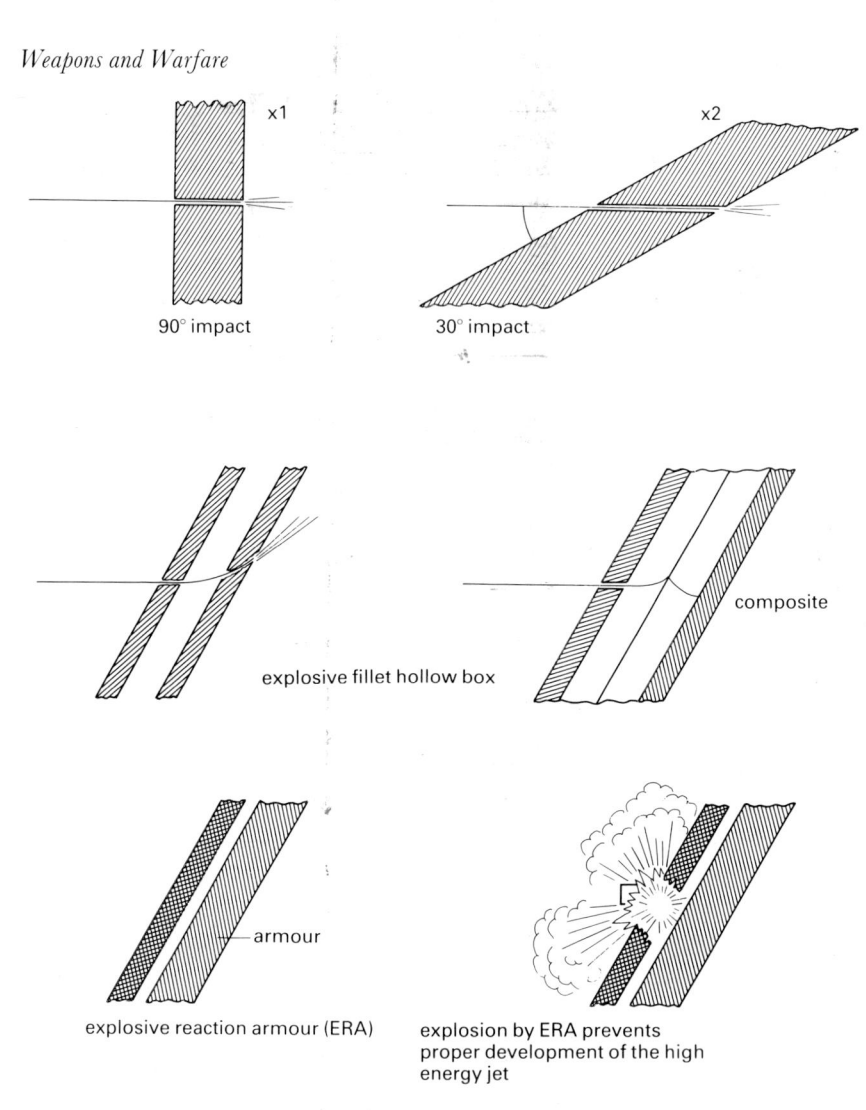

Fig 1.7 Explosion by ERA prevents proper development of the high energy jet.

Hollow charge weapons are at their best when used against armour at right angles to their impact angle. Armour displaced from the normal effectively increases its depth and if the weapon strikes at low grazing angles, the effective thickness of the armour can be increased substantially. Once the jet is formed it is important that it is not unduly disturbed in its passage through the target. Occasionally this can happen accidentally and a hollow charge weapon impacting a pannier or a road-wheel can be activated at the wrong stand-off distances necessary for optimum effect against the main armour. Spaced, or composite armour, gives a similar effect with the jet hitting different mediums

Air-to-Surface Weapons

in its passage and being deflected or dissipated by the confused target composition. Explosive reaction armour, in effect blocks of explosive designed to explode on initial impact, interferes with and dissipates the effect of the jet. This is particularly effective against hollow charge weapons.

Hollow charge heads were favoured for R/P because they do not rely on impact velocity for their effect and obtaining high velocities, or maintaining the velocity with high-drag aerodynamic characteristics, was difficult. The development of better propellants and improved aerodynamics, resulting in part from small overall weapon sizes, has opened the way for the development of high velocity weapons using kinetic energy as the killing mechanism. The Canadians have moved the first step in this direction with their respected CRV-7 weapon which relies upon a modern technology motor and propellant to achieve previously unobtainable velocities from a weapon of 2.75-inch diameter. Ranges up to four times those previously considered normal are possible with this weapon. However, the alternative of trading off some range against greatly increased accuracy is favoured by most operators. The system retains a variety of heads including kinetic energy and hollow-charge.

CRV-7 represents sometimes a natural stepping stone to the more specifically designed kinetic energy effect weapons. These are being developed on both sides of the Atlantic and tend to be smaller and of greater fineness ratio. Very high speeds can be obtained, in the order of Mach 4 or 5, generally referred to as *hypersonic*. Part of the reason the weapon can be smaller is that, relying on kinetic energy as it does, there is no warhead in the conventional sense, no explosive train to ensure its correct detonation and no fusing, all items of complexity, expense and, in some cases, the critical path in the shelf-life of the weapon. In a kinetic energy warhead the effect is usually obtained by use of a penetrator consisting of a long thin rod of very dense material, normally with a length/thickness ratio between 12:1 and 20:1, beyond which it tends to become ballistically unstable, and with the high density and small cross-section giving a high ballistic coefficient. Ballistic coefficient can be looked upon as the ratio of mass against area at the nose of the projectile. It can therefore be increased by making the rod finer or by increasing the mass of the projectile. The easiest way of achieving both is to make the projectile longer but, as explained, flight and penetration considerations limit this to a practical maximum of about 20:1. Consequently, to achieve high ballistic coefficient very dense materials are used for the penetrator. These include tungsten and depleted uranium.

Most high-velocity systems in service or in development are 'dumb' weapons but work is in hand to develop guided versions. A difficult problem is presented to the designer; if radar-based seekers are contemplated, the necessity for high fineness ratios severely limits the area available for antennae. In the case of infra-red seekers there is a problem of developing transparencies which can withstand the high thermal loads generated by hypersonic flight while still maintaining true optical quality. Hypersonic airflows about the nose of the rocket can also cause distortion of the infra-red signal.

Guidance of the small and very high speed rocket is also more complex than with larger and slower missiles. High drag prevents the use of aerodynamic control, with its requirement for fins and the associated weight and complexity of actuators. Instead, thrust vector control and the use of small rocket jets to influence the flight path are more favoured solutions.

Bombs

Unguided, or *dumb* bombs may be looked upon as falling in two main groups; ballistic bombs, the flight path of which is not influenced artificially, and retarded bombs where energy is deliberately dissipated, normally to enable the weapon to be delivered safely from a low altitude profile.

Bomb types have varied considerably over the years. Initially they were small hand-held devices dispensed over the cockpit side and weighing only a few pounds. As specialist bomber aircraft were developed with more substantial carriage arrangements, the weight of bombs increased accordingly. Some very large bombs were developed during World War Two including the heavy and specially-shaped bouncing bomb (arguably, this was an air-dropped depth charge) designed for the attacks on the Mohne, Eder and Sorpe dams. Of more conventional bomb shape were the Tallboy and Grand Slam bombs of 12,000 lb and 22,000 lb weight which relied upon high terminal velocities and deep penetration to achieve *earthquake-like* ground shock effect. The battleship *Tirpitz* and the Bielefeld viaduct both succumbed to this form of attack. To obtain maximum effect, the bombs needed to be dropped from a great height to reach terminal velocity and the only aircraft of the time able to approach this requirement was the Lancaster. Even then the full potential of the Grand Slam was never realised.

Smaller weapons were the norm. While there was a 4,000 lb *Blockbuster* this, in shape and use, was more an aerial mine than a bomb and was useful only aginst the predominantly area targets of the night strategic bomber offensive. More normally, bombs were in the 250 lb to 1,000 lb range, although at the start of the war a 100 lb bomb was fielded and soon found to be inadequate. The British 1,000 lb bomb of today is substantially similar to that developed for internal carriage in the Lancaster in the 1940s. That it is now carried externally on supersonic aircraft to which drag means impaired speed and range may be thought to be a strange contradiction.

Bombs are designated according to their explosive *capacity*. A high-capacity (HC) bomb indicates a high charge-to-weight ratio, resulting in a thin shell unsuited for penetration. Its prime destruction mechanism would be blast and it would be suitable for use against, for example, built-up areas. Conversely, a low-capacity (LC) bomb, would have a low charge-to-weight ratio and would obtain its effect by using the high strength of its case to obtain penetration and

Air-to-Surface Weapons

then relying upon the confined space within the target to magnify the effect of the small charge. A compromise bomb is more usual, the medium-capacity (MC) weapon, where the charge weight is about one-half the total weight of the bomb. The British 1,000 lb weapon is of medium-capacity.

As the tendency to carry bombs externally on high-speed aircraft increases, there has been a move towards producing low-drag bombs. As always, the designer must deal in compromise. A bomb designed for internal carriage can be shaped to optimise its ballistic qualities and this tends towards a fat shape with the centre-of-gravity (CG) about one-third of the way down the bomb. Low-drag bombs require a much better fineness ratio and it is more difficult to get optimum flight characteristics from such weapons. For any given weight, low-drag bombs tend to be longer and this can present problems of loading on some aircraft, particularly the smaller types (Fig 1.8). As most bombs released from high-speed aircraft have to be blown off the aircraft explosively in order to clear the immediate turbulent air flow the difficulty of obtaining a clear release can be greater with the longer weapon. In turn this can produce greater release disturbance and so materially affect accuracy.

Delivery options for the ballistic bomb can vary according to the demands of the aircraft, considerations of vulnerability or on the desired weapon effect on the target. Free-fall bombing, popular in World War Two, is now rarely practised because of poor accuracy and high vulnerability. Very high degrees of air superiority are required to permit large aircraft to operate unmolested on

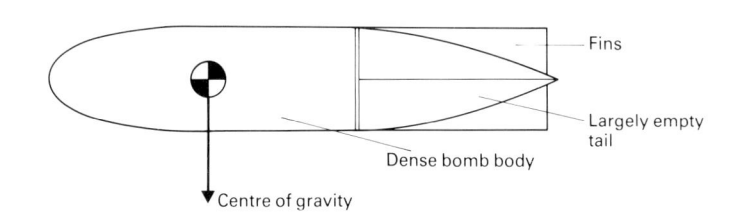

Typical bomb designed primarily for good ballistic flight characteristics but incurring high drag penalties if carried externally.

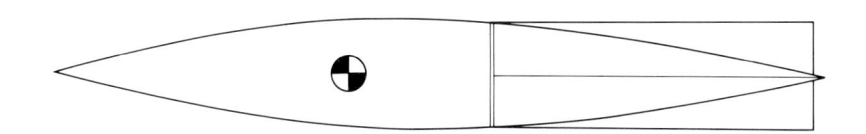

Shape more usual for bombs designed for external carriage and similar to the US low-drag bombs. The extra length militates against internal carriage and the centre of gravity tends to be further to the rear.

FIG 1.8 Bomb shapes for good ballistics and low-drag.

Weapons and Warfare

the profiles necessary to deliver free-fall bombs conventionally. This is not to say that it can be discounted. In Vietnam, for example, the B-52 was successfully used to drop free-fall bombs against assembly areas under the 'Rolling Thunder' programme but in this instance the air opposition in the areas was not extreme and massive supporting defence suppression measures were taken, often involving more aircraft in this role than in the main attack wave.

Releasing from high level, straight and level, means that the bomb has gravity acting at right angles to its initial trajectory. This leads to a complex sighting solution. Further, the bomb then has to drop through an expanse of uncharted air within which wind speed may vary considerably and the direction can back and veer. Although forecast winds can be allowed for in the sighting calculation, these forecasts are rarely accurate enough for bombing small targets.

A means of overcoming some of these problems is by dive bombing, used to good effect by the Luftwaffe *Stuka*. If, in the ideal case, a 90° dive is executed then there is effectively no gravity effect on the trajectory. What effect there is assists bomb velocity, giving higher impact velocities – useful for penetration – and decreased flight time and which, in its turn, reduces cross-wind effects. Consequently, high accuracies are possible by use of steep dive bombing.

The *Stuka* was a purpose built aircraft of its era and was designed to have high drag characteristics, particularly in the dive. It had a large propeller which, when throttled back in fine pitch, acted somewhat as a flat plate air brake; large flaps also helped to slow the aircraft in the dive. As a result, the *Stuka* could get quite close to the target before releasing its weapon and, using its high structural strength to pull out of the dive, could still avoid the bomb blast and fragmentation. Modern aircraft tend to make poor dive bombers because the aerodynamically clean shape of the high-speed designs does not permit speed to be so highly controlled in the dive and this results in lengthy release ranges compared to older aircraft. Shallow dive bombing is therefore more common, although in Vietnam the USAF did practice dive bombing at 60° in aircraft such as the F-4 Phantom and the F-100. The turn-in height was in the region of 20,000 ft and release had to be made at about 10,000 to 12,000 ft to allow sufficient airspace to achieve a safe recovery.

Two other techniques for delivering ballistic free-fall bombs are Loft and Toss bombing. For many years there has been confusion about these terms; to some they were synonymous and to others they were quite different techniques used for different purposes. It is now widely accepted that a toss delivery is one where the bomb is released under a 'g' pull. A loft delivery is there the bomb is released during a steady climb but not under a 'g' pull. To obtain maximum range from a toss attack, the bomb should be released at the 45° point. The principle can be demonstrated convincingly with a garden hose. As Fig 1.9 shows, the bomb traverses through heights where the aircraft has not travelled and can experience wind effects which have not been sensed by the system.

Air-to-Surface Weapons

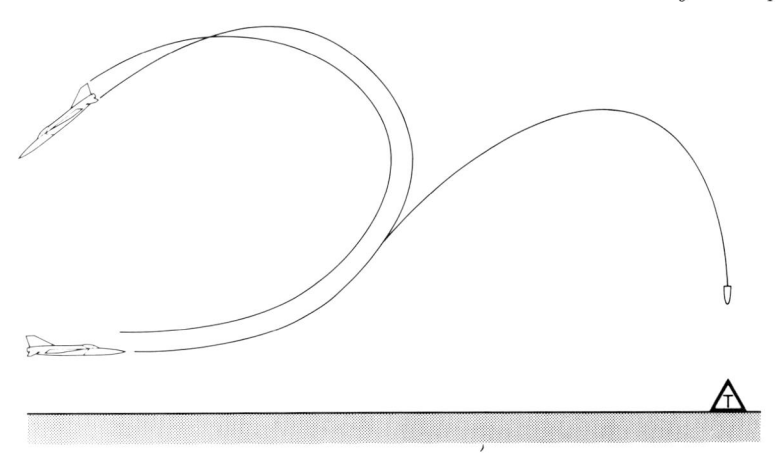

FIG 1.9a Toss attack – The weapon is released under 'g'.

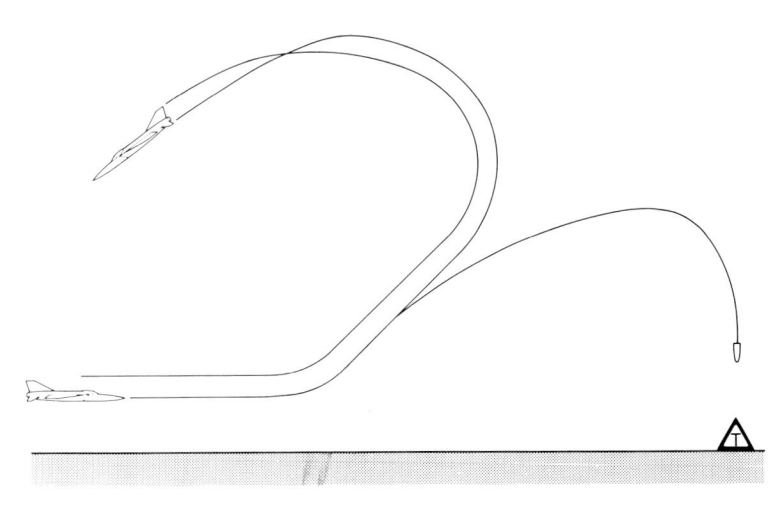

FIG 1.9b Loft attack – The weapon is released in a climb but not under a 'g' pull.

Any such attack is therefore inherently inaccurate and that inaccuracy varies according to the time of flight.

Time of flight will vary in turn with two factors apart from the ballistics of the bomb itself and these will both affect the stand-off range. Toss attacks are normally carried out with the aim of reducing vulnerability and long stand-off ranges are sought after, The higher the speed at release, the longer the bomb will throw. The relationship here is largely the same as is muzzle velocity in the context of a rifle bullet. The angle at which the bomb is released also has an effect on throw distance. Other factors being equal, the optimum distance is obtained, with a release at 45°. However, in the field of practical tactics constraints may work against the high speed, optimum angle attack. The high speed may so increase vertical turning radii that the aircraft is forced to get closer to area defences even if not closer to the target itself. As turn radii is a squared function of velocity, the sums have to be done; it cannot be assumed that high speed is always advantageous. Where that high speed is obtained by the use of afterburners, as is increasingly the case with high speed aircraft encumbered by external stores, the effect on fuel consumption – hence on range – and the beneficial effect to defensive missile systems working in the infra-red band has to be considered. Similarly, the higher the angle of release, the higher the aircraft will be thrown skywards and into the sensor cover of defending missile systems. Most weapon attacks involve compromises and the pros and cons have to be argued out in each case.

A weapon, rather than tactical, consideration arguing for the use of the toss attack is that it is the only way of delivering bombs from low level which overcomes two major disadvantages, those of ricochet and penetration. Ricochet depends on a number of factors, not least of which is the individual target characteristics and the shape of the weapon itself but, depending on the type of bomb, ricochet can occur at impact angles of 20° and below. (In the extreme case, ricochet can occur at up to 40° if all the many factors prove adverse.) Attacks can be completely negated if the bomb was expected to penetrate a target to obtain effect and fails to do so. Toss bombing can be used to increase the impact angle beyond that which would be vulnerable to ricochet. Equally, with penetration, relying as it does to a large extent on impact velocity, the toss attack can produce impact velocities much in excess of those normal in retarded deliveries, even if they are generally less than the terminal velocities which would be common from high-level free-fall attacks.

Against hard targets, impact velocity must be considered in the context of the bomb-casing strength. Above a certain velocity the bomb casing can fracture on impact with a hard target and, as the bomb relies much on the confinement of the charge to produce its effect, a split casing can result in a *burning* of the charge rather than an explosion.

Retarded Weapons

The closer a weapon is released to the target and the less time it is in free air, the more accurate it is likely to be. Unfortunately, if the separation distance between bomb and aircraft is too little, the aircraft itself is likely to be destroyed either by blast or fragmentation. From a low-level delivery, where the bomb time of flight can be as little as three to four seconds, the ballistic bomb has insufficient time to slow appreciably and will explode when the aircraft is still nearly overhead. At such close quarters the aircraft could easily be destroyed.

An answer to this problem is the retarded weapon and these come in two forms; the *retarded bomb*, which is similar in most aspects to the free-fall version

Air-to-Surface Weapons

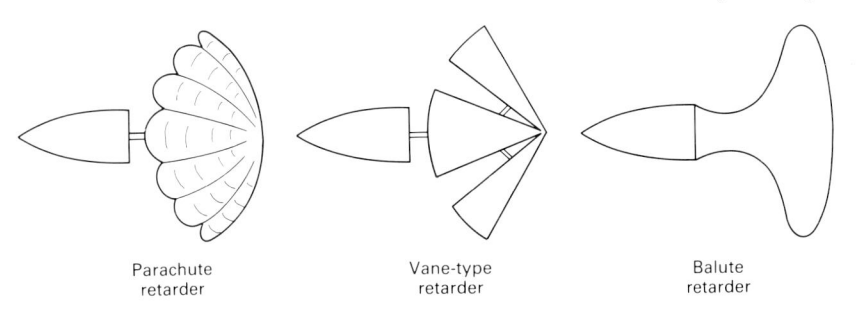

Parachute retarder   Vane-type retarder   Balute retarder

FIG 1.10 Retarder mechanisms.

but has attached to it a retarder tail; and the *cluster weapon* designed with a different function in mind but also delivered in a retarded mode.

Once released, a short time will elapse to allow the weapon to fall clear of the aircraft before the retarding mechanism is activated. There are various ways of achieving the retardation, all involving greatly increasing the drag to slow the bomb markedly from the initial forward velocity. One version deploys a parachute device while another uses vanes. Becoming popular is the 'balute' which is similar to a balloon, inflated by compressed air and presenting a much enhanced area to the airflow. There can be advantages in using 'balutes' on weapons with high fineness ratios typical of those used for external high speed carriage. Not only are there space and packing advantages with the smaller cross-section of the weapons but the opening shock at high speed can be better controlled (Fig 1.10).

Time of flight will vary with release height. For a typical attack with a 1,000 lb weapon it is only 3.4 seconds. Wind errors can be small over this timescale being only the difference between the actual wind velocity and that allowed for. If the attack is flown to position the aircraft's velocity vector over the target, azimuth errors are usually very small; as the impact angle is small, typically in the order of only 10°. Any vertical extent of the target should prevent any large range error building up. The simplicity of the attack is an attraction. A competent fighter-bomber pilot of some experience should be able to execute a fairly accurate attack even if his main weapon-aiming system is inactivated.

Because the impact angle is below that normally associated with ricochet it is always assumed that ricochet will occur and retarded bombs are invariably contact fused, that is, fused to explode immediately the shock of ground contact is sensed. Retard bombs cannot be relied upon, therefore, for penetration and a wide range of targets are ruled out for retard attack for that reason.

An interesting effect has been noticed during weapon trials when, for various reasons, the bomb has not exploded on contact. The tail tends to fall away and the bomb spins and bounces great distances until the very considerable kinetic energy is dissipated. Throughout this path destruction is wrought

Weapons and Warfare

PLATE 1.1 **BL755.** A shaped charge, anti-armour sub-munition which is dispersed in large numbers from a bus vehicle carried beneath the aircraft. *(Hunting Engineering Ltd)*

most effectively against any soft target struck. Against some targets, the concrete-filled practice bomb should not be entirely discounted.

The cluster weapon capitalises on the reduced vulnerability and increased accuracy of the low-level approach but instead of having one warhead, as in the case of the bomb, has a 'cluster' of smaller warheads, each having a lethal effect on the designated target. A typical weapon of US origin is the Rockeye and of UK origin the Hunting BL 755.

BL 755 is currently the main anti-armour weapon of the RAF and consists of a 'bus' vehicle containing 147 shaped-charge sub-munitions. These are dispersed over an elliptical pattern which is dependent upon the speed and height of delivery. Weapons can be delivered in sticks to achieve over-lapping and denser patterns of bomblets.

The effectiveness of cluster weapons varies with a wide range of factors and is difficult to assess. The large number of bomblets produces a 'shotgun' effect and argues for high probability of hit. Against this, the area over which the bomblets are dispersed is also large. The target, a tank, is not particularly large, although there may be more than one tank or other armoured unit within the pattern. A typical Soviet tank is 22 ft long, 11 ft wide and a little over 7 ft high. As with retarded bombs, the impact angles of the bomblets tend to be

Air-to-Surface Weapons

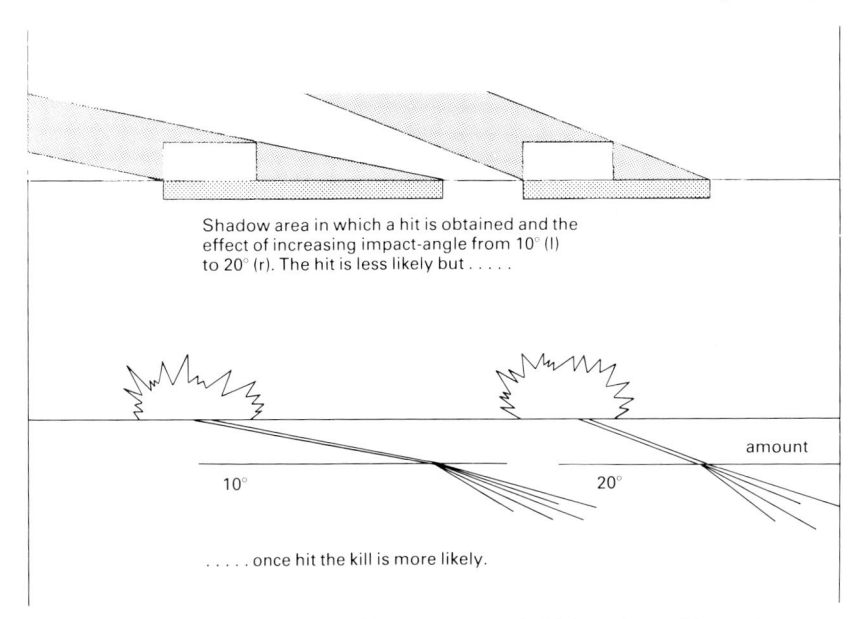

[Figure with labels: "Shadow area in which a hit is obtained and the effect of increasing impact-angle from 10° (l) to 20° (r). The hit is less likely but . . . . ." "10°" "20°" "amount" ". . . . . once hit the kill is more likely."]

FIG 1.11 The conflicting P_{HIT} and P_{KILL} arguments for higher sub-munition angles.

shallow and the effect on the tank can be dependent upon the orientation of the target. The bomblets tend not to be of very high diameter, because this would reduce the number carried. In consequence, if the impact is on the front of the tank – tanks are designed to take punishment from the front – then it is doubtful whether the armour would be defeated. If the impact is on the top or on the less well-protected sides and rear of the vehicle then penetration may be achieved. As we have already seen, a strike against armour at shallow grazing angles makes it effectively thicker. One method of increasing the effect of the bomblets is to improve their retardation and thereby to increase their striking angle. Unfortunately, this decreases the chance of a hit in the first instance by reducing the shadow area effect. This is shown diagrammatically in Fig 1.11.

With Rockeye and BL 755 the weapon bus vehicle is dropped from the aircraft and the sub-munitions are dispersed from that vehicle. In the case of Rockeye the bus spins as a result of offset fins at the tail and the sub-munitions are dispersed centrifugally. In the case of BL 755 the outer skin strips off and the bomblets are dispersed by being ejected by compressed gas acting upon a bladder. In both cases, however, the bus vehicle has fallen off the aircraft and the process of dispersing occurs independent of the aircraft.

Modern developments in technology are causing more attention to be given to cluster weapons and bus vehicles. As accuracy increases and terminal seekers and homing devices can be miniaturised and made highly capable, by the use of new data processing techniques, so the need for large warheads has decreased. The balance between warhead size and accuracy is one of the

Weapons and Warfare

PLATE 1.2 **JP233.** An airfield denial weapon seen here being dispensed from a bus vehicle beneath a Tornado. *(Hunting Engineering Ltd)*

fundamental compromises to be struck by the weapon designer and the greatest pay-off, by far, comes from increased accuracy. In the extreme case, if accuracy can be made so good that a direct hit is possible, the warhead can sometimes be dispensed with. This is the case with the Rapier anti-aircraft missile which is sometimes referred to as a *hitile*.

Another factor favouring cluster weapons and their generally small submunitions is the recent advance in warhead technology which has resulted in a given weight of explosive producing a greater overall effect through being applied more selectively than in the multi-directional manner of the conventional bomb. Hollow charge weapons show this to effect as do the new double-acting warheads where an initial charge makes a path for the emplacement of the main charge deep inside the target. This technique is used on the JP 233 cratering munition and will undoubtedly find application in anti-tank weapons of the future.

Two cluster weapons developed in the US show the trend. The CBU-89/B GATOR is based on the 450 kg Tactical Munition Dispenser and each weapon contains seventy-two anti-tank mines and twenty-two anti-personnel mines. Another application of the same dispenser, the Direct Airfield Attack Combined Munition (DAACM), carries eight Avco boosted kinetic energy runway penetrators and twenty-four Hunting HB 876 area-denial mines. In the CBU

87/B form, the dispenser is used as a Combined Effects Munition (CEM) and contains 202 sub-munitions, each containing a shaped-charge warhead with a casing producing fragmentation for a good secondary effect and generating an incendiary effect from a zinconium ring. The sub-munition weighs 1.54 kg. In these forms the munition dispenses 'dumb' sub-munitions and this will be dealt with later.

The German MW-1 and the British JP 233 weapons are of different operating principle but are generally accepted as 'cluster' weapons. Here the 'bus' vehicle remains attached to the aircraft and the sub-munitions are dispensed from it; in the case of the JP 233, when the sequence is complete, the bus vehicles themselves fall off the aircraft to reduce the drag for the return flight. Both weapons are very large and expensive; the cost of JP 233 is estimated to be well into six figures and the Tornado GR1 can carry two. Each dispenses thirty tandem-warhead runway cratering munitions and 215 area denial mines, the whole weighing in the region of 5,000 lbs. The MW-1 weapon disperser has the capability to accept a wide range of mines and other sub-munitions and is based on a different philosophy to that of JP 233 which was designed specifically for anti-airfield use. Despite this, the use of both weapons to create or to exploit choke points could be contemplated.

Smart Weapons

While the definitions of *dumb* and *smart* bombs can be separated by the straightforward dividing line between those which follow the laws of physics and ballistics uninfluenced by artificial guidance, and those which do not, the field of *smart* weapons presents a more difficult problem. In the simplest case, a smart bomb may be a *dumb* bomb with an add-on kit; cheap and rather crude by fine engineering standards and, perhaps because of this, imposing tactical restrictions on its use. The Paveway series of bombs, at least in their initial form, may be considered to have started at this point. The Maverick family, on the other hand, was conceived as a complete weapon from the outset. The warhead, propulsion, seeker and guidance were engineered simultaneously. Simplistically, the smart weapons could be sub-divided into these two categories but, as the electronic revolution continues apace, developments suggest the need for a third category the *super-smart*, where data processing of the sensor output takes place. In these, massive data processing may be involved and, while not making it a thinking missile in the human sense of that word, nevertheless makes it highly discriminatory.

Strap-on

On 9 September 1943 two armour-piercing 1,400 kg bombs hit the Italian battleship *ROMA* as she sailed in the Straits of Bonifacio. The effect of the bombs and the secondary explosions they caused soon overcame the ship and

Weapons and Warfare

she was lost. Yet another battleship to fall to air power. However, in the case of the *ROMA* there was a difference. She had not been attacked by squadrons of aircraft fighting their way through the hail of anti-aircraft fire which a capital ship and her escorts could produce, nor had the attacking aircraft experienced any losses for they had remained at high level and had not come within range of the defences. Instead, they had used the Luftwaffe's PC 1400X – the Fritz X – radio-controlled bomb for the first time and with devastating effect. Nearly eighty ships, from major combat units to freighters, were sunk or damaged before the Allies developed electronic countermeasures to jam the weapon's control frequencies. It was in 1943 therefore that the era of smart air-to-surface weaponry could be said to have started.

Other guided weapons were developed later in the war and both the USAAF and the US Navy used guided bombs to attack point targets and shipping in the Pacific before the end of the war in 1945. Thus it was surprising that the US was left without good and effective precision munitions to use against high value and heavily defended point targets when the Vietnam war escalated. There may be two reasons for this, and they are common to both sides of the Atlantic. First, democracies are easily lulled into the 'peace-in-our-time' syndrome and it was understandable that following yet another *war-to-end-all-wars* there should be a natural resistance to major programmes of weapon development. Weapon development tends to require a definable and recognisable threat to prosper and immediately after World War Two that incentive was absent. Second, when the Soviet threat became apparent in 1947/48 the West turned to its nuclear potential to guarantee peace and for many years NATO relied upon a policy of nuclear tripwire in which any aggression would be met by a massive and overwhelming nuclear response. This policy was extant until the mid to late sixties when Soviet nuclear parity caused it to be questioned and replaced by the policy of flexible response current today.

During the period of tripwire, little attention, and fewer resources, were expended on conventional weaponry and it was to the dismay of the US that they found themselves deeply involved in a conventional tactical war in the 1960s with poorly optimised aircraft and, above all, the wrong weapons. The effect on aircraft of the Vietnam experience can be seen in the inventories today because it was the requirement for a highly agile air superiority aircraft, identified from the deficiencies experienced over North Vietnam, which led to the specification for both the F-15 and F-16. Equally, much of the design of the A-10 was influenced by the experience of close air support over South Vietnam.

The Thanh Hoa road and rail bridge some sixty nautical miles south of Hanoi was the catalyst in the re-birth of smart weapons. Considerable effort had been expended, and many losses occasioned, in an attempt to interdict this important element in the North Vietnam communication system. Its importance was not lost on the North Vietnamese themselves and once the US intentions became clear, the bridge was heavily defended by anti-aircraft systems. This caused the USAF to bomb from higher and faster profiles with

Air-to-Surface Weapons

the result that damage to the bridge was either minimal or was quickly repaired. It was this problem which sparked the development of the Paveway series of laser-guided bombs (LGB). On 13 May 1972 a weapon was used successfully to drop a span on the bridge for no loss to the 14 F-4 Phantom aircraft which executed the attack.

The Paveway Bombs

The Paveway laser guidance kit is a strap-on system which can be fitted to a variety of bombs. Most popularly it is fitted to the US MK 84 2,000 lb, the US MK 83 1,000 lb and the US MK 82 500 lb bombs in addition to being fitted to the British 1,000 lb bomb. It is a simple system consisting of a detector array in four quadrants mounted in a universal-joint housing which is designed to stay aligned to the airflow. The guidance unit receives the reflected laser signal from the target, assesses its direction by comparing the output from the four quadrants, and then signals the movement needed from the four control fins to the actuators. The target can be designated from the ground by forward area troops or by air control parties using equipment such as the Ferranti laser target designator, or from the air using any of a series of laser target designator pods. The RAF uses the Pavespike pod of US origin and on US aircraft can be found Pave Knife, Pave Tack and, shortly, the LANTIRN pod. Most western military lasers work in the 1.06 micron wavelength and this can be coded to prevent interference between different targets and bombs.

The Paveway series of bombs has benefited from incremental development. Paveway 1, for example, had *bang-bang* control; so called because any signal demanding a control input is satisfied by the control going fully hard-over in the required direction. This tends in most occasions to result in an over-correction and the next signal is again met by a hard-over control movement in the opposite sense – hence 'bang-bang'. This results in a disturbed flight path and a considerable loss of energy which in turn affects accuracy and range. When dropped from high level, the energy of the bomb tends to be augmented by gravity and the problem is less but from low level deliveries, the flight path can be highly oscillatory and can lead to bombs falling short of the target, not through any loss of guidance but through insufficient energy to fly the corrections.

Paveway 2 was an improvement on Paveway 1 and is in RAF service. Paveway 3 introduced a more sophisticated control law and signal processing, resulting in proportional guidance. In this case instead of correcting by a hard-over command the control surfaces are moved only proportional to the measured offset from the laser return. In consequence the bomb flies more smoothly and energy is retained for longer. Further, as the corrections are small and continuous, accuracy is much enhanced (Fig 1.12).

Although the laser guidance ensured high terminal accuracy in comparison with unguided bombs, the LGB does impose its own constraint on the delivery

Weapons and Warfare

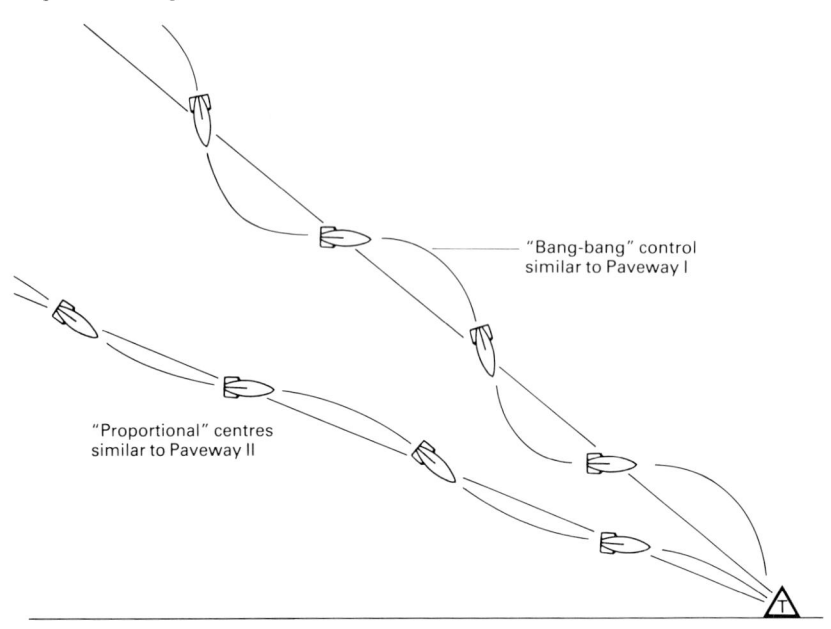

FIG 1.12a Laser Guided Bomb – Guidance Law effect on energy.

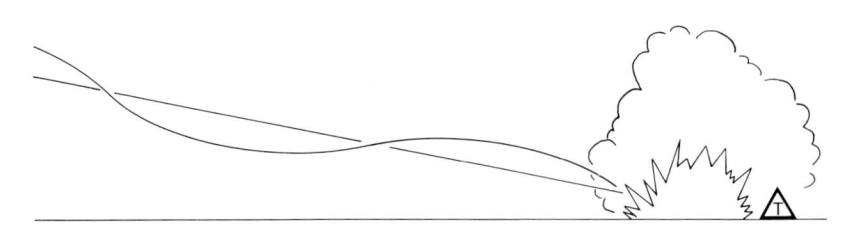

FIG 1.12b 'Short' bombs can result from low angle approaches using 'bang-bang' control laws.

profile. The bomb must eventually arrive at the position where it can both see the reflected laser energy from the target and has sufficient range – or energy – to reach it. This is the so-called *basket* and is best seen in the use of the LGB to take out the terminal errors of toss bombing.

Fig 1.13 shows the major considerations in using the LGB in a toss bomb attack. The laser detector on the nose of the bomb has a finite look angle, typically in the order of 15° semi-angle. It will only receive signals when the target is in the 30° cone on the nose; until then it will not guide. However, it may still be undesirable for the bomb to guide as soon as the target falls within the 30° cone because this may have the effect of making the bomb fly lower and it will dissipate energy faster, the two effects combining to result in a short

Air-to-Surface Weapons

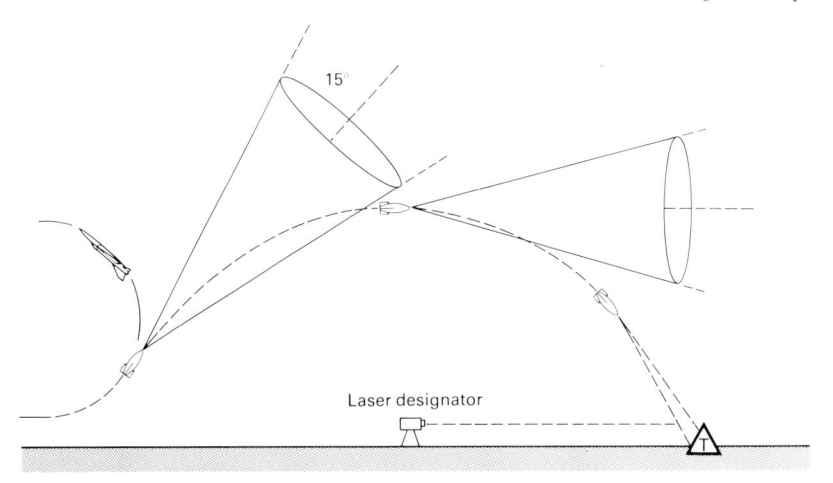

Fig 1.13a High Toss – LGB approaches high and picks up target returns late.

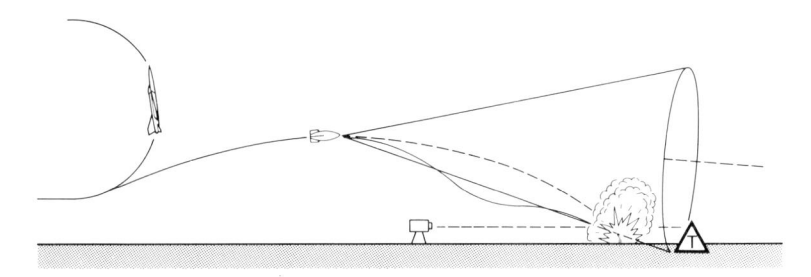

Fig 1.13b Low Toss – LGB approaches low. When target is acquired, bomb tends to approach directly, losing energy and can impact short.

bomb. This can be overcome by the target designation being delayed until a pre-computed time before expected bomb impact.

To prevent the bomb losing energy and falling short, it is tempting to toss for a long bomb and rely upon the bomb to guide back into a steeper descent, so helping to conserve energy. This technique can be used under some circumstances but must be applied with great care if the bomb is not to fail to obtain a reflection and to continue ballistically. This is because of the shape of the seeker look angle on the ground (Fig. 1.14) which favours an acquisition in the long, rather than the short sector. The shape of this area is an ellipse on anything other than a vertical delivery and it can be seen that the more shallow the angle, the more elliptical the ground pattern. Consequently, if the bomb is deliberately thrown long, it is easy to exceed the look angle in the short sector.

Once illuminated, the target reflects laser energy in many directions and, because of this, more than one bomb can be launched to home against the

Weapons and Warfare

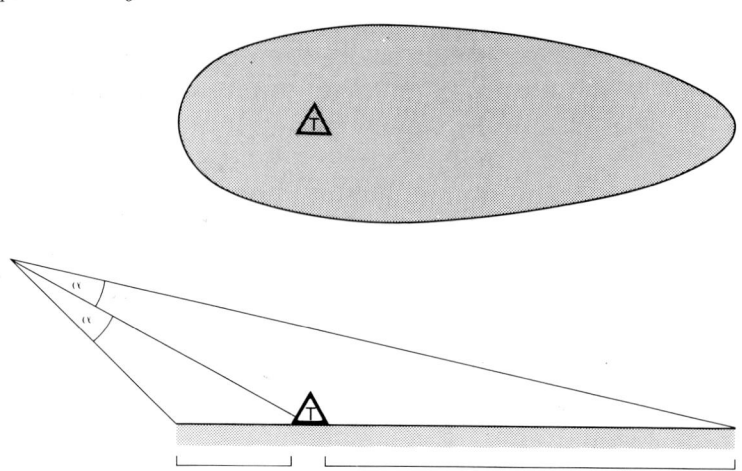

Fig 1.14 Footprint of LGB seeker head showing tendency to seek long at shallow angles.

target. Provided the timing of the attack is co-ordinated, sticks of LGBs from a number of aircraft can be launched against a target utilising a single designation. This technique can be useful for attacking resilient point targets which may require more explosive effect to ensure destruction than may be available from one weapon. Some modern autobahn bridges, for example, are massive structures and would demand more charge weight than a single bomb would provide. As all the bombs would impact the target nearly simultaneously there is the possibility of a synergistic effect similar to that produced by marching men on less substantial bridges.

Although a suitably equipped aircraft can self-designate, this is a complex task effectively ruled out at low level by terrain screening and restricted look angles. More normally, a formation will consist of 'bombers' and 'designators' operating in a highly planned and co-ordinated manner in the target areas. The amount of time separation which needs to be allowed will depend on the time of flight of the bomb. This in its turn is dependent upon delivery speed and release angle. Typically, from a 540 knot entry and a 30° release angle, an LGB may fly for about 30 seconds before reaching the target while the delivery aircraft will commence the manoeuvre some 4.3 nautical miles removed. Clearly, if the designator is flying with the bombers, it will be level with, or even slightly past, the target as the bomb arrives. It is important that the laser, working on straightforward optical principles, is able to reflect from the target to the LGB. The spatial relationship between designator, target and LGB is critical and must be planned with the target characteristics firmly in mind.

As part of an incremental development programme, the Paveway 3 weapon was proposed. This was aimed at removing the necessity for the delivery vehicle to pull up from the safety of low level flight to impart a toss on to the

Air-to-Surface Weapons

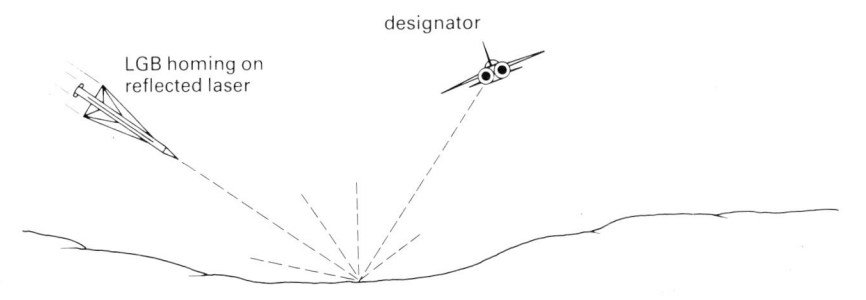

Fig 1.15a Flat, reflective target giving comprehensive signals over a wide azimuth.

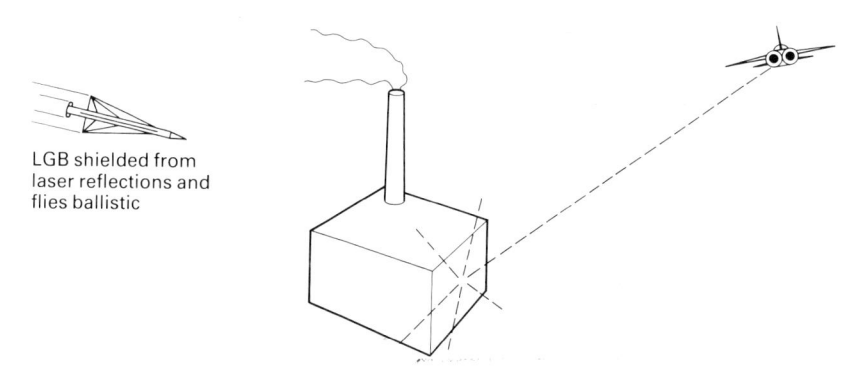

Fig 1.15b Targets with large vertical extent can shield the LGB from signals.

Plate 1.3 **Paveway.** Laser-guided bomb destroying a moving vehicle. *Texas Instruments)*

Weapons and Warfare

bomb. The Paveway 3 system uses a computer package on board the bomb to allow it to fly to the target at a pre-set height, decelerating as it uses its kinetic energy but flying in such a controlled manner that the use of energy is minimised. Because of this, greater stand-off ranges are obtainable. At the end of the fly-out the seeker head homes onto the reflected laser from the target, as previously. Paveway 3 was developed to enhance stand-off and to lower aircraft vulnerability. There is also a version of Paveway in which a conversion package, built by Emerson, is added to the basic Paveway and consists of a rocket motor which doubles the range of the weapon. This was developed at the US Navy weapons centre at China Lake and is known as the AGM-123A SKIPPER II. The Paveway series and the AGM-123 development are all based on laser guidance; a similar weapons philosophy is involved in the GBU-15 weapons although the guidance in this case is different.

GBU-15

In the mid-1960s development started at China Lake on the WALLEYE (AGM-62). This was a guided bomb with a stabilised TV camera in the nose. Once the pilot had locked the TV camera to the target, the weapon could be launched and required no further assistance from the aircraft; it was *launch-and-leave*, a technique much preferred by aircrew. The first WALLEYES were used in 1967 against targets in North Vietnam including military barracks and the Hanoi Thermal Power Plant. In 1971 an improved version, WALLEYE 2 (AGM-62A) became available, doubling almost all the important parameters including launch weight, warhead weight, and range, which was increased to 55 km.

On much the same lines, Rockwell were developing the GBU-15 for the USAF. This was a project which from its inception visualised a modular approach and was to be based on a choice between TV or IR guidance and between the MK 84 2,000 lb bomb, or a sub-munition dispenser, the SUU-54 which can disperse 1,800 grenade-type devices.

In its TV form, the GBU-15 is similar to WALLEYE and, once locked-on, can be launched and left to its own devices. Alternatively, the system can be fitted with a data-link which transmits pictures back to the launch aircraft and allows for mid-course corrections to be made in-flight. This in-flight correction

	WALLEYE I AGM-62	WALLEYE II AGM-62A
Length	3.34 m	4.06 m
Weight	510 kg	1,089 kg
Warhead	386 kg	907 kg
Range	26 km	55 km

FIG 1.16 The Walleye Series.

makes GBU-15 generally more accurate than Paveway. An added advantage is that the data-link can be operated by an aircraft other than the launch aircraft.

The use of the Imaging Infra-Red homing head from the Maverick missile helps to keep costs under control and follows on from the philosophy which spawned many of the new generation of weapons – that of using existing, off-the-shelf equipment and technology whenever possible. As a result unit costs for this type of weapon have proved to be low, with an initial price of $194,000 reducing with series production to $128,000 over a five-year period; this can be further reduced to $100,000 if the data-link facility is removed.

As with the powered version of Paveway, an increased range GBU-15 is now under development to allow greater stand-off from highly defended targets. The powered version, designated the AGM-130, will come in two forms; the AGM-130A, with the MK 84 2,000 lb warhead, and the AGM-130B based on the SUU-54 sub-munition disperser. This later version will be optimised for aircraft attack and will varry AVCO boosted kinetic energy runway penetrators and area denial mines similar to those used in the Hunting JP 233. To overcome the problem of case fracture when hitting hard targets, an improved version of the MK 84 bomb was produced with a much stronger casing. This weapon, first known as the 'improved-2000', is now designated the BLU-109B. When fitted to the powered version of the GBU-15 it becomes the AGM-130C.

In addition to the rocket motor, the fitment of an altimeter allows for trajectory control. The weapon is released initially in the glide mode and remains so until the speed decays to Mach 0.55 at which point the motor is fired to maintain energy. The weapon can be made to fly at set heights and there is a facility to step-down cruise height in increments to maintain a flight path clear of cloud. When burnt out, the motor is jettisoned to reduce drag and to conserve energy. Range is dependent upon release conditions but initial estimates put the range at about three times that of the GBU-15; this would put the weapon into the 20 to 30 kilometre class.

The AGM-130 development of the GBU-15 exemplifies the grey area which can exist between the strap-on enhancement of fairly basic weapons and the true missile. Is not the AGM-130 a missile? It flies, it can mid-course correct, it terminally homes. Perhaps there is becoming a need for some agreed definitions if only to ease the task of future arms control negotiators.

Air-to-Surface Missiles

Air-to-Surface is used advisedly because not only does this section deal with both *Air-to-Ground* missiles but also mentions *Air-to-Sea* missiles. Further, while not necessarily optimised for a naval target, many of the missiles mentioned could have application over sea if the circumstances were suitable. Against most naval surface targets quite small warheads can have a disproportionately destructive effect, as the case of HMS *Sheffield* in the Falklands Island conflict

Weapons and Warfare

proved; in this instance it is suspected that the warhead itself did not detonate and the ship was lost through the effect of the unburnt rocket motor fuel.

There is a profusion of air-so-surface missiles made by a variety of manufacturers throughout the world. It is not the purpose here to present an inventory of such missiles; this is available in standard reference works such as the Jane's Annuals or occasionally in missile directories produced by the more reputable aviation magazines. Nor is it necessary to outline the method of operation of each because, once the general principles of one are understood, the others follow the same pattern closely.

AGM-65 Maverick

As an example, the AGM-65 Maverick makes a good case. It is in service, is continuing a product improvement programme, is in use by more than one nation, and is an excellent example of the exploitation of a sound basic design by modularisation. The Maverick is made by the Hughes Corporation.

The Maverick programme started in 1965 and Hughes were awarded the contract in mid 1968. First production missiles were delivered to the USAF in 1972 and the first 17,000 missile contract was completed in 1975. Since then follow-on contracts for new versions of the missile have kept the programme in series production.

The first version of the missile was the AGM-65A; a TV seeker gave a 5° field-of-view (FOV) and, when locked-on to the target, the missile homed by relying upon target-to-background contrast. Once the pilot had locked the missile to the target by reference to the TV display in the cockpit, the missile could be fired and required no further assistance from the aircraft. It is a *fire-and-forget* missile and the manufacturer claims that, because of this, more than one missile can be fired per pass. However, this capability is very much dependent upon the circumstances of the moment.

It was probably the difficulties in obtaining reliable target acquisition with the wide 5° FOV that led to the first of the development models, the AGM-65B with the same TV seeker but with a 2.5° FOV. Although the initial localisation of the target had to be better, the increased magnification in the electro-optics allowed larger ranges to be utilised against typical battlefield targets.

The problem with relying on TV on a modern battlefield is that, increasingly, night is becoming less of a problem to ground forces. TV-based equipment, even the low-light variants, are essentially light enhancers and rely on the presence of some light. Modern low-light TV equipments are remarkably good and will give good useable pictures down to no-moon, starlight conditions but there remain many occasions when even this light level will not exist. Alternatively, the light conditions may be present but obscured by overcast cloud. This often happens in North-West Europe (NWE) during the winter months. Yet another problem is that TV systems can suffer badly from 'flare' when a bright light enters the FOV. Bright lights can be common on the

Air-to-Surface Weapons

active battlefield from such sources as gun flash, weapon explosions and flares. In such circumstances the TV seeker can lose its picture.

During the winter months some two-thirds of the twenty-four hour period can be 'night' in NWE and in the higher latitudes, North Norway for example, the majority of the twenty-four hour period is effectively 'night' in winter. There was some pressure therefore to develop a seeker head which, if not independent of the conditions, would be less susceptible to them than TV. The answer was to move into the infra-red spectrum and the AGM-65D Imaging-Infra-Red (IIR) Seeker version of the Maverick was born. Where TV Maverick could be used in the NWE winter perhaps thirty per cent of the time it is estimated that the IIR version will be useable up to ninety per cent of the time; a considerable improvement.

The development of a IIR seeker sparked interest in the Maverick from the US Navy. Ships have large and very distinct IR signatures which are very difficult to conceal against a highly contrasting and uniform sea background. Imaging Infra-Red is more difficult to decoy than the more simple early infra-red seekers and the combined characteristics make the missile attractive to navies. The first flight of the AGM-65F for the US Navy was in September 1983. As the target was so different, the 125 lb shaped-charge warhead of the previous versions of the missile, designed for battlefield use, has been replaced by a 300 lb blast/fragmentation warhead. This is a large warhead by missile standards, being larger in terms of explosive content than in some bombs. The effect against even large ships would be considerable, particularly as the high impact velocity would give a high chance of penetration with the consequent enhanced internal explosive effect.

The US Marine Corps (USMC) have also recognised the merit of the missile and in having commonality with the US Navy from whose ships they expect to fight. The USMC saw the need for a precision guided munition to engage enemy strong points on the battlefield in close support of the Marines on the ground. A missile capable of homing onto targets designated by laser was required and the AGM-65E laser guided version of the Maverick was developed. With their particular targets in mind, the USMC have retained the larger blast/fragmentation warhead from the US Navy's AGM-65F. The missile can operate against targets designated from either the ground or from the air.

Designation	Service	Seeker	Warhead	Remarks
AGM-65A	USAF	TV	130 lb Shaped-charge	5° FOV
AGM-65B	USAF	TV	130 lb Shaped-charge	2.5° FOV
AGM-65D	USAF	IIR	130 lb Shaped-charge	
AGM-65E	USMC	Laser	300 lb Blast/Frag	
AGM-65F	USN	IIR	300 lb Blast/Frag	

Fig 1.17 The AGM-65 Maverick family.

Weapons and Warfare

Maverick is an excellent example of a basically sound design being incrementally developed over a long period and having all the long and short-term advantages of series production over large batch sizes. It has been sold widely overseas and combat experience adds to the extensive test data to justify the claim that eighty-five per cent of all Mavericks fired have been successful. This is an impressive figure for a weapon of this complexity and figures half as good as this, or even less, are not uncommon with systems of comparable sophistication.

While not detracting at all from the worth of Maverick as a missile, for other missiles of similar design suffer equally, there are still problems in using it successfully on a modern highly defended battlefield. This derives from the dynamics of the attack and the practical difficulties of target acquisition. Consider the Maverick attack.

On approaching the target area, the pilot selects a missile; this applies power to the guidance gyroscopes which start to run-up. When up to speed, a Ready light indicates that the missile is ready to fire. The pilot then has to acquire the target. He can do this by either staying fast and low for safety and relying on seeing the target far enough away to execute his attack, or he can pull-up to search for the target from a better vantage point. While staying low is a useful technique when delivering retard weapons from a target overflight, it will rarely allow sufficient target acquisition to enable a forward-firing attack to be made. Too often classroom calculations are made to prove the contrary but often are based on the theoreticians 'flat earth' and do not credit that the standard 7.5 foot high tank can be perfectly concealed from low-angle view by the standard NWE hedge.

The pilot may therefore elect to pull-up to a height which gives a better chance of direct line-of-sight to the target, maybe between 500–1,000 feet. Once there, he will have to search for and acquire a target visually. As the target is acquired, he will uncage the missile, activating the electro-optics and the video circuitry; this will bring up a TV picture on the monitor in the cockpit. Referring to this picture, the pilot then slews the video onto the target, centres the cross-hairs, locks the system, and fires the missile.

Some estimates suggest that from pull-up to firing may take some fifteen to twenty seconds, that the missile range is up to twelve nautical miles and that normal lock-on ranges are in the order of two to three nautical miles. From this it can be seen that the vulnerability of the delivering aircraft will be affected by the range at which it is possible to acquire the target visually.

If the missile is to be fired at two nautical miles and the search, acquisition, missile lock and firing sequence is to take, say, ten seconds then when the search sequence starts a 480 knot aircraft will be 3.3 nautical miles from the target. A tank will subtend the same angle as a pin-head at nearly nine feet away and even at firing range will subtend only the same angle as a pin-head at an extended arms length. It is likely therefore that reliable shots will be obtained only if fast aircraft get quite close to the target. In this instance the

Air-to-Surface Weapons

extended turn radii will mean that the aircraft will rarely be able to avoid overflying the forward battlefield defences. The radius of turn of a 480 knot aircraft at 6 'g' is nearly 3,500 feet and at 540 knots, a speed many would consider more desirable, this radius is increased by almost 900 feet to 4,376 feet. In terms of the total geometry of the attack, the advocates of the A-10, which will field Maverick as part of its inventory, claim that the tighter manoeuvre which is possible in the slower aircraft eases target acquisition and does not increase vulnerability overall.

The target acquisition problem is greatly eased against surface shipping and much greater ranges could be expected than those possible against small battlefield targets. Unfortunately for the airmen, the lack of confusion in the maritime battlefield aids the ship defences so that stand-off ranges adequate for the land battle are inadequate against major surface units which have been heavily armed against air attack. For this reason, air-to-sea missiles tend to have longer ranges than battlefield missiles.

AGM-84 Harpoon

Just as Maverick can be taken as typical of the modern generation battlefield missiles, so can Harpoon be used as a similar example for air-to-sea missiles. As with the Maverick, Harpoon has been in series production for a long time, is being incrementally improved and has found favour with a large number of customers.

Harpoon started life as a private venture by the McDonnell Douglas Corporation but was put on an official footing after the sinking of the Israeli destroyer *Eilat* by a Styx missile fired from a fast patrol boat in 1967. The Harpoon entered service in 1976 as a surface-to-ship weapon; two years later the AGM-84A air-launched version was fielded and in 1981 the third variant, submarine-launched, entered service with the US Navy. Over 3,500 missiles have been ordered to date by the US forces and for export.

The air-launched version is 3.84 metres long with a body diameter of 34.3 centimetres; it weighs 522 kilogrammes of which 227 kilogrammes are in the blast/fragmentation warhead. A range of about 60 nautical miles was specified and this drove the design into the use of an air-breathing turbo-jet. By studying a variety of missiles a general rule on range and power requirements can be determined. For ranges up to around 8 nautical miles the kinetic energy can be utilised if the weapon is released at high speed, even at low level. Paveway 3 is an example. If released from high level, this range can be almost doubled while still relying on the kinetic energy. From about 8 nautical miles to ranges in the order of 20 to 25 nautical miles, kinetic energy, augmented by some simple rocket motor arrangement, will suffice; the AGM-130 and the Skipper are examples. Above 25 nautical miles the use of an air-breathing engine becomes cost-effective but once this expensive step is taken, range is dependent only on

Weapons and Warfare

fuel load or type. Harpoon uses a turbo-jet engine to achieve 60 nautical miles but the Boeing air-launched-cruise-missile (ALCM) AGM-86, uses a similar design to achieve ranges in excess of 2,000 nautical miles. The Teledyne CAE turbo-jet engine in Harpoon produces 600 pounds of thrust, weighs only 98 pounds and produces its 60 nautical miles range from about 100 pounds of fuel. An update planned for Harpoon includes replacing the present fuel with the JP-10 high-density fuel used in the AGM-86B ALCM. This enhanced performance fuel will increase the range performance by an estimated fifteen per cent. A further improvement will be to increase the size of the fuel tank itself by some two feet which will double the range of the weapon.

Other than fuel, motor and warhead, Harpoon has a three-axis altitude reference system and an auto-pilot which allows for mid-course guidance. A radar altimeter is fitted to allow close control of height throughout the flight profile. Following launch, and after a short period when altitude control is achieved, the missile descends in a programmed dive until the cruising height is reached. At this point the missile levels out and commences its *sea-skimming*. At a pre-determined distance from the target the radar sensor is activated and the missile searches for its target. The original versions of the missile were designed to pull-up short of the target and to dive onto it; this was with small targets in mind, such as fast patrol boats, where there is a risk that the target could be so low that it would not interfere with the missile at *sea-skimming* height. In later versions of the missile this facility has been removed; it is unnecessary against all but the smallest target and these would only rarely be considered to be a legitimate Harpoon target.

Modification to the search pattern and the en-route navigation can be made using the facility of the on-board data processing. One update under consideration is to provide the facility to route through a number of way points. This helps to protect the position of the launch vehicle from back-plotting by the target and would also allow attacks to be made around land features, for example, round islands or within inlets.

As has been seen, once the decision has been made to use a turbo-jet motor, range is merely a matter of making provison for extra fuel. Air carriage can restrict the amount of stretch undertaken but with the new generation of motor and high calorific value fuels, quite moderate stretch confers major increases in range – in the case of Harpoon a two foot stretch results in an increase of range in the order of 60 nautical miles. The problem the missile designer faces is not so much range as targeting. When ranges exceed the prudent maximum that the delivery vehicle itself may obtain, and these may be constrained by reasons of vulnerability or of concealment, then third party targeting may be required. This can be provided by a variety of means; conventionally from a reconnaissance aircraft such as the P-3C, Nimrod or Bear D; or through triangulation of the target's electronic emissions (ELINT); or through analysis of its signals traffic (SIGINT); or from space using a variety of sensors including infra-red or photography; or even by sightings from friendly forces.

Air-to-Surface Weapons

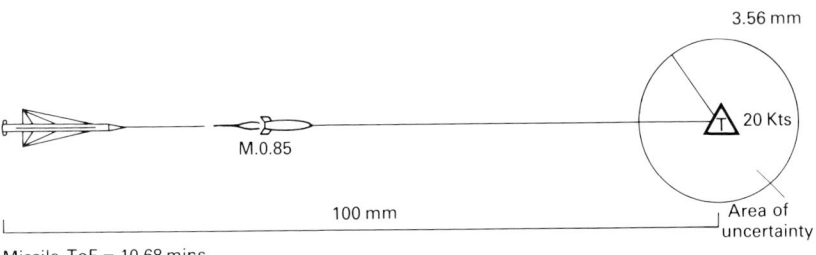

FIG 1.18 Target area of uncertainty is a function of missile time of flight and target speed.

Once detected, the missile has to be fired with sufficient accuracy in the en-route phase so that at the point of going active with the on-board seeker, the target is within the search pattern.

Consider a simplified situation. A missile with a speed of Mach 0.85 (562 knots at sea level) is fired against a 20 knot target. If the worst case is assumed, at the point of firing the target could turn in any direction. Target position will therefore be an area of uncertainty equivalent to target speed and missile time of flight (Fig 1.18).

In this instance the missile would have to search for a target up to 3.56 nautical miles either side of its last known position. Assuming the sector head has a 45° total look angle, the missile would have to go active not later than 9.3 nautical miles from the assumed target position, giving the target a maximum possible reaction time to the missile emissions of 59.6 seconds (Fig. 1.19).

There is a requirement to achieve greater stand-off against major surface fleet units for two reasons: first, the modern shipborne surface-to-air missile is long-ranged and can pose threats well in excess of 60 nautical miles; second, when operating with fighter combat-air-patrol, either ship-based or land-based, the threat to the delivering aircraft can be some hundreds of miles from

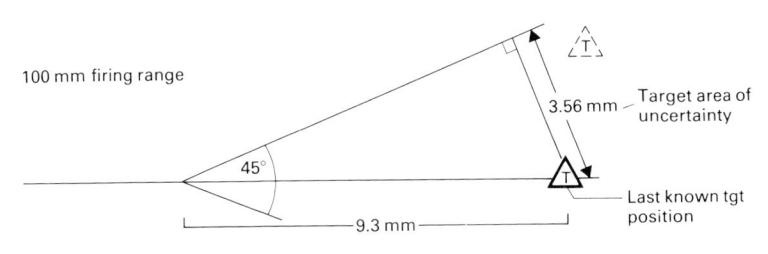

Area of Uncertainty Determines Missile Search Requirement.

FIG 1.19 Area of uncertainty determines missile search requirement.

Weapons and Warfare

PLATE 1.4 **Sea Eagle.** A 'super smart', long range, sea skimming anti-ship missile. It is seen here carried beneath the VSTOL Harrier. *(British Aerospace)*

the target. For this reason, the Soviets have tended to develop large long-ranged missiles for use against the heavy air defences of the US Carrier Battle Groups and the development of modern long-range cruise missiles will obviously have an effect on the maritime battle. From the example above, however, the problems can be determined. If a missile is fired from 300 nautical miles, the seeker (in the example) would have to activate nearly 28 nautical miles from the target at nearly three minutes flight time from impact. This gives the defences considerable warning and more than adequate time to react. Such ranges can also present a further problem. At sea-skimming heights, the seeker may be too low to detect a low-lying target if the active-seeking range gets too large.

The designer has alternatives, all having pros and cons. He may decrease the time of flight by increasing the speed but to do this beyond subsonic speeds at low level is costly on fuel, motor and hence total missile size. With missiles like the very large AS-4 (over 30 feet long and about 6,000 kilogrammes) the Soviets have gone for a high level (60,000 feet plus), very high speed (Mach 3.5) approach followed by a high angle terminal dive. Although the missile approach can be detected, time of flight is relatively short and the terminal profile makes it very difficult to intercept. Further, from such an approach

Air-to-Surface Weapons

there is no obstruction from earth curvature to interfere with its homing system. There is much to be said for such a solution.

Another approach is to provide target position update during the en-route phase. This has many advantages in that at each update the area of uncertainty of the target is commensurately reduced and, with it, so are the problems. It also enables the missile to stay passive for longer, so reducing its vulnerability. Once the system of continuous update of target position is perfected, the time of flight becomes largely irrelevant and very long ranged missiles can be used. In this case the need for airborne or seaborne launch platforms must be questioned and land-based ballistic missiles, or cruise missiles, become feasible systems for the attack of surface shipping in distant oceans.

Anti-Radiation Missiles (ARM)

Anti-aircraft defensive systems have many inherent advantages over their intended targets. They are less constrained by weight, size, power sources, crew complement and their weapons have the benefit of many of the same advantages. Because air power is so dominant on the battlefield, the resources invested in its counter have been great and nowhere more so than in the Warsaw Pact where quick-reaction NATO air was seen to be the greatest threat to both the surprise attack and to the use of manoeuvring armour, the primary arm of the Soviet Army.

In earlier days the answer to the surface-to-air (SAM) threat was to fly below its sensors and the current expertise in ultra low level operations, generally within NATO and more particularly in the RAF, resulted from this situation. But the capability of modern SAM systems to operate at even the lowest levels has steadily improved. Better control over the problems of radar multi-pathing has emerged, antennae design has improved, as has signal processing, and fixed SAM sites can be positioned carefully with aerials raised on masts or on earth bunds to improve the radar horizon. The problems of missile fly-out at low level has been eased by the use of vertical launch with the missiles approaching the target from above. This does something to negate terrain screening tactics. Missiles with active heads mean that, once fired, the missile is the threat rather than the ground site or the whole system. This limits the counter-measure options.

The cost of modern aircraft makes a reasonable investment in their protection sensible but of greater import is the fact that unless the ground defences can be neutralised, or at least diminished, air power may not be able to be applied effectively and the whole massive investment in it could be negated. The airman therefore has to fight first for his airspace before fighting anything else and it is the anti-radiation missile which largely enables him to do this.

The impetus for ARM development came from the Vietnam war where high local concentrations of SAMs were encountered. The AGM-45 Shrike missile was used extensively. Shrike is a 10 foot long, 8 inch diameter missile with a

Weapons and Warfare

ARM	Length	Dia	Wt	Speed	Range	Warhead
Shrike AGM-45	10 ft	8 in	390 lb	M 2.0	20 nm	IUS Blast/Frag.
Standard ARM AGM-78	15 ft	13.5 in	1,400 lb	M 2.5	30 nm	Blast/Frag.
HARM AGM-88	13 ft 8½ in	10 in	796 lb	≃M 3.0		

FIG 1.20 The major US ARM.

range variously up to about 20 nautical miles and having a 145 pound blast/fragmentation warhead. Shrike suffered some inadequacies; it was controlled by a 'bang-bang' system and suffered the problem of falling short as seen on the early Paveway bombs. It was also pre-set to certain frequencies which meant it was inflexible in its use, the crew not being able to reprogramme to new threats in the air. The range and speed of the missile, despite the latter being close to Mach 2, made the delivering aircraft approach closer than desirable to the SAM target.

These inadequacies were addressed in the follow-on Standard ARM, the AGM-78. As Fig 1.20 shows, it was a much larger weapon. Standard ARM has a broad-band seeker able to operate against search, SAM and GCI radars and gave the delivering aircraft the capability to turn away before entering the target's lethal envelope. The missile can be programmed to react to specific targets while in flight.

AGM-88 HARM is the latest in the US development of ARM. It is a high-speed missile designed to engage targets before they can be switched-off and to have the ability to strike the target before the aircraft can be engaged by the SAM. This later mode is one of three, the others being a *Target of Opportunity* mode where the seeker locks onto any target answering certain requirements, and a pre-briefed mode where the missile is launched against a target with specific parameters.

It is interesting to see the difference in philosophy building up between the US and Europe, particularly the UK. The UK approach to ARM in the form of ALARM is based on a quite different operational concept. ALARM was conceived to be carried as a target defence suppression weapon to be fired into the target ahead of the attacking force. When fired, it climbs to around 35,000 feet where it deploys a parachute and descends slowly searching for signals over a wide footprint. If a signal matching the threat data base is detected, the parachute is jettisoned and the missile free-falls and guides on to the emitter.

It is clearly seen, however, that no matter how fast the missile may ascend to 35,000 feet if it is to hang on a parachute and then free-fall to the target there is little chance of it engaging the SAM before the SAM will engage the on-coming high-speed aircraft.

An option suggested is for the attacking formation to orbit until the ALARMs have had chance to engage the defending SAMs but orbiting over enemy territory in war is not a tactic likely to endear itself to operators. This

Air-to-Surface Weapons

PLATE 1.5 **ALARM.** Anti-radiation missiles on Tornado. In this case seven such missiles are carried. Carrying fewer ALARM would permit other weapons also to be carried. *(British Aerospace)*

limitation will force the RAF into two concepts: the first will be to use the weapon not as a self-defence weapon but as an area defence or 'campaign' weapon for supporting defences in general rather than in the specific; the second will be to use aircraft ahead of the main strike force to launch the ARM in sufficient time to suppress the defences without delaying the attack aircraft on route.

In turn this may force the RAF to reconsider another decision. From operational experience the USAF have long considered that the task of defence suppression demanded specialist and highly trained crews; further, that it demanded equally highly specialist and extensively equipped aircraft. So was born the specialist WILD WEASEL force which served so well in Vietnam and now is equipped with the F-4G. The extent of the modification of the F-4G is some measure of the complexity of the role and those who have worked with the Wild Weasels can testify to their effect on the battlefield. They attribute this success solely to the specialist nature of their equipment and training. It is undoubtedly a full-time task and one unlikely to be optimised if looked upon as a strap-on secondary capability. It will be interesting to see how the RAF handles this problem when ALARM is fielded shortly.

An effective defence against ARM is to switch-off the emitting radar. This is a two-edged sword because the radar is rendered inoperative while the emitter is suppressed. From the viewpoint of the attack pilot, this is quite sufficient even if it is not so profitable from a 'campaign' standpoint, where the destruction of the SAM is clearly highly desirable. Much of the ability of the SAM to switch-off depends on seeing the missile en-route or alternatively receiving some indication of launch. Large missiles such as the AS-4 could be expected to show on radar; smaller missiles such as HARM, or ALARM which will approach from the near vertical, detection may be far more problematical.

ARM used as part of an integrated attack package against a high value target is an attractive offensive option. Against warships, for example, the coincident arrival of anti-ship and anti-radiation missiles would give the commanding Admiral a difficult choice of which systems to keep on line and which to suppress. It is this sort of practical tactical problem which is sparking renewed interest in detection devices using parts of the spectrum other than emitting radar.

Cruise Missiles

At what point an AGM-130 rocket-powered GBU-15 or an extended range AGM-84 becomes a *cruise missile* may be debatable until some acceptable definition is agreed, probably based on an arbitrary range capability. Without entering that argument, it is generally accepted that the General Dynamics Ground-Launched-Cruise-Missile (GLCM), the Boeing AGM-86B Air-Launched-Cruise-Missile (ALCM), and the new range of Soviet cruise missiles, of which the new AS-15 is the air launched version, without doubt are *cruise missiles*. They are weapon systems with great implications for both offensive and defensive warfare and offer great scope for development and improvement in a number of areas as technology proceeds apace.

Taking the AGM-86B (ALCM) as a case example, it can be seen to follow a trend which had existed for a long time. Cruise missiles are said to have been under study in the US before the end of World War Two, as well they may have been, because the German V-1, albeit in crude form, was a GLCM and had been conceived originally as an air launched weapon, indeed it was tested initially on the Focke-Wolf-Condor. Both Mace and Snark testified to continued interest in cruise missiles and it was in the mid-sixties that the Boeing AGM-86 was first suggested as a decoy to assist in B-52 penetration of the Soviet defences. After a somewhat convoluted history, which included being involved in the argument that there was little point in penetrating with a decoy when the decoy could be armed. Later, being involved in the politics of the B-1 bomber, the AGM-86B eventually emerged as an armed missile in its own right.

The AGM-86B ALCM is a weapon of about 3,000 pounds weight, over 20 feet long and cruises at M 0.85 for ranges variously estimated around 2,000 nautical miles. An air-breathing Williams turbo-jet of 600 pounds static

Air-to-Surface Weapons

thrust, running on JP-10 high calorific value fuel, accounts in part for its excellent range characteristics. Warhead details are rarely given but a nuclear capability is acknowledged and simple first-order estimations of the weight from published line drawings would put it in the order of 300 kilogrammes. The ALCM can be carried by the B-52 and is planned to be carried by the B-1; the B-52 will carry twelve externally on two inboard wing pylons of six each and an additional eight in an internal rotary launcher fitted in the bomb bay; a total of twenty missiles. The B-1 will utilise the same eight missile rotary launcher internally and mount fourteen additional missiles externally on fuselage pylons for a total of twenty-two missiles.

To some the cruise missile offers a cheaper method of providing a national strategic deterrent than the Trident programme although such people place too little importance on the near invulnerability of the nuclear submarine, or on the equally near invulnerability of the multiple and decoyed ballistic missile warheads. However, it is also true that the advocates of the Trident, in defending their young, have tended to decry the cruise missile too much and too far. Even the first generation cruise missiles, typified by the Tomahawk and the ALCM, present a formidable target for an air defence system. They are small targets to detect in the first place and equally difficult to engage with a missile optimised for fusing and warhead effect against much larger aircraft-sized targets. When long range capability is taken into account, both in the missile itself and in the launch aircraft, be that B-52 or the Soviet Bear H, then all-round attack is a possibility against most targets. Defence against all-round threats is expensive in terms of resources and a look at the situation in the United Kingdom is instructive.

Air defence against stand-off weapons is largely a matter of circumferences. As stand-off missiles are difficult to intercept, either because they are small and stealthy (cruise missiles) or they are high and fast (Soviet AS-4), it is advantageous to intercept the carrier aircraft. If the stand-off capability is limited, say to 200–300 nautical miles, and is directional within a limited arc a passable defence can be fielded by using long loiter fighters supported by AEW and tankers (Fig 1.21).

This is accomplished at some cost, however, and it is important to the understanding of the worth of long ranged cruise missiles to have some knowledge of this cost. Modern fighters can cost $30 million and may cost more, their missiles in the era of AMRAAM may cost $300,000 each and a load of between four and eight will become the norm. Tankers will cost upwards of $80 million and AEW aircraft will approach $120 million or, with enhancements, much more.

The aggressor has one considerable advantage over the defence which he must optimise and exploit to the full; he can choose the time of his coming and can concentrate his attack to achieve defence saturation. Conversely, the defence must be forever vigilant and when the intercept geometry cannot be solved from ground alert, then the expensive option of airborne combat-air-

Weapons and Warfare

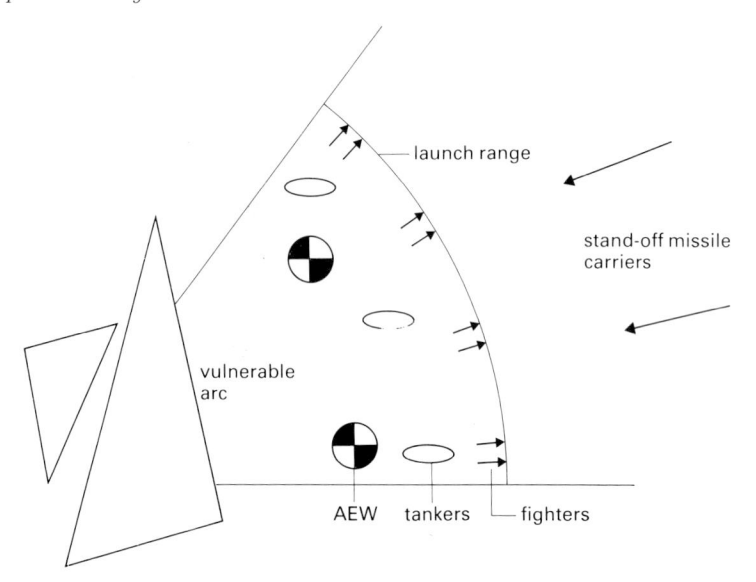

FIG 1.21 Defence against Stand-off missiles over a restricted arc.

patrol (CAP) has to be used. The mathematics of the resources needed to maintain a single unit on CAP is illustrated in Fig 1.22.

With these in mind, consider the geometry of a cruise missile defence over, for example, a 90° arc at a 300 nautical mile intercept range (Fig 1.23).

To cover a 471 nautical mile arc when an AEW could detect a cruise missile at 50 nautical miles – giving a 100 nautical mile 'cover' – would require:

$$\frac{471}{100} = 4.71 \text{ CAPs}$$

Using the parameters above, *each CAP aircraft* at 300 nautical miles will require 3.33 serviceable aircraft per position. In turn, the serviceability factor must be taken into account and at seventy per cent the requirement becomes:

$$\frac{4.71 \times 3.33}{0.7} = 22.4 \text{ aircraft}$$

This covers the continuous CAP at 300 nautical miles by only one aircraft per CAP position. As the wise offensive planner will attempt to obtain defence saturation it would be unwise to have such a thin CAP manning and two aircraft might be considered to be a prudent minimum. This would double the requirement to forty-five aircraft.

It can be seen from this simplified first-order mathematics that transit time is a major factor in the calculation and that if this can be reduced, major advantages accrue. It is in this area that tanker aircraft truely become *force multipliers*.

Air-to-Surface Weapons

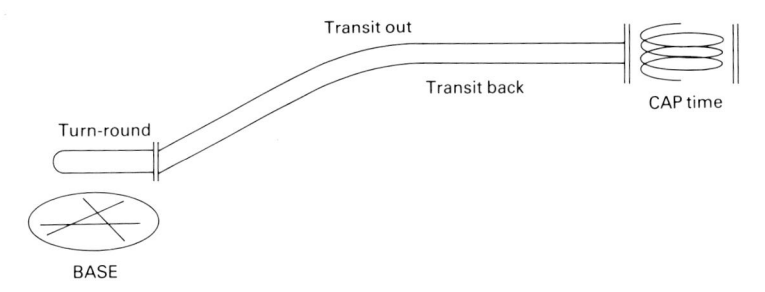

FIG 1.22 Basic Combat Air Patrol (CAP) mathematics.

Consider the in-flight refuel which gives a CAP aircraft another two hours on CAP. Cycle time then becomes:

$$2 + 0.75 + 0.75 + 3.5 = \underline{7}$$

Aircraft required per CAP now becomes:

$$\frac{7}{3.5} = \underline{2 \text{ acft/CAP}} \text{ (in lieu of 3.33)}$$

Aircraft required to cover the 90° sector at 300 nautical miles with tankers becomes:

$$\frac{4.71 \times 2}{0.7} = \underline{13.46 \text{ aircraft}}$$

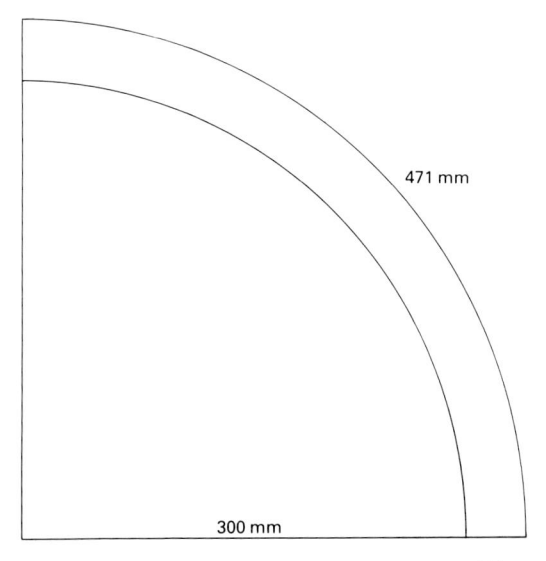

FIG 1.23 The radius to be covered for an intercept at 300 nm.

Weapons and Warfare

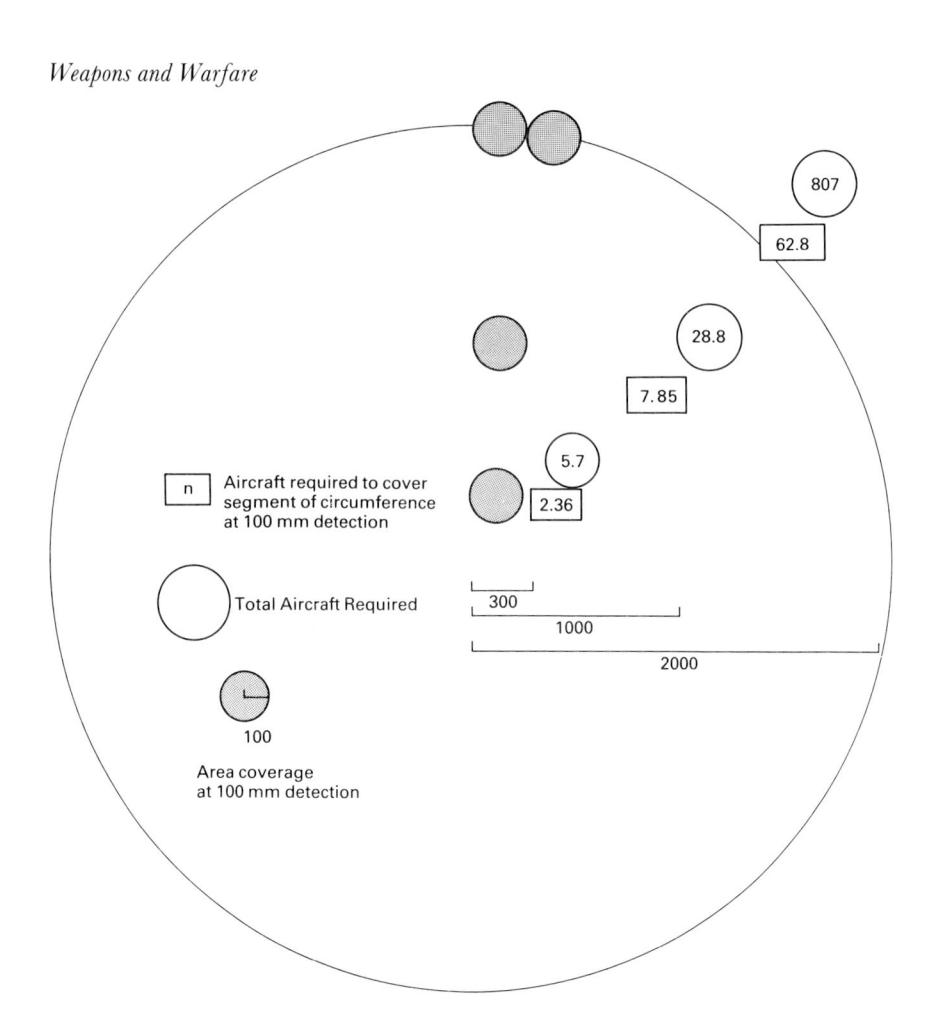

Fig 1.24 The mathematics of long distance combat on patrol.

When compared with the 22.4 aircraft required without tankers, it can be seen how highly cost-effective tankers can be.

Such fighter CAP considerations may prove to be somewhat academic in the age of stand-off improvements over the 200 nautical miles of the old AS-4 to the 1,800 nautical miles of the AS-15 or the 2,000 nautical miles-plus of the AGM-84B.

Fig 1.24 shows some relationships over a 90 degree sector looking at AEW cover at three different ranges, 300, 1,000 and 2,000 nautical miles. If an AEW aircraft was deemed able to detect a target at 100 nautical miles, giving it a total frontage of 200 nautical miles, and assuming the best case of no overlap of cover with adjacent AEW patrols, the figure gives some idea of the mathematics involved. It can be seen that in the case of a 1,000 nautical mile

Air-to-Surface Weapons

patrol, and given a six hour turn-round – not unreasonable for long-term operation of a complex system aircraft – and a twelve hour total flight time, then 2.57 aircraft are required in total to man every CAP position. To cover the 90° segment at 200 nautical mile frontage requires 7.85 stations and the total number of aircraft required at a seventy per cent serviceability rate amounts to 28.8. The purpose here is to give some idea of the macro mathematics rather than the suggestion of any particular scenario but it is worth noting that it would take a very good AEW aircraft to detect a stealthy cruise missile at 100 nautical miles and long-range cruise-missile carriers can envelope targets so extending considerably the 90° segment. It can also be seen that to attempt to intercept aircraft which can release their stand-off missiles 2,000 nautical miles from target is a practical difficulty and an economic impossibility. On the other hand, few scenarios present such a purely mathematical situation as the attempt to fit 2,000 nautical mile radius circles to a globe will soon, and convincingly, demonstrate.

Fig 1.25 considers the variation of the aircraft required under conditions of differing endurance. It is apparent that whenever *dwell* or *loiter* is required, the high endurance typically associated with the larger aircraft shows great advantage. As in AEW aircraft so much of the total cost is tied up in the system rather than the aircraft, the long-endurance airframe pays off handsomely and quickly. The seventy-two hour endurance acknowledges the airship as a contender in the field and this may be an understatement of the endurance possible from a large airship using modern technology. Clearly there is a point when time on station is counteracted by long transit times.

If, however, it is decided that intercept of the missile carrier at long stand-off ranges is impracticable then shortening the circumference to intercept just off the UK coast would result in a 1,650 nautical mile circumference. Here it can be seen that the high endurance of the airship gives the possibility of great savings on the total system. Detecting the cruise missile is only the first part of the problem; the second being the successful engagement. Each of the AEW stations outlined above would need to be supported by a fighter CAP to make good the intercept. A closer study of this difficult problem may lead to the conclusion that the intercept timescales are so tight that both detection and intercept must be conducted by the same vehicle. Another path to the same conclusion could be the numbers of fighters required to maintain twenty-four hour watch over an extended perimeter. The resource mathematics of the long-endurance AEW aircraft have been demonstrated; they pale into insignificance when compared with the requirement for the much shorter range fighter aircraft.

But there is another set of factors which must be taken into account and that is the possibility of the fighter obtaining a kill against the cruise missile, given a successful detection by the AEW.

Fig 1.26 shows some suggested percentage serviceabilities, or reliabilities. The figures used are meant to illustrate the mathematics involved rather than

Weapons and Warfare

Endurance can be improved by specialist aircraft design, by air-to-air refueling or by innovated utilisation of devices such as airships.

Range	Total Acft Req'd at twelve hour endurance	Total Acft Req'd at eighteen hour endurance	Total Acft Req'd at seventy-two hour endurance
			(1)
300	5.7	4.9	4.6
1,000	28.8	20.7	39.7
2,000	807	269	NA

(1) Assumes a transit speed of 40 knots and is airship orientated.

If, however, it is decided to defend close-in and airship basing can be close (2 hours) from patrol position the situation changes:

Circumference to be covered	= 1,650 nm
Acft Req'd on station at 100 nm detection range	= 8.25
Acft on average 300 nm from patrol point (12 hour period)	= 14.1
Acft Req'd available	
Total Acft Req'd at seventy per cent scramble	= 20.2
Total Acft Req'd at 18 hour endurance	= 17.14
Total Acft Req'd at 72 hour endurance	= 13.52
Weapon system reliability (i.e. radar and weapon control system)	90%
Probability of successful launch	95%
Probability of successful guidances	90%
Probability of successful fusing. (Air-to-air missile fusing is normally optimised against the much larger target of the full sized aircraft)	80%
Probability of successful warhead activation and effect on the small target (see comment under fusing)	60%

Total single shot probability of kill

$$= 0.9 \times 0.95 \times 0.9 \times 0.8 \times 0.6$$
$$= 0.369$$
$$= 37\%$$

At a PSSK of 37% a four-missile salvo against a target will give the following probability of kill:

$$P = 1 - (1 - PSSK)$$

where

$$n = \text{no. of events (or shots)}$$
$$= 1 - (1 - 0.369)^4$$
$$= 84\%$$

FIG 1.25 Variation of aircraft required according to endurance.

relate to any particular system and the reader is invited to substitute figures of his choice. It can be seen that even assuming what some may say are generous figures against such a small and difficult target, the single shot possibility of a kill (PSSK) is not particularly high. It also shows that if the PSSK is in the order of thirty-seven per cent a four-missile salvo will give only an eighty-four per cent chance of a kill against a single cruise missile target.

If two aircraft are on CAP then two cruise missile targets can be engaged

Air-to-Surface Weapons

Alternatively a four-missile load could be expanded against the separate targets giving a probability of kill against each:

$$P = 1 - (1 - 0.369)^1$$
$$= 0.60$$
$$\text{or } \underline{\underline{60\%}}$$

NB. In mathematical terms this is not a high probability of kill.

FIG 1.26 Probability of obtaining a kill against a cruise missile target.

with an eighty-four per cent probability of successful engagement but what situation pertains against a B-52 or B-1 firing a salvo of twenty or twenty-two missiles? Cruise missiles offer the offensive airmen an excellent means of obtaining defence saturation.

Modern cruise missiles can be formidable adversaries for air defence systems. When the US are probably flying stealth fighters (the F-19?) and even stealth bombers, how will such technology applied to the much smaller cruise missile affect detection ranges? In the examples used previously, a detection range of 100 nautical miles was assumed but by use of extensive composites, radar-absorbent material and by careful shaping of the aerodynamic design, great improvements can be made in radar-cross-section reduction over current designs which themselves are small enough. The effect of smaller detection ranges on the resource mathematics outlined previously are easily calculated and soon show the high cost of defence against the threat.

The efficacy of the threat is largely a function of accuracy and warhead size. Warhead size has tended to be small in cruise missiles in the past and accuracy considerations have tended to lead to nuclear warheads. However, a proposal was made to equip a Tomahawk AGM-109 derivative with fifty-eight tactical airfield attack sub-munitions. In this form the 2,900 pound missile would have had a range of 472 kilometres. The small size of cruise missiles makes the range/payload relationship quite critical but the advent of more capable conventional warheads is making this constraint less of a hindrance to the designer.

Accuracy is the all important factor. There are two aspects to the problem; route navigation, and target acquisition and terminal homing. The problem of route navigation is to know where the missile starts from, where it is going, and knowing where it is en-route, to enable it to make navigational corrections. Clearly, the system used should be as jam-resistant as possible, be reliable and accurate.

Most cruise missile navigation systems rely on large scale data bases of the en-route and target terrain against which a comparison of the sensed en-route conditions is made. There are different methods of doing this, depending on which characteristics are selected for comparison. For example, one system is terrain *profile* comparison. In this the profile of the terrain, measured from a radar altimeter returns, is compared to a data base contained in the missile and

Weapons and Warfare

a matching of the two can give accurate positions to a few tens of metres accuracy.

Another system relies on a similar matching of signal to stored data base but this time using terrain *characteristics*. These may be land or water, road or woodland, built-up area or barren mountainside.

In the past a problem with cruise missile navigation has been to achieve accurate en-route navigation over water and to achieve landfalls within the stored data base. This is becoming less of a problem. Not only are inertial navigation systems becoming more accurate at less cost but advances in modern data storage is allowing greater data bases to be carried in the cruise missiles. Apart from this, the advent of the Satellite navigation system GPS (Global Positioning System), allows navigation in three-dimensions to impressively small errors. Theoretically, the system can be jammed when the missile is in close proximity to the target but it is more unlikely to be jammed in the en-route phase over an ocean leg.

Terminal accuracy is already high. Digital scene matching area correlation (DSMAC) is a well-established technique which operates along the same principle as the en-route navigation systems in that it compares the target scene, as viewed by the sensor, with a stored image. The ability to match one with the other is dependent on the accuracy and extent of the stored information and the speed of processing the mis-match into a control correction. Modern electronics are advancing on both fronts; storage capacity is increasing substantially and processing speed is improving by orders of magnitude. The result is that accuracy against a target on which there is good intelligence should be measured in the small number of metres by the mid-nineties, indeed some enthusiasts will claim that the direct hit will be the norm against all but the most difficult targets.

Such accuracy has an immediate beneficial effect on warhead size and targets previously ruled out as unsuitable for conventional attack can now be viewed afresh. Cruise missiles can carry, for example, warhead sizes suitable to allow the use of large modern unitary warheads – one proposed for a Tomahawk derivative was 937 pounds weight – and modern developments such as fuel-air explosives could be utilised against a variety of targets to good effect well within this weight.

Fuel-air explosives (FAE) work on the principle of dispensing a fine mist or aerosol-like cloud of fuel before detonating it. A very high-pressure shock wave is produced and this is followed by a fireball. A 500 kilogramme FAE based on methane can result in an overpressure up to 0.9 kilogrammes per square centimetre (kg/cm^2) at a distance of 130 metres from the cloud; at 190 metres the pressure is still sufficient to cause damage to tank optics and aerials. Severe damage to soft structures such as aircraft can be caused at pressures as low as 0.42 kg/cm^2. As a comparison, 0.8 kg/cm^2 is sufficient to sink, or at least severely damage, a medium-sized warship.

Current FAE technology can produce an effect three to five times as great as conventional explosives of the same weight. Peak overpressures of up to 100 kg/cm^2 are considered possible with development and this would involve a pressure wave travelling as fast as 2,200 metres per second. Such weapons could prove to be up to ten times as effective as conventional explosives.

FAE have an application for use with cruise missiles because of their relatively high effect per unit of weight and because many of the targets which cruise missiles could be used against would be vulnerable to high blast overpressure. Aircraft in the open are obvious targets, and the Warsaw Pact still have large numbers of unsheltered aircraft, particularly their heavy types. Sheltered aircraft could also be vulnerable to high overpressures as could elements of modern railway systems and power generation plants.

A further technological advance stemming from the electronic revolution which will benefit the cruise missile designer is the *super-smart* sub-munition.

The 'Super-Smarts'

The *smart* weapons can be locked onto their target, fired, and left to complete the task unaided by the crew. But the crew have to first acquire the target, recognise it as hostile and lock the missile to it. The *super-smarts* achieve this input by use of the data processing of their own sensor information. This has become possible by advances in the miniaturisation of high speed and high capacity data processing devices suitable for use in the airborne missile, and the development of millimetric-wave sensors.

Millimetre-wave (MMW) radar fits between the infra-red and the centimetric bands in terms of resolution but it works in a part of the spectrum, 35 MHz to 200 GHz, which is difficult to counter. The short wavelengths are not particularly good for penetrating the atmosphere over long ranges but their application tends to suit the shorter range and there is no major disadvantage in practice. The short wavelength does allow the use of small antennae and this is an advantage in missile and sub-munition applications.

Although still in the development stage, it is already clear that millimetric-wave seekers will be able to produce signals which will be able to be processed to determine far more detail about a target than was previously thought possible. Not only will it be possible to identify armour from soft-skinned vehicles but, eventually, their seems no reason why tanks cannot be located within an array of APCs.

The Hughes WASP project was one of the first to utilise this technology. It has been followed by a variety of projects since many of which, it must be said, have not been fielded because the practice was too far behind the theory of the laboratory in what is still a relatively new and immature field of knowledge. However, some major decisions have been based on the technology succeeding, including the Phase 3 munition for the Multiple Launch Rocket System

Weapons and Warfare

(MLRS) fielded in the US and Europe and a number of European ideas on air-launched anti-tank weapons.

An early project envisaged a pod weighing in total about 2,000 pounds containing twelve Wasp mini-missiles. Each mini-missile would operate independently after being fired from the launcher and would seek for, identify and then guide onto the selected target. In this approach each sub-munition was a mini-missile and had to have its own propulsion and guidance. Later approaches to the same problem suggested an unpowered sub-munition descending on an eccentric parachute to produce a seeker scan, the warhead, using forged-fragment technology, fired when the data processor calculated that the range and orientation to the target was correct. This resulted in a smaller, simpler, and therefore cheaper, sub-munition but also allowed the great advantage of packaging far more sub-munitions into a pod or bus vehicle.

Developments along this theme are not difficult to imagine. For example, the bus vehicle, a cruise missile or whatever, could have its own integral millimetric seeker and would locate a suitable target array before dispensing the sub-munitions to conduct their own individual target search and attack. The size of the bus vehicle could be such as to permit pre-programmed search patterns to be flown or even searches along approach routes to the battlefield. A *smart* bus-vehicle, dispersing *super-smart* sub-munitions, may be the path to the future for a variety of targets including airfields and those targets on the immediate battlefield and its hinterland.

Cost will be high and this may frighten those concerned solely with budgets. However, the technology can fulfil its early promise, such weapons will surely be *cost-effecive*. And what price failing to deter the next World War?

Note
[1] Report of HOIC Defence Committee P4/P5 Vol 2, p. 796

Introducing Chapter 2

THE shape of war is continually changing and nowhere more drastically than in the air where modern missiles have completely altered the nature of air combat. Dog fights may still occasionally occur but more by accident than intention in an environment where the principal weapons are designed to be fired at ranges of many kilometres. Nevertheless, air combat now is no less demanding than in the days of the Red Baron; nerve and speedy reflexes are still at a premium but for different reasons and purposes. The next chapter shows why. The author, an experienced airman, takes us through the theory and right into the cockpit.

2

Air-to-Air Weapons

AIR VICE MARSHAL J R WALKER CBE AFC RAF

THE development of large formations of heavily armed aircraft to prosecute the strategic bombing offensive in daylight during World War Two probably provided the incentive for the development of air-to-air guided weapons. Certainly the Luftwaffe fighter losses were heavy and increasingly so with the advent of the P-51 Mustang, used in the long-range escort role. Two missiles were well into development when the war stopped in 1945; one, the Henschel HS 298 was radio command guided, and the other, the Ruhstahl/BMW X-4 was wire guided. Perhaps fortunately, they were not used operationally.

During the late 1940s and the 1950s most of the leading aviation nations pursued the development of air-to-air missiles. The US started development of the Sparrow, Falcon and Sidewinder series, France produced the radar-guided MATRA 511 and the radio command AA20, the Soviet Union fielded the radar guided AA-1 Alkali and the UK produced the Firestreak IR missile.

There is a comprehensive collection of AAMs world-wide and there is little value in cataloguing them here; there are excellent missile directories produced from time to time by the leading aviation magazines. What is more useful is to consider some of the factors common to missiles of a particular group and to see how these strengths and weaknesses affect the use of those missiles in a combat environment.

Infra-Red (IR) Missiles

When discussing IR missiles the unit of wavelength used is the micron (μm) which is one-millionth part of a metre. Fig 2.1 shows the pattern of radiation across the infra-red part of the electromagnetic spectrum of a body at a temperature of 5,000°C, 3,000°C and 500°C. It can be seen that at the higher temperature the peak emission is in the visible range and the body would appear *white hot*. As it cools, so it moves further towards the red end of the visible spectrum and becomes visibly *red hot* until it cools beyond the visible spectrum but still emits radiation in the invisible *infra-red* part of the spectrum.

The wavelength of the maximum intensity of radiation increases as the

Weapons and Warfare

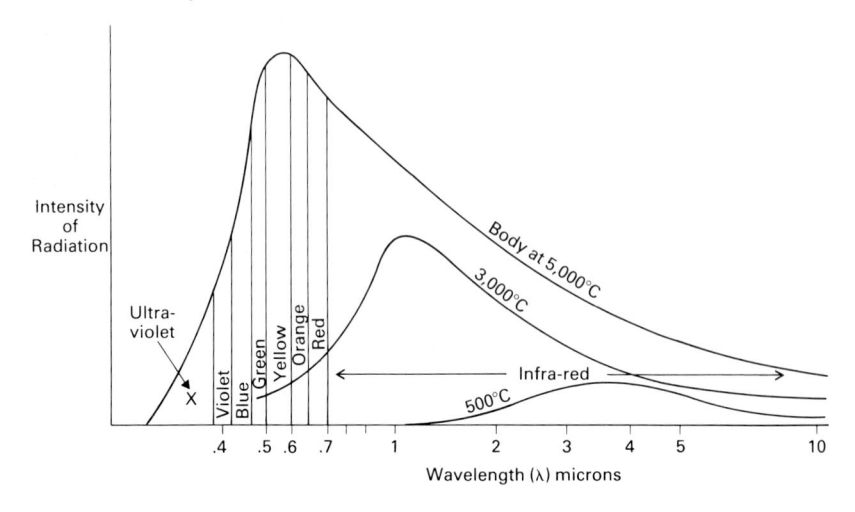

Fig 2.1 Radiated electromagnetic energy of a body at varying temperatures.

temperature of the body decreases and this can be seen by Wien's law which states that the wavelength of maximum radiation is:

$$\lambda_{max} = \frac{2900}{T}$$

where T = the absolute temperature of the body.

From Wien's law it can be seen that the wavelength of radiation from the hot metal of a jet pipe, typically 500°C, would be:

$$\lambda_{max} = \frac{2900}{500 + 273}$$

$$= 3.75 \ \mu m$$

The hot metal of the inside of jet pipes is commonly viewed from anything up to an angle of 30° off the tail and missiles optimised for this frequency, such as the early IR missiles, were restricted to attack from the rear over this small angle of 30° each side of a dead astern. Further, jet pipes can be concealed by structure, particularly during manoeuvre, and designs such as the F-4 Phantom and the Jaguar show how overhanging tail planes can provide concealment of the jet pipes under some conditions.

The limitation caused by reliance on jet pipe emissions can be overcome in part by homing on the emissions emanating from the exhaust plume. The carbon dioxide in the exhaust radiates around 3 μm and the water vapour at around 4.2 μm. The exhaust plume radiates in all directions and theoretically gives an all-round detection capability but in practice the exhaust plume is

Air-to-Surface Weapons

also shielded from ahead and from the sides. Effectively, exhaust plume seekers will have an enhanced rear angular capability but not a head-on or all-aspect capability.

Another source of radiation from the target can be the skin heating which results from air friction at high, normally supersonic, speeds. An aircraft flying at Mach 1.25 at low level, or one flying at about Mach 1.7 at high level will exhibit a skin temperature rise of about 65°C. The higher skin heating at high level is partly compensated by the lower ambient temperature. Wien's law shows that the wavelength of maximum radiation for this temperature is much higher than the 3 to 4.2 μm of the exhaust plume and is in the 8.6 μm range.

Chemicals capable of reacting to IR radiation are required in the missile head. Such chemicals need to react quickly, to be able to detect small amounts of IR radiation and to have high cut-off points. 'Cut-off' is the point at which the chemical ceases to react to IR radiation and can be increased, normally by about one micron, by cooling the head by about 200°C. Two commonly used chemicals in IR missile heads are Lead Sulphide (PbS) and Indium Artimonide (InSb). Lead Sulphide cuts off at about 3 μm uncooled and 4 μm cooled while Indium Antimonide cuts off around 6 μm; cooling does not improve this but does enhance the detectivity. Indium Antimonide heads can therefore detect the exhaust plume radiations at 3 μm and 4.2 μm, most of the hot metal radiation and a good deal of the leading edge radiation.

Just as hot carbon dioxide and water vapour radiate IR energy, so do the cold gases present in the atmosphere absorb IR energy. This atmospheric absorption affects the transmissivity of IR radiation and the pattern seen at Fig 2.2 shows a series of transmission windows.

It can be seen that thermal imaging devices working at normal ambient temperatures of about 15°C (10 μm) are little affected by atmospheric

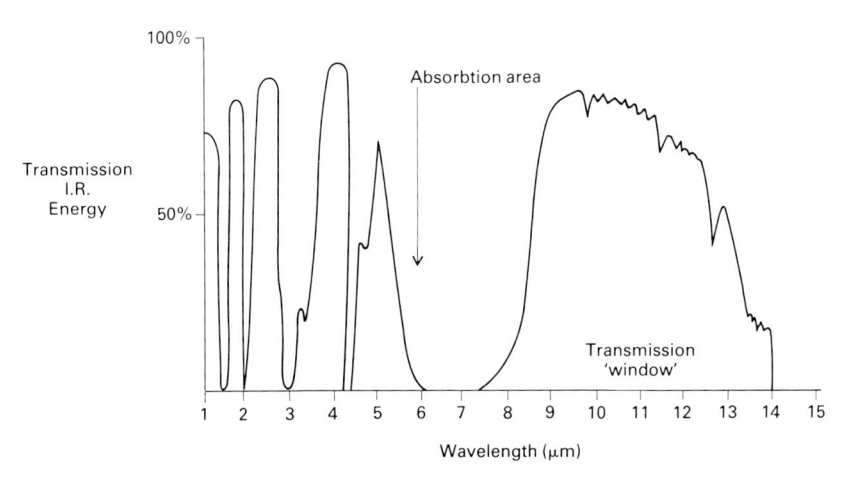

Fig 2.2 IR transmission – a 1 μm path at sea level.

Weapons and Warfare

absorption. The emission from leading edges between about 5.5 and 8 μm are badly affected and it is likely therefore that missiles optimised in this area would be looking at the 4 to 5 μm band and relying upon high detectivity in this band to produce reliable head-on acquisitions. While the general pattern of the transmissivity remains the same, at higher levels the percentage of energy transmitted increases. It can also be seen that a higher speed target will help in acquisition as the shorter wavelengths from its hotter leading edges will bring the emissions out of the poor band between 5.5 and 8 μm.

IR emissions are also affected by atmospheric scatter caused by particles or droplets in the air. The closer the droplet size is to the wavelength, the greater the losses through scatter. IR generally punctuates haze or smoke, which has small droplets or particles, better than optical wavelengths but both are equally affected by large particles found in rain or cloud.

This gives rise to one of the major disadvantages of IR weapons over radar weapons – they are not all-weather capable. They are, however, highly discriminating and IR missiles will have less difficulty than radar missiles in selecting one of a number of targets on which to home. Radar missiles can, under some circumstances, receive radar returns from two or more targets and home to a mean point, missing all the targets.

Before dealing with radar missiles and from that leading on to some new and interesting aspects of the modern air battle, consider some of the constraints in the use of missiles. It is too easy to look upon the air-to-air missile as the wonder weapon but the limited history of air warfare in which missiles have been used tends, if anything, to prove the reverse. First, the air-to-air missile is a complex weapon and depends on a number of complicated functions to operate reliably and effectively and to give a successful result. Some are outlined in Fig 2.3 and it can be seen that even if individual functions operate at high probabilities, the number of functions involved still gives quite low overall probabilities of success.

It is seen that in this example overall probability is only seventy-three per cent despite high probabilities being assumed for the individual component events. Many would argue that overall probabilities as high as seventy-three per cent could only be looked for in new generation missiles and then only in

Event	Probability of Success	Cumulative Probability of Success
Aircraft system produces valid firing command	0.95	0.95
Missile fires	0.95	0.90
Missile guides	0.95	0.86
Missile within valid parameters	0.95	0.81
Fusing operates successfully	0.95	0.77
Warhead activates	0.95	0.73

FIG 2.3 The effect of a variety of individual high probabilities on overall probability of success.

Air-to-Air Weapons

fairly benign combat, or test, conditions. Few commanders would bank on better than sixty-five per cent, the prudent ones would at least consider thirty to forty per cent and those conscious of the Vietnam experience would not be surprised at overall figures of ten per cent.

There were many reasons for the Vietnam experience not least of which was the decision taken by the US to send everyone to Vietnam once before anyone went twice. This was highly equitable but resulted in a massive cross-training programme because the throughput of fighter pilots was greater than any other. Consequently, not only were the experienced fighter pilots 'tour-expended' early on but thereafter the type and role experience of the crews in Vietnam was much less than the ideal. With the equipment of the time, the very difficult judgement on whether a valid missile firing could be made was almost completely pilot orientated and in this very tricky area, experience was all-important. As a result, many missiles were fired outside their capability, so artificially affecting the results. A further factor was the situation arising from a poor identification capability and the need for positive identification that a target was hostile before firing. By the time the range had closed to the point where that could be done, the opportunity to use the head-on radar Sparrow missile was squandered. This artificial rule of engagement, at a stroke, did much to negate the major technological advantage possessed by the United States. Yet another problem was the confidence factor. For whatever reason, missiles were being fired and obtaining no, or few, hits. Pilots then took to firing more than one at a target – a standard *salvo* was two AIM-7 Sparrow for example – yet if the shot was outside parameters, this merely served to make the overall figures look even worse.

The judgement of missile firing envelopes is a difficult task requiring experience and regular practice. Fig 2.4 shows a typical missile firing envelope for a rear-hemisphere IR missile with a capability over a thirty per cent semi-angle. The minimum range is determined mainly by safety considerations; the missile has to be fired from the aircraft with locked control lest a control hardover should jeopardise the aircraft. In addition, the warhead is inhibited for a period to allow it to clear the aircraft sufficiently so that an inadvertent detonation would not cause self-damage to the aircraft. A time must also be allowed thereafter for the missile to guide satisfactorily to the target. Together, these factors constitute a minimum range. Typically, such a range may be in the order of 300 metres.

The maximum range tends to be a factor of either the ability of the seeker to acquire a sufficiently strong signal from the target to allow guidance or, alternatively, the ability of the missile to actually fly the distance between launch aircraft and target. This latter ability will be determined by the altitude – missiles tend to fly longer at height – the speed of the target and the overtake speed of the launch aircraft. A well designed IR missile will try to match a number of these parameters; for example, if the pilot receives an indication of seeker lock then at that range the missile should be able to fly the distance.

Weapons and Warfare

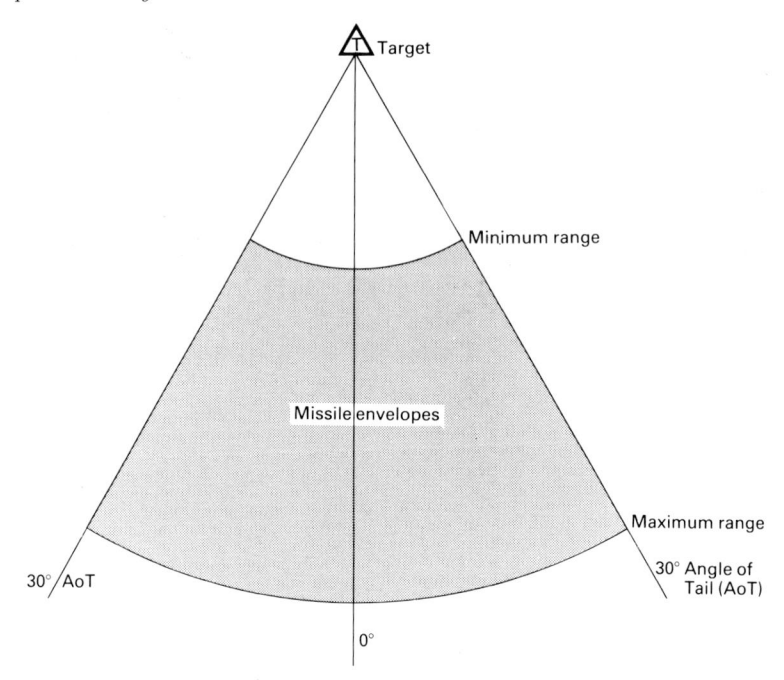

FIG 2.4 Typical missile firing envelope against a non-manoeuvring target.

Fig 2.5 shows the complication occasioned by a manoeuvring target. In this simplified case it is seen that as the target turns so does its vulnerable tail area move with it until it may cease to coincide with the launch aircraft, thereby denying an acquisition.

This situation can be further complicated if the missile has some form of proportional navigation law in its guidance system. Modern AAM have the capability to pull high lateral 'g' loads, typically in the order of 35 'g'. Although this sounds more than enough to defeat an aircraft restricted at best to 9 'g', it is important to realise that it is the turning radii which largely determines the ability to execute a successful engagement and a 9 'g' aircraft at 400 knots will have a considerably smaller turning circle than a 35 'g' missile travelling at Mach 2.5.

Under certain engagement geometry the missile can be placed in circumstances demanding of it a *square corner* which could be outside even the high 'g' capability it possesses. Such a case is illustrated at Fig. 2.7 where a high speed missile is fired in the forward quarter against a target with the missile attempting to keep the target at its dead-ahead position throughout the engagement. This is not utilizing proportional management and it is said to have a navigational constant (K) of 1. In other words, a sight-line spin of, say, 1°/second is accepted at face value by the guidance system. By introducing

Air-to-Air Weapons

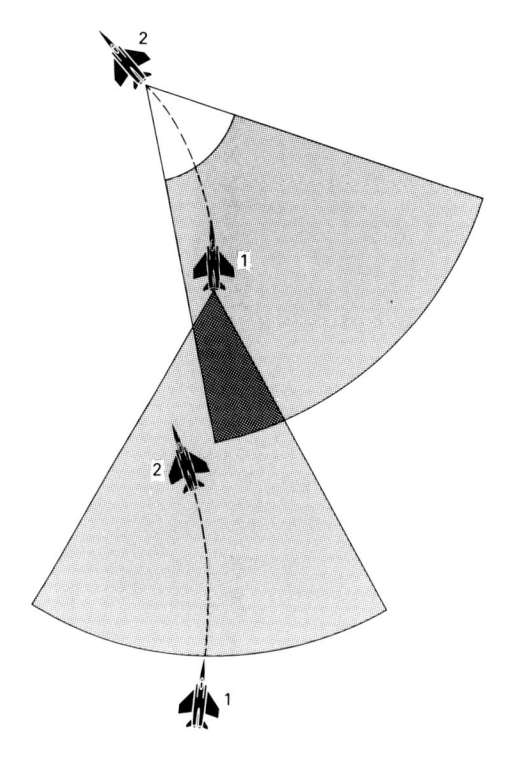

Fig 2.5 Target manoeuvre negating a missile acquisition.

various degrees of proportional navigation and by increasing the K-factor, much more efficient profiles can be flown and the *square corner* can be avoided. A K-factor of 2, for example, would involve the guidance system assuming a sight line spin rate of 2°/second for an actual case of 1°/second. In this way a *lead* is built into the flight path.

A proportional navigation law with a K of infinity would seem to be the ideal and equates to a full lead prediction profile in which the angle between missile seeker head and the target is kept constant throughout the interception. Unfortunately there are technical reasons for not using such high constants and K-factors of between 4 and 7 are common in practice. Fig 2.7 also shows a further advantage of using proportional navigation in that the missile flight

Vehicle	Speed	'g'	Turn Radius (ft)
Aircraft	400 kts	9	1,588
Missile	M 2.5	35	6,929

Fig 2.6 Turn Radius at low level.

Weapons and Warfare

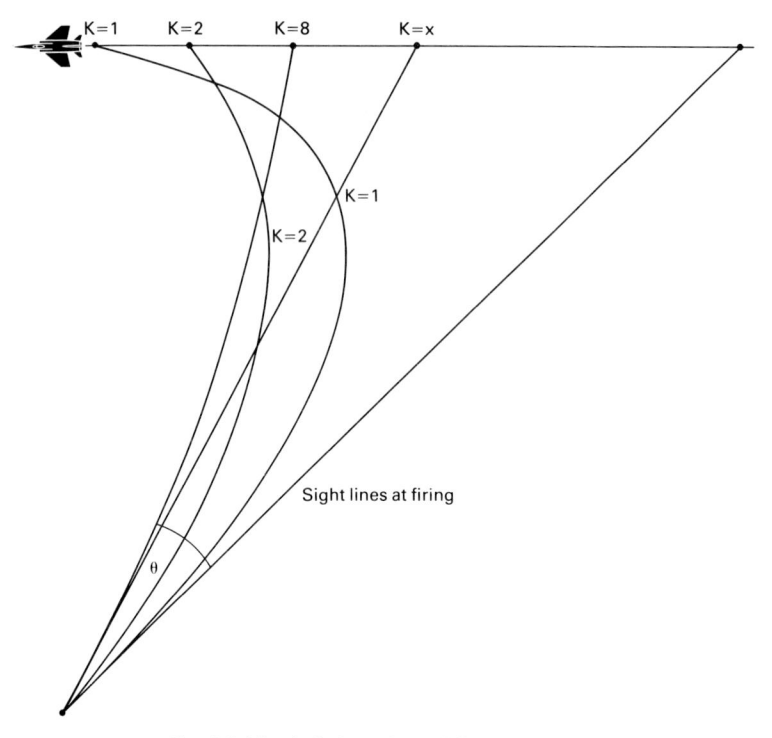

FIG 2.7 Missile flight paths at different k-factors.

path to the target is shorter, so effectively increasing the range of the missile. Comparatively, the missile impacts earlier which, in modern air combat conditions, can be an important advantage.

The individual characteristics of the missile and the geometry of the attack will have to be taken into account in determining whether the missile seeker head has sufficient gimbal capability to keep the target sighted throughout the flight path. A missile with a K-factor of 1 will effectively be looking dead-ahead and keeping the target in its near-12 o'clock position. As the K-factor increases so does the missile seeker head have to be offset to keep the target in view. It can be seen from Fig 2.7 that in the case of the extreme K-factor of infinity, the seeker head would spend its whole time in flight offset at the angle θ.

The firing envelope against a manoeuvring target tends to be highly skewed and this can make the accurate determination of valid firing opportunities even more difficult in the air. Envelope diagrams always appear to be very pure but in practice they apply only to the specific conditions outlined. They also assume perfect knowledge of the target's flight conditions, something which is rarely better than an estimate in practice. Fig 2.8 nonetheless shows a typical skew of the firing envelope against a manoeuvring target and the shape is influenced for two reasons: the first is that the missile can 'cut-the-corner' and

Air-to-Air Weapons

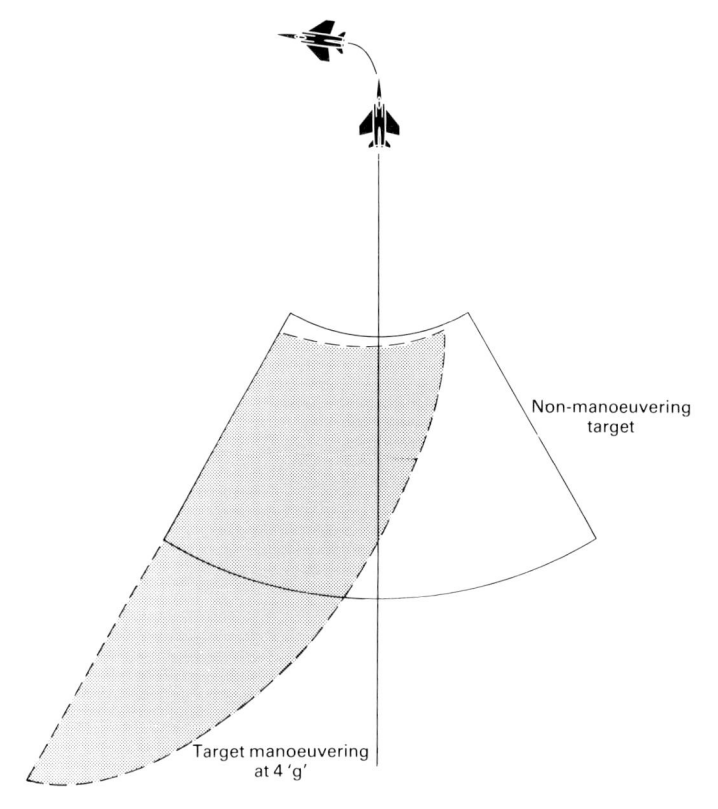

FIG 2.8 Skewed envelope against a manoeuvring target.

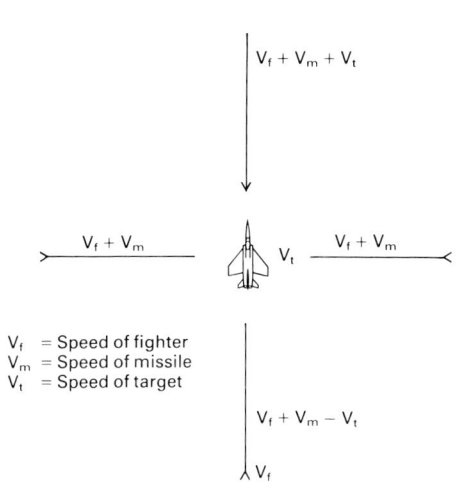

$V_f + V_m + V_t$

$V_f + V_m$ V_t $V_f + V_m$

V_f = Speed of fighter
V_m = Speed of missile
V_t = Speed of target

$V_f + V_m - V_t$

V_f

FIG 2.8a Missile closure speeds.

therefore the flight path will be shorter than in the straight and level case. The second is that the target turn effectively increases the missile speed. This can be seen better by reference to Fig 2.8a which shows the relationship between target, fighter and missile speeds in accordance with firing aspect.

It is this later relationship which gives the different shape for engagement envelopes of missiles capable of head-on attack, be they IR missiles capable of sensing leading edge heating, or radar missiles. Such an envelope is seen at Fig 2.9a. At Fig 2.9b the envelope which results from a high speed target can be seen. This shape is caused by the possibility that high sight line spin rates on beam engagements may exceed the seeker head limitations and also that the 'g' requirement on the missile may exceed the aerodynamic limitations. At Fig 2.9c the envelope resulting from the extreme high speed case shows that the target may actually be getting away from the missile and that the only valid shot may be to engage where target speed is additive to the total engagement. These considerations could apply to aircraft of the SR-71 type which are capable of flight in the Mach 3 region.

Although modern IR missiles have a capability at all-aspects against supersonic targets, and for those missiles the envelopes mentioned above are equally valid, the more normal missile to use at all-aspects, particularly against subsonic targets, is the radar missile. The term *radar missile* covers a variety of different types all having their strengths and weaknesses. These will be examined briefly, restricting comment to those suitable for air-to-air use but not forgetting that the surface-to-air missile has many of the same strengths and weaknesses and should be borne in mind when dealing with the general principles.

The IR missile, already discussed, is an example of a passive homing device in that it senses the IR radiation from the targets. Passive homing can also be utilised in torpedoes in the acoustic band and can be used similarly by a radar missile to home onto a radar emission from the target. This can take the form of an Anti-Radiation-Missile (ARM), designed to home on to a ground radar or an airborne intercept radar, or a Home-on-Jam system, designed to home up the beam of a jamming source which could be used to deny accurate range or bearing information to an aircraft or missile system.

As with IR homers, passive radar homers have the advantage of increasing accuracy as they approach their target because the energy of the homing signal increases the closer they get to it. Further, as no assistance is required from the launching aircraft, once the missile is fired, the fighter can withdraw – a 'launch-and-leave' weapon. The lack of any fighter emissions also means that the target is not warned of the approaching threat. On the other hand, passive homing missiles can be countered fairly easily; the target emission can be stopped or simple decoys deployed. Furthermore, passive homers can lack resolution under certain circumstances and tend to attack the centroid of a raid rather than home onto a specific target.

Semi-active missiles home on the energy reflected from a target illuminated

Air-to-Air Weapons

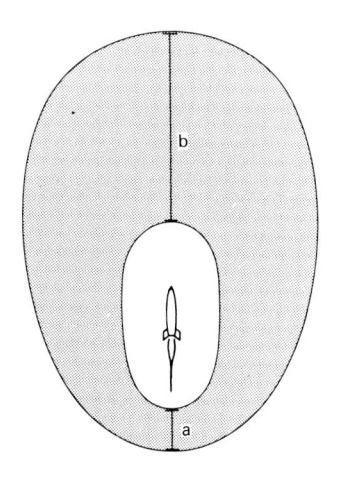

FIG 2.9a All-aspect missile envelope.

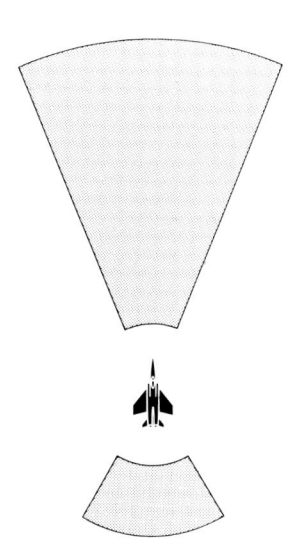

FIG 2.9b All-aspect envelope against a very high speed target.

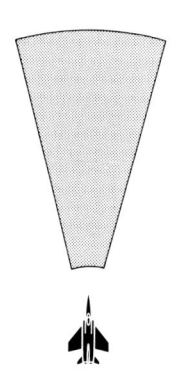

FIG 2.9c Degraded envelope against a very high speed target.

Weapons and Warfare

by the missile system's own radar. This can be in the form of a ground-based illuminator, in the case of a SAM, or can be a function of the Air Intercept (AI) radar in an airborne system (Fig 2.10). Target returns again increase as range is closed and long ranges can be obtained if the target illuminating radar is of sufficient power. Countermeasures are possible but are generally more complex than in the passive homing case. The semi-active radar missile can be tuned to a particular frequency and this can include a factor for target doppler effect. Jamming is consequently more difficult. Even if a jamming situation exists, it is possible for an engagement to succeed if the illumination is powerful enough. Throughout flight the missile continues to rely upon the reflected energy from the illuminating radar and this means that a semi-active missile is not *launch-and-leave*. This can have serious side-effects in the total beyond-visual-range (BVR) air combat. A problem over the resolution between formations of targets can arise. Furthermore, the energy may be altered when his passive warning receiver is illuminated.

To overcome some of these problems and to strive for a greater engagement range, which is becoming increasingly necessary, AAM are now tending towards active homing. The AIM-54 Phoenix in use with the US Navy on the F-14 was an early active homing missile and the Advanced Medium Range AAM (AMRAAM) currently under development also uses active homing. In an active missile a self-contained radar within the missile head transmits when close to the target and homes on to the reflected emissions of its own illumination. Active missiles tend to be complex and can be expensive; the size can be further increased because the need for active homing is derived from the long-range capability. In consequence, the motor and guidance (including provision for mid-course guidance, which can be inertially based) can be large and complex in their own right. Phoenix, for example, is over 13 feet long, has a body diameter of 15 inches and weighs nearly 1,000 pounds; it costs over 0.5 million.

Missiles of this size can present operational problems particularly when associated with carrier-based aircraft where recovery to the ship will often be weight critical. In air defence operations from a carrier group, where combat air patrols tend to be the norm, aircraft will probably return to the ship with unexpected munitions more often than not. An F-14 with a maximum load of, say, six AIM-54 Phoenix will therefore have to land-on with nearly 6,000 pounds of Phoenix alone, before gun ammunition and IR missiles are considered. Add to this the weight of prudent fuel reserves to cater for battle damage or poor weather and, even from super-carriers, landing weight limits can be, or come close to being, exceeded. The option of jettison is not practicable at the cost or the scarcity of such missiles. Such large and heavy weapons also produce an aircraft performance penalty. Although an aircraft may be tasked to engage at long range, it may become involved in shorter ranged, high-agility combats in which high weights and drags could determine the outcome.

Air-to-Air Weapons

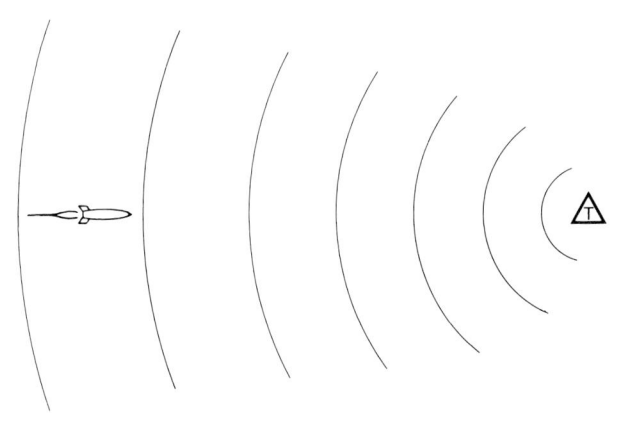

FIG 2.10a Passive homing.

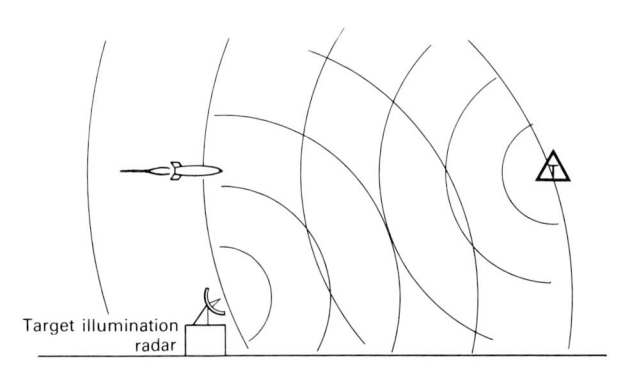

FIG 2.10b Semi-active homing.

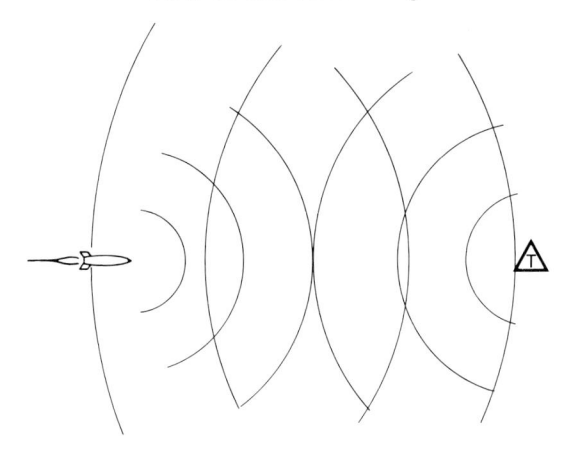

FIG 2.10c Active Homing.

FIG 2.10 Homing methods.

Weapons and Warfare

PLATE 2.1 **Skyflash.** Skyflash missiles fitted aerodynamically under the fuselage of a Tornado. *(British Aerospace)*

Such considerations affected the design specifications for AMRAAM. While this missile is unlikely to have the extreme range of Phoenix, which has been launched at over 100 nautical miles, it will be much lighter and will have less drag. Body diameter is more than halved at 7 inches and the launch weight will probably be one-third that of Phoenix. The lower frontal area results in less drag and this assists in producing higher speed – another increasingly important aspect in air combat at long range. It has been calculated that an F-16 fitted with the AIM-7 Sparrow missile – in use on F-4, F-15 and other types – instead of the preferred AMRAAM, would suffer a ten to fifteen per cent penalty in acceleration times and in fuel consumption.

Technology is close to the point when it can produce the missile specified by the operator. Phoenix at one end of the spectrum and the new AMRAAM and Advanced Short Range AAM (ASRAAM) at the other, show the wide variety of options available. It may be that the prudent operator should specify a weapon as advanced as possible but, on the other hand, this may not be a cost-effective thing to do. Indeed, it could be most wasteful because in the complex and highly interactive business of air combat, it is rarely one factor which dominates but the combination of many. In the beyond-visual-range (BVR) engagement it is important that systems are matched; aircraft performance can be negated by poor radar performance; an excellent radar, in its turn, can be under-exploited for lack of missile range.

The provision of a *matched set* of aircraft performance, radar performance and missile capability is too often taken for granted yet it is a major task falling upon those involved in the specification of operational requirements and procurement. The old saying that fifty per cent of the cost is involved in achieving the last ten per cent of the performance, while debatable in the absolute, is generally accepted as about right.

Many air forces remain without full control over their own fate. A force updating its missiles may be offered a long-range missile but lack the funds to purchase this and, at the same time, to undertake the radar update necessary to exploit fully the improved missile performance. An aircraft, once fielded, normally has a fixed volume available for the radar and, more particularly, a fixed radome size. It may not be possible to change the dimensions of antennae materially even when the minaturisation of electronics allows for greater data processing to be undertaken in any given area than was previously possible. In this there may be more scope for radome modifications on the slower, older aircraft than on the newer high speed designs where air flow about the nose area, affecting intakes and wing roots, can be most critical. A look at the nose treatment of the Nimrod AEW 3 shows the liberties which can be taken with the slower, more tolerant designs but the possibility of undertaking the same surgery on F-16 or F-18 would be unthinkable.

Within the constraints of a minor work, let along a chapter within it, the detailed examination of the complex interfaces between the individual items in the BVR air combat 'matched-set' cannot be tackled without some simplification. Even allowing for the lack of purity which such simplification brings about, the main relationships can be investigated and, where interest is sparked, more detailed investigations can be initiated. Consider therefore, the archetypal BVR missile combat and examine the major factors which apply.

Clearly aircraft performance is important – but how important? Radar detection range is equally important, for this is effectively the eyes of a BVR engagement and it has been long proved that, to the human, the eyes are by far the primary sensor – so is it with radar in a BVR situation. But the mechanisation of the weapon system is also an important factor when closure speeds can be numbered in the multi-Mach regime. From a first detection, how long does it take to lay an attack and to release the missile? Too long and the opponent gets away the vital first shot which, if the missile has an active homing head, effectively doubles the odds against. Then there is missile range.

Weapons and Warfare

PLATE 2.2 **Magic 2.** Shown here being fired from a Mirage 2000. *(Matra)*

A long range detection matched to a short range missile merely accentuates anxiety.

Consider the situation in the cockpit of an interceptor which picks up a return ahead. A modern air intercept radar and its associated data processing system should quickly give a fair approximation of the target speed and height. The first, and by far the most important, decision to be made is whether or not the target is hostile. Much has been talked of JTIDS and NIS[1] and IFF MK 10 and the like (all Identification Friend-or-Foe (IFF) devices) yet such black boxes remain less glamorous in the procurement priorities than the more tangible, and understandable, EFAs, ATFs etc[1] yet without an effective IFF, regardless of which exotic fighter is being flown, *time* starts to be squandered following the initial radar contact. In any air combat *time* is the vital ingredient of success; it is the life-saver or life-taker and cannot be sacrificed needlessly. One senior NATO commander has said that his fighter force would be twenty-five per cent more effective with a reliable IFF; his staff only disagreed with him on the extent of the disadvantages – they thought he was being conservative. Over a force of 3,000 aircraft at $25 million each even a large sum is invested wisely if it can improve effectiveness by such an impressive factor as twenty-five per cent.

So is the contact hostile or not? If in any doubt, the fighter must accelerate from the cruise speed on Combat Air Patrol for two reasons: first, fighter speed

Air-to-Air Weapons

adds to missile speed and increases missile reach; second, if the BVR missiles miss, and a prudent fighter pilot will always assume this, then the speed is needed to convert to what could be a stern chase or even into a high agility dog-fight. In this very demanding arena, however, there is nothing done without a penalty and the acceleration will use fuel, will commensurately reduce CAP time and could reduce the time available for close combat, where *persistence* is becoming more important.

The next major decision needed is when to convert the radar from a scanning to a tracking mode. Here knowledge of the enemy is important. Will the enemy have a radar warning device which tells him that he is within the scan pattern of an interceptor? Will it be sufficiently advanced to tell that the returns received come from a potentially hostile fighter? When the target is locked-up for missile launch, will this too be displayed? If it is, what counter will the target have availble to it? Can it turn 90° to exploit the 'doppler-notch'? Will it turn away, hoping to make the missile manoeuvre or extend beyond its range limit? Will the target's mission allow it to divert from track and still achieve its offensive purpose? Offensive tasking agencies are the same world-wide and customarily task to the full declared range capability of offensive aircraft and combat fuel packages.

When to fire first? It is a bold and confident pilot who does not launch at first opportunity. The single-shot-kill-probability of missiles is not sufficient to trust to only one and a number of missiles may need to be despatched; with some weapon systems this takes time, and if the radar detection has been late, the need to arc off to position for the line astern re-attack may put pressure on to launch radar-missiles early. This will be even more so if the target must remain illuminated by the fighter radar to permit semi-active guidance and when radar gimbal limits could become critical if the launch is left too late.

Then there is the enemy. Is he an offensive aircraft reluctant to get engaged in a missile dual lest the main purpose of the offensive mission is compromised? Or is the target blip an escort fighter with every bit as capable a BVR missile system as the CAP fighter? If so, he probably has an inestimable advantage; while the fighter has doubt about the identification of the target blip – is it an offensive aircraft, or escort, or even returning friendly – the escort fighter, if only from the profile of the CAP pattern, almost certainly knows that his blip is hostile.

Such considerations must weigh on the mind of the fighter crew. Answers to some can be found by equipment, some by procedures, even more by instinct or intuition but, regardless, they take *time*. Such is the source of *reaction time*.

To attempt to identify some of the relationships and to seek a vehicle for discussion, consider a *simplified* and *stylised* BVR missile engagement. *Stylised*, because the direct head-on engagement is considered; *simplified*, to avoid a mathematical treatise where inappropriate but, for example, assuming a figure for missile *average* speed when, in fact, a missile would fly more to the profile in Fig 2.11. Consider an engagement in which:

Weapons and Warfare

> Fighter speed   = Mach 1.0
> Target speed   = Mach 0.8
> AAM speed   = Mach 2.5 over launch speed
> Fighter Radar Range   = 50 nautical miles
> AAM fly time   = 60 seconds
> System reaction time = 30 seconds

Then the following engagement would result:

Fig 2.12a shows that of the 50 nautical mile radar range 4.77 nautical miles and 30 seconds are taken up by the reaction time. The AAM fired at that time will impact 90.42 seconds after first detection at 38.47 nautical miles down range. At this point the fighter has closed to a point 14.4 nautical miles down range. The AAM range (based on a 60 second flight time), while a marginal short fall, is quite well matched to the total geometry of the attack.

Could the *marginal miss* be corrected by a higher launch speed? Fig 2.12b shows the effect of an increase in attack speed to Mach 1.2, which improves a *marginal shortfall* into a *hit* with some range in hand.

But what is the effect of aircraft performance? Consider the case when reaction time, AAM performance and radar range is the same but aircraft speed is different. Look at the situation where BLUE is twice as fast as RED at Mach 1.5. As AAM flight time to impact is a function of fighter speed, AAM speed and target speed, it can be seen that, at least to a first approximation,

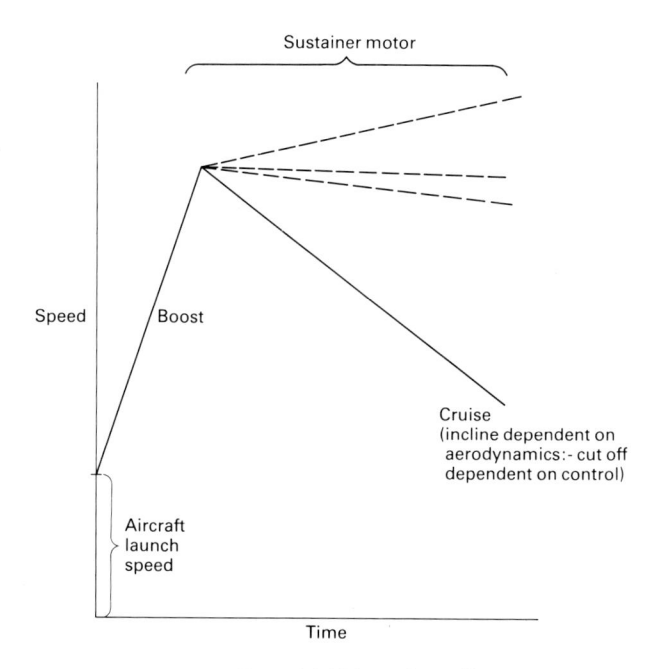

FIG 2.11 Typical AAM missile profile.

Air-to-Air Weapons

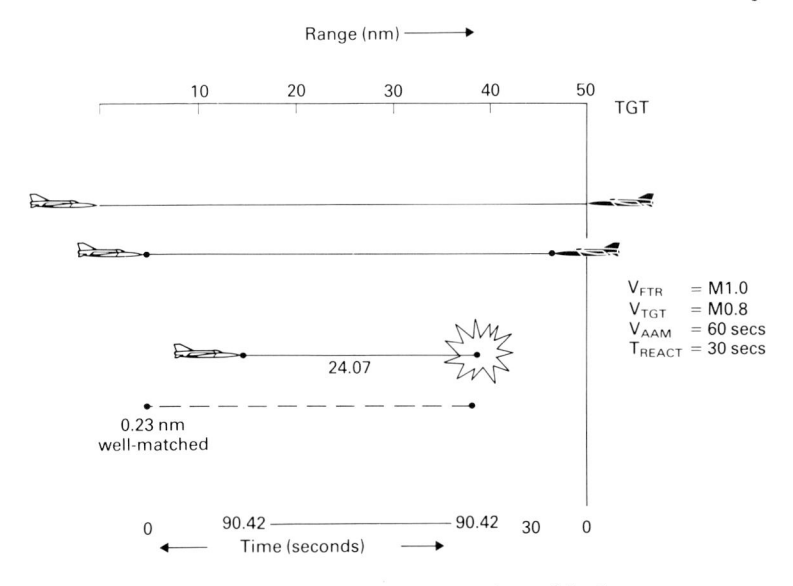

Fig 2.12a BVR missile engagement – missile just falls short.

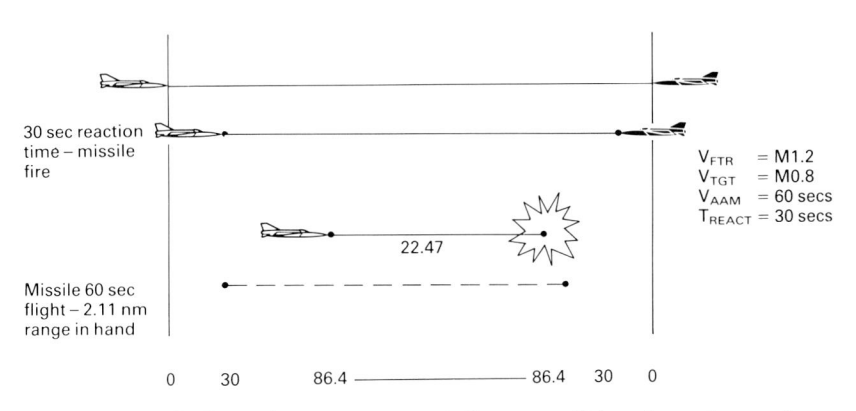

Fig 2.12b BVR missile engagement – missile range sufficient due to increased fighter speed.

there is little difference between the missile being fired from the fast aircraft or from the slow aircraft. There is a small increase in missile reach when fired from the faster aircraft (Fig 2.13). This tends to suggest that there is something in the suggestion that, in the technological age, weapons and systems are more important than vehicles.

What, therefore, if the Blue side place their investment in the aircraft while Red update their old slow aircraft with a longer-ranged, faster missile and

Weapons and Warfare

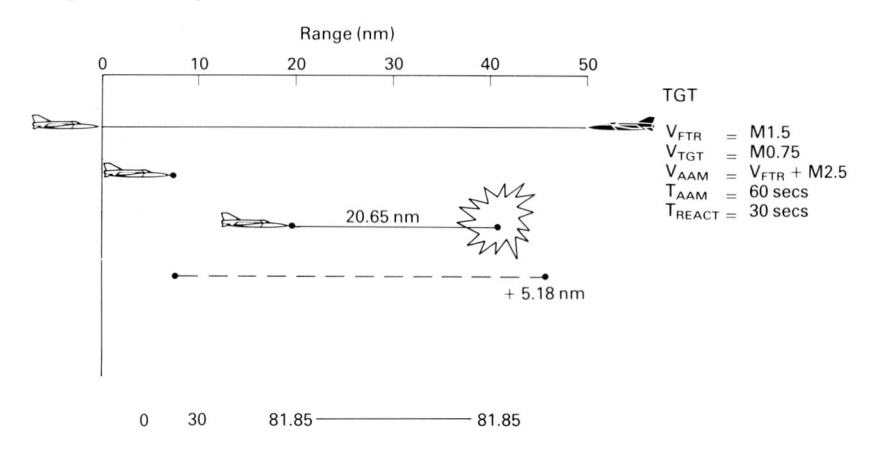

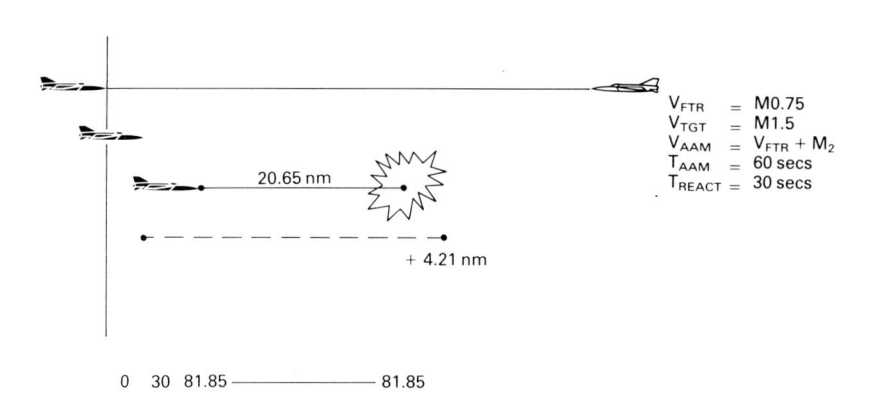

```
                    Range (nm)
        0    10    20    30    40    50
                                           TGT
                                           V_FTR   = M1.5
                                           V_TGT   = M0.75
                                           V_AAM   = V_FTR + M2.5
                    20.65 nm                T_AAM   = 60 secs
                                            T_REACT = 30 secs

                                + 5.18 nm

        0   30    81.85 ———————— 81.85
```

```
                                           V_FTR   = M0.75
                                           V_TGT   = M1.5
                                           V_AAM   = V_FTR + M2
                    20.65 nm                T_AAM   = 60 secs
                                            T_REACT = 30 secs

                                + 4.21 nm

        0   30  81.85 ——————— 81.85
```

FIG 2.13 BVR engagement showing effect of aircraft performance.

some data processing – or an IFF system – to reduce the reaction time. Fig 2.14 shows that the parameters for Blue stay as before but Red, by increasing missile speed by Mach 1.0, thereby increasing reach, and by reducing reaction time by 15 seconds, now impacts Blue at 63.7 seconds, some 18.15 seconds before Blue's missile would impact Red. If the Blue missile was relying on the Blue radar emissions for semi-active guidance, the Blue missile would stop guiding after Red's missile impact. If, however, the Blue missile was an active homer and had gone active before the 18.15 seconds time difference, Red would still be faced with a threat notwithstanding the destruction of its opponent's aircraft.

The active missile will introduce a new dimension to the air combat arena.

Air-to-Air Weapons

Diagram labels (top):
Range (nm): 0, 10, 20, 30, 40, 50

Red
V_{Blue} = M1.5
V_{red} = M0.75
$V_{blueAAM}$ = V_{Blue} + M3.5
T_{AAM} = 60 secs
T_{REACT} = 30 secs

0   30   81.85 ———— 81.85

Diagram labels (bottom):

Red
V_{Blue} = M1.5
V_{Red} = M0.75
V_{RedAAM} = V_{Red} + M3.5
$T_{AAM(red)}$ = 90 secs
$T_{REACT(red)}$ = 15 secs

0
15
63.7 ———————— 63.7

Red's investment in a better missile range and speed is under-exploited by the limitation on radar range. The system is not well 'matched'.

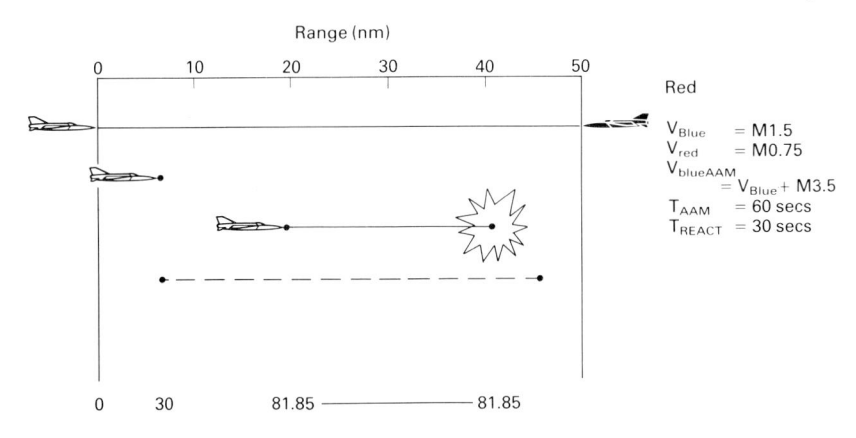

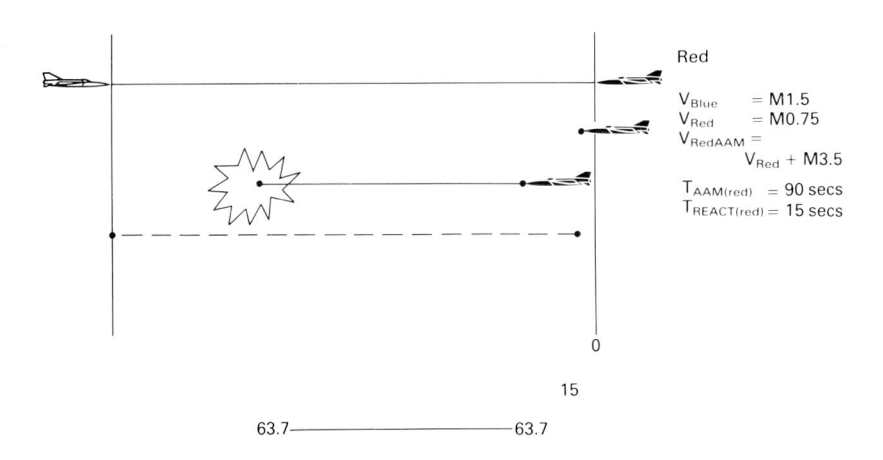

FIG 2.14 BVR engagement showing effect of missile range and speed enhancement.

In a trial of multi-aircraft combat, conducted some time ago, it was found that some tens of missiles were launched and in flight within a few seconds of the start of the engagement. Semi-active models would go ballistic if the launch aircraft was destroyed but active missiles, in quantity, could be difficult to counter, particularly if other threats were present – SAM and AAA – causing the formation to manoeuvre. Discussion on missile air combat too often presupposes a single fighter engaging a single target when, in practice, this is the least likely case. The factor most feared by combat pilots is the one most difficult to quantify – that of confusion. Studies of past air combats have shown that this is truely the killer. One study concluded that eighty per cent of aircraft shot down during a conflict had been engaged by unseen opponents. Another, leading from the analysis of gun camera film, suggested that seventy per cent of the aircraft engaged had less than 30° of bank applied when hit; hardly desperate evasion. The World War Two poster warning against '*the-Hun-in-the-Sun*' indicates that the basic lessons hold good with time. In the modern BVR battle electronic *eyes* may have to reinforce the human eye but the principles remain the same.

Progressing from the BVR combat into the modern high agility visual combat will call for quite different piloting skills and technical equipment. The BVR battle is largely a conflict between systems and sensors and, as such, electronic warfare will have a large part to play. The high agility air combat will be less the game of chess and parallel more the physical strains of the rugby scrum.

Increasingly modern fighters can not only achieve 'g' loadings in the region of nine but can, under a wide range of circumstances, sustain such levels. Even given 'g' suits, reclining seats, physical fitness and, above all, regular practice there are few, if any, pilots who can sustain such high 'g' levels for anything more than a few seconds. Those air forces operating such high performance equipment are finding new problems; one claims that a term of duty on a squadron of high agility fighters results in a collar size one larger than at the start due to the physical strain imposed on holding aloft the body's single most heavy object, the head. Others are becoming increasingly concerned at the so-called *'g'-induced unconsciousness* where, unlike the gradual onset of blackout associated with normal 'g' loadings, and its rapid relief when the load is reduced, a sudden onset of very high 'g' may cause an equally sudden loss of consciousness and, more seriously, an extended period of some ten to fifteen seconds before consciousness is regained. Few scenarios in combat or in flight close to the ground would permit such long periods of unconsciousness without serious consequences.

High 'g' in visual combat may therefore have to be used sparingly and sustained 'g' restricted to levels in the order of five or six. The higher 'g' loads may be limited to those occasions when the nose must be drawn on to the target to sight guns or missile heads for the kill, or for the *in extremis* avoidance of attack.

Two new factors are emerging in the close air combat scene. In the past, the ability to disengage was the prerogative of the passably competent fighter pilot. To engineer a head-on pass, or to develop some angular difference in a low energy situation, was enough to depart the combat before the opponent could react. Sufficient distance could be gained to prevent any parting shot. With high agility aircraft, however, even a 180° angular difference can be taken out in a matter of nine seconds or so and a missile can be fired even earlier than

Air-to-Air Weapons

PLATE 2.3 **Skyflash.** Skyflash air-to-air missile being launched form an F16.
(British Aerospace)

that if the aircraft has an off-boresight capability. Once engaged therefore, is there any escape short of a result? Has gladiatorial combat arrived at the point at which the winner survives and the loser invariably does not? In a field with no recognisable means of surrender, or indeed of offering quarter, the situation concentrates the mind. It also places added emphasis on *persistence*, or the ability to stay engaged, usually dependent upon the available fuel. Economical engines, high fuel-fractions and the skill to use thirsty after-burners economically, will weigh heavily on the ultimate outcome.

Modern aircraft design is tending to favour the Infra-Red missile. Compare the long jet pipes of aircraft such as the Hunter, through the shorter but airframe-shrouded jet pipes of aircraft like the F-4 Phantom and the Jaguar, to those of modern designs where unstable control technology allows weight to be placed further aft and engines can have very short jet pipes right at the end of the fuselage. The jet pipes of F-15, F-16 and F-18 show the trend well. The opportunity for IR shielding is consequently less and this is exacerbated by the trend in engine design itself. Modern materials and, even more significantly, turbine blade cooling, have allowed turbine inlet temperatures in the order of some 1500 degrees centigrade in the more advanced designs. In short jet pipes this heat dissipates only a little and metal parts in a modern jet pipe, such as the after burner galleries, can be operating at temperatures which only a few years ago would be found only on the turbine disc itself. The IR signature is likely to be very large indeed.

IR decoy flares will help, although these can prove to be less useful against high agility missiles approaching from the beam angles. Data processing in the missile heads themselves, made possible by the advances in miniaturisation, can give the modern missile great discrimination by including logic or *behavioural* circuits. Few if any flares, for example, retain the velocity profile of an aircraft and can thereby be discounted by logic circuits as a valid target.

IR jammers which emit pulsed IR transmissions offer the best option in the short term but good intelligence on the missile operating frequency is required. In the longer term,. it is not impossible to conceive a missile head with a *home-on-jam* facility similar to the technique used widely on radar missiles.

Against *missiles*, rather than *hitiles*, there may be scope in seeking countermeasures to the fusing circuits. A proximity fused warhead is no threat if it does not initiate. In some respects this can be easier than attacking the guidance heads from a distance because fusing circuits activate close to the aircraft and size and power requirements for a counter may prove more manageable.

Any modern combat is going to be a highly lethal affair, be it BVR using long-ranged radar missiles, or in the close visual combat more usually associated with IR missiles. Missile expenditure will be high if only because the cumulative kill probabilities are low enough for the wise pilot to seek the insurance of numbers; also that, in the multi-aircraft situation, some missiles are bound to be laid on the wrong target or will be confused. With the modern missile in a high agility close combat, some aircraft will be presented with numerous firing opportunities and may fire-out rapidly. The contradiction of needing large missile loads of both radar and IR missiles while not wishing to accept the weight and drag penalties in combat, is a problem to designer and pilot alike.

Smaller, lighter missiles, typified by the trend from AIM-7/Skyflash to AMRAAM, and semi-buried or conformal carriage will have to be the path to the future for the smaller high-agility fighters but the threat of the very long-ranged missile, fired from the large, even ponderously slow platform, cannot be ignored altogether. For this later design the integral rocket/ram-jet is a natural choice for the motor and it will be interesting to see how this technology proceeds – and which nation embraces it. Ultimately they may have the trump card.

Note
1. Joint Tactical Identification and Display System (JTIDS)
    NATO Identification System (NIS)
    European Fighter Aircraft (EFA)
    Advanced Tactical Fighter (AFT)

Introducing Chapters 3 & 4

*I*T *was as true in the days of early air combat as it is now that the aircraft is but a platform for the weapons. When, during World War One and World War Two, the weapons were very similar for friend and foe, the outcome depended in the main upon the quality of aircraft and the skill of their pilots. The advent of a great variety of missiles of variable characteristics and quality has by no means reduced the importance of the platform from which they are fired or the skill of the aviator, but there is a different emphasis. The need now is for a properly integrated system with well matched missiles and platform. In addition to the pure flying skills of earlier days, the requirement is now for air crew to operate a complicated piece of electronics.*

Although fixed wing aircraft and helicopters have separate highly specialised roles, their capabilities overlap in the close support of land and naval forces. Helicopters may be equipped with much the same weapons as high performance fixed wing aircraft and in operations over land may be less vulnerable in some circumstances by reason of their ability to make the best use of ground to provide cover from view and fire.

The ability of helicopters to operate from confined spaces gives them another advantage over fixed wing aircraft in that the latter require long runways which are themselves vulnerable to enemy action. The Harrier, nicknamed the 'jump jet', *minimises this vulnerability in that it can take off from short, hastily prepared strips and land vertically. It is thus an ideal aircraft for close support of an army in the field and operation at sea from carriers. However, its* 'jump jet' *characteristics inevitably detract from other aspects of its performance so that aircraft needing fixed long runways will remain an essential part of an air force inventory for the foreseeable future.*

3

Fixed Wing Aircraft

AIR VICE MARSHAL H A MERRIMAN CB CBE AFC FRAEs RAF

AIR power will play a vital part in any armed conflict between NATO and the Warsaw Pact countries. As an example, due to the peace-time deployment of NATO ground forces, a surprise attack by Warsaw Pact forces will mean that fixed wing combat aircraft will be the only source of substantial retaliatory fire-power able to bear while the NATO forces are redeploying to make contact. During this period Warsaw Pact aircraft will be employed on a large scale with the objective of disrupting that redeployment. Therefore extensive air operations will be pursued by both sides not only on primary air-to-ground missions but also to deny the use of the air to the opposite side. Where possible, surface-to-air missiles will also be used for this purpose by both sides; but air-to-air combat can be expected to predominate, if for no other reason than that of the practical difficulty in regulating the airspace for missile and aircraft allocation.

AIR-TO-AIR COMBAT

Air-to-air combat could possibly start with missile launches at aircraft separation distances beyond visual range (BVR) taking advantage of look-down, shoot-down capabilities. Given no external interference, the accuracy of these missiles will invariably mean that the aircraft which launches first will destroy the opponent. Hence the importance of denying the opponent information which will enable early launch, and also to be able to disturb the flight of the missile once it has been launched. During the time of flight of any BVR missile exchange, the aircraft will close towards each other with the object of firing a short range missile at the first opportunity should the BVR missile not achieve its objective. Calculations show that, in all probability, the pilot will then be in visual contact with the adversary. Air combat manoeuvring will ensue in order to position the opponent within the firing envelope of the missiles being carried. The ultimate short range weapon is the cannon and firing opportunities for this weapon will also be in the mind of the pilot during the air combat manoeuvres.

Weapons and Warfare

The performance of both the missile and the aircraft play important parts in the outcome of air combat. For any particular missile, the aircraft performance can be vital if success in a one-versus-one situation is to be reasonably assured. Analysis of the numerous parameters of an aircraft design which contribute to the aircraft's combat performance has established beyond doubt which are the most important. New aircraft designs will take advantage of this research; the shape, size and power plant installation will all be determined principally on this vital performance in order to give the aircraft the best possible chance of survival.

The Current Front Line Aircraft

Today's high performance combat aircraft in the front-line squadrons of the West, with only a few exceptions such as the F-16, F-18 and Tornado, have their origins in the late 1950s and early 60s. The F-4 Phantom and F-104 Starfighter, used widely in NATO, successfully completed military acceptance flight tests at the end of the 1950s and entered service shortly thereafter. The Mirage 3, from which the present Mirage 2000 descends, was similarly undergoing service testing during the same period. The prototypes of the Harrier and Jaguar were flying in the mid-1960s and they were followed closely by the F-15. Although improved over the years, these aircraft were founded upon technologies at least thirty years old. At the time of their debut, they represented a remarkable advance over the aircraft of thirty years earlier, typified by the piston-engined biplane such as the Hawker Fury and Fairey Swordfish. In their turn, the next generation of fighter combat aircraft to enter service will, in terms of military cost-effectiveness, provide a comparable progression over those currently in front line service.

The Advance of Technology

Even the most recent aircraft to enter service with the West were designed in the 1960s and inevitably incorporate technologies of that decade. The results of the past twenty years of research are awaiting orders for new front line aircraft. Certainly, wherever possible, the fruits of those research programmes are used to enhance the capabilities of existing aircraft through improvement programmes. But if the maximum synergistic benefit is to be achieved, only a completely new design can permit the introduction of radically new concepts. The European Fighter Aircraft (EFA) is one aircraft which is being designed on this principle.

Although combat aircraft research work is spread across many disciplines and centres of activity, it can conveniently be classified into five major fields which embrace the most important elements of a modern aircraft weapons system: structures, aerodynamics, power plant, avionics and weapons. In some of these areas striking advances have been made over the past ten years.

Fixed Wing Aircraft

In others, taken by themselves, the improvement may be modest. But theoretical studies have indicated that when combined in a design optimised to take advantage of all this research, substantial synergy is achieved. The performance, operational capability, reliability and cost benefits are considerable.

The next generation of fixed wing combat aircraft such as EFA, will be based on these advanced technologies. The result is likely to be the biggest step forward in one generation since the introduction of the transonic jet fighter of the Fifties.

Structural Materials and Aircraft Structures

Over the years we have all become familiar with the manufacture and properties of fibreglass. However, because of its relatively low stiffness, it has had only limited application to fixed wing aircraft structures, largely being confined to radomes and aerial covers. The need for a radiation 'window' dictated the use of such a material. However, if the silicon glass fibres are replaced by carbon fibres, an immensely strong and lightweight material results. Moreover, it shows practically no tendency to fatigue with cyclical loading. The value of this material for aircraft structures can readily be appreciated. Other benefits, such as low radar reflectivity, are gained at the same time. But perhaps the most exciting feature is that by tailoring the direction of the warp and weft of the many layers of fibres which make up the desired thickness of material for the structure, the bending and twisting which occurs under load can be directed favourably. For example, the deformation of a wing under high 'g' loads can be transferred through the structure so as to re-shape the aerodynamic surface appropriately for the high incidence airflow conditions which could be expected in such a manoeuvre.

On the other hand, carbon fibre composite (CFC) does have distinct limitations. It does not stand up well to high temperatures. This makes it unsuitable for use in close proximity to engine hot parts. Minor impact damage impairs its strength and this has to be taken into account in the design. Also, the construction methods are more complex and new skills have to be acquired by the workforce. Indeed, the large scale introduction of CFC could lead to considerable redundancy both in metal working plant and skilled operators. These additional costs, together with limited knowledge of long term ageing effects, such as a life time exposure to ultraviolet radiation from the sun and moisture absorption over the years, may limit the wider use of CFC. Moreover, battle damage effects, repair problems, electromagnetic compatability, electrical continuity, aerial installations and lightning strike hazards are still undergoing assessment and will have to be balanced against its otherwise attractive properties.

Where metal continues to be used in the structure, new methods of construction, such as superplastic forming and diffusion bonding, have been developed to produce large and complex unitary structure components. Fewer individual parts are required in the aircraft and greater strength is achieved at lighter weight. Significant cost savings (up to fifty per cent) are possible through the reduction in production man hours. New alloys are also becoming available having the same strength characteristics of the more conventional aluminium alloys but lighter in weight.

These new materials and methods of construction, used in combination, will enable higher levels of performance to be obtained from a given design; conversely, a desired performance will be achieved from a lighter aircraft. When the snowball effect of the lighter mass is taken into consideration (a process known as *scaling*) the end product is a noticeably smaller aircraft.

Aerodynamics

During the past ten years, aerodynamic research has explored some very new techniques to develop aerofoil sections responsive to varying conditions of flight. These methods have now become possible because of the extraordinary growth in digital computer capabilities, in capacity and speed of operation. Using the results of this work, today's aircraft designers can produce aerofoil sections which will maintain high efficiency over an exceptionally wide range of flow conditions: high Mach Numbers, incidence and Reynolds Number. These effects can be extended by reshaping the wing section automatically (the Mission Adaptive Wing (MAW)), described in more detail under Avionics.

This determination of airflow patterns of computer calculation has also led to the design of low drag installations for the external carriage of weapons and the prospect of ensuring that when the weapons are launched from the aircraft they are subjected to the minimum disturbance from the aircraft's own airflow pattern, substantially improving the aiming accuracy and lethality of these stores.

Computer airflow calculations will additionally greatly assist the achievement of low base drag in aircraft design. Poor flow around the rear of the aircraft has affected many designs in the past, leading either to lower than predicted performance or costly and time consuming design changes.

Engine Technology Improvements

Compressor and turbine efficiencies have reached such high levels in contemporary engines that it is difficult to foresee much improvement over the next decade in this area. Better prospects will be obtainable from being able to use higher turbine inlet temperatures. By this means considerably more power can be produced from the same size of engine. Several metallurgical and manufacturing techniques are now making this possible for the next generation of engine. Amongst them are the use of *blisks*, a process in which the turbine blades are formed as an integral part of the turbine disc; and single crystal

Fixed Wing Aircraft

PLATE 3.1 **Harrier.** Powered by a single vectored thrust turbo fan engine, the Harrier takes off and lands vertically or within a very short forward run. It is seen here in the Falklands campaign where it sometimes operated from the decks of merchant ships. *(British Aerospace)*

molecular structure within the blade material. Both methods offer greater structural integrity at elevated temperatures. Turbine operating temperatures several hundred degrees higher than those currently in every day use will be possible with concomitant improvements to engine thrust, specific fuel consumption and reductions in the number of compressor and turbine stages required. For a given thrust, the engine size and weight can be reduced, as will the quantity of fuel needed for a given mission.

The means by which the right amount of fuel is fed into the combustion chambers over the very wide range of engine operating conditions and pilot demands, has always been complex. The solution has been provided in the past by large, complicated hydro-mechanical fuel control devices. They have not always proved very efficient or reliable. More accurate and faster responses, giving better engine handling and fuel efficiencies over the complete operating range of the engine, can now be achieved by using a digital electronic computer to control the fuel flow. Modern computer design techniques also mean the full authority digital electronic control (FADEC) unit will be smaller, lighter, more reliable and easier to maintain than its mechanical counterpart of yesterday.

The high thrust-to-weight ratios achievable from these engines, together with knowledge developed from the work done on the Pegasus engine as used in the Harrier, make possible the employment of thrust deflection techniques which can be used for enhanced manoevrability in the air as well as take off and landing performance. On the other hand, vertical flight capability in conjunction with level supersonic speeds approaching Mach 2 will be difficult to attain for several years yet and is not likely to be seen on a front line fighter this century.

Avionics

The impact of the rapid advances in digital computing techniques has already been mentioned in relation to aerodynamic improvements and fuel control. The enormous strides being made in all aspects of advanced electronics, ranging through the measurements of quantities, the handling of data and the presentation of information to the crew, open up prospects of aircraft performance previously unattainable. Indeed, aircraft electronics (Avionics) are becoming a key feature of almost every aspect of combat aircraft design and operation. For ease of description, the influence of avionics can be divided into the areas of flight control operations, the gathering and handling of data and the man/machine interface.

The use of electrical signalling, even with some limited computer assistance, to transmit the pilot's control movements out to the primary flying control surfaces (fly-by-wire) is in use on a number of present day combat aircraft. But the introduction of digital techniques to active control technology (ACT) provides additional capabilities way beyond the reach of the older analogue systems. Perhaps the most significant of these is to provide artificial stability on every axis of aircraft movement. By eliminating the necessity to design the aircraft with natural aerodynamic stability, the tailplane, fin and fuselage length (the tail volume) can be smaller and hence of lower weight and drag. Moreover, the tailplane (or horizontal stabilizer) can now be designed as an upward lifting surface making a positive contribution to the support of the aircraft's weight. (In an aircraft designed with natural stability, the tailplane normally produces a down force which the wing must then counteract.) Hence, for any given normal 'g' manoeuvre design point, the wing can be smaller, saving yet more weight and drag. Moreover, by placing the horizontal stabiliser forward of the wing (canard layout) the positive lift generation enhances take off and landing performance. Careful design of this layout can also achieve favourable airflow patterns over the wings, providing additional performance benefits.

Natural aerodynamic stability always opposes aircraft manoeuvres demanded by pilot input to the controls. Artificial stability can be designed so that it does not. In these circumstances, aircraft response to control inputs, on all axes, can be made faster, greatly improving the air superiority fighter qualities. The active flight controls can also be programmed to provide gust alleviation, relieving fatiguing jolts on both crews and airframe, lengthening the life of the aircraft and contributing towards higher aiming accuracy.

Fixed Wing Aircraft

Electronic automatic operation of secondary flying controls can enhance the manoeuvre performance significantly. This is achieved by changing the aircraft's wing section with flight conditions so as to ensure optimum lift/drag ratios at all times. This mission adaptive wing (MAW) utilises leading and trailing edge full span flaps, so designed that a continuous and smooth upper surface to the wing is maintained over a large portion of their operating range. The flaps are positioned automatically by programmed digital computers fed by the parameters of the flight conditions. Pilot intervention is available when required.

Active control technology of this order readily offers the designer the potential for ensuring that no pilot input to the flight or systems controls (e.g. full back stick) can cause the aircraft to exceed its design limitations. The concept of *carefree handling* removes from the pilot that large element of work load, sometimes under critical combat conditions, devoted to ensuring the safety of the aircraft at all times. Moreover, it offers the prospect of operating the aircraft to different limits by switch selection. Lower limits can be used in peace time so as to prolong aircraft life through reduced airframe fatigue and lower engine temperatures. A simple switch operation can make available a higher level of performance for use in combat or emergency. Pilot overrides to the limiter can readily be provided for emergency situations. While this may damage the aircraft, an overwise fatal accident may be avoided, e.g. during a rapid pull-up to avoid an obstacle.

In the post World War Two era, military aircraft have progressively evolved into a complex integrated weapons system. From a flying machine to which weapons and their associated aiming devices were added, the modern combat aeroplane now fully integrates radars, electro-optical systems, navigation aids, aiming systms, automatic weapon release, electronic defensive aids and the flight controls to achieve maximum accuracy and operational effectiveness whilst alleviating the workload on the crew. Linking these systems together has, over the years, become a progressively difficult design problem. Intricate electro-mechanical and electro-hydraulic devices were used and, in order to pass commonly required data freely between elements of the system, cable looms have grown in size and weight, opening up the risks of mutual interference and the prospect of failure of one or several of myriads of connections. Meanwhile, the danger of random induced currents from powerful electro-magnetic radiation sources has created its own design and engineering problems in efforts to provide adequate screening protection. Most of these shielding solutions introduce weight and space penalties.

Extensive use of digital computers, fed by a digital data bus system, provides considerable relief to this problem. By this method, all the individual elements of every part of the system either requiring data or sending data, operates on a common digital signal format which is distributed on a synchronised time sharing basis along a single main highway extending the length and breadth of the aircraft. Large quantities of data can be passed quickly and extensively to

Weapons and Warfare

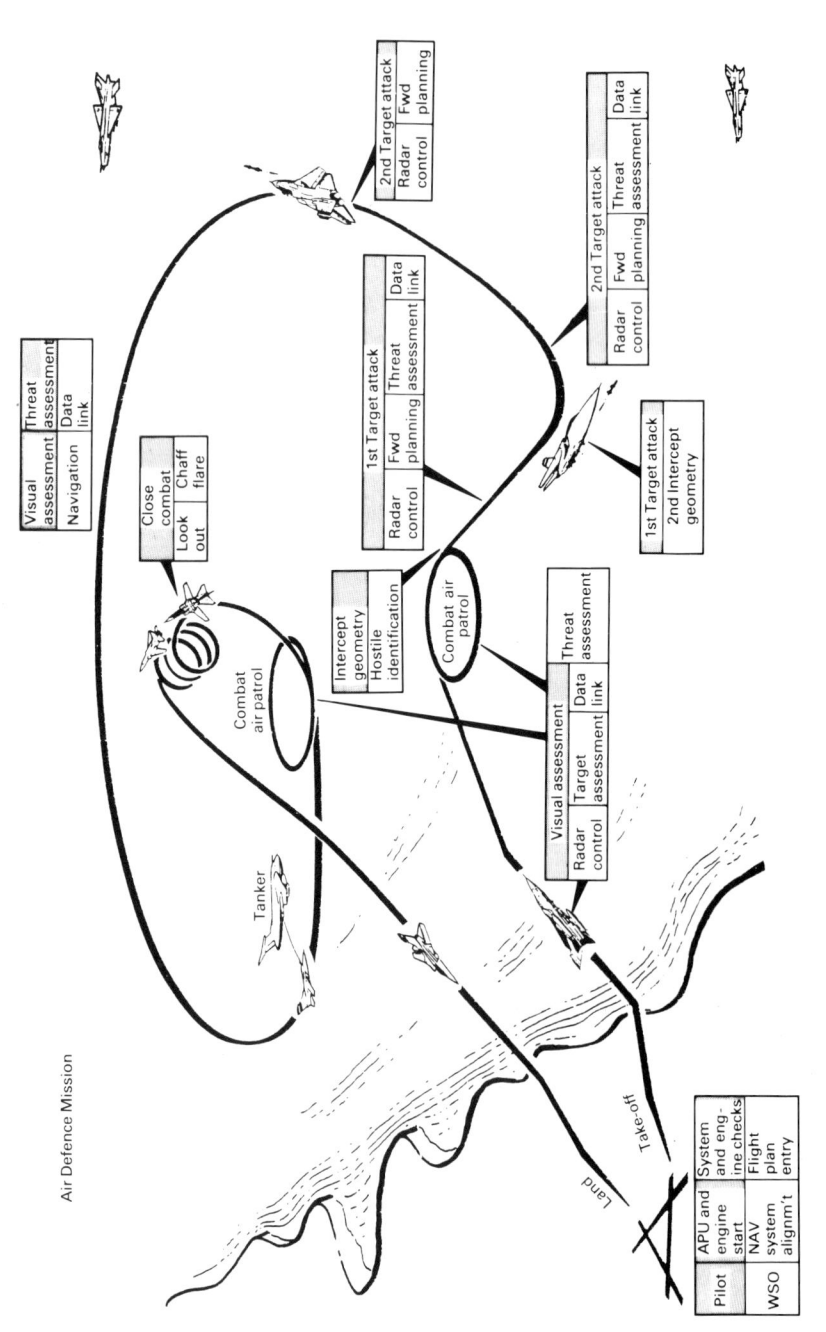

Fig 3.1 Air Defence Mission. *(British Aerospace)*

Fixed Wing Aircraft

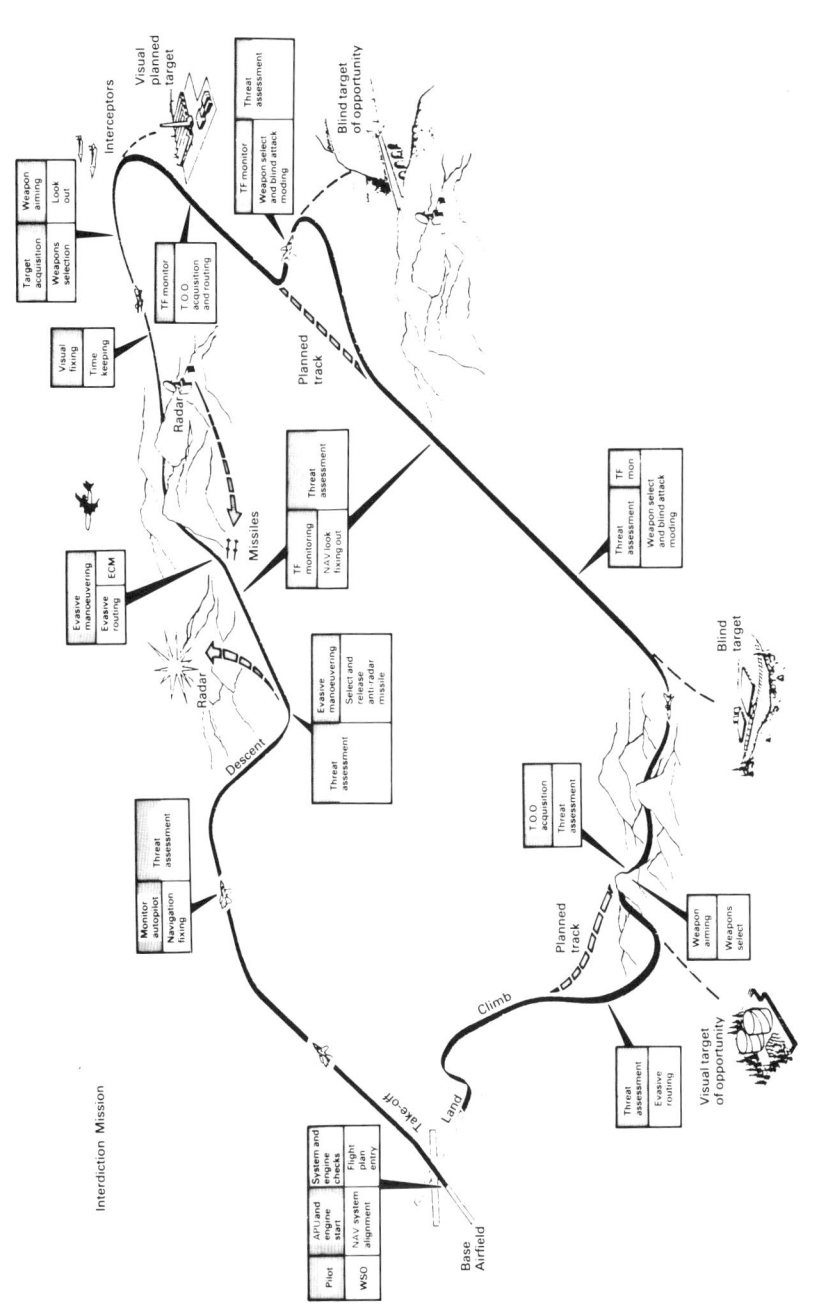

FIG 3.2 Interdiction Mission. (*British Aerospace*)

Weapons and Warfare

PLATE 3.2 **Modern Conventional Cockpit.** Example shown is of a Tornado interdiction and strike aircraft. *(British Aerospace)*

many different parts of the aircraft. One of the biggest operational benefits will come from the flexibility such a system offers. Use of a common international standard for the transmission and reception of all data in the design of avionic systems will offer the potential for easily adding or changing system elements. Provided adequate space, power supply and cooling are available and weight limits are not exceeded, a choice of fit becomes available and the weapon system optimised for any specific mission can be fitted. It also means that within a single aircraft design, individual national equipment preference can be readily handled. Amongst the air forces of an alliance, such as NATO, interoperability is more readily achievable. The digital data bus system is arguably the most important advance in the development of aircraft weapons systems since the advent of the micro-circuit.

Despite the degree of automation which is now possible, only a trained crew can provide the level of decision taking required for the prosecution of airpower in peace and war. The cockpit remains the vital nerve centre of the total machine, and the tremendous advance in information technology in recent years has revolutionised the means of interfacing the crew with the aircraft and its weapon system. New and radical methods are available to pass information to the crew and to enable them to command every facet of the

Fixed Wing Aircraft

PLATE 3.3 **Advanced Technology Cockpit.** Advanced cockpit utilising coloured multi-function electronic displays both head down and head up. *(British Aerospace)*

flight operations. Advanced cathode ray tubes with high resolution full colour and daylight viewing can be used to provide information on the state of the aircraft and the phase of the mission, either automatically or by simple pilot selection, such as a voice command. Each individual display can be multi-functional, offering considerable flexibility and redundancy safety. By using suitable programs, a great deal of automation or semi-automation is introduced into the control of the weapons systems. Therefore multi-role operations can readily be accommodated by the crew without loss of efficiency. Greater automation means less workload for the crew, and the number of crew members can be reduced accordingly. What previously required a two man crew is now feasible with one. Aircraft size and weight can be reduced and greater aircraft performance is achievable for a given expenditure of money – especially in life cycle cost terms. Improvements in information and control flow between crew and aircraft also means better flight safety and more effective mission performance especially in the phase of the detection of targets and their subsequent destruction.

Weapons

A great number of the new and advanced technologies which have been developed for aircraft are equally applicable to the design of new small weapons. Hence in matching weapons to targets, the greater accuracy achieved by advanced guidance techniques, data handling, flight control

Weapons and Warfare

systems, aerodynamics and new materials, mean smaller warheads, less fuel, smaller size and lower weight. Intallation on the aircraft becomes easier and the aircraft's performance with weapons is enhanced as more weapons can be carried. Alternatively, for a given weapon size, more fuel/warhead can be incorporated, increasing the stand off range and/or kill performance. Whichever solution is chosen, a new order of magnitude of targets destroyed per sortie becomes achievable, making air power more effective than ever. These developments have been covered in detail in the weapons chapter.

Stealth

The power and accuracy of modern guided weapons are now nearing the point at which in combat, given no deliberate interference, the combatant who launches his weapon first will achieve a kill and win the battle. When these combatants are engaging each other beyond visual range, information on the target is required by other than visual means. Denying the enemy this information is therefore vital. As radar is the most widely employed system used for this purpose, especially at the longer ranges, some means of defeating enemy radars is essential. Although many techniques can be employed, one effective system that is applicable to new aircraft designs is the incorporation of stealth technology.

Stealth design covers many facets but can be broken down into three main areas: shaping the aircraft to minimise radar reflections, the use of materials which have low radar reflectivity, and electronic devices to interfere with interrogating radars. The first is achieved by careful attention to detail design, principally to eliminate the introduction of corner reflector equivalents in the aircraft structure. This is more easy to say than to achieve, given that there are some aspects of the aircraft which cannot be altered very much, e.g. the face of the engine and the size of the engine intakes. Clearly, the fact that the new generation of aircraft and its weapons installations can be made smaller will be a significant contribution in itself. Radar reflectivity can be reduced by the use of radar absorbent materials in those parts of the structure generating the largest radar response. Electronic devices are numerous and mostly highly classified. By using these technologies, the effective radar cross section of the aircraft can be considerably reduced.

The Experimental Aircraft Programme (EAP)

Over the past twenty years, new technologies have been developed largely in isolation from each other. In some instances the perceived benefits are still theoretical and the practical achievement awaits flight trials. More than anything else, the full benefits will never be known before all the technologies are brought together in one design which takes full account of the synergy obtainable from the combination effects. The virtuous circle that is generated

Fixed Wing Aircraft

PLATE 3.4 **The EAP.** An experimental aircraft programme demonstrator with all moving foreplanes and advanced compound sweep wing with power by two RB199 MK 104 engines. *(British Aerospace)*

from progressive iterations of scaling down the design because of weight reductions, smaller size and higher efficiencies in so many major aspects of the design, can only remain a theoretical calculation until full scale flight tests are made. At the same time it is prudent to develop many of these technologies to the point of full air-worthiness before incorporating them into a new operational aircraft design. This work will provide vital experience to designers and engineers and establish confidence in the techniques. In this way the technologies can be specified for any new combat aircraft with a high degree of assurance. Equally, the experience gained from flight tests will enable an operational system to be designed, developed and proven in less time and with a higher prospect of achieving the desired performance. The Experimental Aircraft Programme (EAP) aircraft has been designed and built for this purpose. Rolled out in a ceremony at British Aerospace Warton in April 1986, it incorporates all the new technologies in one test demonstrator vehicle. From mid-1986 flight tests have provided a wealth of experience in these advanced techniques, starting with design and construction. The next combat aircraft development programmes will thereby be shortened appreciably and go forward with a confidence which would otherwise be lacking. Indeed, without the information obtained from EAP, it is debatable whether Governments would be prepared to invest the huge sums of money involved in a project with so many novel and otherwise untried aspects. The EAP is the cornerstone of future combat aircraft design and development.

Conclusions

Despite technological advances, the manned aircraft will continue for the foreseeable future to be the mainstay of military airpower. Only the man in the cockpit can provide the flexibility of decision and action essential for the successful prosecution of air operations in peace and war. Suitably equipped, the manned aircraft can perform all the desired airpower missions over the complete range of deterrence and graduated response from airspace policing in peacetime to nuclear weapon delivery in war.

Advanced and new technologies offer the opportunity for increased performance across a wide range of roles with a single crew and a smaller aircraft. In general, the flight envelope of the vehicle does not need to be very different from today's front line aircraft. However, several critical parameters, such as air combat manoeuvring and take off and landing distance, can be significantly improved. Considerable enhancements to the weapon system, including the weapons themselves, will also ensure a substantial increase in lethality against air and ground targets.

Meanwhile, smaller size, lower weight, fewer material parts and the reducing costs of computer technology all contribute to lower cost of acquisition. The better reliability trend in successive generations of avionics, as evidenced already in Tornado operations, means lower running costs in manhours and spares, and much greater availability of front line aircraft for operations.

Taken together, the lower costs of ownership in combination with higher effectiveness will result in a new order of cost-effectiveness, offering appreciable savings compared with the present generation of aircraft, especially as the current aircraft approach the end of their lives.

The Longer Term Trend

The smaller size of the next generation of combat aircraft, coupled with widespread employment of stealth techniques, will reduce the vulnerability of the aircraft to defences. However, the constantly changing balance between offence and defence will mean inevitably that at some time in the future the low level airspace will no longer provide the degree of protection which has made it so attractive for air operations over many years. Although this is unlikely to occur much before the end of the lifetime of the next generation of combat aircraft, now is the time to be considering the research and development programmes for the succeeding generation of weapon systems. Threat improvements would indicate that the acquisition of information on battlefield, second echelon or airborne targets, and the launch of weapons against those targets, will have to take place at long range stand off distances. The advances in electronic surveillance techniques should make the former achievable, either by satellite or airborne warning and control systems (AWACS). These systems should also be able to provide mid-course guidance for long range missiles which could themselves have self-contained precision terminal guidance. Considerable energy will be required to give the missile the necessary range and speed of penetration. If launched from a static ground based platform, most of the energy will have to be attached in some form to the missile, making it bulky to store, transport and prepare. Moreover, once launched, the missile is unlikely to be recoverable should circumstances demand a change of plan. Alternatively, a large element of the required energy could be provided by launch from an aircraft flying a high speed and altitude, enabling the missile itself to remain relatively small and hence easier to manage, and less vulnerable to interception. Additional benefits would accrue from secure storage and preparation on airfields; and the fact that for Central European and Northern flank operations, the aircraft could be based in the United Kingdom, reducing their vulnerability on the ground. After take off, the climb to height and acceleration to the launch conditions (say Mach 3+ at more than 70,000 feet) could be made in the direction of the target. Data link control would be in use throughout the mission, including missile release. This would relieve the launch vehicle from carrying sophisticated sensor and computer systems, all of which would be in the larger and fewer in number AWACS platforms. Of course, up to the moment of weapon release, the aircraft can always be recalled if reuqired. The missiles themselves, which are always the expendable element of the weapon system, would be smaller and cheaper than a ground launched system and have considerably greater flexibility of use. The aircraft would provide the rapid deployment and long range over-the-horizon threat flexibility which has been and will remain the hallmark of air power.

4

Helicopters

BRIGADIER GENERAL SAMUEL G COCKERHAM US ARMY

THE world's first practical helicopter – with a full range of controls for power and flight in all directions – made its inaugural flight in Germany in 1936, piloted by a woman. Today, fifty years later, helicopters are indispensable to modern warfare and combat; a fully-fledged member of the combined arms teams of many nations' military forces – Infantry, Armour, Artillery, Aviation, and Engineers; an integral part of commerce worldwide, and are enhanced by the most advanced technology.

It is estimated that the Soviet Union has a fleet of 16,000 helicopters; the United States, 11,000; the United Kingdom, 800; Germany, 700; and other NATO countries, 1,500. Other non-NATO countries own 2,000 helicopters for commercial applications and military uses. Within the Free World, in research, development, and production, the United States helicopter industry (Bell, Boeing, McDonnell Douglas, and Sikorsky) employs 28,000 persons. In France (Aerospatiale), Great Britain (Westland), Germany (MBB), and Italy (Agusta), the industry employs 23,000 persons. Helicopters serve in all major nations as prime movers of military forces, their equipments, armaments, and surveillance sensors.

The helicopter that appeared in Germany before the Second World War, however, did not fly smoothly into the worldwide acceptance it enjoys today. The war effort disrupted research and development in Europe for both Germany and the Allies, and the predominant design, development, and production work continued in the United States. During the Second World War, helicopters served rudimentary military purposes. Still new, with unproven components and limited capability, they flew medical evacuation, rescue, light surveillance, and liaison missions. However, their payload, range, and reliability were not great enough for large-scale logistics and unit operations.

After the War, European firms reinitiated their helicopter development programmes. Since the United States had the lead in the field, however, European firms entered into licensing agreements with United States manufacturers – Bell, Boeing, Sikorsky and later, Hughes, now McDonnell Douglas. The United States introduced newer and larger helicopters late in the Korean

Helicopters

PLATE 4.1 **AH-64 Apache Hellfire Missile.**

War, while simultaneously extending their use to logistics and troop unit deployments. As a direct result of the combat lessons learned in the Korean War, the United States initiated the development of an all new turbine engine-powered utility helicopter, the UH-1 [HUEY], later to become the main-line troop-lift helicopter in Vietnam. The United States also continued development and production of medium-sized and heavy helicopters for equipment, cargo, and large tactical unit movements.

Experience Leads to Innovation

In the United States, the requirement for larger helicopters clearly exceeded availability. European and American firms exchanged technology and the US Army procured European helicopters for test and evaluation in the late 1950s. Two such machines were the French Djinn and Alouette helicopters: light observation and utility machines. Departures from the standard US designs and their variants also began in the 1950s. Aerospatiale (Sud Aviation), Agusta, Westland, and MBB continued their research and development and

Weapons and Warfare

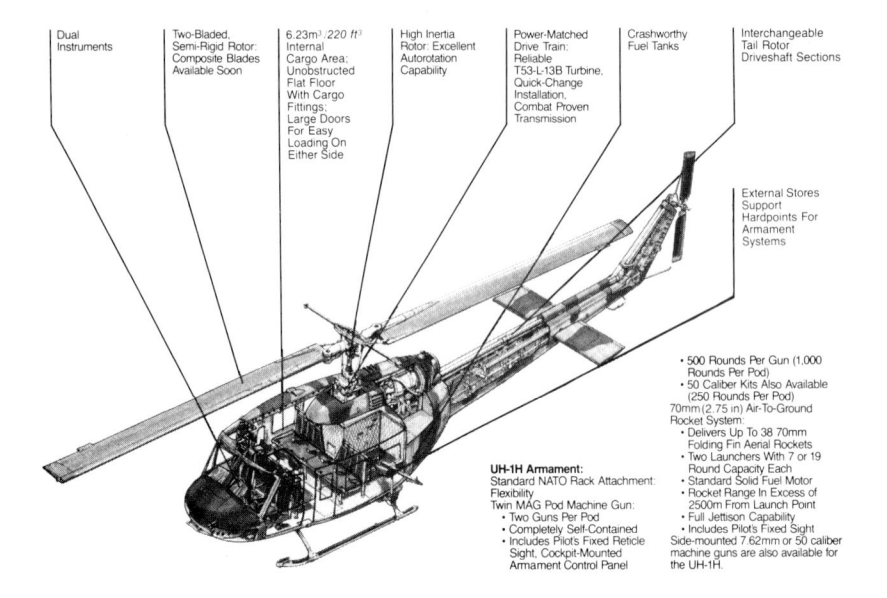

Labels (clockwise from left):
- Dual Instruments
- Two-Bladed, Semi-Rigid Rotor; Composite Blades Available Soon
- 6.23m³/220 ft³ Internal Cargo Area; Unobstructed Flat Floor With Cargo Fittings; Large Doors For Easy Loading On Either Side
- High Inertia Rotor: Excellent Autorotation Capability
- Power-Matched Drive Train: Reliable T53-L-13B Turbine, Quick-Change Installation, Combat Proven Transmission
- Crashworthy Fuel Tanks
- Interchangeable Tail Rotor Driveshaft Sections
- External Stores Support Hardpoints For Armament Systems

UH-1H Armament:
Standard NATO Rack Attachment:
Twin MAG Pod Machine Gun:
 • Two Guns Per Pod
 • Completely Self-Contained
 • Includes Pilot's Fixed Reticle Sight, Cockpit-Mounted Armament Control Panel

 • 500 Rounds Per Gun (1,000 Rounds Per Pod)
 • 50 Caliber Kits Also Available (250 Rounds Per Pod)
70mm (2.75 in) Air-To-Ground Rocket System:
 • Delivers Up To 38 70mm Folding Fin Aerial Rockets
 • Two Launchers With 7 or 19 Round Capacity Each
 • Standard Solid Fuel Motor
 • Rocket Range In Excess of 2500m From Launch Point
 • Full Jettison Capability
 • Includes Pilot's Fixed Sight
Side-mounted 7.62mm or 50 caliber machine guns are also available for the UH-1H.

FIG 4.1 UH-1 Huey. (*Bell Helicopters*)

began production of new helicopter models of original design and performance. Both European and US firms developed new turbine engines, dynamic components (rotor blades, hubs, transmissions, gearboxes, shafting), flight controls, instrumentation, communications, and their accessories that allowed the helicopter to serve many more purposes in business and commercial activities.

In the late 1950s and early 1960s, the US Army began field experimentation with observation and utility helicopters as aerial weapons platforms. It was a trial-and-error type of experimentation using off-the-shelf guns, rockets, fire-control devices, and helicopters. The results were favourable enough to convince the Army that an armed helicopter was feasible, practical, and desirable. During the same period, the European military experimented with the use of helicopters in manoeuvres and field exercises. In addition, the French Army employed helicopters in air assault operations against guerrilla units in North Africa with great success. The French North African campaign was, in fact, the first time that helicopters were used in combat. The French experimented with off-the-shelf guns and rockets fastened to the landing gear and struts of cargo and utility helicopters. They learned that accurate fire control and crew protection from ground fire were key problems requiring immediate solutions if air mobile/assault operations were to be successful.

Helicopters

Crew members were most vulnerable to ground fire; their protection became top priority. Armour plates were placed around crew members, controls, and fuel tanks as an expedient solution. Ballistic protection of crew, components, crashworthy fuel cells and other design features of combat helicopters were ten years in the future at this time.

Meanwhile, the United Kingdom in its campaign in Malaysia, found the helicopter an indispensable combat vehicle. The advantage in mobility offered by the helicopter enabled the British ground commanders to defeat the guerrilla bands and win the support of the people. The helicopter played a most crucial role in the campaigns and contributed greatly to the success of the combat commanders.

United States Develops Attack Helicopter

Based on lessons learned in combat by the French and British Armies, plus its own experimentations, the US Army reaffirmed its requirement for long-term research and development programmes for armaments, fire control, avionics, navigation, and day–night viewers for use on armed helicopters. Thus, in 1964, the US Army began development of a fully integrated attack helicopter – one that was full-systems capable.

With the advent of turbine engines in the 700 and 1,800 shp range, and new airframe dynamic components, the UH-1A and CH-47A helicopters and the OV-1A aeroplane appeared. These were the first in a long line of highly dependable aircraft, which became the prime vehicles for developing the US Army's Air Assault Concept in 1964 and 1965.

The US Army tested the Air Assault Concept using a newly formed 11th Air Assault Division [15,000 men], equipped with over 400 helicopters, and aircraft. Tests and field trials confirmed the value of such a concept. The division, name changed to the 1st Air Cavalry Division, was rushed to Vietnam in 1965, and, based on its success in combat, another air assault division was organised in Vietnam. At the peak of operations, the US Army had 3,900 helicopters in combat operations throughout south-east Asia.

As a result of these activities, the US Army recognised the need for distinct classes of helicopters – Scout, Utility, Attack, and Medium and Heavy Cargo. The scout, utility, and attack helicopters worked closely together in air assault operations. In fact, their integrated effort was imperative for successful combat operations. Compatible communications, roles, missions, and procedures were developed for each helicopter class. Thus, the need for both integration and specialisation in helicopter design had emerged from the US combat experiences in Vietnam

Helicopters Provide Unique Mobility

Battle commanders have long dreamed of being able to move military units

Weapons and Warfare

with ease over the battle area regardless of terrain, weather, and visibility conditions. At the altitude of the Army troop's boot top – twelve inches – and higher, the helicopter is potentially capable of providing freedom of movement at any time, any place, and under any conditions. Helicopters attain maximum protection and efficiency through terrain cover and concealment, known as nap-of-the-earth [NOE] flying. From Army boot top to two main rotor diameters (about 100 feet) above the earth's surface, the third dimension of tactical mobility, the helicopter is in hover-in-ground-effect (HIGE) distance where the air is the most dense. Lift assistance is derived from the rotor down-wash striking the earth's surface, thus lessening the power required to fly. At altitudes greater than two rotor diameters, the helicopter loses the protection offered at lower attitudes by foliage, terrain cover, and concealment, such as folds, reverse slopes, defilades, ridge lines, and avenues of approach; and it is also exposed to surface-to-air missile (SAM), and anti-aircraft guns.

Helicopters require greater power when flying at hover-out-of-ground effect (HOGE) and higher altitudes than when flying at boot top height within the HIGE limits. To exploit third dimension mobility fully, helicopters must be designed to hover both in ground effect and out-of-ground effect. Hovering is to the helicopter as floating is to water craft, or climbing is to land vehicles. Hover flight requires the most power; thus, to operate successfully, helicopters must first be able to hover. Until the helicopter, no vehicle could work in the third-dimension mobility region of air space – that is, with the freedom to take off and land from any point on the earth's surface. All other forms of mobility and firepower enter and exit this area, but none stays and works in it with the ease of the helicopter.

Helicopter third-dimension high-speed mobility, combined with all-weather day–night performance and firepower, makes this vehicle unique. Its combat versatility and flexibility of response expand the area of combat – the helicopter is capable of hovering, flying, and conducting combat on eighty-five per cent of the world's land mass ninety per cent of the time. The foregoing is true if it is designed to hover-out-of-ground effect at 4,000 feet pressure altitude and 95°F; if it is designed to hover-out-of-ground effect at 6,000 feet pressure altitude and 95°F, the usable time and territory increase.

Helicopters Designed to Move and Shoot

The principal determinants of helicopter design and configuration are the following:

1. Atmospheric condition – Altitude, temperature, humidity, and wind. (These affect performance of engine and rotor blades.)
2. Hover performance – Affected by engine power and rotor blade design.
3. Mission profile – Time duration, hover, cruise, climb, and tasks.

4. Payload – Internal, external, stores, armaments, sensors, and other.
5. Survivability and crashworthiness – Affected by threat and parameters of 'g' force.
6. Endurance – Fuel load.
7. Time period – User, threat and technology sophistication.

To succeed in battle a military force must be able to move, shoot, communicate, and sustain better than its adversary. No military force can hope to be successful in battle without accomplishing these four combat functions in a superb and unexcelled manner. (An advantage in any one of these areas of combat power gives a relative advantage over the adversary.) The fighting force must also be able to operate around the clock in all weather, terrain and visibility conditions, without any degradation in performance. If work can be done under all of these conditions as easily as during the day, the force strength increases by a factor of two-plus. Today, the tactical movement of large or tailored forces by helicopter is both practical and feasible.

The full-systems-capable helicopter, an attack helicopter, provides a mobile platform for firepower and the necessary sensors to move with nearly equal ease at night or in periods of reduced visibility as during the day. The innovations making this possible are in the field of Target Acquisition, which includes the following functions:

1. Detection – (Is there a target: 'yes' or 'no'?)
2. Recognition – ('Yes', it is either a tank, truck, armoured personnel carrier, or other.)
3. Identification – (Yes, it is either friend, or foe; and if foe, a tank (its type?)
4. Engagement – (Fire For Effect.)

"If you can see the target, you can kill it." In other words, the probability of Detection, Recognition, Identification, Hit, and Kill are all equal; notwithstanding, Target Acquisition remains the most difficult element in the chain of events leading to a *kill*. The helicopter has made this chain of probabilities more effective through its inherent mobility characteristics. At 150 to 200 knots, the helicopter is capable of movement anywhere in the tactical area within minutes, where formerly ground vehicles (tanks, tracks, wheels) would be almost invariably restricted to man-made roadways, river bridging, or cross country movement, depending on trafficability.

The helicopter alone is able to move with complete freedom across regions of the Arctic, even in summer, for example. The permafrost and semi-permafrost prohibit use of ground vehicles except over existing roadways or trails. In addition, many primitive regions are without roadways. In such regions, the economics of peace-time commerce may not support the building of roadways and communications systems. Therefore, the helicopter is the

Weapons and Warfare

PLATE 4.2 **OH 58D Scout.** The mast-mounted sight enables target engagement from a low hover behind cover. *(Bell Helicopters)*

most economic means of contact, and, in most under-developed nations, is becoming a necessity.

Technology for Today and Tomorrow

The helicopter must no longer be viewed as an end in itself. It has passed at a fast, ever increasing pace from the tinkering, trial-and-error period of the 1910s through the 1930s to the experimental, novelty phase of the 1940s and 1950s, into the systems-integration phase of the 1960s and 1970s. Yet, it still has tremendous growth potential as a prime mover of troops and passengers, cargo and unit equipment, and as an integrated attack helicopter system. Moreover, the helicopter is the vehicle most capable of meeting the tasks of the battle commander.

The helicopter achieved maturity by steady increases in performance of its engines, and dynamic components. There have been technological advances in flight controls, electronics, avionics, and visionics (sensors), which are now more efficient in terms of their requirements and uses of space, weight, power, form, fit, and function. With respect to visionics, in particular, these reductions

Helicopters

have made the *black box* hardware and associated software attractive for use in helicopter warfare. The subsystems can now be integrated into the helicopter without the space, weight, and power limitations and penalties of earlier models in earlier years.

Today's technology requirements for combat helicopters are great: the need is for nap of the earth flight (less than 50 feet above the highest obstacle in 100 feet lateral distance of flight path), in low visibility, at night, in high pressure altitude, and at high speed (200+ knots) with sensors and weapons in search of targets. Much of this capability exists. When targets are found, they can be destroyed with near pin-point accuracy.

The first tanks, and vehicles destroyed in combat by a TOW [Tactical Optical Wire Guided Missile] occurred in April and May, 1972 in the vicinity of Pleiku, Vietnam. The TOW is a precision, point-type weapon with range out to 3,750 metres. Its accuracy, and penetration capability represented the world's first really effective anti-tank weapon. For the first time in history, the mobility and combat versatility of the helicopter were mated with a precision anti-tank weapon. Specifically designed attack helicopters and their mission equipments have greatly improved the combat effectiveness of all combat arms [Infantry, Artillery, Armour, Engineers, and Signals] and especially combat support.

But the threat keeps changing. Helicopters must take hits, keep flying, and detect, recognise, identify, and engage targets at increasing ranges. Also, they must face anti-aircraft guns, missiles, and ground fire. An emerging new threat is other helicopters armed with air-to-air firepower. No helicopter has been shot down by another helicopter, and to date, there has not been a helicopter-to-helicopter fire fight.

Missiles, advanced weapons, radars, electro-magnetic interference, electro-magnetic pulse, chemical, biological, nuclear, laser, and other armaments are all threats to be countered, and the combat helicopter must respond quickly. Helicopters will have to be able to change mission equipments, in less than thirty minutes, and vary tactics to defeat threats if they are to continue to meet mission demands of ground battle commanders consisting of: (1) Command, Control, and Communications; (2) Close Combat; (3) Fire Support; (4) Air Defence; (5) Utility/Cargo; (6) Combat Support; (7) Combat Service Support, and (8) Self Deployment. If the helicopter continues to demonstrate its capability to satisfy the ground battle commanders' mission demands, and to defeat enemy threats, it will become the vehicle of first and last resort on the battlefield. Past Operational Tests have already confirmed an exchange ratio of tank losses to helicopter losses of 20:1.

Movement of combat forces from one point to another and in condition to fight is important for survivability, mission execution, and Surprise. The correlation between speed and Surprise is important – speed here refers to the time required to move the mass of combat force. The helicopter is the vehicle most likely to regain tactical mobility and firepower advantage for the ground

Weapons and Warfare

PLATE 4.3 **UH-60A Black Hawk lifting two 105 mm Howitzers.** *(Sikorsky Aircraft)*

PLATE 4.4 **Stream of UH-60A Black Hawk engaged in troop lifting.** *(Sikorsky Aircraft)*

Helicopters

PLATE 4.5 **UH-60A Black Hawk in attack role.** *(Sikorsky Aircraft)*

commander, and, in the process, gain Surprise. The commander who has lost Surprise will be defeated in battle. Long-range strategic deployments of helicopters have, in fact, been demonstrated at distances equal to the distance of the North Atlantic route.

The Soviet military forces have adopted and expanded the US Army's air-assault concepts devised in Vietnam. Consequently, the Soviet Union now produces large numbers of troop assault, fire support, and anti-armour helicopters; most of these have a degree of air-to-air capability against other helicopters. For example, the new *Kamov Hokum* Soviet helicopter has both an anti-armour and anti-air mission capability with speed in the range of 350 kilometre/hour. At this speed the *Kamov Hokum* far exceeds the speed of comparable United States and European attack helicopters.

It has been said that to build a better helicopter you need only to build a better engine. Though the premise remains valid, there are other more demanding technologies in the non-airframe subsystems area: electronics, fire control, computers, armaments, stand-off-sensors, designators, navigation, countermeasures, avionics, visionics, and smart systems, to name a few. The integration of family subsystems offers the promise of making the attack helicopter the dominant vehicle on the high-technology battlefield. The design frontiers for the helicopter remain in the threat, airborne visibility, all weather, and Mission Equipment integration areas of research and development.

Weapons and Warfare

In the high technology battlefield of the future, the major threat to the ground commander will be the helicopter – not the tank and its armoured vehicle columns.

Introducing Chapters 5 & 6

THE demands of air defence are reflected in the complexities and variety of characteristics of weapons available and the command and control environment in which they are operated. The attacking aircraft has the initiative in all respects and can thus contrive to present the most fleeting and difficult of targets, usually using terrain as cover until the last moment. On the other hand reconnaissance and airborne early warning aircraft may fly at considerable heights and distances hoping to achieve their mission from a relatively invulnerable position. The helicopter and the fixed wing aircraft operate in very different modes and pose quite different problems to the air defence. Thus, a variety of weapons are needed to meet this multiple threat and, for success, they require the minimum of manual operation. Ideally they should be fire and forget. The need to allow friendly aircraft to operate with sufficient freedom poses a difficult problem for command and control. Measured in resource terms, air defence is an unusually expensive business which is why, in the Western world, where for many years armies have not been exposed to an unfavourable air situation during operations, air defence over land seldom receives an allocation of resources commensurate with the threat.

The Falklands campaign demonstrated the perils which attend war at sea. As long ago as the battle of Jutland and more recently when HMS Hood was lost in World War Two, ships and virtually their entire complements vanished in cataclysmic explosions when their magazines were hit. The torpedo, too, brought sudden death, but more generally there was time to appreciate events and make appropriate tactical dispositions. Now, a mere chink in the armour, or a momentary lapse, of no more than two seconds, may well bring instant and complete disaster. To have, as the jargon goes, a man in the loop, may result in a split second's calamitous delay, yet men must remain in control. Chapter 6, in explaining the complexities and technologies involved, highlights the difficulty of providing an effective defence against a missile attack at sea.

5
Land Based Air Defence

R F JACKSON

THE aim of this chapter, which is written from a NATO viewpoint, is to provide some insight into the nature of active land based air defence systems. Passive approaches, such as camouflage, hardened shelters, decoys and the like are not considered. In attempting to do so, it highlights some of the factors that influence their design and procurement. Rather than provide a catalogue of past and present systems, emphasis is placed on current equipments and the way that air defence is likely to evolve in coming years.

Without some understanding of the threat that they face, it is difficult to comprehend the rationale behind the evolution of air defence systems, both as they are currently and as they are being designed for the future. For this reason, after this short introduction, this chapter continues with an appraisal of the air threat to be countered. This is followed by a description of the constituent elements of air defence systems, along with the techniques that they use. Organisational aspects are then treated briefly before the chapter closes with some thoughts for future trends and possibilities.

Ground based air defence can be provided by a range of different weapons from guns, through short range highly mobile surface to air guided weapon (SAGW) systems such as the UK's Tracked Rapier, right up to long range highly sophisticated, but less mobile systems typified by the US Patriot system. The varying level of sophistication and range of action is reflected in the need for varying levels of command and control of these weapon systems.

This chapter deals mainly with SAGW systems as they provide, in the present and for some time to come, the prime land based defence of air space. Guns, radar controlled or otherwise, are in use by some nation's forces for short range low level air defence of vulnerable points or individual Army units; for this reason, a short section thereon is to be found following the treatment of SAGW systems.

In the First World War, the growing use of aircraft for military purposes resulted in the use of guns in a land based air defence role. During the Second World War, radar provided the wherewithal for better fire control of anti-aircraft guns and became the basis for several experimental SAGW programmes in Germany and the United Kingdom. It was, however, in the

Weapons and Warfare

1948/1949 period that SAGW developments really began in earnest, with projects such as Nike in the US and Thunderbird and Bloodhound in the United Kingdom. Emphasis on these systems was the defence against the high and medium altitude bomber threat, which had become so destructive towards the end of World War Two. This thinking was continued in the 1950s with the development of the US Hawk system which, with continuing improvements, still provides a large proportion of the non Warsaw Pact air defences today.

The Threat

Since the Second World War, the threat posed to land based air defences has increased and diversified significantly. At the end of World War Two the threat was mainly from bombers, using free fall bombs, and flying at medium and high altitudes. Technological developments during the 50s and 60s, such as terrain following radar, head-up displays and cluster weapons, made it possible for an enemy to mount an air threat which could penetrate below the radar defences of the earlier SAGW systems and attack targets with precision and great effectiveness. Fighter ground attack aircraft evolved in sophistication using the same technologies in the same timescale and began to pose a great threat to ground forces, both in forward battle areas and rear airfield and supply areas. Thus, the emphasis of the threat changed in the thirty years after World War Two from the medium and high altitude high speed bomber to one which, whilst still encompassing that threat, placed greater and greater emphasis on saturation attacks at low level, flying beneath radar defences and unmasking close to the target; the targets had become not only fixed installations such as airfields, supply points and troop points, but had also come to include mobile battle groups. This trend was continued with the advent of the armoured attack helicopter, exemplified by the Soviet Hind, during the 1970s. In fact, it seems probable that, in forward areas, the helicopter will prove a more significant threat than fixed wing aircraft, which have less potential for all weather close support and a lower chance of survival than the coming generations of attack helicopters. The latter provide difficult targets for the battlefield air defences as they are able to make the maximum use of terrain features to screen their approach, and need to be visible to the defended site only for the short time needed for them to aim and fire their weapons.

This evolution of the threat towards greater emphasis on low level attacks, making maximum use of terrain screening, means that land based air defence systems must be able to react very quickly in order to deal with targets which unmask at short range and are visible for only short periods of time. These limitations of short engagement time and relatively short unmask range, mean that land based air defence systems are required in significant numbers if they are to provide a credible defence over a reasonably large area of the battlefield and, at the same time, provide the required defence of airfields, supply points,

Land Based Air Defence

PLATE 5.1 **SA-6 Gainful.** A Soviet tactical medium range surface-to-air missile.

etc. The answer to this has been the development of a variety of low level, relatively short range, guided weapon air defence systems, with mobility, even portability, and affordability as major requirements. Weapons of this class have included Rapier (UK), Crotale (France) and Roland (France and Germany) in the vehicle mounted category, and Redeye, Stinger (United States) and Blowpipe Javelin (United Kingdom) in the manportable category. In addition to these guided weapon developments, developments of radar controlled gun systems have continued, primarily to provide defence of battle groups in forward areas. The most famous of these is probably the Soviet ZSU 23/4 system; Western developments have included the

$$\begin{array}{ll} \text{Oerlikon Diana} & (2 \times 25 \text{ millimetres}) \\ \text{Otto Melara} & (4 \times 25 \text{ millimetres}) \\ \text{Bofors Bofi} & (1 \times 40 \text{ millimetres}) \end{array}$$

Weapons and Warfare

        Gepard   (2 × 35 millimetres)
        Vulcan   (6 × 20 millimetres)

The threat currently facing NATO land based air defences takes the following form. An assault in massive strength with overwhelming superiority in the sectors chosen for breakthrough is likely. The attack will probably be made in depth and the most successful penetrations exploited by the following echelons of forces. This strategy, if successful, would create a number of corridors through the SAGW belt and the mopping up, in fairly short order, of those SAGW sites in between. Simultaneously, there would be a major effort to suppress all other NATO air defences to a level which would allow the Soviets virtual control of the air. The targets would include command, control and communication (C^3) facilities, while a high priority would be accorded to the NATO airborne warning and control system (AWACS). Concurrently, the Soviet Air Force would also provide direct support to the land battle, the proportion of air effort on each task varying as the situation altered.

For the future, little change is seen in total numbers and varieties of Soviet aircraft, or in operating speeds and altitudes. However, the trend is developing towards stand-off weapons and their extensive use, larger payloads carried over longer ranges and a much improved ability to conduct all weather precision attacks on a wide variety of targets. Already emerging is a new generation of anti-armour all weather fighters with a look down–shoot down capability and an increased threat to our own AWACS. In the forward areas, it seems probable that the helicopter will continue to prove a more and more significant threat than fixed wing aircraft and will develop the ability to stand off at greater ranges from its potential target through the use of longer range fire and forget stand-off weapon systems.

As indicated in the foregoing paragraph, Soviet missiles of all natures will provide a growing threat. The Soviets will introduce into service a wide variety of long, medium and short range missiles; they will be ballistic, cruise and tactical and would be launched from ground and air. Depending on the type and tactical situation, these missiles will feature terminal guidance, terminally guided separating warheads and smart submunitions, the latter particularly intended for armoured targets in forward areas. Delivery inaccuracies, even of the longer range weapons, are likely to be better than 100 m, and as good as 10 m when used against fixed targets.

Many other measures are likely to be integrated into the main Soviet battle plan. Apart from the land based air defence units themselves, NATO radar and C^3 will be the targets of electronic warfare (EW), sabotage by special forces, or airborne assault. One should also anticipate attacks by increasingly flexible anti-radar missiles and the use of remotely piloted vehicles (RPVs). Soviet capabilities would be improved by the use of Stealth techniques and, possibly, by the incorporation of laser soft damage weapons combined with selective control of self-protect jamming.

Land Based Air Defence

PLATE 5.2 **ZSU-23-4.** A Soviet 23 mm air defence system which can be laid either by radar or manual sighting.

The future threat could be formidable and, if one is not to be confused or even overawed, the key features need identifying. Two which stand out are saturation and variety. According to official estimates, openly published in sources such as the United Kingdom's annual Defence White Paper, the Soviets are likely to start with a strategic superiority in excess of 2:1 in aircraft, a ratio which can locally be much improved in their favour by their choice of time and place to attack. Moreover, our air defence systems will be faced with a random arrival, over short periods, of large numbers of air and ground launched missiles. In short, variety of attack will stem from the multiplicity aircraft and missile types, attack in all weathers from all altitudes, arrival angles up to the nearly vertical and speeds from the hover to those in excess of Mach 4. Target exposure times may be as short as 15 seconds; in some battlefield cases it may be even shorter.

With these key features of the present and evolving threat identified, it becomes possible to deduce the operational needs that have driven the evolution of land based air defence to their present state, and which will continue to drive their development into the future. The task facing such systems is a significant one and calls for systems to take full advantage of improvements in technological capability, whether as mid-life improvements to existing systems, or in the form of the development of completely new

Weapons and Warfare

PLATE 5.3 **Tracked Rapier.** A highly mobile low level defence system for the defence of armour in the forward areas. This system, which is in service with the British Army, carries eight ready to fire missiles and it can be brought into action in thirty seconds. It is operated by a crew of three. *(British Aerospace)*

systems to provide a defence against an ever increasing variety of target types, sizes, speeds and attack directions in an ever more hostile countermeasure environment.

Major Elements of Air Defence Systems

Active land based air defence systems, whilst they may be capable of operating autonomously, are normally integrated into a total air defence network. This requires that they possess the requisite communication links and that they operate within a defined command and control structure. The total air defence network is able to call on specialist resources to report on movements in the air space with which it is concerned; these resources provide the individual air defence units with early warning of potential attacks on the assets being defended. An example of such reporting systems is the NATO air defence ground environment (NADGE) providing radar surveillance of a wide belt of air space stretching from North Cape, in Northern Norway, through Scandinavia and Central Europe, on through Italy, Greece and Turkey, ending with the radars on Mount Arrarat. Other examples of altering systems

Land Based Air Defence

are the UKADGE (United Kingdom air defence ground environment) and various airborne early warning systems, such as AWACS. These warning systems are not active in themselves, i.e. they cannot destroy targets, they simply report on their movements. It is the active air defence elements that form the subject of consideration for the remainder of this section.

All active land based air defence systems involve to some degree, the wherewithal to perform the following functions.

Surveillance/Search
Fire Control
Kill
Kill Assessment

Search and surveillance may be carried out by a variety of means, ranging from the unaided use of the human eyeball, through the use of optical aids (including thermal imagers), passive infra-red surveillance devices, small highly mobile radars (such as those used in the British Aerospace Rapier system) and, for long range air defence systems, large radars. Whatever the means employed, it is frequently alerted by having data passed from one of the reporting sensors mentioned in the previous paragraph. In some cases, radars are of such a size that they are fixed installations in themselves, such as those used in the Nike Hercules system, which has provided the high and medium level long range air defence of large areas of Europe for many years. In the more sophisticated and larger modern systems, such as the US Patriot, a single radar may be used to carry out several of the functions. The Patriot radar is used for search, providing tracking data for threat assessment and fire control and, when a missile is in flight, for tracking both missile and target and for providing mid-course guidance data to the missile, as well as for illuminating the targets so that the missiles in flight can home on to it in its terminal phase, using the missile borne radar seeker.

At the other end of the scale, simpler manportable systems, such as Short's Blowpipe and Javelin, use the operator's eye to search for and find the target, track it, using an optical sight throughout the engagement and, finally, use the operator's eyes to assess whether or not the engagement resulted in a target kill. The same could be said to be true of a human operator using a machine gun in an air defence role.

Where radar, especially of a more complex variety, is used to provide surveillance, search, threat assessment and fire control data, one such radar can be used to control several sets of launchers, guns or fire units. This is done in systems as diverse as the American Patriot and the French Shahine. The radar data obtained is used to allocate particular launchers to engage specific separate targets with their missiles.

In some earlier SAGW systems, several radars were used to carry out the different functions. A rotating high power radar would provide data on movements in its airspace, in terms of range and azimuth; a separate height

Weapons and Warfare

PLATE 5.4 **Patriot.** Missile at launch. *(Raytheon Ltd)*

finding radar would then provide information on the height of selected potential targets. The data so obtained, together with responses to the identification friend or foe (IFF) system would be used to determine whether the object being tracked was a threat and, if so, whether it would be entering the possible engagement zone covered by any of the launchers of the SAGW system. Where several engageable targets were under surveillance, the data would also be used for threat ordering – providing a list of engagement priorities allocated to different launchers. Once a target had been allocated to a particular fire unit, the tracking radar of that fire unit, used for missile guidance, would be dedicated to track that target until the engagement was completed. Thus, in systems using this principle, such as the United States Hawk system, there were many radars for a battery of several fire units. Such batteries, therefore, involved many vehicles and, whilst mobile, were only so to a limited extent, taking some considerable time to get into and out of action in a mobile mode. Recent advances in radar and data processing technology have made possible track-while-scan (TWS) radars, using phased arrays of antenna elements, which enable radar beams to be formed and steered in an agile manner electronically. Thus, a stationary antenna may rapidly scan its beam over a wide arc of at least plus or minus 45° in azimuth and elevation, and be used in both search and tracking mode. At the same time, the radar beam

Land Based Air Defence

may be narrowed or widened to adapt to the electronic countermeasures environment, and to search the air space in the optimum way. Where full 360° azimuth cover is required, it can be obtained by using four such radar antennae or by rotating a phased array antenna such that it is able to search the whole of the 360° of air space, particularly at low level, in one or two seconds.

The use of radar for surveillance has the advantage of giving good range in all but the severest weathers; it is adaptable and can provide automatically precise data on target azimuth, elevation, range and speed, all of which is needed for efficient threat assessment and fire control. It does, however, suffer from the disadvantage that it is active, i.e. it radiates energy, and can be detected by an enemy, who may then use countermeasures such as electronic jamming or even anti-radiation missiles to home automatically on to the radar to destroy it. Thus, whilst radars are used in most SAGW systems where good range performance in all weathers is required, some consideration is being given to passive surveillance means for those SAGW systems intended for the defence of forces in the more forward battle areas. These systems are generally more concerned with providing air defence against general support fighters, fighter ground attack aircraft or armoured helicopters coming in at low level. As the target is likely to use the terrain to screen his approach, the appropriate air defence system requires only to have a range of some 50 kilometres or so. For this passive infra-red (IR) surveillance devices are capable of providing good azimuth and elevation data on targets, at least in those weather conditions in which the enemy is likely to be able to amount an effective aircraft or helicopter attack against moving ground forces. Passive surveillance is not a new idea. Not only has it been provided by the human eye for many years, but passive acoustic sensors were used with some success in early anti-aircraft gun systems.

Whereas radar is particularly appropriate for defence systems in which all weather performance is required, and which need to deal with a large number of potential targets at any given time, passive surveillance is more appropriate to short range more mobile systems used for defence in forward areas, where disclosure of the presence of units would be a problem, and for which individual units do not defend a very large air space and do not need to handle a large multiplicity of targets simultaneously.

The purpose of all air defence systems is to be able to destroy or, in some way, render targets ineffective. The range of consequences of an air defence engagement has led to a whole class of what are called *kills*. The normal means of achieving these kills is by delivering a projectile to impact the target in such a way as to destroy it structurally. This may be done by delivering a projectile (a bullet, shell or missile) so as to achieve a direct hit with a target and kill it by means of the kinetic energy associated with the impact (KE warhead). This obviously requires that the projectile fired from the ground makes a direct hit. Another approach is to kill the target by using the projectile to place an explosive charge surrounded by fragments (semi-armour-piercing warhead) inside the target and to use the blast and fragments from the explosion to cause the kill. This again requires that a direct hit be achieved. Another, much more commonly used approach, is to deliver a projectile to the close vicinity of the target and to detonate the warhead close enough to the target to kill it by means of some method of proximity fusing (proximity fused warhead).

These different methods, all of which can be used either with shells fired from a gun, or with guided missiles fired from a ground based launcher, have their own advantages and disadvantages:

▷ The kinetic energy warhead, containing no explosive, needs no safety and arming unit and no proximity fuse. It is, therefore, inherently lighter and cheaper than other forms. When used in a guided missile, this has a significant effect in keeping the missile cost relatively low. The weight advantage makes this suitable as the kill mechanism in manportable air defence missile systms.
▷ The semi-armour-piercing (SAP) warhead possesses the same advantages, except that there is need for a safety and arming unit. The size of the warhead of the type needed to cause a given level of kill is smaller than that needed to produce the same level of kill when detonated outside the target. Consequently, the use of an SAP warhead results in lower projectile weight for a given kill and lower cost than a proximity fused warhead. At the same time, it can provide higher lethality than a KE warhead for lower impact speeds (on a weight for weight basis). An example of a system which takes full advantage of these factors is the British Aerospace Rapier system in its various versions. The lack of a proximity fuse in both the KE and SAP warheaded systems enables both to be used in engagements against targets of very low level and ensures that the missile fired in such a way as to fly close to the ground will not suffer premature fusing as a result.
▷ The proximity fused warhead has the advantage that it does not require the projectile to hit the target in order to destroy it. It is, therefore, appropriate for use in projectiles fired to engage targets against which it would be difficult to guarantee a hit – such as small RPV's, cruise missiles and targets which are particularly highly agile.

Proximity fuses take various forms and have become highly sophisticated in their design. Since World War Two, the majority of fuses in use have been based on radar principles, in which the radar is set to respond only to the presence of targets at short range, and in which a prediction is made of the best time to trigger off the warhead in order to cause the maximum of damage to the target. Indeed, the study of fuse, warhead and target interaction has now progressed a long way. Nowadays, other methods of fusing, using miniature laser radars or capacitance sensing devices, are also in use, as are some passive infra-red sensors. In missiles with homing heads, the latter can be adapted to

Land Based Air Defence

provide the fusing data. The final choice to be made is dependent upon the relative priorities to be accorded to cost, performance and weight.

The last-mentioned in the list of functions on page 117 is that of kill assessment. Normally, this important function is carried out by the same means as are used to provide the threat assessment in the first place. However, where a separate means of target tracking is used as part of the process of engaging the target, this too can normally provide data on which an assessment can be made as to whether or not the target has been killed. A radar may provide data indicating a sudden change in target speed, or the fact that what was one object has now become several; an optical tracker or thermal imager may provide more convincing evidence; some method of kill assessment is required if the threat priorities are to be properly allocated to subsequent engagements by the air defence system.

It is in the methods that have been developed for getting the warhead from the ground to the target that most progress has been made, and a great variety of means have been employed, over the last forty years or so. In the case of air defence systems based on guns, the basic methods have remained the same – namely the use of a ballistic course for a projectile aimed at a predicted point of impact. In the case of guided weapon systems, a whole host of different techniques have been used to ensure that the warhead is delivered at the target and some discussion of these techniques forms the subject of the next section of this chapter.

Missile Guidance

There are some four main methods of guidance used in guided missile systems. These are:

Command guidance
Beam riding
Homing
Inertial.

Each may be used either separately, or in combination. This section deals mainly with the first three, as the fourth, the inertial guidance mode, is simple in principle and may be used on its own to guide missiles towards a point at which one of the other guidance methods will take over. Given target co-ordinates, the missile employing inertial guidance uses its own on-board inertial equipment to determine its own position and velocity, either in absolute terms or relative to the known target position. From this information, it computes its own steering commands which are used to modify its flight in such a way as to place the missile in the general vicinity of the target, from which point it may home onto the target, using one of the methods described later.

Weapons and Warfare

```
Command
Tx
```

Main guidance functions

○ Target tracking
○ Missile tracking
○ Guidance command computation
○ Command link transmission/reception

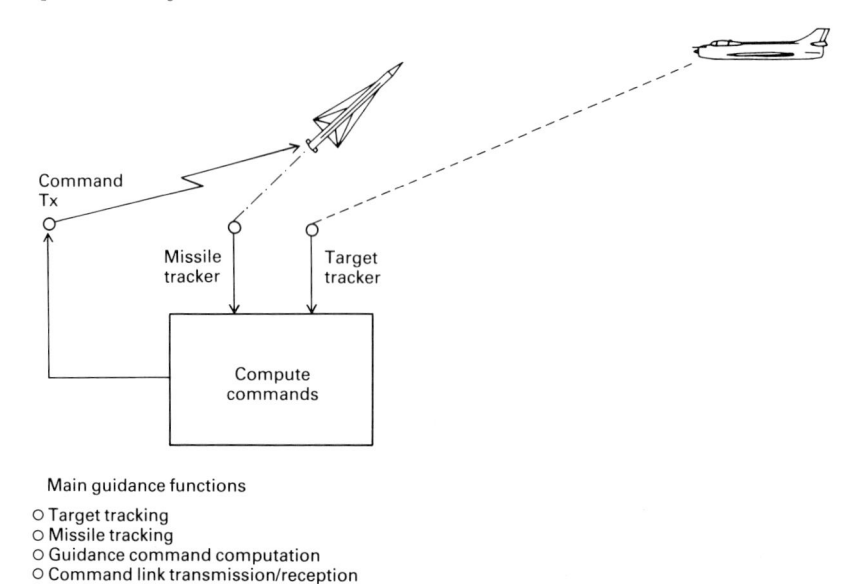

Fig 5.1 Command guidance.

Returning to the first of the guidance methods listed, Fig 5.1 shows the essentials of a command guidance system. In this, the target is tracked by some device, such as an optical sight or radar tracker. The missile is tracked by a similar device. Data on missile and target tracks is used to form guidance commands which are transmitted to the missile in flight, in such a way as to cause the missile to intercept the target. The main guidance functions are, therefore, target tracking, missile tracking, the computation of commands to be sent to the missile to cause it to intercept the target (called guidance commands), the transmission of these guidance commands via a command link transmitter to the missile and, finally, the reception of these commands by the missile in flight and the use thereof to operate actuator systems in such a way as to steer the missile on the correct course. Some of the early wartime experiments by the Germans used guidance systems of this type; they continue to be used right up to the present day. The American Nike Hercules system, referred to earlier in this chapter, makes use of separate radar trackers for the target and the missile; the missile radar tracker uses a coded beam to send instructions to the missile in flight; missile and target tracking data are fed into a computer which provides the commands to the missile in such a way as to bring it to the target on a predicted impact course; as the missile and target tracking information show the coincidence, a command is sent to the missile warhead to trigger it at the appropriate point. In this way, the requirement for a separate missile-borne proximity fuse is avoided, the warhead of the system being large, can be triggered with sufficient accuracy by this method.

Land Based Air Defence

Guidance computer

Command Tx

Main guidance functions

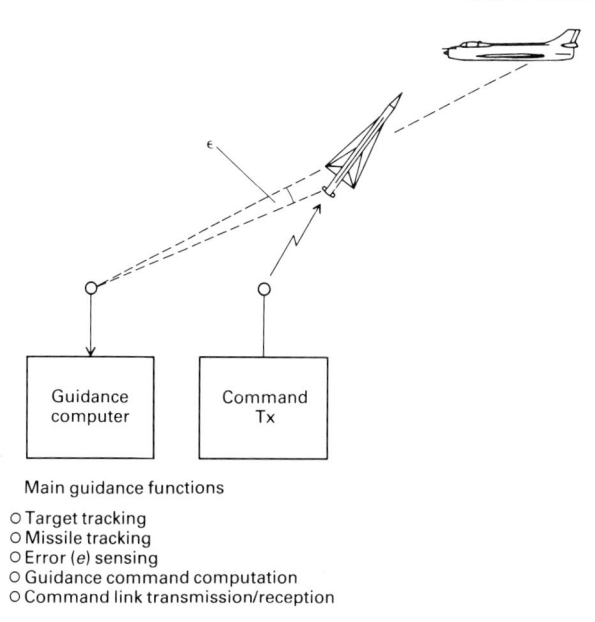

O Target tracking
O Missile tracking
O Error (*e*) sensing
O Guidance command computation
O Command link transmission/reception

FIG 5.2 Command to line of sight guidance.

Since the time of the Nike family, the most common form of command guidance has been that shown in Fig 5.2. This is known as command to line of sight guidance (CLOS), because the commands transmitted to the missile in flight cause it to steer a course to remain positioned on the line of sight which exists between the target tracker and the target. In such a system, there should be no angular error between the line of sight from the tracker to the target and the line of sight from the tracker to the missile. Any error which may occur, designated as *e* in the figure, is used in the computation of guidance commands, which are transmitted to the missile. These guidance commands are then interpreted by the missile to cause it to steer in such a way as to reduce the error *e* to zero. This command to line of sight system is inherently simple. Its advantages over other command systems are that both missile and target can be tracked by the same device, enabling surveying and collimation problems to be kept to an absolute minimum. The main guidance functions in the command to line of sight system are seen as tracking of the missile and the target, sensing the angular error between them as seen by a command tracker, calculation of the guidance command to be sent to the missile in flight, the transmission of these commands and, finally, the reception of the commands by the missile. The Rapier, Roland and Crotale systems, already referred to, make use of this guidance principle.

The techniques that can be used in target and missile tracking for a CLOS guidance system include optical, infra-red, radar and active laser tracking

Weapons and Warfare

principles. So far as the target is concerned, optical trackers rely on the normal optical image and, therefore, apply to daylight operation only. The missile image is normally enhanced for an optical tracker by equipping it with flares; missile optical tracking can take place, therefore, in clear weather day or night conditions. The main advantages of optical tracking are passivity, relatively low cost and reasonable resistance to countermeasures. The other forms of tracker overcome the problems of operation at night-time and, in the case of radar tracking, in conditions of bad weather. Infra-red tracking systems, like optical systems are entirely passive. The use of one common tracking system to track both missile and target has the advantage that it provides the means to avoid collimation errors which might otherwise exist. Where optical trackers are used, the final sensor employed may well be the human eyeball; alternatively, it could be some form of opto-electronic detector. In the former case, the error between the sight line to the target and the sight line to the missile becomes apparent to the human operator, who then generates commands by moving some form of joystick. These can then be sent to the missile in flight by a laser or radio command link. This principle was employed in the earlier versions of the British Blowpipe missile. The use of automatic detection of the error between target and missile sight lines, such as can be obtained from radar, infra-red array and television array sensors, enables the speed of the response of the guidance system to be significantly enhanced over that which makes use of the human operator. It is for this reason that most modern anti-aircraft and anti-missile systems provide for an automatic method of error sensing.

Various methods can be used to transmit commands to missiles in flight; radio links, from UHF to microwave frequencies, lasers and coded radar transmissions are all used in current SAGW systems. The laser link offers light weight and is suitable for portable and short range good weather systems. Radar and radio links provide all weather performance, but the lower frequency radio links are more susceptible to counter measures.

Another form of line of sight guidance is that known as beam riding. This differs from CLOS guidance only in the way in which missile control signals are derived. In place of having a missile tracker, a beam is transmitted into space as the result of signals received by a target tracker, see Fig 5.3. The missile carries a receiver which detects the angular position of the missile with respect to the transmitted beam centre. The beam is positioned in space so that if the missile flies along a particular part of this beam, it will be guided to intercept the target. Therefore, the main guidance functions are target tracking, the use of target track data to calculate the position of the beam in space, the actual projection of a beam into space in the correct direction and, finally, the sensing of missile position with respect to the projected beam by means of a missile borne sensor. The majority of these functions need to be carried out automatically and the techniques used are either radio/radar or electro-optical. The advantages and disadvantages of the two techniques are much the

Land Based Air Defence

Fig 5.3 Beam riding guidance.

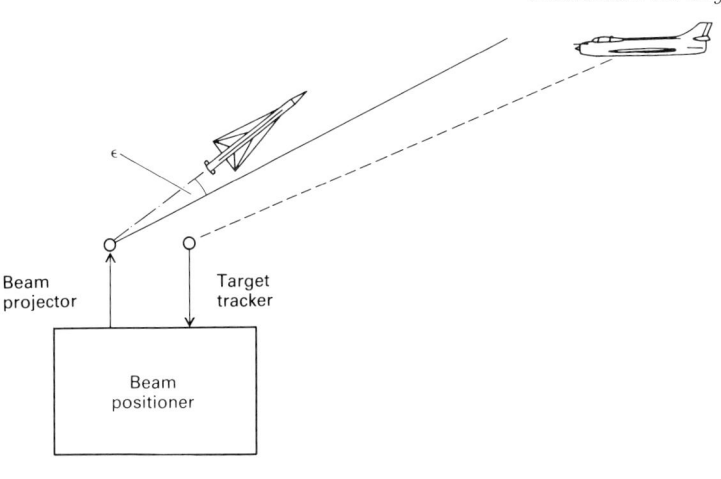

Main guidance functions

o Target tracking
o Beam positioning
o Beam projection
o Missile borne beam sensor

same as quoted before in relation to command to line of sight systems. Compared to a CLOS system, the beam riding system has the advantages that missile borne equipment may be simpler and cheaper (there is no need for a missile borne beacon or transponder) and there is no need for a groundbased missile tracker. The disadvantages, on the other hand, are that there is need for accurate collimation of the beam projector with respect to the target tracker, there are some difficulties in providing feed forward command compensation for rapid angular accelerations of the target (which may arise as a result of target manoeuvre, or an attempt to engage target crossing at high angular velocity) and passivity of the fire unit is not possible. The Swedish RBS70 provides an example of an SAGW of the beam riding type.

The need to keep missile size and hence cost and complexity of the system to a minimum means that command and beam riding systems find their application mainly in SAGW with an engagement range capability in the bracket up to 15 kilometres or thereabouts. The reason for this is that all such systems result in a terminal guidance error which increases as a function of engagement range. Even where one attempts to overcome such increases in guidance error by the use of a proximity fused warhead, the maximum useful engagement range is likely to be in the region of 15 or 16 kilometres if the system is to remain a fully mobile one. The previous exception to this, Nike, overcame the problem of larger terminal guidance errors from long range by virtue of the fact that it was extremely large and carried a very big warhead. New developments along

Weapons and Warfare

these lines are highly unlikely. Longer range SAGW now tend to be smaller and lighter and make use of homing guidance principles.

In homing guidance systems, the missile carries its own target tracking system, frequently called its homing head or seeker. This tracks the radiation received from the target and the output from this tracking system is used to guide the missile's flight in such a way as to cause it to intercept the target. Generally, three types of homing guidance are identified. These are:

▷ Passive homing, in which the missile in flight receives radiation emitted by the target itself. This may be heat radiated by the target and received by a missile borne infra-red homing head, or it may be radiation received from equipment such as radars, altimeters or jammers on board the target.
▷ Semi-active homing, in which a radar or laser transmitter, based on the ground, illuminates the target and the missile receives the reflections of that radiation from the target in its own homing head. The missile is normally so equipped that it can receive radiation direct from the ground transmitter so as to enable it to correlate the signals reflected from the target with those sent out by the transmitter. In so doing, it avoids locking on to, and homing on to, radiation reflected from, or originating from, sources other than the target.
▷ Active homing guidance, in which the missile carries its own transmitter. The radiation from the missile transmitter reflected from the target is received by the missile homing head. Thus, in this case, the missile is required to carry its own complete radar system.

These three homing guidance methods can be used by a missile for its entire flight, or they can be used during the terminal phase of flight only, see Fig 5.4. In this latter case, inertial guidance or crude forms of command guidance can be used to place the missile in the general vicinity of the target, target tracking data can be transmitted to the missile to enable it to point its homing head in the direction of the target, the missile can acquire the target with its homing head when it comes within range and good terminal accuracy can be achieved through the use of a final terminal homing phase.

Passive homing may be accomplished through the use of infra-red radiation sensing homing heads, which home onto the radiation from a target induced by aerodynamic heating, or by the heat produced by the engines. This technique is used in some short range manportable systems, such as the American Stinger, or the Soviet SA-7, intended primarily for defence against low level air attack. They provide good day and night-time defence under conditions in which an effective air attack might be mounted against forward battle groups. Passive radar homing systems are primarily found as a revertionary mode for semi-active or active radar homing systems, enabling them to home on sources of countermeasure radiation and combat the effects of self-screening jamming. Passive homing offers passive operation in a completely autonomous, or *fire and forget* mode when used to provide guidance for the full flight of the missile.

Land Based Air Defence

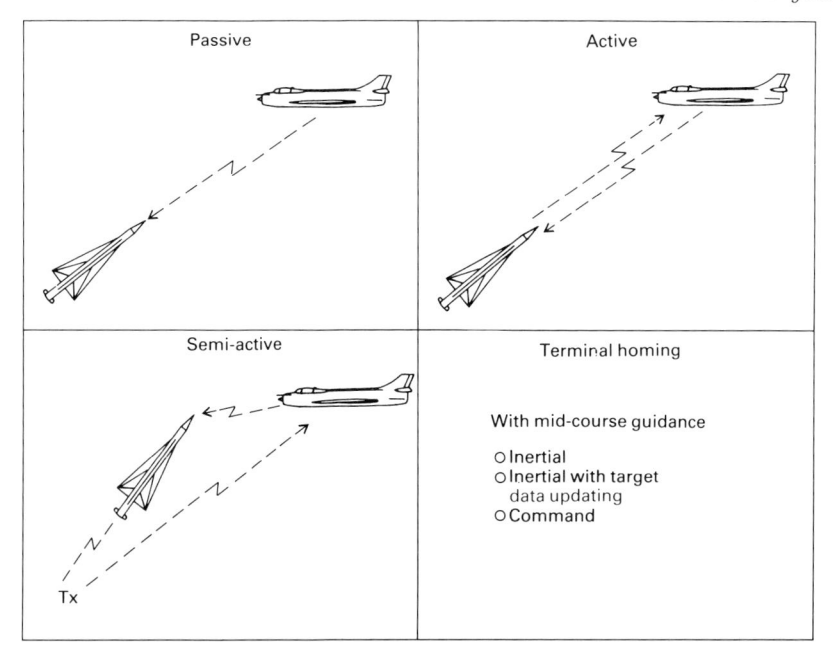

FIG 5.4 Homing guidance.

Semi-active homing makes use of either laser or radar elimination of the target. To date, few laser semi-active applications have been noted, whereas many of the world's SAGW use semi-active radar homing. Examples include the American Hawk and the British Bloodhound and Thunderbird systems. Such systems provide good all weather long range potential, but do suffer the disadvantage in that they tie up the use of a radar tracker/illuminator for the whole period of an engagement. The firepower, and hence saturation resistance, of such systems is, therefore, limited by the number of tracker/illuminator channels available. This limitation can of course be overcome, at least in principle, by the use of active radar homing.

In practise, the transmitter power that would be required on an active radar homing head, to allow it to function in an adverse countermeasures environment, would be above the level that would be practicable for all except relatively short range systems. For this reason, active radar homing is normally considered viable only for terminal homing in conjunction with some other form of mid-course guidance being used to navigate the missile to within a few kilometres of the target, at which point the active homing process takes over. Whilst such systems have, so far, been realised only in air-to-air guided weapon systems, the next generation of medium range SAGW is likely to make use of this compound form of guidance also. It is by these means that future SAGW systems will provide high saturation resistance. The use of active terminal homing (or passive terminal homing, if complete all weather performance is not required) allows for missile automomy and, therefore, the number of engagements is not limited by the number of ground based illuminators or target and missile trackers, as would be the case for semi-active terminal homing and all the way command guidance systems respectively. In terminal active homing SAGW systems, the only real limitation on fire power and saturation resistance is that imposed by the need to track a number of potential targets in order to provide the data required for the midcourse guidance of missiles in flight. As midcourse guidance does not require to be carried out with anything like the same degree of accuracy as that required to kill a target, it can be accomplished quite satisfactorily with only occasional updates of information from the ground, a single multi-function radar is perfectly capable of controlling a very large number of such engagements.

The American Patriot system is an example of a current system which goes quite a long way towards providing improvements in firepower over and above the conventional semi-active radar homing systems such as Hawk and Bloodhound. The Patriot system makes use of a multi-function radar to provide mid-course guidance of a number of missiles at the same time. However, the terminal homing phase is accomplished using semi-active homing, with illumination of the target taking place on the basis of radiation from the same multi-function radar. This illumination is time shared, on a rapidly switched basis, between a few targets; so that, whereas conventional semi-active homing systems require one illuminating radar for each engagement, the American Patriot system can engage a number of targets for each multi-function radar.

Guns and Missiles

Until the advent of the SAGW system, land based air defence relied entirely on guns, particularly radar controlled guns. The guided weapon, by its very nature, is more likely to find its target than an unguided shell, particularly beyond 1 kilometre or 2 kilometres range and so, ever since the 1950s, guided weapons have taken on the bulk of the land based air defence role. As the first SAGW systems tended to be rather bulky and involve several vehicles, radar controlled guns maintained a position for short range or unit air defence, and this is still the case with many armies. However, with the continuing reduction in size of short range guided weapon systems being made possible by advances in technology, the overall economic balance is tending to move in the direction of the use of SAGW systems for all types of land based surface to air defence. This movement has been hastened to some extent by the fact that many ground attack aircraft and helicopters are now becoming armoured to the level at which, to be fully effective, a gun system needs a calibre of at least 35 millimetres and, even then, may require several hits or proximity bursts before it can bring an aircraft down.

Land Based Air Defence

There is, of course, a possibility that this trend away from the gun may be reversed if technology makes possible some form of terminal guidance that can be applied to shells launched from an anti-aircraft gun. This is certainly a possibility in the future and may provide air defence guns with a new lease of life.

Guns do have some advantage over guided weapons in so far as morale is concerned. The pilot flying low over the battlefield may be unaware that he is being engaged by a missile, even given aircraft warning devices, until his aircraft is hit; it may require the cumulative effect of casualties over a period of time before the attrition rate has an effect on pilot morale. The pilot will, however, be aware whenever he is being engaged by tracer shells and his concentration is likely to be affected. Tracer is not only a deterrent to the enemy; the sight and sound of the gun firing is a morale booster to the defending troops.

Despite these morale advantages, the logistic and economic problems generally favour guided weapon deployment over that of radar controlled guns for even short range air defences; at ranges beyond a few kilometres, the SAGW systems have, and will maintain, a commanding overall domination of the land based air defence field.

Organisational Aspects

As indicated earlier in this chapter, land based surface to air defences can be classified as being of medium range, short range or unit air defence. Put somewhat oversimplistically, the medium range systems, all SAGW, provide general defence of the air space; the short range, or SHORAD systems, provide low-level air defence of limited areas and vulnerable points which can be attacked by aircraft penetrating other air defences, either by flying at low enough level to remain unscathed, or simply by running the gauntlet; the unit air defence is specifically concerned with the defence of battle groups from air attack, generally launched by aircraft at relatively short range and in the forward battle areas. The proper control of these systems requires the right degree of hierarchical organisation. In Western Europe, the NATO integrated air defence system has resulted in the deployment of medium range SAGW in belts. These belts were formed initially from the Hawk and Nike systems; currently they are being updated with Patriot replacing Nike and improved Hawk equipments resulting from a progressive improvement programme. In addition, NATO fighters operate between the two belts, on the flanks as gap fillers and above the Hawk engagement zone.

Command and control of these medium range SAGW, and of the defensive fighters, is from the air defence control and reporting centres. Thus co-ordination between the SAGW and the fighters, with their air-to-air missiles, is reasonably well assured. In addition, Patriot provides facilities for significant direct interchange of data between neighbouring sites, in order to assist

Weapons and Warfare

target handover from one SAGW unit to another, but this does not materially affect the overall C^3 system.

SHORADS, as national assets, are deployed with each Army Corps for area defence of the field forces and to defend vital point targets and airfields. Command and control of the field army SHORADS is by the Corps air defence organisation, who have communication rearwards to the air defence operation centre at Allied Tactical Air Force Headquarters, and forwards to the battery command posts. SHORADS defending airfields are controlled through the Station Operation Centres, safe lanes being declared when the Station's own aircraft are returning to land.

Unit air defence systems, are necessarily the most loosely controlled of all. They will normally be allowed to fire only when an aircraft is identified as enemy, or when it commits a hostile act.

Many nations, the United States and West Germany in particular, are planning a C^3 improvement programme for their SAGW systems. This is likely to result in the netting of all available surveillance systems and ensuring that all levels, down to Battery levels, receive a complete air defence picture of the area of interest. The surveillance systems will include AWACS, which relays the situation to the control and reporting centres and hence, through its SAGW operations desk, to the medium range SAGW and through Allied Tactical Air Force to the Corps air defence desk.

Future Trends

Modern developments in micro-electronics and in related fields in information technology are capable of significantly improving the performance of land based air defence systems and of providing them with a good defence capability even in the presence of ever more sophisticated evolutions of the threat and countermeasures scenario. Modern electronics make possible more accurate missiles; this in turn means that they can maintain lethality with smaller warheads and hence the overall size of guided missiles is reducing for the same overall system capability. This results in an enhancement of mobility and reduces logistic problems. Greater electronic sophistication is making possible, even today, active terminal homing of missiles that can acquire their target in flight, given a minimum of information from the ground launching site. This has its benefits in increasing firepower and, through exploiting the possibilities of such techniques as trajectory shaping, provides a means of overcoming some of the effects of enemy countermeasures. Thus, in the future, for every given operational range, future SAGW systems are likely to be more mobile, have better counter-countermeasures performance, have greater firepower, require reduced manning and ease logistic problems compared to systems of the past.

As stated in an earlier section, micro-miniaturisation of electronics is holding out the possibility of having guidance in shells fired from rapid fire anti-aircraft guns. Whilst such systems are unlikely to be fielded much before the turn of the century, they may prove to be highly effective in the unit or short range air defence role.

Other possible contenders, though, for the short range air defence role must include beam weapons. The idea of some form of *death ray* has been talked about for very many decades. With the advent of high power lasers, the possibility of soft damage weapons is becoming very real. Such weapons would be used to damage the sensors used by attacking aircraft, missiles or other devices, thus rendering the systems inoperative. The ability of lasers to effect a structural kill of a missile in flight has already been demonstrated, but the advent of practical battlefield systems of this type is still likely to be some years away.

Damage to equipment on board attacking aerial vehicles can be inflicted by other means; the use of *beams* or high levels of electromagnetic energy, at frequencies other than those pertaining to laser beams, may also find application in future land based air defence systems.

Despite these possible developments, it seems certain that land based air defence of larger areas will remain the province of medium range SAGW for many decades and that the main trends to be expected in these systems are those indicated earlier.

6

Shipborne Air Defence

CAPTAIN W R CANNING DSO RN

As the preface to this book suggests, armed conflict today is a complex and highly technological business in which electronic warfare techniques and their countermeasures play an increasingly dominant role in the dictation of tactical doctrine. Indeed, Electronic Warfare (EW) is an integral part of shipborne defence and is inextricably related to air defence in particular. Nowhere would its influence be more keenly felt than in any future war at sea involving modern naval forces. However, the threat to ship survival exists at virtually any level of maritime confrontation as the conflict between the United Kingdom and Argentina over the Falkland Islands clearly showed in 1982. Even so, this well documented campaign was limited in involvement; there was no significant clash of naval surface forces which might have led to an exchange of MM 38 Exocet *broadsides*, although a major confrontation between ships and aircraft of the British Task Force and Argentine air power led to losses on both sides, often resulting from the employment of weapons of elderly vintage such as the 500 kilogram bombs widely used by the Argentinians. Nevertheless, the threat posed by the air launched AM39 Exocet missile was taken very seriously by the British forces and revealed some fatal chinks in the Navy's armour. As history shows, there is nothing new regarding the susceptibility of ships to air attack although the means of both attack and defence have perforce kept pace with the advancing science of modern warfare. Guided glider bombs were used by the German air force against Allied naval forces during the landings in Sicily in 1943 at a time when British naval gunnery was still predominantly tailored to meet the needs of surface action. Even as late as the early part of World War Two, there were surprisingly few medium calibre guns in ships of the Royal Navy with a primarily AA function, and an almost total lack of any effective fire control system to serve them; conversely, the American and German navies understood the need for dedicated weapons and recognised that guns were only as good as the system that controlled them. On the other hand, manually operated close range weapons of 20–40 millimetre calibre were widely fitted in the Royal Navy to provide last ditch defence. The wars in Korea and Indo-China did not involve air defence at sea on any scale and it

Shipborne Air Defence

PLATE 6.1 **HMS Sheffield hit by Exocet.** HMS Sheffield disabled and on fire after being hit by Exocet.

took the sinking of the Israeli destroyer *Eilat* by Egyptian Styx missiles in 1967 to drive home the importance of shipborne air defence. Interestingly enough, the Royal Navy had discarded most of its small calibre guns by 1982 but re-introduced them as the result of experience gained during the Falkland Islands conflict of that year.

An appropriate starting point, therefore, is to review the present and projected air threat at sea and to see how this influences the doctrine for countering it.

The Developing Threat

It is generally acknowledged that there are more than 800 vessels in the navies of the world today with the ability to launch anti-ship missiles. Some of these platforms are submarines and many are small, fast attack craft displacing no more than a few hundred tonnes. In addition, anti-ship missiles may be delivered by both fixed and rotary wing aircraft, and may be launched from land where appropriate. Today's missiles are relatively benign when compared with those likely to enter service within the next ten years. Surface skimmers of the Exocet type fly at subsonic speed a few metres above the sea (subject to sea conditions) but with limited manoeuvre capability; divers approach at high level (20,000 metres perhaps) but attack their targets in a steep terminal dive of 60 degrees or so; others combine low level approach with

Weapons and Warfare

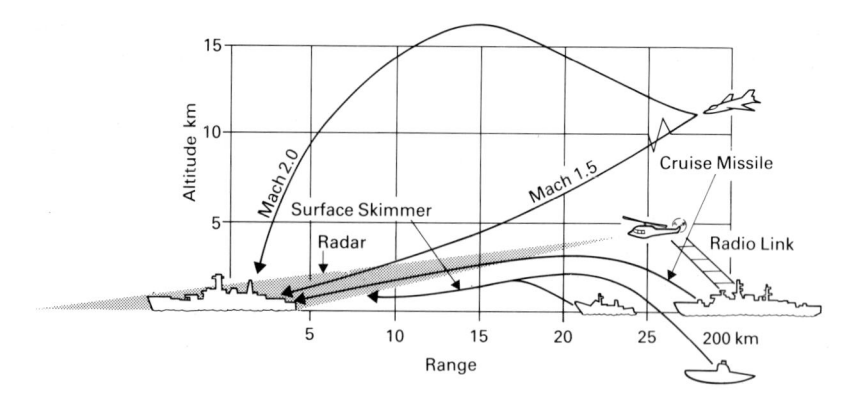

FIG 6.1 The threat.

a terminal bunt. Target seeking employs either active radar or passive homing techniques or, occasionally, a combination of the two. While formidable enough today, future development in anti-ship missile technology will introduce a threat of even greater potency (Fig 6.1). Surface skimmers will soon be flying at Mach 2 or more while divers could approach at Mach 3. Many will also have the ability to manoeuvre in both horizontal and vertical planes as a means of defeating defence systems. In addition, 'hardening' of the missile body against counter fire and an ability to discriminate between seduction devices and the intended target will further enhance the effectiveness of the next generation of anti-ship missile. Add to this the ability to programme several missiles to reach their target from different directions at the same moment and the task of the defence is seen in stark proportion. It is against this canvas that anti-ship missile defence (ASMD) is studied in the following paragraphs although, for this exercise, ASMD should be deemed to embrace defence against other, less sophisticated weapons.

Philosophy for Air Defence at Sea

The provision of air defence for a force of ships at sea is a corporate matter with the burden falling on ships with a specialised air defence capability in terms of sensors and weapons. Extreme examples are the Aegis system in the *Ticonderoga* class cruiser of the USN and aircraft carriers operating air defence aircraft. The overriding criterion for air defence must be to neutralise the threat at the longest possible range from the force, accepting that some submarine-launched anti-ship missiles (typically the Soviet SSN7) may be fired at short ranges of less than 25 kilometres and that some missiles launched from long range will penetrate the defence for a variety of reasons. In order to illustrate the structure of force air defence it is worth considering a typical NATO task force at sea during hostilities in the North East Atlantic. The

Shipborne Air Defence

predominant air threat is posed by anti-ship missiles of advanced design although the use of other air launched weapons from land or carrier based aircraft cannot be ruled out.

The first consideration for the Force Commander is to review his mission and to decide whether to adopt an overt or covert posture. While it is difficult to evade surveillance by satellite, tactical considerations may suggest that a covert, silent policy may best serve his purposes until he is certain that his presence is known to the enemy. However, a range of options is open varying from total silence on all communications, radar and sonar transmissions, through selective release to unrestricted use of emitters. The selection of an emission control (EMCON) policy can call for fine judgement in weighing the pros and cons of active or passive sensor operation bearing in mind that passive detection nearly always outranges detection by active transmission although the target information gained by the latter is invariably more precise.

The selection of the right posture must therefore take full account of the objective, the threat and the capability of the force to counter the threat. Although primarily disposed to meet the threat, the selected EMCON policy will directly influence the disposition of ships within the force although, for the purposes of this chapter, the underwater elements of force tactics will not be considered further. Force disposition is the art of deploying a group of ships in such a way as to maximise individual and collective capability and to make the enemy's task of target identification as difficult as possible.

The Need for Defence in Depth

Assuming that the NATO force being considered as an example includes carrier borne aircraft, ships with medium range surface to air missiles (SAM) and those with a mix of short range SAM and gun systems, it will immediately be apparent that air defence fighters, in close association with airborne early warning (AEW) aircraft, provide the pivotal element of an air defence disposition; they are able to operate several hundred kilometres towards the threat and, therefore, can intercept aircraft targets before the latter release their missiles. An AEW/fighter combination thus provides an outer ring or layer of defence which becomes the exclusive preserve for air operations beyond the range of shipborne SAM systems. This is known as the Fighter Engagement Zone (FEZ). Air defence aircraft aggressively operated and competently directed will deplete incoming raids, particularly if the enemy is restricted in the direction from which his attack may be mounted. However, penetration of the FEZ by a proportion of *leakers* is inevitable and these will enter the next layer of defence, namely that of the Missile Engagement Zone (MEZ) to be taken on by *area* SAM systems. Since these may have a minimum range of several kilometres, a third, inner layer of defence is provided by a mix of short range SAM, gun and so-called *soft kill* systems involving the use of chaff or electronic techniques that displace, obscure or falsify the radar echo of

Weapons and Warfare

a target ship. However, deceptive techniques of this nature are by no means confined to last ditch defence and may apply throughout the area of interest to simulate, for example, ghost ships or formations in order to confuse the attack. In the jargon of air defence, short range SAM and guns are referred to as *point defence* weapons since, in general terms, their effectiveness is limited to directly approaching targets, whereas *area* SAM systems enjoy a much wider engagement envelope.

In this way, *layered* air defence is achieved and this is illustrated in simplified form at Fig 6.2. Within this framework, individual ship capability is dependent

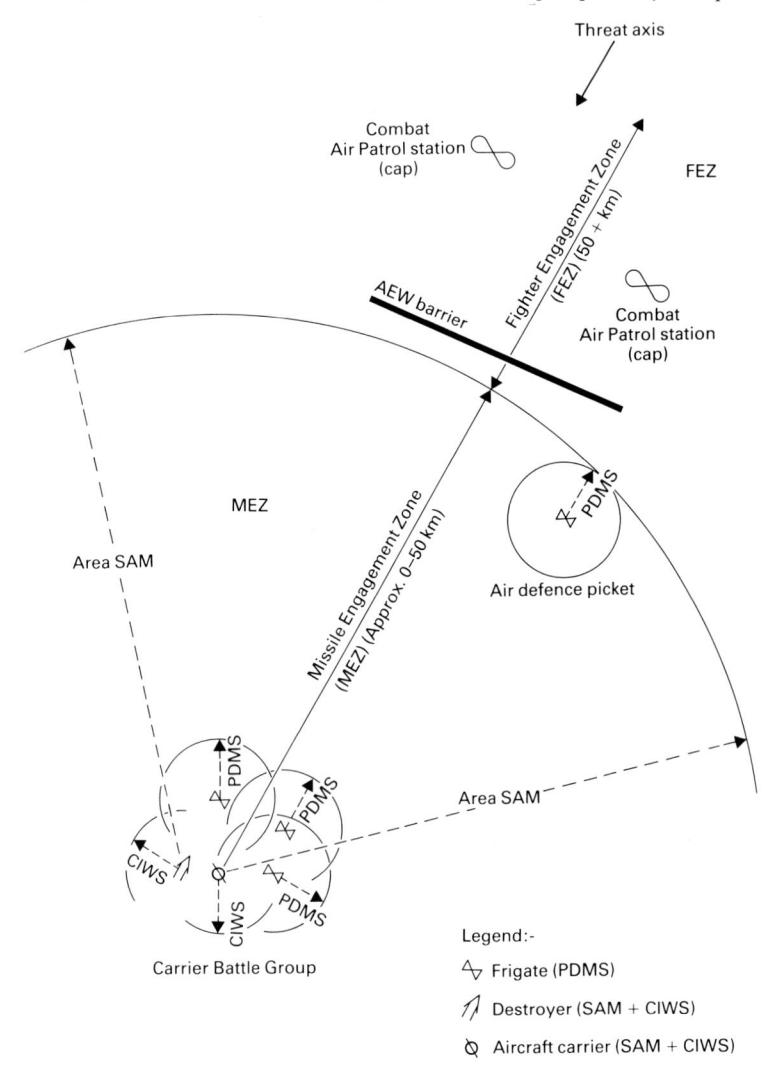

Fig 6.2 Conceptual air defence – plan view.

Shipborne Air Defence

on two important characteristics; all round cover of sensors and weapons, in order to obviate the need for ship manoeuvre for the purpose of bringing these to bear, and multi-channels of fire, enabling simultaneous multi-target engagement. However, all round coverage tends to be costly in terms of space, power and servicing and is therefore a facility that is likely to be confined to large frigates/destroyers and upwards. Conversely, multi-channels of fire may be enjoyed by ships of less than 1,000 tonnes mounting, for example, a 76 millimetre gun and a Phalanx close in weapon system. The use of EW techniques applies throughout the whole spectrum of air defence, from the earliest indication of a threat to the final moment of missile evasion, and must be perfectly understood. For example, timing in the active use of radars and jammars is a matter for precise judgement and tight control in a developing threat, since attacking weapons may have the ability to home in on these emitters. The relationship between radars, jammers, passive EW sensors and even communications is also a major consideration in view of the degradation in passive sensor performance that can result from poor harmonisation. This was dramatically illustrated by the loss of HMS Sheffield in the Falklands campaign when the use of satellite communications at a vital moment blanked out the ship's passive warning system which would otherwise have heralded the approaching Exocet missile. Hence the firmly held view that EW is a fundamental element of the fabric for air defence; its neglect is a perilous option.

Against this philosophic backdrop, it is now appropriate to consider the employment of individual weapon systems within the MEZ. Air defence fighters, crucial though they are to air defence as a whole, have been covered in earlier chapters and will not be further discussed here.

Area Defence

Definition of the inner and outer limits of the MEZ is imprecise. The outer limit must clearly delineate between MEZ and FEZ and must be preserved to avoid interaction, albeit with safe lanes established for use by returning friendly aircraft.

The inner limit is dependent on system minimum ranges but is blurred by an operating overlap between area and point defence missile systems (PDMS). However, in general terms an area weapon MEZ may be bounded between 5 and 50 kilometres from the force disposition centre or from an individual unit. In a sense, the prosecution of the anti-air battle in the middle distance is relatively straight forward; reaction times are less critical than closer in and the essence of good defence lies in firm co-ordination of the available assets by the Force Anti-Air Warfare Co-ordinator – as he is known in NATO circles. By contrast, point defence (sometimes referred to as local area defence) can become something of a free-for-all unless the tightest weapon discipline is enforced. By the nature of things, point defence is intensely personal, since a

Weapons and Warfare

Fig 6.3 Examples of shipborne area defence missile.

Missile	Country of Origin	Approx Range (km)	Guidance	Remarks
Masurca	France	40	Semi-Active (SA)	
SAN.2	USSR	45	Radio Command	
SAN.3	USSR	30	Radio Command	
SAN.6	USSR	60	Probable mid-course guidance with terminal homing	Vertical Launch (VL)
SAN.7	USSR	25	Probable SA	
Sea Dart	UK	45	SA	
Terrier	USA	35	Beam Riding	Obsolescent
Standard 1 (Med Range)	USA	18	SA	
Standard 1 (Extended Range)	USA	55	SA	
Standard 2 (Med Range)	USA	50	Mid-course guidance with SA homing	For use in Aegis System (VL)
Standard 2 (Extended Range)	USA	100	Mid-course guidance with SA homing	

Note: Details from *Janes Weapons Systems* and *Flight International*.

particular ship is directly theatened and is concerned almost exclusively with her own survival. As suggested earlier, PDMS are generally tailored to defend the ship in which they are mounted – in other words they are optimised against directly closing targets. However, some also offer a degree of capability against crossing targets depending on system reaction time and missile agility; hence the expression *local area defence.*

Fig 6.4 Examples of shipborne local area and point defence missile systems.

Missile	Country of Origin	Approx Range (km)	Guidance	Remarks
Sea Sparrow	USA	18	SA	
Aspide	Italy	18	SA	
SA-N-1	USSR	15	Beam rider and SA	
SA-N-4	USSR	12	Command	
Crotale	France	10	Command Line of Sight (CLOS)	
Barak	Israel	10	CLOS	
Seawolf	UK	5	CLOS	
Sadral	France	5	IR	
RAM	USA/Germany	5	Radar homing and IR	
RB70	Sweden	5	Laser beam rider	
SA-N-8	USSR	5	Not known	VL
Sea Cat	UK	3	CLOS	
Javelin	UK	3	CLOS	
Stinger	USA	5	IR	

Note 1. Details from *Janes Weapons Systems* and *Flight International*.
Note 2. Ranges claimed by manufacturers vary between maximum flying range obtainable and that at which full operational performance is retained.

Shipborne Air Defence

Local Area Defence

Given the threat posed by anti-ship weapons, the surest defence can only be provided by weapon systems optimised to meet it. This means that the minimum requirements of a suitable weapon system must include not only quick reaction but also reliability, accuracy and lethality. Opinion regarding the best, most cost effective way of achieving the necessary level of kill assurance is varied and has led to the debate between the ability of PDMS and close in weapon systems (CIWS), such as the Vulcan Phalanx or Goalkeeper, to provide the required level of defence. Either way, the use of jammers to disrupt and chaff to confuse and distract the radars of homing missiles is entirely complementary but requires timing to perfection if these are to play their part effectively without adding to a situation that is certain to be quick moving and confused. Indeed, some will argue that the co-ordination of the close-in battle is one that demands computer management. However, this means additional loading of already strained tactical communications circuits

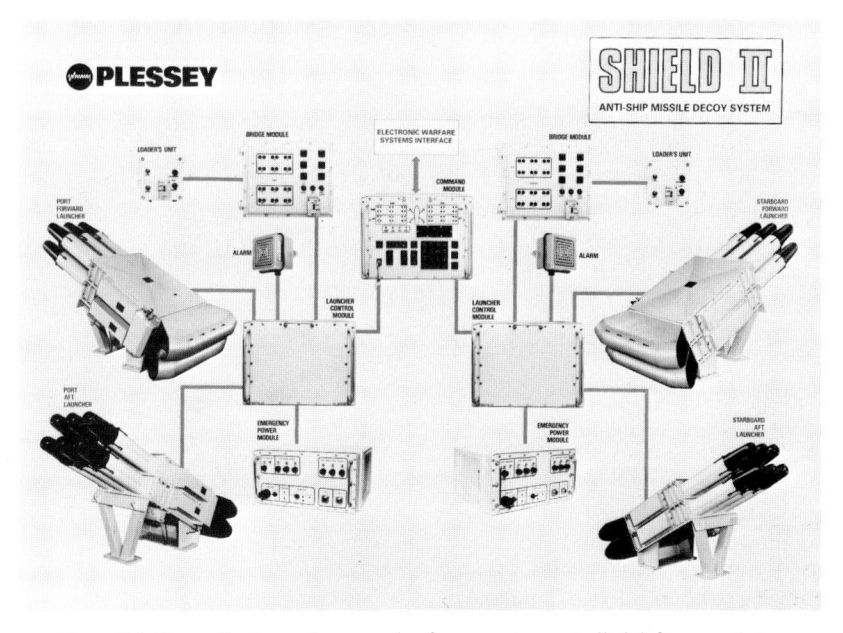

PLATE 6.2 **Decoy Systems.** An example of a computer controlled defence against missiles fitted with radar or infra-red homing devices. It assesses the latest navigational and threat information, comparing this data with decoy profiles stored in its tactical memory and thereby enabling it to select the optimum response. Its response time is less than one second. This includes variations to the fuse setting prior to the launch of the chaff rocket, thus ensuring accurate deployment of the decoy. There are two modes of operation; deployed close to the ship, in order that there is a smooth transfer of missile 'lock' from ship to decoy, or some two kilometres from the ship, in order to distract missiles before they have selected their target.

(Plessey Aerospace)

139

Weapons and Warfare

PLATE 6.3 **Sea Wolf.** The vertical launch version of the air defence and anti-missile system so successfully used during the Falklands campaign by the Royal Navy.
(British Aerospace)

which are themselves vulnerable to jamming. Opinion, therefore, is likely to be based on subjective judgement.

Comparison of the merits of PDMS and CIWS is not a strictly valid exercise. On the one hand, a PDMS is designed to engage its target at a safe distance from the ship while, on the other, defence by CIWS is centred on the 'wall of lead' principle at close range. As the table at Fig 6.3 shows, several PDMS are at sea or are in development. Among these, Sea Sparrow, which is widely fitted in older USN and some NATO warships is an adaption of an air-to-air missile; Crotale was originally designed as an anti-aircraft missile but has since been modified to provide some capability against sea-skimming anti-ship missiles. Seawolf was the first to be designed from the outset as a truly anti-missile missile. Barak arrived later and the Rolling Airframe Missile (RAM) is still some way from reality.

Shipborne Air Defence

Fig 6.5 Examples of close-in weapons systems.

System	Country of Origin	No of Barrels	Calibre	Rate of Fire/Mounting (Approx)
Goalkeeper	Holland	7	30 mm	4,200 Round per minute
Seaguard	Switzerland	4	25 mm	3,400 Round per minute
Vulcan Phalanx	USA	6	20 mm	3,000 Round per minute
Dardo	Italy	2	40 mm	600 Round per minute
Meroka	Spain	12	20 mm	9,000 (theoretical)
Air Defence Gun	USSR	6	30 mm	NK

Even within the PDMS school, there is a divided view between the virtues of a short range, high speed missile (e.g. Seawolf) and a longer range but slower missile such as Sea Sparrow or Barak. The case in support of the former is based on the fact that, at sea skimming height, the horizon of surveillance radars is limited to about 15 kilometres in a frigate sized ship and that effort devoted to achieving long missile range is therefore superfluous; it follows that speed to the target is vital. The advocation of long range/slower speed turns on the requirement to be able to deal with aircraft targets at greater height and which are, therefore, *visible* by radar at much greater range. A combination of both virtues in one missile appears an obvious solution but the requirements to counter the surface skimming missile threat are highly specialised and do not blend sensibly without compromise given the limit of technology today.

As suggested earlier, CIWS rely on massive output of shot fired in short bursts at close range (less than about 1,500 metres) to kill the target. For example, the seven barrel 30 millimetre Gatling gun produced by General Electric and used in Hollandse Signaalapparaten's Goalkeeper CIWS achieves a prodigious output of 4,200 rounds per minute – or 10 rounds per barrel per second. Goalkeeper uses discarding sabot ammunition releasing a hardened tungsten alloy penetrator for target killing. By comparison, Vulcan Phalanx fires 20 millimetre ammunition and relies on the use of depleted uranium in the composition of the penetrator to provide the necessary punch. Anti-ship missiles can be *killed* in a number of ways. The most effective is to achieve warhead detonation but damage to control surfaces or guidance systems will also achieve the aim by causing targets to ditch. A missile flying at high speed a few metres above the sea only requires a small deflection to cause this. Again, the killing techniques of PDMS and CIWS differ. The former, using fragmentation warheads will rely on system or control surface damage for success whereas the latter aim specifically for penetration of the warhead to achieve detonation; anything less incurs the real risk of the ship being struck by debris, which may arrive in significantly large pieces. Hence the strongly held view that PDMS and CIWS are complementary weapons with the latter fulfilling something of a last resort role.

Weapons and Warfare

PLATE 6.4 **Goalkeeper.** The close in anti-missile defence system featuring a General Electric 30 mm Gatling Gun with an automatic radar weapon control from Signall. *(Hollandsc Signaalapparatn bv.)*

Missile Guidance

Several guidance options are available and selection depends largely on the role of a particular missile. For example, long range missiles generally employ a combination of mid-course guidance or inertial navigation to reach a point in flight from which a seeker in the missile can be laid on the target for the terminal phase of flight. Seekers may use active radar, semi-active (SA) or passive techniques. Active radar is self-explanatory; semi-active homing relies on reception of energy reflected by the target from an illuminating radar in the parent ship; passive seekers home on IR or radar emissions from the target. Medium range missiles are likely to use SA guidance throughout flight while some older missiles still use beam riding techniques here, the target is held by narrow beam radar and the missile flies itself up the beam to the target. Laser beam riding is a later development of this technology and its inherent resistance to jamming could mean wider application in future.

Command to Line of Sight

Most short range SAM use Command to Line of Sight (CLOS) guidance whereby the missile is commanded via a radio link to fly along a target sight line generated by radar or electro-optic means.

A dedicated radar for target tracking or illumination is needed for each target being tracked by SA or CLOS systems; thus channels of fire become limited by the number of trackers available. This would prove a severe operational limitation, given the likely numbers of missile targets to be handled in the air defence battle of the future. The trend is therefore towards *fire and forget*, using multi-function radars and missiles equipped with homing heads; but radars of this generation tend to be heavy and expensive equipments requiring large platforms to accommodate them.

Warhead Technology

The application of warhead design, whether for area or point defence missiles is similar in principle although size may differ significantly. Generally speaking, large, long range missiles can expect to suffer greater miss distances in view of their size and comparative lack of agility. They compensate for this by employing a bigger punch. Conversely, the accuracy and mobility of small missiles such as Seawolf enable the use of very small warheads displacing only a few kilogrammes. It is not brute force that counts but rather the ability to focus the charge in the right direction at precisely the right instant in relation to the target.

Apart from nuclear *tips*, with which the Soviet SA-N-2 missiles may be equipped, the type of warhead is limited to the use of *expanding rod*, blast or fragmentation techniques. In the former, a bursting charge forces sections of thin steel rod radially outwards. These are optimised to damage aircraft control surfaces by a cutting action. Blast warheads rely on a heavy charge of HE for their effect while those using fragmentation heads generally employ some form of shaped charge round which is wrapped a collar of pre-fragmented steel. Detonation of the charge will produce a directional shower of fragments that may be numbered in thousands and with sufficient energy to inflict mortal damage over a distance of several metres all round. This is unlikely to produce a warhead detonation but will kill the target just as surely.

Fuse Technology

Destruction of small, fast and manoeuvrable targets calls for precise interception geometry in order to optimise the effect of the defending missile warhead. To achieve this, fuse and warhead are matched so that detonation occurs when the relative position of target and missile is such that damage can be brought to bear on vulnerable parts of the target, e.g. control and guidance sections. Given that point defence systems will, in general terms, approach their targets in a head-on aspect, it will be appreciated that fuse trigger must be delayed by some milliseconds after initial target sensing by the fuse in order to achieve maximum effect. With optimisation designed for a head-on engagement, warhead effect will reduce proportionally as the aspect moves towards a right angled intercept. In these circumstances, not only in the fuse *window* minimal but the directional burst of the warhead is 90° out of phase with the designed optimum. All missiles will incorporate some measure of fuse/warhead matching but it is a particular requirement of the small missile where space and weight considerations dictate some constraint in engagement geometry.

A further problem that besets designers of radio frequency (RF) fuses for missiles operating at sea skimming height is the very proximity of the sea itself since RF reflections from waves can cause fuse trigger. The options are either to fly at a height above the sea which is greater than the sensitivity, or activation range, of the fuse itself, or to reduce that sensitivity. The former implies the need for a terminal dive to a surface skimming target and runs the risk of reducing kill probability; the result of reducing fuse sensitivity speaks for itself. Designers are being forced to seek alternative fuse technology in a bid to avoid the RF fuse dilemma at ultra low level and it may be that the use of infra-red sensing will provide the solution for the future. Indeed, the continuing development of anti-ship missile technology imposes ever more stringent demands in the field of defence and is worth some speculative comment.

The Future

While manned combat aircraft are likely to be flying for many years to come, it is reasonable to assume that the threat from stand-off weapons will increase. Their launch from other platforms, both surface and sub-surface, certainly will not diminish. The need, therefore, for effective anti-ship missile defence will assume even greater importance if surface ships are to survive.

In Western democracies, limited military budgets are assailed by competing demands for Research and Development (R & D) funds and the supply is unlikely ever to match the demand. Compromise and value-for-money will continue to be the watchwords of the defence trade. Another highly relevant feature in military R & D is the time taken to introduce a new weapon system into service. Seventeen years between inception and final acceptance is by no means unusual with the result that *new* systems are already obsolescent on entering service.

Looking to the future, the threat of saturation attack by anti-ship missiles in a hostile EW environment must point towards the increasing need for highly automated defences relying on vertically launched fire-and-forget weapons controlled by multi-function radars as developed for the Aegis[1] air defence system. However, considerations of size and cost rule out the viability of this option for less well endowed navies. Nevertheless, a scaled down version of Aegis to meet the needs of local area defence is a practical proposition, particularly if the costs can be spread over a number of subscribers in a collaborative venture. Future refinements in ASMD may also see a move away from missiles to *hittiles* (i.e. a missile which is designed to hit and explode on contact, as a means of countering *armoured* warheads) and the use of significantly higher weapon speed.

In other directions, researchers are looking at the possibility of guided munitions whereby the trajectory of a shell is corrected in flight by command signal in order to improve the effectiveness of gun defences. Directed energy weapons are also likely to be under consideration for shipborne use.

Summary

There is no easy solution to the challenge that lies ahead in countering the next generation of anti-ship missile. Funds for development programmes will remain strained and, logically, this will tend to lead towards the need for overseas collaboration. However, with the notable exception of the Tornado aircraft programme, collaborative projects within NATO do not enjoy a particularly successful track record, due to differences in interpreting the requirement and the jealous guarding of national interests. The one certainty is that the threat will continue to develop from sea skimming missiles and that failure to provide adequate defences will again raise the question of the viability of surface ships in any future conflict.

'Note
1. A reduced capability version of the SPY-1 radar/VL Standard missile system as fitted in the *Ticonderoga* class cruiser.

Introducing Chapter 7

BY the end of the Second World War, artillery was exercising a predominant influence over the battlefield. In the British Army, for example, some thirty per cent of the manpower was devoted to artillery and, although the air defence of Great Britain and anti-tank tasks accounted for considerable resources (commitments now undertaken by the Royal Air Force and Royal Armoured Corps respectively), a tremendous weight of artillery was available for the land battle. Since then, in the Western world at least, artillery has been relegated to a position of lesser importance for reasons quite unconnected with the realities of war. The British and American armies have been involved in counter insurgency campaigns where fire power is of less importance than men on the ground or the mobility which helicopters afforded them. Indeed, in some places such as Northern Ireland, artillery was positively not required, while infantry were in very short supply indeed. Much of the military effort in the West has gone into NATO where, on exercises, the tactical movement of armour and infantry has provided a more obvious measure of military capability than regiments of artillery which are only pretending to fire. Thus, in the struggle for resources, artillery has suffered and, in the absence of intensive war on any scale, tactical doctrine has become unbalanced. In the Soviet Union, the lessons of World War Two seem not to have been forgotten and artillery plays as large a role as ever.

The next chapter should be read against this recent historical background which explains why developments in indirect fire weapons seem somewhat pedestrian. In fact, the major new developments in artillery in recent years concern target acquisition and the production of target data. Quite apart from the varied means of target acquisition now available, the forward observer no longer relies upon a pair of binoculars and a map; he has devices, such as the thermal imager, which turn night into day and enable him to obtain the target position with accuracy. At the gun end, computers enable the rapid handling of large amounts of data, allowing increased flexibility from what was always a flexible arm, and a higher probability of first round effectiveness. These developments partially offset the reduction in the quantity of artillery now available. It is doubtful, however, whether logistics, another casualty of peace time soldering, will be able to shift the vast quantities of ammunition with the facility which peace time manoeuvres suggest would be required. It is to be hoped that, in the British Army at least, the experience of the Falklands campaign will remind our present generation of generals that real operations, unlike those on the North German Plain, take their pace from the speed or otherwise at which ammunition can be replenished.

7

Mortars, Artillery and Rocket Systems

B A HILL BSc MPhil

MORTARS have never been pretentious weapons for their value lies in their simplicity and ruggedness, two attributes any soldier would put high on this list of desirable weapon characteristics. Simplicity is born out of a construction comprising only a barrel, a mounting and base plate, and a sighting arrangement. With just three major elements, stripping and re-assembly are straightforward, as is the method of operation. A simple construction means ease of manufacture and requires unsophisticated ammunition which together make for a low cost weapon system. High trajectories of fire give the mortar considerable flexibility, enabling it to be fired beyond hills from reverse slopes, from inside trenches and to give overhead support. The bomb has a near vertical descent, producing a circular beaten zone, and with a rapid rate of fire, good destructive effects.

It is, therefore, not surprising that mortars have performed well; in World War Two they were reckoned to have accounted for about half of all ground troop casualties. Mortars were ideally suited to the battles of that war in which fronts were well defined, advances deliberate and without any great emphasis on the need to move equipment. But modern combat is based on manoeuvre and, as a consequence, the nature of tomorrow's war will be very different from that of yesterday. Frontal assaults will still take place but the lines will be blurred as Warsaw Pact forces seek points of penetration for the development of axes of advance onto which operational manoeuvre groups can be inserted.

Such will be the conditions of battle that fire must be rapid and accurate with a highly destructive quality so that delivery will be complete before any counter-fire is incurred. If the mortar is to have a continuing role, it must meet these objectives of modern warfare in a scenario where its traditional role is less evident.

Like all other weapons, the mortar has become more effective as advances in technology have been incorporated into its design. A comparison of two British mortars, the old 2 inch and the new 51 millimetre light mortar illustrates the point. Modern technology benefits the light mortar through improved target-

Weapons and Warfare

ing, made possible by the inclusion of a bubble sight, and through better ammunition, the bomb being formed from serrated steel wire which induces greater fragmentation. Yet it must be admitted that, in overall terms, the potential for technical development of the mortar is limited. A sudden implant of high technology could very well change its whole character.

Other weapons, without the same constraints on development, have been able to use the new technologies to broaden their range of applications so encroaching on that sphere of operations which was previously the sole domain of the light mortar. Among those that have the potential to replace the light mortar, rifle grenade launchers, like the American M203 used with the M16 Armalite and the Soviet AGS 17 mounted on the AK 74, compared very favourably over the shorter ranges. During the Falklands campaign, the 51 millimetre mortar was not issued but the British, applying a little ingenuity, obtained excellent results using the Milan ATGW instead. Through the development of new ammunition, the Carl Gustav anti-tank recoilless gun can also engage a wider variety of targets. It can fire an anti-infantry round which sprays hundreds of steel balls in all directions and a high explosive multi-purpose round intended both for defeating armour and for attacking other targets such as bunkers.

There is a clear trend towards diversifying the applications to which weapons can be put. Although no one weapon can match the performance of the light mortar, collectively they can achieve the same result, just as the Milan and the 81 millimetre mortar did in the Falklands. A combination of the rifle grenade and anti-tank weapons firing high explosive rounds could produce similar results. While the mortar would still have the advantage in terms of weight, this could well be offset by a change of tactics made in the light of the multiplicity of roles of which modern infantry weapons are now capable. Such trends could well spell the demise of the light mortar.

While the future of the light mortar is uncertain, so too is that of the heavy mortar, if for different reasons. Clearly the heavy mortar has none of the range and target damage limitations of the light mortar, at calibres above 120 millimetres they are capable of reaching out to 10 kilometres and those like the 240 millimetre Soviet M-240 will inflict widespread damage. But against these desirable characteristics must be set a number of limitations. Inevitably, rate of fire will diminish as calibre and hence ammunition weight increase; weapon weight will also increase and the greater recoil will demand a more rugged weapon carrier. Away from its carrier, heavy mortar engagements will become less practical as the re-supply of large calibre bombs becomes increasingly difficult. Even in a manoeuvre war, operations away from the carrier would be frequent as obstacles such as fallen bridges, dense woods and uncompromising terrain have to be negotiated. In Vietnam, when the Americans encountered these problems, a dearth of rapid and sustained fire resulted which did little to enhance the reputation of the heavy mortar. One of the main difficulties was that the mortar had to be carried forward for if it were left behind to fire

Mortars, Artillery and Rocket Systems

overhead it became easy prey to raiding parties. Mobility is important in mortar operations for other reasons as well. Particularly its high angle of fire makes it easily detectable by mortar locating radars like Green Archer and Cymbaline, opening it up to counter-battery fire and necessitating rapid changes of position.

Every weapon has its shortcomings but what makes these shortcomings acceptable is the fact that there is no other weapon which could fulfill its role in battle any better. When that position becomes less tenable so does the viability of the weapon in question. In the case of the 120 millimetre mortar that situation arises when it is compared to an artillery piece like the 105 millimetre Light Gun. As far as the effect on an unprotected target is concerned, on a weight for weight basis the mortar will prove more lethal, a condition enhanced by the higher rate of fire of muzzle loaded mortars. But in terms of range, guns are better, the Light Gun, for example, has a range of 17 kilometres while all heavy mortars are ballistically limited to 10 kilometres in normal operation. Unlike guns, mortars are restricted to sub-sonic muzzle velocities by the firing stresses the weapon can withstand and it is this that sets a lower limit on range. Accuracy also suffers as a result of lower muzzle velocities, for the bomb has a longer time of flight making it more subject to wind effects and other weather conditions.

Rocket assisted projectiles (RAP), using rocket thrust to obtain continuous propulsion in flight have enabled the mortar to reduce its range disadvantage. Thompson-Brandt in France, using RAP, have extended the maximum range of their 120 millimetre rifled mortar to 13 kilometres and predict increasing it further to 17.5 kilometres as the technology develops. But rocket assistance is only a part answer for if projectile weight is to remain the same, about 30 per cent of the warhead explosive must be given up for rocket propellant. Increases in range can be achieved but at the expense of reduced target effects.

In general terms there is little to choose between the smaller calibre gun and the heavy mortar and the particular role to be filled will determine which weapon is selected. One application for which the 120 millimetre mortar has been considered is as part of a Rapid Deployment Force, a force capable of intervention at any trouble spot world wide. In such a force, the mortar could be used instead of the gun as the basic heavy support weapon for mechanised infantry. The fact that a 120 millimetre mortar would be half the weight of, say, the Light Gun and have three to four times its rate of fire, makes it an attractive proposition for operations where speed is of the essence. To maximise mobility, the mortar can be vehicle mounted along the lines of the French AMX-10P trials. Although it would then be necessary to compare it against the possibilities of a self-propelled (SP) gun with its potential for increased rate of fire through the use of an automatic loading system.

If rate of fire becomes crucial, mortars can also be made automatic although, due to ammunition bulk, probably not at heavy mortar calibres. The Soviets, for example, have in the Vasilek, an 82 millimetre medium mortar capable of firing at 120 rounds per minute. It uses a form of breech loading, and probably belt feeding, to fire both high explosive and anti-tank rounds, the latter being fired horizontally. The Vasilek is something of a mystery in the mortar world for although it was first noted in 1971, it was not until its deployment in Afghanistan in 1983 that visual confirmation of its existence was obtained. When it did appear, it was vehicle mounted on the BTR, BMP and BMD as well as being towed. This gave the first real evidence of vehicle mounted mortars being used by the Warsaw Pact forces. Until then it had been thought that the Soviets had little interest in that method of mortar employment. So, for several reasons, the Vasilek came as something of a surprise to Western military observers.

Medium mortars like the Vasilek and the British 81 millimetre offer what is best in compromise. They have good range, approaching 6 kilometres, sound consistency of fire and are easily vehicle mounted to avoid counter bombardment. Alternatively, they can be broken down and manpacked by their crew, the weight of ammunition at around 4 kilogrammes being the most restricting factor. As yet there is nothing to match the fire characteristics of the medium mortar and recent technological advances in mortar support equipment will help to maintain that position. In the past, accuracy has not been one of the mortar's strong points but with the advent of the laser range finder and fire computers for solving the ballistic equation, that will change. Another weakness technology should be able to strengthen is the inefficient use of propellant due to the loose fit of the projectile in the barrel necessary in a muzzle loaded weapon. Research offers the possibility of an expanding guide band to provide forward obturation, thus preventing loss of gas pressure past the projectile as the propellant burns.

Just as ammunition has been developed for other weapons to attack targets which were the sole province of the mortar, so too has ammunition been developed for the mortar so that it can attack a wider variety of targets. In this category, the most significant are the anti-tank projectiles, the West German 120 millimetre Bussard and British Aerospace's 81 millimetre Merlin, which take advantage of the mortar's high angle of fire to effect top attack. The Bussard is a *smart* projectile in that it incorporates a laser detector to enable it to home in on the laser light reflected off the target when illuminated by a laser designator operated by a forward observer. The more advanced Merlin is a *brilliant* system. It is a true fire-and-forget munition using its own millimetre wave radar to home in onto the target before detonating its shaped charge warhead.

In the longer term liquid propellant developments should further improve mortar performance. Greater accuracy and simpler operation should result from not having to use clip-on type charge increments to achieve different ranges. Instead, a precise quantity of propellant would be delivered into the breech for each firing. Using liquid propellant would save storage space inside vehicles since caseless ammunition would be employed and the liquid propel-

Mortars, Artillery and Rocket Systems

PLATE 7.1 **Merlin.** A terminally guided anti-armour projectile designed to be fired from a standard 81 mm mortar. *(British Aerospace)*

lant kept in an external tank. Manufacturing costs would also be reduced, since the present demand for precise propellant grain sizes would be obviated. However, there are safety problems associated with liquid propellants which must be taken into account.

Technology has supported the mortar and while this may not be to the same extent as for other weapons it is sufficient to ensure it has a role on the modern battlefield. Medium mortars will continue to provide infantry support through their high angle of fire; but even so if a prominent role is to be maintained there must be further progress. Mortar crews are, by and large, more exposed to bullets, shell splinters, chemical weapons and nuclear fallout than any other vehicle mounted weapons team. There are solutions to mortar crew protection, as illustrated by the French armoured AMX 10 PAC. Such an option is one that few armies can afford to pass up if their mortars are to be fully effective in mobile warfare. By contrast, the future of the light mortar is very uncertain as other weapons threaten to replace it. Indeed the future of the mortar may lie predominantly in the medium calibres, for while some armies will prefer the heavy mortar to the gun in specific circumstances, the converse will provide the majority verdict.

Weapons and Warfare

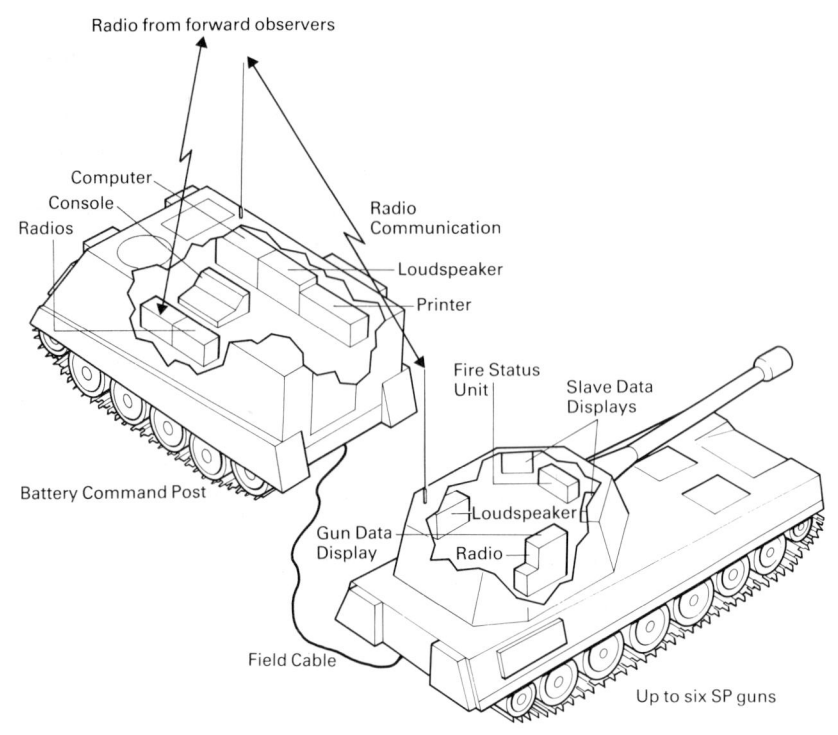

Fig 7.1 Field artillery fire control system. Developed by British Aerospace and Zelleeger Uster Telecommunications. *(British Aerospace)*

The point has been made that RAP techniques can bring heavy mortar ranges up to those of artillery guns. In truth though, this gives the mortar no real edge for guns can and do use RAP ammunition in just the same way. The United States have in the M549 155 millimetre artillery round, probably the commonest RAP ammunition in service. When fired from the M109 SP gun it has the effect of increasing range from 17 to 30 kilometres. Similarly, liquid propellants have more applications than just in mortar ammunition. Guns, particularly SP guns, can reap the benefits of liquid propellant in exactly the same way. Indeed, it could be that the greater specific impulse which can be obtained from liquid propellants under uniform deflagration conditions will improve the firing characteristics of gun ammunition to a greater extent.

In Canada, Space Research Corporation of Quebec are pursuing the technique of base bleeding as another means of increasing the range of gun fired ammunition. Base bleeding concentrates on the effects of the partial vacuum created at the rear of a shell in flight which generates an aerodynamic drag force thus limiting maximum range. Combustible material is incorporated into the base of the shell with the property that as it burns it generates oxygen deficient gas products. When these are emitted through the base of the

Mortars, Artillery and Rocket Systems

shell into the airstream, extra oxygen becomes available, enabling these products to burn and so increasing gas pressure in the base area. Such an increase reduces base drag by as much as 80 per cent to the extent that the range of the M109 is increased by 6.5 to 23.5 kilometres. While base bleeding does not give the same range extension as RAP techniques, the percentage of payload that must be given up is considerably less. Guns can clearly benefit from base bleeding but, unlike other methods of increasing range, its applications elsewhere are limited. Only rifled mortars could possibly take advantage for the drag factor involved is associated only with spin stabilised ammunition, mortars, in the main, are smoothbore using fin-stabilised projectiles.

Base bleeding is, as yet, still in the development phase, it will be several years before it can be incorporated into service ammunition. At the present time, only RAP provide an effective method of range extension. This means that mortars, at least in the short term, can compare favourably in terms of range with smaller calibre guns. Mortars also have a weight advantage but when these factors are taken into consideration in deciding on their use, they must be set against the greater accuracy of the gun and the bigger payload of its ammunition. Also the ability to helicopter-lift the gun offsets some of its mobility disadvantage, as the British demonstrated with the Light Gun in the Falklands. There it worked exceptionally well, gaining the reputation of being a battle winning weapon.

Many armies on tight defence budgets will find it propitious to choose between the heavy mortar and a smaller calibre gun. Making this choice will not be easy, there is an old adage that armies must fight where least expected. Such was the case for the British in the South Atlantic where the vote for the Light Gun was vindicated; they would without any doubt have been less well served by large calibre mortars. But where the mortar is accepted, guns at calibres around 105 millimetre will be squeezed out between the mortar and heavier 155 millimetre artillery. This is because the place of 155 millimetre guns is well established, it has been since the Quadrupartite Ballistics Agreement of 1965 when NATO armies, and as a consequence many others, affirmed a concentration on the 155 millimetre calibre.

Artillery

In artillery circles the gun debate surrounds not the question of calibre, the contentious issue now lies in the choice between towed or self-propelled (SP) guns. As far as the soldier is concerned, SP guns offer a number of advantages. On tracked chassis, SP guns are tactically more mobile and are able to change their location quickly thereby reducing their susceptibility to counter-battery fire; this improved mobility over difficult terrain also means that they can achieve more inaccessible fire positions. Because SP guns can be, and almost invariably are, provided with armoured protection, the crew is much less vulnerable to shell splinters. In the design of the gun system itself, SP versions

Weapons and Warfare

PLATE 7.2 **AS90.** A self-propelled 155 mm gun developed by Vickers Shipbuilding and Engineering Ltd.

are more amenable to automatic gun operation, as in the case of the Swedish 155 millimetre FH 77, which maximises the rate of fire so shortening the duration of fire needed to saturate the target.

Despite the relative shortcomings of towed guns, they still have some mitigating characteristics. For example, while they do not lend themselves to automatic operation, they will, under manual operation, be simpler and, almost by definition, more reliable. Since they are not confined to a particular chassis size, there is greater freedom of design which can employ the reduced constraints on breech size, recoil and weight to produce longer ranges. With a separated propulsion unit, survivability increases for if the towing vehicle were to be hit, a straight replacement would keep the gun operating with unimpaired efficiency. Furthermore, the technical advances in wheeled system survivability, particularly the development of run-flat tyres, have closed the mobility gap. Cost is another factor which cannot be separated from operational considerations. Since towed guns are cheaper, more can be procured which on the battlefield will make for greater weight of fire. However, lack of crew protection may militate against these advantages.

Despite the perceived advantages of SP guns, national defence budgets will inevitably determine how many can be acquired. In combat terms what will

Mortars, Artillery and Rocket Systems

then matter is getting the correct numerical balance between SP and towed guns. Just as in tank design, artillery make-up will be a compromise between firepower, mobility and protection, even if for very different reasons.

Determining the correct artillery order of battle in times of economic restraint is important, ensuring that the weapons in service represent the latest in technology is crucial. This is particularly true in NATO since against the Warsaw Pact forces it faces a numerical disadvantage of 3 to 1, not only in artillery but all weapon types. Technology can offset that disadvantage, indeed it is NATO policy to use technology to overcome the deficit. It must, therefore, be of considerable concern within NATO that it does not have artillery of superior performance at the present. The ubiquitous M109 came into service in 1964, since when it has undergone two retro-fit programmes to improve its range and targeting. Even so, it falls short of its Soviet counterpart, the 2S3 with its range of 18.5 kilometres. To compound the range deficiency, the 2S3 also has full NBC protection and an automatic loader, giving a higher rate of fire. Similarly, the new Soviet 203 millimetre M1975 is believed to have a range of 30 kilometres whereas NATO's 203 millimetre M110 has a standard range of only 21 kilometres. Even when using RAP it can only reach 29 kilometres. These range shortcomings are typical of the NATO artillery problem, one which will not be resolved until the successful conclusion in the USA of the Howitzer Improvement Programme. Then NATO will have a 155 millimetre gun, 45 calibres in length, with a range capability of 25 kilometres (or 30 kilometres using RAP). Ammunition for the new howitzer will employ fully combustible cartridge cases with a high rate of fire achieved through either semi- or fully-automatic loading. Only when this weapon becomes operational will the balance be substantially redressed. Retro-fitting provides a useful method for upgrading weapon performance but it can seldom be relied on to provide a complete solution. Such was the case when the BM4 international turret was fitted to the M109. Its 45 calibre gun, with its larger chamber, allows for slower and smoother acceleration and gives an improvement in performance overall. But whether this gun provides an optimum match with the charge system is open to question. It is, in fact, quite possible that a 54 calibre gun would improve performance further.

There is little doubt that, on current performance, NATO artillery lags behind that of the Warsaw Pact. However, it would be quite wrong to infer from this that, in the West, there is any shortage of technical expertise. The FH 70, the European consortium's 155 millimetre towed gun, reflects this with its range of 24 kilometres. But its self-propelled version, the SP 70, highlights the NATO problem. While the FH 70 started its acceptance trials in 1976, the SP 70 will not reach the same stage of development until the late 1980s. In simple terms, gestation periods are overlong, to the point where the nettle of technical advantage is not fully grasped.

During the 1980s, a number of European manufacturers have marketed, as private ventures, state-of-the-art systems incorporating the latest in materials

PLATE 7.3 **FH70**. The European Consortium's 155 mm gun.

science. Noricum in Austria are typical, having produced the GHN 45, a long barrelled 155 millimetre towed gun but without the usually associated problems of droop, whip and overheating. Range is 30 kilometres, 39 kilometres with RAP, and a base bleed projectile on one occasion travelled 45 kilometres. In France, Giat have produced the highly respected 155 millimetre GCT SP gun with fully combustible cartridge case ammunition and an automatic loader with an accompanying high rate of fire.

Private concerns seem able to avoid the inertia which appears inherent in national and international arms production. But if any blame is to be apportioned for the long time it takes to get new weapons into service, none should fall on the military strategists. As long ago as the 1960s it became evident that the Soviets were concentrating on manoeuvre warfare and that artillery would have an important role to play in blunting any mechanised thrust. Since then a much clearer understanding has been formed of the Soviet concept of echelonment and the use of the operational manoeuvre group. NATO has responded with the doctrine of follow-on forces attack (FOFA) within which artillery provides the method of deep attack. At the hub of FOFA is the need to engage Warsaw Pact formations beyond the forward edge of the battle area before they can be committed to the attack. Engagements must be short, high volume fire operations, for it is during the first 20 seconds of the attack that artillery fire is most effective. The effects then begin to diminish, after a minute all the enemy will have gained cover and artillery locating systems will enable enemy counter-battery fire to start up.

Defeat of Soviet armour by traditional artillery ammunition has a poor prognosis. Guns at long range cannot provide the degree of accuracy needed to hit individual vehicles or the volume of fire necessary to saturate the target area in order to overcome the accuracy limitation.

Precision guided munitions have emerged as one of the more profitable means of attaining the high kill rates essential if FOFA is to succeed. A leading system is the Martin-Marietta produced 155 millimetre Copperhead, one of the group of *smart* munitions. At 63 kilogrammes Copperhead is a heavy projectile, a consequence of the on-board laser seeker, the associated electronics and the propulsion unit for a projectile 1.37 metres long. As a result, range is curtailed, although the use of mid-body wings holds it to 16 kilometres. In common with many guided anti-armour weapons, Copperhead carries a shaped charge warhead, taking advantage of the weight saving offered by economical use of warhead explosive. Shaped charges, although having questionable behind-armour effects, have an adequate armour-defeating capability at calibres of 155 millimetre. But it is a factor which requires constant monitoring as the Soviets continue to increase the thickness of their tanks' top-armour protection. Copperhead, being designed to the main NATO artillery calibre, can be fired from a wide variety of guns including the M109, M198 and the FH 70.

Within FOFA, Copperhead has an important role to play but its characteristics of being a single warhead system and only being able to operate in conjunction with a forward observer, define its limitations against massed targets. Multiple target attack needs to be based on cluster munition principles, a subject of the search-and-destroy armour (SADARM) programme. Designed in the context of the 203 millimetre M110, these munitions represent a parent vehicle transporting anti-armour sub-munitions to the target area. Once above an armoured formation, the sub-munitions would be released to be self-homing, attacking the tops of individual targets with self-forging fragments. These are the *brilliant* systems and represent the next generation up from the *smart* weapons.

Artillery, using the cluster munition approach, provides an excellent means of remotely delivering mines into deep areas. Already there is the remote anti-armour mine system delivering units of nine mines over distances up to 17 kilometres. Various types of mine can be used, depending on the desired effect, including the M741 mine with a short self-destruct time and the M718 with a self-destruct time of more than 24 hours. These will have widespread application, for wherever they are dispersed, operational havoc will be created. If this is over an artillery battery, fire operations would be slowed and counter-battery fire effectiveness reduced as movement becomes more difficult and dangerous.

Weapons and Warfare

Rocket Systems

The advantage of larger calibres in the use of cluster-type munitions is self-evident, for bigger calibres mean that a greater number of sub-munitions can be delivered. Cluster munitions, with their greater area of coverage, also go some way to counter the problems of wider fire dispersion at longer range. But it is essential in the deep attack that area saturation be rapid as well as complete if enemy forces are to be denied mobility. This can only be manifested through high rates of fire – the reason why NATO forces will get the Vought Multiple Launch Rocket System (MLRS). Firing 233 millimetre rocket projectiles to ranges of 31 kilometres in ripples of up to twelve in under a minute, MLRS will be preferred by many armies to large calibre guns. Nevertheless those armies which are able to employ both will have a wider set of long range options born out of the complementary nature of guns and MLRS. Guns will provide greater accuracy of fire and the capability to deliver nuclear weapons as well as standard high explosive rounds. MLRS will provide area saturation but will, with its anti-armour munitions, concentrate on the attack of armoured formations.

MLRS is very much part of the emergent technology; it makes for a fundamental improvement of FOFA, replacing tactical fighter bombers flying short range fire support and interdiction missions. Tactical air losses will be reduced as the problems of bad weather, night flying and the highly efficient Warsaw Pact air defence systems are circumvented. Additionally, MLRS will give support to hard pressed NATO forces where typically one United States division must, on a 40 kilometre front, deal with between five and nine Warsaw Pact divisions with an advantage of up to 6 to 1 in all types of equipment.

It has been a long haul from the late 1960s when the threat was first realised. MLRS is only one of a number of otherwise abortive attempts to improve NATO's deep attack capabilities. A tripartite arrangement between the UK, Italy and West Germany formulated the RS-80 project, specifying six 280 millimetre rockets with a range of 60 kilometres based on the SP 70 chassis. But in 1976, the UK and Italy withdrew their support after a definitive move by the USA the previous year which was to lead, ten years later, to the Vought MLRS being accepted into NATO service. West Germany, with its more positive commitment to rocket launchers, was left feeling somewhat disenchanted, a situation that was later to affect the phased development of the Vought system. France, around the same time, was developing the SYRA rocket system but that too was abandoned as the USA sought international development of its own multiple rocket system (MRS) programme. In the event, the UK, West Germany, Italy and France were all to be involved with the USA in the MLRS project.

At the sharp end of the Vought MLRS is a self-propelled loader launcher (SPLL) built around the M2 Bradley MICV chassis, and having two launch pods each with six rockets. In contrast to the NATO choice, many countries,

Mortars, Artillery and Rocket Systems

PLATE 7.4 **Multi-launch rocket system.** The Vought system developed for NATO. *(Hunting Engineering Ltd)*

including the Soviet Union, have opted for a wheeled chassis for their MRS. Wheeled chassis offer better strategic mobility, suiting the Soviet concept of a future battle in Europe in which long distances are covered quickly. Conversely, tracks give better tactical mobility and allow for greater armoured protection of the crew, factors which NATO envisage as making more efficient use of the weapon in battle. These advantages should help repair the numerical discrepancy even though wheeled chassis are cheaper, enabling the Soviets, for the same capital outlay, to put more units in the field. The choice between wheeled and tracked chassis is not clear cut but for NATO, with fewer systems, survival is a more important criterion tipping the balance in favour of tracks. It means that all twelve rockets can be fired, followed by a rapid move to a new position, within one minute and before counter-battery fire arrives. Not that wheeled mobility has been totally discarded for the Americans have adopted a wheeled re-supply vehicle. Each participating country is to develop its own re-supply vehicle but it would be surprising if they did not follow the American lead.

Before engaging the target, accurate target data must be communicated to the crew, effected on MLRS by an in-cab radio linked to the fire direction centre. When used in conjunction with the vehicle's stabilised land navigation system, the data enable the on-board computer to determine range and azimuth. For firing, the launcher module is then automatically elevated and positioned on the line of fire.

Weapons and Warfare

The Phase 1 rocket ammunition for MLRS contains 644 M-77 sub-munitions in each round with a fragment inducing feature for the anti-personnel role and a shaped charge for the defeat of armour. At a calibre of 30 millimetres, these warheads have a limited anti-armour capability, but area coverage is a 300 metre diameter circle at maximum range, so the disruptive effect on armoured formations will be considerable. When a full ripple of twelve rockets is fired, the volume of fire will be sufficient to compensate for the reduced accuracy of free flight rockets.

West Germany will be almost entirely responsible for the second phase of MLRS ammunition development, a rocket containing twenty-eight German AT-2 anti-tank mines. Mines, delivered as rocket cluster munitions, can very quickly generate an effective barrier along the axis of march of an armoured column especially when sown in a bottleneck or in such a way as to create one. However, West Germany, apart from being the sole developer, will also be the only user of Phase 2 ammunition except for a token delivery to Italy. That the other main partners in the MLRS consortium will not be involved in Phase 2 suggests a concession to West Germany following the acrimonious termination of the RS-80 project.

For the majority of MLRS users there will be a direct transition to the third phase, the M-77 sub-munitions being replaced by the emergent technology SADARM sub-munitions. These *brilliant* munitions will be of the self-homing type, operating within a 2 kilometre by 1 kilometre area, using individual millimetre wave radars to locate and attack armoured targets. SADARM munitions, however, are presently in an embryo state and predictions of in-service dates can only be made on a speculative basis. To cover for any possible development delays, an interim Phase 3 munition delivering the Paveway 3 '*smart*' bomb is now very much in prospect.

By the second half of the 1990s, MLRS will be a highly effective system incorporating the very latest of the emerging technologies. But from the outset the *dumb* M-77 munitions, despite their simplicity, will give NATO a significant step forward in indirect fire. Considering the accuracy and density of fire imposed on the target, it is calculated that two SPLL firing all twelve of their Phase 1 rockets in two alternate salvos will be sufficient to neutralise an area 300 metres in diameter, roughly the area occupied by an artillery battery or armoured mechanised platoon. By comparison, it is reckoned that twenty-four 155 millimetre guns would be needed to neutralise an artillery battery in fifteen seconds while seventy-two guns would have to be used against an armoured mechanised platoon to achieve the same effect. The arrival of the Vought MLRS has generated considerable euphoria in NATO circles but it is the euphoria born out of relief in finally getting MLRS into the field rather than anything to do with a major technical breakthrough. That NATO has dithered in coming to terms with the MLRS requirement becomes all too evident when looked at in the broad European context.

West Germany has long appreciated the value of MRS. Since 1970 the

Mortars, Artillery and Rocket Systems

Bundeswehr has fielded the 110 millimetre LARS (Light Artillery Rocket System). Mounted on a truck chassis, LARS fires its thirty-six rockets in maximum ripples of twelve out to 14 kilometres, each ripple taking no more than eighteen seconds to launch. It can fire various types of rocket munition including fragmentation and smoke. In addition, there is available a rocket which dispenses five AT-2 mines, a feature which has clearly had an influence on the second phase of the Vought MLRS. LARS also operates a DM 39 radar target rocket, with a radar reflector, in conjunction with the Contraves Fieldguard system for assessing the accuracy of trajectories. Fieldguard is used by many artillery systems, both gun and rocket, for increasing first round accuracy. Usually, a round is fired and the Fieldguard system plots the flight path of the projectile to determine the accuracy of trajectory. The projectile then self-destructs before reaching the target area so denying the enemy warning of attack from an inaccurate first round. Such is the value of Fieldguard, that its potential is being assessed with a view to NATO employing it in concert with the Vought MLRS.

In Europe, the German Army is not alone in having an MRS in service. The Spanish Army has three types in the field including the 140 millimetre Tervel, a twin twenty rocket system with a range of 25 kilometres. Tervel also has a spread of rocket munitions available, including an 18 kilogramme high explosive warhead and cluster types with rockets containing forty-two anti-personnel grenades, twenty-eight shaped charge anti-armour grenades or twenty-one smoke grenades.

Nor has the private sector of European arms manufacturing underestimated the value of MRS with systems emanating from Austria, Belgium, France, Italy and Switzerland. All these incorporate technology at the leading edge of research and demonstrate a munitions range wider than that available to the Vought users, suggesting that they are as yet unable to get the best from their system. But when it comes to a full assessment of any NATO weapon, the acid test is a comparison with its Soviet counterpart.

Soviet artillery rockets, like so many other Russian weapons, demonstrate a continuous long term development process which, in the case of MRS, goes back at least to World War Two; in 1941, the truck-mounted MB 13 was firing salvos of between thirty and forty-eight Katyusha rockets. During the 1950s, the BM 13 was replaced by the 140 millimetre sixteen round BM 14 and the much heavier 240 millimetre twelve round BM 24. In 1964 the BM 21, firing forty 122 millimetre rockets came into service and was to be combat proven by the Egyptian Army during the Arab–Israeli conflict. So successful was the BM 21, that the Israelis reacted by producing their own rocket system, the 160 millimetre LAR, as well as refurbishing captured BM 24. Ammunition for the BM 21 included high explosive, fragmentation and smoke rounds as well as a chemical round containing the blood agent hydrogen cyanide which causes death at any time between thirty seconds and fifteen minutes of inhalation. The BM 21 was superseded in 1977 by the BM 27, the current Warsaw Pact

Weapons and Warfare

MRS. Equipped with sixteen 220 millimetre rockets, it has a maximum range of around 40 kilometres and its warhead types include high explosive, chemical and fragmentation bomblet munitions. These are similar to those of the BM 21 but also in the inventory are rockets carrying incendiary bomblets and minelet sub-munitions. By comparison, the NATO system, in fire effects terms, barely matches the BM 27. It is the BM 27 which makes almost complete use of ammunition types. Again, when it comes to range, the Vought system falls behind, being outdistanced by some 8 kilometres. In mitigation, it must be remembered that NATO and the Warsaw Pact see somewhat different roles for their rocket launchers. In NATO they have a strong anti-armour orientation while in the Warsaw Pact Armies it is a more general purpose role. Even so, it is difficult to deny that the BM 27 is the better system.

MLRS has allowed NATO to close the artillery gap by what at first sight appear to be paradoxical means, since MLRS struggles to match the BM 27 in performance. But the paradox is only illusory for MLRS has been able to bridge a gap in NATO's deep attack structure which simply did not exist on the Warsaw Pact side. What the BM 27 does is to maintain that long Soviet tradition of progressively developing its weapon systems. It is important to get things into proportion but at the same time not denigrate those NATO artillery developments like the MLRS. In MLRS NATO now has a conventional weapon system which can produce target effects previously only possible through the use of nuclear weapons. Not least its introduction will have the effect of raising the nuclear threshold.

Even so, comparisons between MLRS and the BM 27 illustrate only too well the common shortcomings of NATO artillery. Should it come to general war in Europe, NATO will, in every sense, have an artillery disadvantage. Deficient technology is not the cause, instead it is the familiar problem of financial restraint. The whole issue of artillery funding warrants very careful scrutiny. After all, winning the ball game depends on having a fair share of good possession.

Introducing Chapter 8

THE demise of the tank has been predicted for twenty years or more but has yet to come about, even though recent conflicts have exposed it to modern anti-tank technology. The fact is that the land battle, for success, requires the close co-operation of all arms, one of which is armour with its high velocity, direct fire, heavy gun. The infantry would feel naked without its presence just as the tanks would feel unhappy without infantry and artillery to winkle out or suppress short range anti-tank weapons in close country or built up areas. This next chapter explains why the dinosaur, although no longer supreme, will be with us for a long time yet.

8

The Last Decades of the Dinosaurs

RICHARD SIMPKIN

Perspectives

For three score years and ten the tank has aspired to coronation as Queen of the land battle. Four times it has nearly fulfilled that ambition. The tank symbolised both the triumphs of blitzkrieg and the Red Army's defeat of the Wehrmacht, becoming for the Soviet soldier what the tractor had been for the first generation of Bolsheviks. This impetus carried the tank high into the 60s to become, for the Warsaw Pact and NATO alike, the conventional linchpin of the nuclear battlefield. At about the same time, the genius of that *Great Captain* Moshe Dayan even seemed to prove that tanks alone could win wars. Ironically it was on the banks of the Suez Canal just seven years later that this British–Israeli heresy finally came home to roost.

Even since it came of age with the Soviet T34/76A, the tank has retained essentially the same form. The only successful innovative concept has been Sven Berge's S Tank, and this was rejected by the users of the main NATO armies as a tank destroyer rather than a tank. In fact one can trace five stages in the life of the tank so far. As an infant it was technologically precocious, mechanically unpredictable, and widely misunderstood – most of all by its parents. As a teenager, it went in search of an image, popping up all over the advanced world in a variety of wildly improbable guises. The T34 not only stabilised the tank's form but embodied the first two great leaps forward – one in survivability (a horrid word but a necessary one), the other in firepower. It was reasonably well protected against the specialised anti-tank weapons which came into service in the late 30s, as well as against shell splinters and small arms fire. And it mounted a gun capable both of taking on other tanks with solid shot and of delivering offensive and general support fire with high explosive (HE) shell of useful calibre.

The next major step, again in firepower, came in the British Army shortly after the end of the Second World War. Up till then, towed anti-tank guns had been more powerful than any gun a turreted tank could mount. The Centurion

Weapons and Warfare

PLATE 8.1 **The Soviet T34/76,** introduced in 1940, has set the pattern for most tanks since.

tank (1946) mounted first the 17 pounder, the same gun that was currently in use with the infantry and about the heaviest that could be manhandled in forward positions; and a little later the 20 pounder (83 millimetre) gun, designed to be mounted on a tank and to fire the then novel armour-piercing discarding sabot (APDS) ammunition. (Later still this tank was upgunned with what was to become the '*NATO 105 mm*'.) In the British and United States Armies, politically bound to the defensive and militarily wedded to the attrition theory of war, the result of this advance was to make anti-tank defence the tank's primary role. In the event, there was a generation of well-balanced designs of *medium tank* – Centurion, M60 (USA), and T54/55 (USSR) and, with an equally valid design balance albeit a different one, Leopard 1; and the Soviet Union stayed in this parish. But concentration on the anti-tank role in static defence – the antithesis of what the tank concept is about – led NATO to the *main battle tank* (MBT) concept and its dinosaurs of today.

The next swing of the pendulum came in the anti-tank field, with the introduction of the French SS10 system, the first of what we must now define as *low velocity cruise anti-tank guided weapons* (ATGW). For three reasons, these ATGW had very little effect on tank design – apart from shifting the design balance of Leopard 2 heavily (in every sense) towards armour. Initially, tanks had no protection against them. Then, quite apart from grave and persistent teething troubles, this whole genre was found to have a number of fundamental tactical limitations. The major vehicle-mounted systems were hard enough to handle even by advanced armies in positional defence; only the Soviets have ever seriously attempted to come to grips with their use in support of mobile

Tank Warfare: The Last Decades of the Dinosaurs

PLATE 8.2 **Leopard 2,** closely resembling the M1A1 in current performance, but with a higher development potential thanks to the use of more advanced subsystems.

actions; and they have not found a really satisfactory solution. Until quite recently, manportable systems lacked the range and punch required in the high-intensity all-arms battle. And by the time they acquired these, the introduction of compound armour (of which more later) was offering the tank a substantial measure of protection against the hollow charge warheads all these missiles carried.

By contrast, the effect of cruise ATGW on tactical concepts, force structure, and even – as we now know – operational concepts was radical in the extreme. In the opening phase of the Yom Kippur War, the Egyptian Army's Soviet Sagger system devastated Israeli armour operating with little artillery and less infantry support, and very nearly won the war for the Arabs. In the Israeli Army, oddly enough, this led to a great debate, won by the tank men, on the retention of an élite armoured corps, but only to a belated and mimimal response in the shape of properly equipped mechanised infantry. In the Federal Republic, this was probably one of the factors that led the Wehrmacht-trained officers still in the saddle to accept and even promote the 1973 Army Regulations, which imposed positional warfare. In the British and United States armies, it seems to have encouraged armour and infantry at least to start talking to each other in realistic terms.

But in the Soviet Army, analysis of these actions, doubtless linked to Marxist–Leninist paranoia, seems to have engendered a near-hysterical fear of the NATO anti-tank defence. A reliable first-hand report has it that a key senior officer in the Group of Soviet Forces Germany (GSFG), asked what he thought about attacking the NATO centre, observed: *"Well, we'll do it if we're*

167

Weapons and Warfare

told to because that's what we're here for. But it'll be a bloody massacre!" Admittedly such thinking was carried on the ebb tide of the battlefield nuclear heyday. But the outcome was a reversion to the *all-arms battle* concept first preached by Tukhachevskii in the 20s, before he turned from *broad front* to *deep battle*. If the emphasis given by *Voennyi Vestnik* to the various aspects of the land battle is anything to go by, promulgation of this concept has taken almost a score of years. The change has been reflected in progressive shifts of the tank and mechanised divisions towards a balanced tank–infantry structure, and may well soon culminate in their being merged into a single type of balanced *shock division*.

Now the firepower and rotary wing revolutions depicted in earlier chapters, and in particular *top attack* (the ability to attack the roofs of armoured vehicles), seem likely to put paid not only to the conventional tank, but to the high-density mechanised all-arms battle of which it once claimed to be Queen. Certainly the breadth of the anti-armour threat spectrum, both geometrically and in its variety, rules out monarchy for the tank. Such future as it has must lie in a diarchy or, very possibly, a triumvirate.

Historical analysis of weapon systems shows that a particular form of system, such as the battleship or the piston-engined aircraft, has a life of give or take fifty years. What is more, there are many specific indications that this form of tank has passed the peak of its evolution in biological and technological terms alike. It has become over-specialised – a tank destroyer in tank's clothing. And it has become so complex as to cast doubt on its cost-effectiveness *vis-à-vis* competing weapon systems – notably the helicopter and the armoured artillery gun. This is hardly surprising. Despite its unrivalled capacity to generate emotion – surely due in part at least to its phallic appearance – the tank is simply the concept of mobile, protected firepower expressed in terms of mid-late 20th century technology. What matters is the weapon system concept, the tactical and structural concepts surrounding it, and the operational concept surrounding those. The problem is that the creation of *tank regiments*, *armoured corps* and so on has knit the tank, in the form of a heavy tracked vehicle, into the social structure of armies. The cavalryman whose grandfather would not deign to sully his hands even on an armoured car now embraces his *sauroid* of a tank as ardently as that grandfather – or even a show jumper unseated by a refusal – ever clutched his horse.

Weighing the driving power of logic and love of innovation against the combined retarding force of conservatism, organisational inertia and peacetime financial stringency, one might reasonably predict that advanced armies will retain a manoeuvre element based on heavy tracked vehicles for forty or fifty years. In terms of serviceable weapon systems, that means a major product improvement of existing tanks and infantry fighting vehicles (IFVs), worth ten to fifteen years of service life, and probably one new generation, giving another thirty to thirty-five years. Technologically, the first of these stages means using technology available in developed, even engineered, form

Tank Warfare: The Last Decades of the Dinosaurs

now; the second would require sub-system technology now out of research and into development. One would thus expect to see a switch of funding away from research programmes associated with armoured vehicles and towards helicopters, and indirect fire and (fixed-wing) air-to-surface weapon systems. This has certainly happened in France and the United States; it is happening in the Federal Republic; and there are very strong indications, both positive and negative, that things have been moving this way for some time in the Soviet Union. One odd man out is Israel. She patently cannot risk the short-term weakness implicit in a major transition. In any event – another of those fascinating analogies between defence and marketing and perhaps the real meaning of '*like fights like*' – she must retain a capability roughly matching the expectations and habits of her opposition. The other exception is Britain – no comment!

The First Division

Not too long ago one could speak of the *tank producing countries* – and count them on the fingers of one hand. Then, as the third world developed its industry and its taste for dangerous toys, one had to single out the *tank developing countries*. Now one must pan in on the *tank innovating countries* – the 'first division' – to which I shall confine this chapter. For a broader view I would commend the reader to General Dr von Senger und Etterlin and Rolf Hilmes.[1,2]

Drawn from the common fount of the Third Reich, East's and West's post-war armoured vehicle technology is extraordinarily similar. In fact, though, given that a country has adequate scientific and technological resources and industrial bases (by no means the same thing), neither the military requirement nor the available technology appear to be decisive in the fielding of a successful armoured vehicle. Money matters of course. With Centurion, despite its woeful shortcomings below the waist, the United Kingdom briefly gained a world lead of a good half-generation; in thirty years she has scrooged herself into almost a full-generation lag. (Although she invented the tank, Britain's real contribution to both the military and the technological aspects of mechanised warfare has lain in armoured reconnaissance.) But the critical factors are evidently procurement procedure and – even more than in most fields – a touch of genius.

The United Kingdom and the United States both bog down on the first of these. The adversary procedure being, it would seem, the only thing that makes Britons tick, British procurement can be summed up as *User vs. Designer, Financier Presiding*. And for our closest allies, I can only quote a report I recently made of what one of their own leading experts had to say: "*Not for the first time in the history of United States procurement, the Soviet Union and/or her clients might go to war with tanks and guns, while the United States leapt to defend her interests armed mainly with a bunch of Operational Requirements. At least the rigidity of these documents might*

Weapons and Warfare

then prove an asset rather than a liability." As the United States Army would be the first to admit, the field of light armoured vehicles is a long-standing disaster area for it. But the extent to which its procurement procedure pushes the state of the art is best demonstrated by the fact that both the M1 Abrams tank and the M2/M3 Bradley infantry/cavalry fighting vehicle only emerged as viable and serviceable vehicles after coming up for the third time, with the wasting of a good decade of time and astronomical sums of money. While money, scale and available technology keep the United States in the first division, she has never so far been a pioneer in any aspect of armoured warfare. On the one hand this may change with her 1982 switch to manoeuvre theory; on the other, the retirement of designer Clifford Bradley, and the apparent lack of a successor of his quality, may hold her back.

By way of justifying this last statement, one notes how the retirement from the hot seat of Sven Berge, unquestionably the West's leading expert on armoured vehicles, seems to have knocked much of the innovative stuffing out of Swedish armour. Having put his country firmly – surprisingly perhaps – in the first division with the S Tank, Sven kept it there with the VK155 1A armoured artillery gun, and left it well placed with the UDES XX 20 articulated tank destroyer and the UDES 19 (*alias* UDES 40) tank concept. Immensely respected as a person, he was at the nub of a circle of close personal friends encompassing the general staff, the armoured user, the procurement executive and top management in the key firms – in fact the tightest and most effective (and most congenial) *old boy net* I have ever encountered. His engineering expertise as a consultant is still available; but, valuable as this is to his country and the West, it was evidently not the key to his success. Without the centripetal force of his personal influence, the circle seems to be coming apart. This specific example makes a trenchant general point – good tanks are sired by a genius who is also an inspiring team leader.

It may well be for lack of one that Soviet tank development seems to have lost its way over the past ten years or more. From the earliest days of the Bolshevik era, the Russians have been perfectly well aware that the principle of collectivism and decision making by committee, which they enshrined as a dogma of Marxism–Leninism, was not a good way of getting things done. For the things that really mattered, they found a way round the system. In summer 1918, Trotsky dispatched Tukhachevskii, as a *military specialist*, to set up the Red Army's first field formations. And it may well have been Tukhachevskii, as Deputy Defence Commissioner for Procurement in the early thirties, who set up the Soviet system for armoured vehicle development. Certainly it was Chief Marshal of Armoured Forces Babadzhanyan who put the thing in a nutshell fifty years later when he observed that, since the designer inevitably had the last word, there seemed little point in not giving him the first as well!

As far as one can see, the Soviet practice is to write a matching set of outline general staff requirements for weapon systems and vehicles which have to operate together. These are as different from Western *operational requirements* as

Tank Warfare: The Last Decades of the Dinosaurs

PLATE 8.3 **The Swedish UDES concept study for a future main battle tank has come to represent the 'Topless Tank' concept.** Offered 30 ton and 40 ton versions, the Swedish General Staff opted for the better protected design (whence this project is also known as UDES 40).

chalk from cheese. They confirm the tactical role(s) briefly and broadly enough not to interfere with the unspoken shared understanding of them. (Like many Germans of Wehrmacht vintage, the Soviets believe that such ideas may be paralysed by the fetters of formal wording.) And they set out a minimum of absolutely rigid constraints, mainly logistic, such as maximum battle mass, loading gauge, and road range without refuelling. This outline requirement is handed to one or more *design studios* (roughly equivalent to a firm of consulting engineers), which are told to get on with it. The Soviets owed their world lead in tank design to *the two great Ks* – Koshkin who fathered the T34, and Kotin who was responsible for the world's only successful series of heavy tanks. Now these men must have retired and are probably dead. Koshkin, or his team, may well have developed the excellent T54/55 (admittedly after the T47 had proved a total disaster); and the T72 appears to have come from the same stable. Powerful fighting machine though it may be, the Soviets probably classify the T72 as a medium tank, like T54/55. Certainly they regard it as a hack tank, suitable for satellite armies and third world clients, and for low to medium intensity operation, often in extremes of climate and/or terrain.

By contrast, recent evidence confirms one's subjective impression that the innovative T62 and the advanced but problem-packed T64A were main battle tanks with the feel of the Kotin studio – though surely no longer of the man himself – about them. And the same goes for the T80, which began to replace the T62 (*sic*) in two armies in the southern part of the Group of Soviet Forces Germany (GSFG) late in 1984. The clue to the puzzle is that, about a year

Weapons and Warfare

PLATE 8.4 **The Soviet T64** was fielded at the same time as the T72. It is a more advanced design but was plagued with teething troubles. The T64, shown here, has the best ballistic and NBC projection of any proven tank in the world.

later, in the other three armies of GSFG, the T64B began to replace the potent but temperamental T64A.

The T64B and T80 are virtually if not completely identical above the waist. They lack the multi-sensor ballistic inputs of modern NATO tanks, but definitely have a facility for firing a guided projectile from the 125 millimetre gun, as well as the existing unguided natures. The Soviets may have gone this way for one or both of two goods reasons. For them at least, it may offer a more cost-effective way of optimising accuracy on very small hard targets with subtenses of only 0.3 to 0.5 mils at long ranges (eg the Merkava turret front). And for anybody it is almost certainly the best way of using the tank gun against the helicopter. Extrapolating from German data, it should be possible to put a proximity/impact fused FSDS/FRAG sub-calibre round into the target area at times of flight to 4,000 metres of 4 seconds or better.

Tank Warfare: The Last Decades of the Dinosaurs

PLATE 8.5 **The Israeli Merkava Mk 2** represents the first stage of further development of the first breakaway from conventional design to retain top traverse. It is looked on with great enthusiasm by experts in other countries, and may well point the way to the remaining future of heavy tracked armoured vehicles.

It is thus in mobility that the T80 offers a step forward. The running gear and probably the transmission appear to owe a great deal to Leopard technology. For the present, the nature of the 735 kW (1,000 horsepower) engine seems to depend less on intelligence information than on whether the commentator concerned is a supporter of the M1 or of Leopard 2! To make a shaft turbine worthwhile at this rather modest rating would suggest a breakthrough to a *fin* rather than a *tube* type of heat exchange. Leopard-like once more, the T80's engine could be a diesel with an exhaust turbocharger boosted from an external combustion chamber for response to acceleration loads.

Whichever is right, the Soviets now seem to have achieved just the kind of strong multiple springboard they like for a leap to a radical design concept which could be their Army's last heavy armoured vehicle.

But it is above all Israel that exemplifies the need for a good tank to know its father. General Israel Tal was one of Moshe Dayan's bright young armoured commanders – a first-rate tank soldier with solid battle experience. Starting from scratch, he has personally masterminded the design, development, testing, production, employment and further development of the Merkava tank. This is the first radical post-war innovation likely to find acceptance outside its country of origin, and we shall be examining

Weapons and Warfare

it in depth later. Israel Tal is more than capable of expressing his ideas on all aspects of armoured warfare; he is a spellbinding speaker. But it may well be freedom from the need to explain and justify himself in formal words, to which he would then be committed, that has sustained his vast and versatile creativity.

The exception to this seeming need for proven paternity is the Federal Republic. Here one must first take on board another of those paradoxes that seem to haunt the world of armoured vehicles. It is equally true to say that, in the T64B, the Soviet Union has the best fighting tank in the world – and that, with Leopard 2, the Federal Republic quickly re-established a world lead in the field of armoured vehicles. The explanation of this lies in what one might, by analogy with the term *infrastructure*, call the *inframilitary requirement* – a hotchpotch of political will and intention, economic resources, demographic and anthropometric statistics, and ergonomic factors, which merits a book to itself. The Soviet Union has enough men of combat age and suitable size to recruit tank crews from men little over five feet tall. Her operational concept features frequent formation reliefs, say after forty-eight to sixty hours; and she has the resources to do this. And if every Warsaw Pact tank killed just one NATO tank, it would more than fulfil its norm; thus the Soviets can forego the agility which is such a key factor in survival, and use a smaller power train. These factors together allow her tank designers to work at a battle mass between one-quarter and one-third lower than their NATO opposite numbers, and – still more important nowadays – a turret volume as much as two-thirds smaller. By contrast, NATO tanks must accommodate nine out of ten of the large Anglo-Saxon and Nordic men available, and tank and crew must live to fight another day – and another and another – without the advantage of freedom of manoeuvre. Whence the fastest dinosaurs in the West!

In tanks, as in most other fields, the Third Reich's war production was marred by internecine strife of every kind. But when she came to rearm, the Federal Republic seemed to have acquired the ability for genuine team work. Perhaps this is a result of the *Wirtschaftswunder*. Certainly it manifests itself at many levels – in the ability of research workers and designers of different disciplines to communicate with one another; in a relatively harmonious (or at least constructive) relationship between designer and user; and above all in the readiness and ability of industry to group and regroup for individual projects, either in a single concerted effort or in consortia shaped to produce the most fruitful kind of controlled competition. One has the impression that openness of information, high professional standards, and the scope and quality of the technical press all play their part in this success – along of course with an outstanding technical information base. On the other hand – again as in other fields, and as many Germans readily admit – the Federal Republic's talent lies in development, application and a *systems approach* rather than in creativity and innovation as such.

The Technical Threat to Armour

Tukhachevskii observed that, historically, the conduct and outcome of military operations seemed to have had less effect than many other factors in determining the first outcome of wars. By the same token, we are now at a stage where, for as long as a need for heavy armoured vehicles continues to exist at all, the specific *military requirements* must come rather a long way down the list of factors that determine their characteristics and configuration. Given that a group of such vehicles remains a necessary and effective means of gaining forward momentum, sustaining it in the face of opposition, and posing a threat in depth, one first needs to examine the scope and nature of that *opposition*, and *the interaction of these with the design of the target vehicle*.

From the T34 onwards, the *weight pie* of a conventional turreted tank has remained much the same (Fig 8.1). Rather under half the battle mass contributes to direct (armour) protection; and roughly half of this goes to protection against specialised weapons over a horizontal frontal arc of some 60° or 70° (Fig 8.2a(i)). The frontal aspect of a tank's armoured envelope is about ten per cent of the surface this presents to the wide wicked world (Fig 8.3). So very roughly, to give this extra protection, the front has to be over ten times as thick as the rest.

The first element in the escalation of the threat is an extension of its horizontal arc (Figs 8.2a(ii)–(iv)), thanks partly to dismounted and individual anti-tank weapons partly now to *amiable mines* (surely a misprint worth preserving), partly to top attack – but mainly to the helicopter using cruise ATGW and nap-of-the-earth (NOE) tactics. There are as yet no definitive published data, but the indications are that the helicopter's primary arc of attack centres rather forward of the flank (Fig 8.2a(ii)), so that full protection against it has to be extended to the sides. This trebles the horizontal arc and means that the large sides of the tank have to be protected against *normal* attack (ie perpendicular to the surface attacked).

Although convention played lip service to a small vertical arc, this was never taken very seriously. Now the possibility of top attack creates a cone of threat,

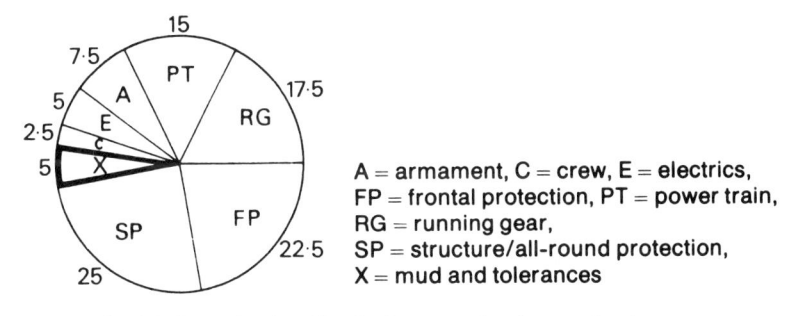

A = armament, C = crew, E = electrics,
FP = frontal protection, PT = power train,
RG = running gear,
SP = structure/all-round protection,
X = mud and tolerances

FIG 8.1 Generalised weight pie of a conventional turreted tank.

Weapons and Warfare

A. Future Horizontal Arc
(estimated, not to scale)

i   ii   iii   iv

Classical (72°)   HELS   OP   Total (~210°)

B. Future Vertical Arc
(estimated, not to scale)

Top + 50° to 90°
120 mm Mort-Group-Merlin
Copperhead, etc.
Sadarm, Bill, etc.
Smart rockets (Soviet MBRL, etc.)

Med
+ 15° to + 50°
HEL
Chain
Gun
≯ 35 mm
APDS

Low
+ 5° to + 15°
Fixed-wing
+ HEL
Cruise ATGW's +
A-TK rockets

Classical
− 5° to + 5°
Direct fire guns
cruise ATGW's.

Mines

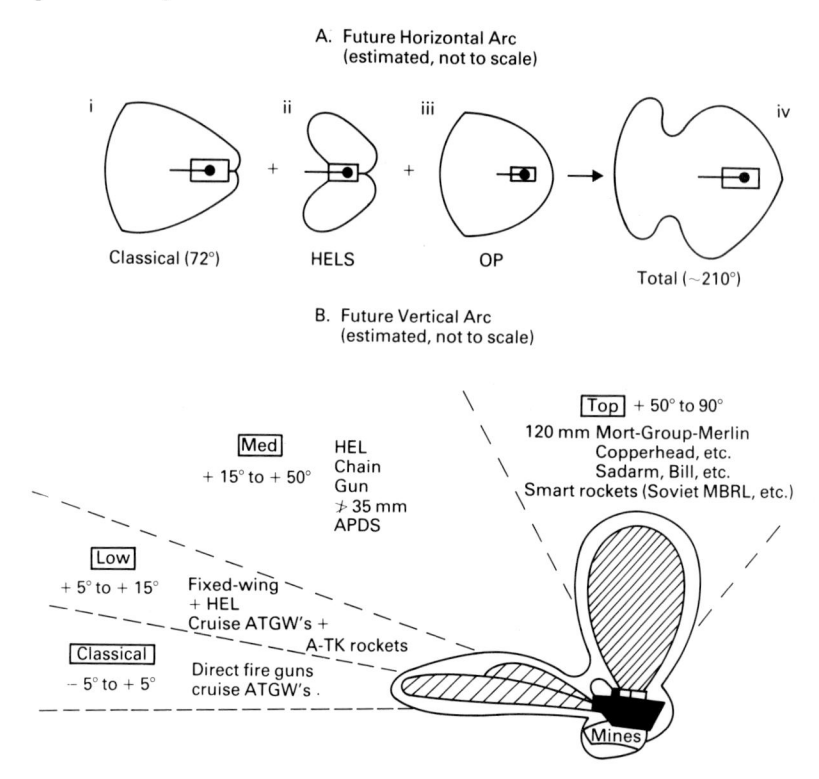

FIG 8.2 The anti-armour threat envelope (a) horizontal – (i) classical, (ii) helicopters, aimable mines etc, (iii) top attack, (iv) combined; (b) vertical.

again perhaps with an included angle of around 60° to 70°, and somewhat biased towards the front (Fig 8.3b). Then there is the small matter of lethal scatterable minelets (as opposed to the track-cutting variety). Informed common sense would suggest that there is a reduction in threat at about 45° in both horizontal and vertical planes, so that one is really looking at a threat envelope with four rather similar lobes (Figs 8.2a(iv) and 8.2b together). (On the other hand, cruise ATGW which attack obliquely downwards, Bofors' Bill for instance, are already undergoing trial, and the same principle could be applied horizontally.) Simplistically assuming, just for a moment, that the power and nature of attack is the same for all lobes, we see that the extra *thickness* of armour that was on the front now has to be spread over the large sides and roof as well – with a bit on the belly too. So we are almost exactly "back to square one" – back to the all round thickness.

To penetrate beyond this naive assumption, one needs to explore the natures of attack of armour. Here again there have been great leaps forward, both in delivery means and in attack mechanisms. Being defeated by any form of spaced armour, high explosive squashhead (HESH) has long been water

Tank Warfare: The Last Decades of the Dinosaurs

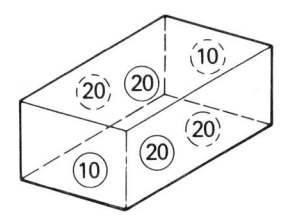

FIG 8.3 Generalised approximate distribution of the surface of a conventional tank's armoured envelope between the various aspects.

under the bridge. Now experts maintain that simple hollow charge (Fig 8.4a) must be seen as a bunker-busting nature rather than as a primary means of attacking armour – though it is still of course devastating against light armoured vehicles. Complex hollow charge (Fig 8.4b) has been with us for nigh on forty years, during which time it has unwaveringly shown boundless promise and minimal performance. The attack of armour by conveyance of stored chemical energy to the target now turns mainly on the explosively formed projectile (EFP). This has evolved from the old *beehive* charge used by the Sappers, via the Misnay-Chardin effect (as used in the French Micah aimable anti-tank mine) and self-forging fragment (SFF) attack against aircraft and light armour. An EFP is in effect a single self-forging fragment. The principle is extremely simple; it is just a matter of putting a wide-angle lid on the narrow-angle funnel of a hollow charge liner (Fig 8.4c). The practice is extraordinarily complicated and not as yet fully understood.

A hollow charge *jet* is in fact a stream of particles. The ones at the tip are extremely small and travel extremely fast (Table 8.1); as you go back down the jet to its origin, the particles get larger, maybe with one or more sizable slugs, and an order of magnitude slower. One can fairly think of a hollow charge jet as being consumed from the tip backwards by the armour it is penetrating. And this high-density particulate stream behaves like a fluid; it can be persuaded to disperse, to deflect, even to turn back on itself. This characteristic makes it relatively easy to defeat by sleight of hand.

By contrast the EFP slug is a kinetic energy (KE) penetrator, depending on energy of movement for its power of attack. A large HE, squashhead, or hollow charge shell does in fact have considerable kinetic energy – likewise, of course, large guided missiles. But up till now the only way of delivering a serious kinetic energy attack has been a high-pressure gun, since the late forties normally mounted on a tank or tank destroyer; we now have to call this *gun-delivered KE attack*. One alternative, now in an advanced state of development in the United States but possibly generating more euphoria than real promise, is the *hypervelocity* cruise ATGW; as far as effect on the target is concerned, the parameters of this are similar to those of the gun-delivered penetrator. The EFP, by contrast, is carried to the target – or at least to the immediate target area – together with the explosive charge which at once

Weapons and Warfare

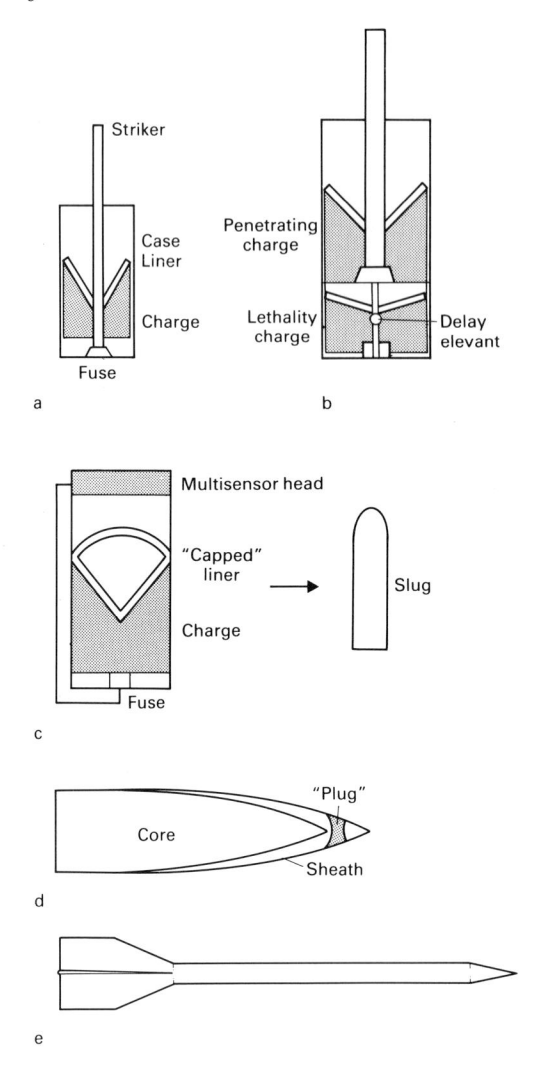

FIG 8.4 Mode of attack – (a) simple hollow charge (HEAT), (b) complex hollow charge, (c) explosively formed projective (EFP), (d) sub-calibre penetrators – (i) spin-stabilised (APDS), (ii) fin-stabilised (APFSDS).

forms it and imparts its energy of attack. To compare EFP attack with gun-delivered attack and hypervelocity missiles, we must explore the mechanism of KE attack and the characteristics of EFP more closely (Tables 8.1 and 8.2).

If we take a thick steel plate as representing *resistant* armour (see below), penetration basically depends on kinetic energy (E_5, Table 8.1). This is, however, subject to two key conditions. To produce the state of hydrodynamic

TABLE 8.1. *Approximate/estimated/predicted figures for some gun-generated and projectile-generated KE attacks – L/D = length/diameter ratio, VS = velocity of strike (velocity of EFP plus delivery velocity of shell/warhead where applicable); ES = (kinetic) energy of strike; QS = cross-sectional loading on strike; MS = momentum of strike. Figures for the Rheinmetall 120 mm smoothbore tank gun and matching EFP attacks are emboldened.*

				Parameters			
Type/conditions	Data mass (kg)	L/D	VS (m/s)	ES (MJ) (% 120 mm)	QS (kJ/cm^2) (% 120 mm)	MS (kN.S) (% 120 mm)	Remarks
Gun-delivered projectiles							
90 mm AP	10.97	3/1 (?)	853	4.0 (41)	63 (7)	9.4 (80)	
105 mm APDS	6.48	4/1*	1,478	7.1 (73)	563 (66)	9.6 (82)	*Estimated
105 mm APFSDS	6.12	15/1*	1,501	6.9 (72)	857 (87)	9.2 (78)	
120 mm APFSDS	**7.1**	**20/1***	**1,650**	**9.7 (100)**	**950 (100)**	**11.7 (100)**	
Explosively formed projectiles (EFP)							
Steel, present, static							Velocity see Note 2; no published data to confirm present maximum mass
Fragment	0.048	4/1	2,200	0.12 (1)	94 (10)	0.1 (1)	*12.7 mm bullet
slug	0.1	4/1	2,200	0.23 (2)	75 (8)	0.22 (2)	
slug	1.0	4/1	2,200	2.42 (26)	264 (28)	2.31 (20)	
slug	2.0	4/1	2,200	4.84 (49)	324 (34)	4.28 (36)	
Steel, present, shell/missile-delivered							Shell/warhead velocity 800 m/s
Fragment	0.048	4/1	3,000	0.22 (2)	175 (18)	0.14 (1)	*12.7 mm bullet
slug	0.1	4/1	3,000	0.44 (5)	140 (15)	0.29 (3)	
slug	1.0	4/1	3,000	4.5 (46)	490 (52)	3.14 (27)	
slug	2.0	4/1	3,000	9.0 (92)	602 (63)	5.83 (51)	
Steel, future, static							Most optimistic forecast
slug	5.0	8/1	3,000	22.5 (232)	1,331 (140)	15 (128)	
Other modes							
155 mm HE splinter[12]	0.0014	(var)	1,800	0.0023	(var)	0.0025	
HEAT 'jet' tip			10,000 (±)				For comparison NB sharp velocity gradient along 'jet'

179

Weapons and Warfare

TABLE 8.2. *Guideline thickness/calibre (t/d) ratios, based on penetration of homogeneous rolled steel plate, for various modes of attack.*

Type of attack	50s	70s	80s/90s	Remarks
Gun-generated KE	2.0	3.0*	4.5*	Optimum figures, *wrt gun calibre
Hypervelocity ATGMS	–	–	?	Terminal ballistics as for gun
Hollow charge	3**	4	6.5	Optimum figures, **unspun, spun=1(+)
EFP	–	–	1	US current 'practical' figure[3]

Notes *including skirt; Israeli figure is 1.0 m^2
**estimated

flow in the target material on which substantial penetration depends, the force per unit area, or *cross-sectional loading* (Q_5, Table 8.1), must reach a certain minimum. This makes the density and length/diameter ratio (L/D) of the penetrator crucial – whence the move from full bore solid shot through sub-calibre APDS (Fig 8.4d, L/D say 4/1) to fin-stabilised APFSDS (Fig 8.4e), with L/Ds of up to 20/1 and still growing.

The second condition is penetrator mass. Why this is important is still not fully understood, but along with the need for high density it dictates the use of a heavy material such as tungsten. The best opinion would probably include two points. Like a hollow charge *jet*, the material of the penetrator appears to be *consumed* by the act of penetration; or, if you like, there has to be enough mass to keep the attack going. And while it is energy that determines the thickness of armour defeated, it is momentum (M_5, Table 8.1) which is generally thought to determine the minimum effect on the target – the predicted lethality. The respective parts played by energy and momentum in damaging the target are far from clear; it has never mattered too much in the past and, with the switch from *resistant* to *destabilising* armours, it may not matter too much in the future. The point is that the gun man thinks Energy, while the tank and armour designer tends to think Momentum.

Gun-delivered APFSDS penetrators can be fired either from a rifled tube by using a slipping driving band (*decoupling*) or from a smooth bore. In the one case the *slow* spin required to ensure consistency, despite production variations, is imparted by residual friction, in the other by angled gas ports in the fins – the latter at a cost of some 50 metres per second in muzzle velocity in the case of the Soviet 125 millimetre APFSDS of T64 and T72. The penetrator of a hypervelocity missile is similar to that of a gun; the missile can be either a slow roller or roll stabilised.

In comparing the EFP slug with the gun-delivered penetrator, we need to look at another parameter – the thickness/diameter ratio (T/D, Table 8.2). Against resistant armour, hollow charge has a T/D of some 6.5/1, as against the optimum of 4.5/1 (referred to *gun* calibre) for APFSDS. EFP slugs are now achieving a T/D of 1/1. This means that an EFP medium artillery shell at likely angles of arrival would defeat any Western tank's glacis plate with a com-

Tank Warfare: The Last Decades of the Dinosaurs

fortable margin for lethality. The question is whether EFP will show the same growth in T/D as the other modes of attack. Historically, one would expect it to, but there are a number of good reasons why it may not. There is undoubtedly a theoretical limit for the velocity of an EFP (ignoring the velocity of its carrier), just as there is for the muzzle velocity obtainable from a conventional gun using solid propellant. Current German thinking (Table 8.1) suggests that this may lie at some 3,000 metres per second, with an L/D of 8/1. What this means in terms of T/D ratio is impossible to say at this stage; but for a 5 kilogramme slug it gives a kinetic energy over twice as great as that obtained from today's *model* tank gun, the German 120 millimetre smoothbore. Increasing the energy of EFP beyond this probably depends on mass (a function of the carrier rather than of warhead design), and/or on the possibility of using heavy metals. While the Germans have doubts on this last move, the Americans consider it to show great promise and lay great stress on the pyrophoric effect of molybdenum and DU (depleted uranium) in attacking diesel fuel. But perhaps the most important unknown is the extent to which the velocity developed by the EFP itself can legitimately be summed with that of its carrier in estimating penetrative performance.

It is the combination of EFP and top attack which has revolutionised the attack of armour and shattered the survivability of today's agile monsters. This depends on the ability to score direct hits – with shell and mortar bombs fired indirect, with ballistic (as opposed to cruise) missiles, and with sub-projectiles carried by all these, in every case with terminal homing guidance; and, less important in the long run, with oblique and downward-looking attack by cruise missiles with full-course guidance. *Smart* projectiles, such as the United States 155 millimetre Copperhead shell, employ semi-active homing; they depend on the target being marked, typically by a laser beam. For three reasons they are limited in application, and, in the view of many, no more than a flash in the pan. They depend on radio communication between observer/marker and gun or launcher position. The use of a single type of radiation lays them open to passive countermeasures, both pinpoint and area, such as multi-component smoke. And the impingement of detectable radiation on the target at least unit seconds before impact makes them easy to counter by aggressive means, such as self-forging fragment grenades fired from the tank's roof. It is the advent of the *brilliant* top attack projectile and sub-projectile, using multisensor *passive* homing responsive to at least two components of the target signature, that poses the real threat. We now have to think in terms not of a smart hollow-charge Copperhead but of a brilliant EFP one!

Armour and Survivability

Fig 8.5 sets out the ways in which the chance of a crew-vehicle system surviving on the battlefield may be enhanced. By far the most important for the future is indirect protection – notably reduction of the *fair hit* area (of which

Weapons and Warfare

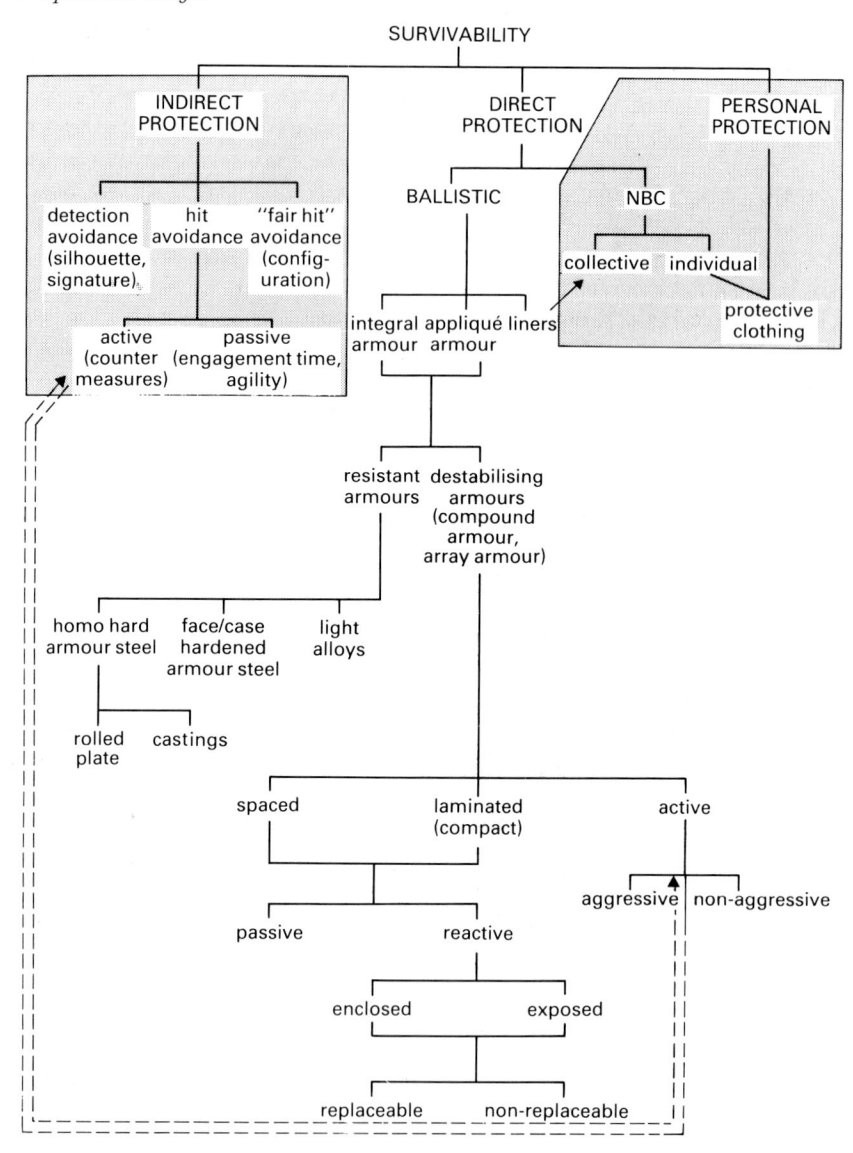

```
                              SURVIVABILITY
        ┌─────────────────────────┼──────────────────────┐
    INDIRECT                   DIRECT                PERSONAL
   PROTECTION                PROTECTION             PROTECTION
        │                        │                      │
  ┌─────┼─────┐           ┌──────┴──────┐        ┌──────┴──────┐
detection  hit   "fair hit"   BALLISTIC      NBC         
avoidance avoidance avoidance                    collective  individual
(silhouette, (config-                                            │
 signature)  uration)                                       protective
     │                                                       clothing
  ┌──┴───┐       integral appliqué liners
active  passive  armour   armour
(counter (engagement time,
measures) agility)
                            ┌────┴────┐
                       resistant  destabilising
                       armours    armours
                                  (compound
                                   armour,
                                   array armour)
              ┌──────────┬────────┐
         homo hard   face/case   light
         armour steel hardened   alloys
                     armour steel
              │          │
           rolled     castings
           plate
                ┌──────────┬──────────┐
              spaced    laminated    active
                        (compact)
                                    ┌────┴────┐
                                aggressive non-aggressive
              ┌────┴────┐
           passive    reactive
                    ┌────┴────┐
                enclosed   exposed
                    ┌────┴────┐
               replaceable non-replaceable
```

FIG 8.5 Elements of armoured vehicle survivability, highlighting ballistic protection. (*Reprinted from Military Technology by kind permission of the Mönch Publishing Group.*)

more below), and of firing and movement exposure times. A small but important point within ballistic protection is the adoption of boronated polyethylene liners (so far only in T64, which, in fact, uses leaded plastic). These at once absorb some neutrons (hydrogen and boron both having very high neutron capture cross sections), act as ballistic longstops, catch spall and ricochets, provide thermal insulation and reduce minor injuries from contact with metal. The main thing here, though, is the swing from integral resistant armour to destabilising *appliqué* armour systems, hung on a structural shell – or even a frame. This opens the way to re-armouring a vehicle to meet a new threat. While an armour system must always contain a substantial resistant element, there is virtually no hope of keeping out modern attack over an extended arc with a wholly or mainly resistant system.

Destabilising armour systems depend on interaction between the attack and a succession of interfaces, each designed to inflict some specific kind of harm on it. The design of destabilising armour systems is an art; in fact it is not only for reasons of secrecy that it can fairly be called a mystery! One important variable is spacing: the great difference in density between air and other components is significant; and some destabilising effects need time, and therefore space, to develop. The materials are almost any you like to name – steels, a touch of titanium maybe, light alloys, possibly lead, ceramics, GRP, heavy-duty nylons, metal and plastic housings, water, diesel fuel (in pressurised self-sealing tanks). Broadly speaking and weight for weight, these compound armours give an advantage over homogeneous rolled steel plate of about 2:1 against hollow charge and 1.4:1 against KE attack (including EFP). As current NATO tanks demonstrate, their bulk may be something else again!

This step forward may not be enough though; many feel that modern powers of attack demand an energetic response. The Israeli *Blazer* system is an early and successful example of reactive armour – a sandwich of an explosive charge between two plates. More recent proposals integrate the explosive as a layer within a compound system. Reactive armour, like some passive arrays, in effect destroys hollow charge attack by turning it back on itself. Its effect against KE attack is more limited. At high angles of attack it tends to deflect the penetrator; at lower obliquities its effect, like that of passive resistant armours, is related to the energy of attack. There may also be problems with discrimination between attack of armour and normal artillery fire. To start with, reactive armour looked like a dramatic advance. But the switch from hollow charge to EFPs, its one-shot nature and its possible tactical limitations now seem to make reactive armour no more than another material for the creator of destabilising systems to play with.

Much play has also been made with active armour. But one can sum up active armour as, at best, tomorrow's response to yesterday's attack. Despite its tactical limitations, it would have been a logical and fairly effective answer to *smart* attack. But *brilliant* attack sets both technological and tactical problems. Both the single guidance impulse of a primary projectile and the detonation of an EFP warhead may take place at a slant range of as much as 300 metres from the target. The ability of a non-aggressive active armour system to deploy a multi-component smokescreen at this distance within tens of milliseconds is at best questionable! Thus the defender would be forced to

Weapons and Warfare

PLATE 8.6 **Blazer reactive armour on an Israeli Centurion;** this is an excellent way of uparmouring an existing tank against a mainly hollow-charge threat.

smother his area in smoke and lose his fields of view and fire. Aggressive active armour (SFF grenades) can attack closer in and thus gain time to respond. But it would appear to offer such a threat to vehicle commanders, with their heads out, and to men on their feet, as to make it incompatible with the high density all-arms battle concept now favoured by advanced armies.

A Three-Tiered Defence

If one considers the combined threat to armoured vehicles from helicopters, *brilliant* projectiles delivered by indirect fire or fixed-wing aircraft, and oblique or downward-looking cruise missiles and direct-fire shell, the most promising approach appears to lie not in the type of countermeasure described as active armour, but in a three-tiered low-level air defence of the kind the Germans, for instance, seem to be contemplating against attack helicopters. This comprises point defence of a small group of vehicles, *local area* defence aimed specifically at protecting, say, a combat team, and area tactical air defence proper. As we shall see, this approach has a fundamental effect on force structure, tactical groupings and requirements for armoured vehicles.

Let us concentrate here on point defence. The tank gun, firing proximity/impact fused FSDS/FRAG can do the job. But the tank has other things to do; it already carried far too little ammunition (typically forty rounds of 120 or 125

Tank Warfare: The Last Decades of the Dinosaurs

millimetre); superimposition of an air defence sub-system on its already complex fire control system would be psychologically unacceptable, even if feasible and affordable; and giving a tank turret and mounting sufficient traverse rates, and elevation rates and angle, would not be easy. On the other hand, the optically sighted cannon, typical of IFVs, is in no way man enough for the job. Likewise, the 60 millimetre guns now fashionable for light armoured vehicles probably cannot deliver a worthwhile sub-calibre fragmentation projectile; and the sub-calibre principle must be employed to minimise time of flight. A very interesting Italian proposal is to apply their 76 millimetre naval gun, probably firing FSDS/FRAG, to this role. One does not yet know exactly what they have in mind, but this armament on a suitable mounting marches very well with the German concept of an *escort vehicle (Begleitpanzer)*.

Configuration

Deeply as it may shock the informed reader, I do not propose to take up any of the limited space allotted to me with further discussion of firepower, or with any discussion at all of mobility as such. The prospects and problems these areas present are dwarfed by the need to find a configuration which is at once viable and acceptable to the user. A glance at Table 8.3, read in conjunction with Fig 8.6, leaves one in no doubt of the urgency of doing this, of the excellent use to which Soviet designers have put the advantages outlined earlier in this chapter, or of the reason why so much play has been made in recent years with *topless* concepts like UDES 19 or the United States TTB1.

Technologically the only remaining argument against these designs is that optics still give better resolution than any optronic vision and sighting system, to an extent which is significant in the critical matter of detecting and acquiring targets on the dirty battlefield in daylight with average North European cloud cover. But recent advances in charge coupled devices (CCDs), notably in the Federal Republic and Sweden, combined with existing technology in multisensor heads and image processing, are likely to overcome this drawback, leaving the interface of ergonomic requirements and display

TABLE 8.3. *Approximate 'fair-hit' target areas above hull roof level – turret (or equivalent) front, side and roof.*

Vehicle	front (m^2)	side (m^2)	'turret' roof (m^2)
M1	2.7	3.5	12.0
Leopard 2	2.1	3.9	10.7
Merkava MK 1	1.6*	3.5	5.3
T72	1.6	1.9	5.1
UDES XX 20	0.06**	0.25**	2.0**
'Nacelle concept'	0.5**	0.5**	1.75**

Notes *including skirt; Israeli figure is 1.0 m^2
**estimated

Weapons and Warfare

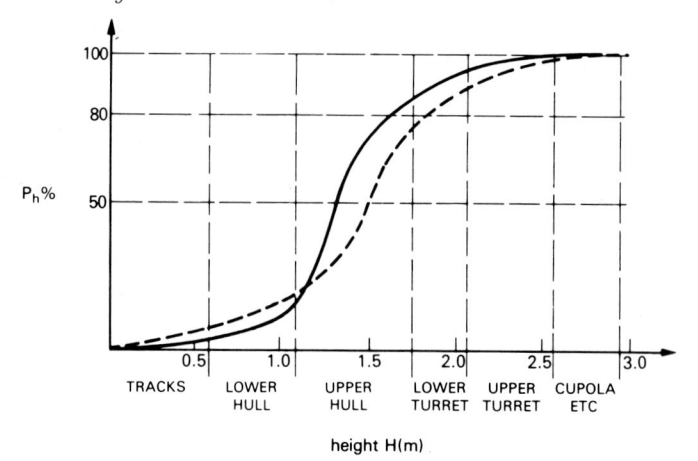

FIG 8.6 Height and exposure probability (key heights based on Chieftain), with non-tactical driving (broken line) and with good tactical handling (full line, estimated).

technology as the sole problem area. Since combat and service support costs vary roughly as the cube of battle mass, the high cost of these sub-systems would probably be more than offset by the savings resulting from a reduction of up to one-third in battle mass, and thus in system support costs.

The crunch point is the commander's station. The United States user is still exploring the problem, so we must look to West German and Israeli user opinion as the most articulate and, in the West at least, the most authoritative. While there is now some wavering over the need for tank commanders normally to work head out to *sense the battlefield*, there is absolute insistence on the need for tactical commanders from platoon upwards to do so. And the ability of tank (and IFV) commanders to work turret down – that is to observe through optics without exposing the turret (or equivalent) to observation and direct fire – is seen as indispensable. Any experienced user will agree that these stipulations are very hard to refute.

The two, though related, are separate; so let us take the head-out problem first. Such is the difficulty of selecting and training tank commanders that the Wehrmacht is the only army ever to have come near to solving this problem; in fact with the convergence of the relevant aspects of tank and helicopter technologies, the requirements may even come to approach those for attack helicopter crews. One basic Soviet artillery norm for neutralisation of a defensive position puts down one 122 millimetre HE shell (or the equivalent) per 7 to 8 metres of real estate; and they may fire three or four such norms. The total plan area of modern NATO tanks is some 20 square metres. Enough said! On the other hand, one must accept that a direct hit on the commander's station itself, hit with a medium HE shell or any form of specialised attack, is curtains for the commander, even if he is closed down.

Tank Warfare: The Last Decades of the Dinosaurs

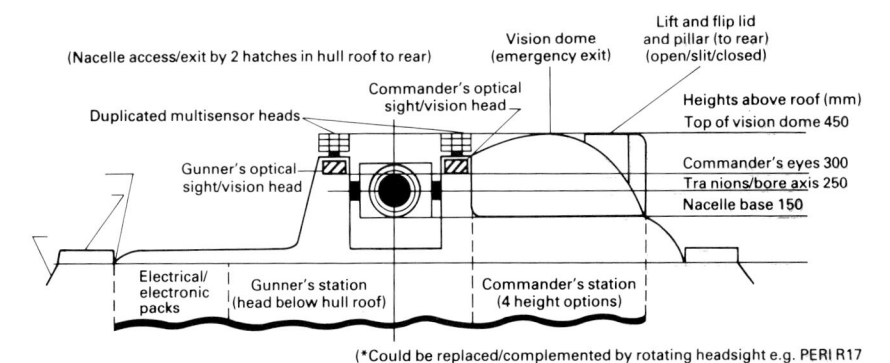

FIG 8.7 Concept schematic of an externally mounted gun with a commander's 'nacelle'. (*Reprinted by kind permission of the Mönch Publishing Group.*)

There is in fact a feasible compromise between these two extremes, in the shape of what one might call *armoured dual glazing* – a combination of armour glass and polycarbonate material – backed up, of course, by a steel lid providing slit vision and fully closed positions. If such a transparent armoured dome or nacelle (Fig 8.7) was associated with an emergency escape route only, as opposed to a normal access hatch, there would be no difficulty in heating, washing and wiping it to provide the kind of vision offered by a modern car or aircraft cockpit. As long as the dome was large enough for the use of hand binoculars, this would provide *head-out* vision with protection against artillery and small-arms fire.

However, the concept indicated in Fig 8.7 runs up against two further user objections, one of them valid but the other due largely to prejudice. While accepting the desirability of stowing ammunition externally or separated from the main armoured envelope by fireproof bulkheads, and of making the physical process of loading automatic, the *model* users insist on manual loading in emergency – and the Israelis on human control of loading. The second requirement, of highly questionable validity, in the face of solid evidence from Swedish trials, is for the breech end of the gun and the loading process to be under armour.

The Merkava Concept

For these reasons and the increasingly evident need for a pair, or perhaps a trio, of matching vehicles, the one path down which progress seems possible is evolution of the Merkava concept. The Mark 2 as it stands is undergunned and underpowered by modern standards; but it is to be upgunned with an Israeli 120 millimetre smoothbore, and up-engined from 675 to 895 kilowatts (900 to 1,220 horsepower). The Israelis seem to consider a power–weight ratio of 14.7 kilowatts per ton (20 horsepower per ton) adequate for their conditions and

Weapons and Warfare

lengths of operational moves; and the tank already has an outstanding transmission and running gear of Israeli design, which will make full use of this extra power. Merkava has the power train at the front, forming part of an integrated armour system with a steel shell and appliqué packs of destabilising armour (probably reactive) outside it. The cunning, bred of battle experience (and battle analysis!) and superb attention to detail has resulted in some form of spaced or compound armour on almost every aspect of the tank, *and* on utilisation of the space for stowage, thus at once saving volume and further increasing protection. In the Mark 2 tank, the proportion of battle mass that contributes to survivability has been increased from the conventional 45 per cent or so to almost 80 per cent – and still rising. Using Rolf Hilmes' yardsticks, this design philosophy should more than double Merkava's ability to survive KE attack and almost treble survivability against hollow charge – both as compared with an equivalent conventional design with steel armour.

But it is the hull rear that makes the Merkava concept unique in terms of *crew* survivability and, for the future, of versatility. In the existing tank, there are two rear doors, giving onto a compartment which will take six fully equipped infantrymen seated and eight at a push. A Merkava battalion can carry a company and retain its full stow of ammunition, or a battalion by removing the ammunition from this rear compartment. In battle, the compartment has been used for evacuating wounded, lifting Sapper detachments and explosive stores, and many other purposes. Above all, though, it provides the shocked and probably injured crew of a crippled tank with a genuine chance of escape – something no tank with top hatches can do. Rolf Hilmes, the technical brains of the Leopard team, expounds fully and enthusiastically on this layout. What he does not point out, though, is that Merkava's hull, with a large turret ring and a quasi-box bodies rear, provides an ideal basis for the vehicles that must surely partner the tank in future.

Let us look first, though, at the turret. The frontal area (Table 8.3) has been reduced by one-half as compared with NATO tanks, to the same figure as T72; and in fact about one-third of this area is a skirt right down by the turret ring. The turret roof area has also been halved (again to match Soviet practice); But the large slab sides remain. The question is how much further one could go towards the estimated figures for the *nacelle* concept (Fig 8.8 and Table 8.3).

Quite a long way, I believe – and from this point on I am expressing unproven personal opinion. Given the rear doors, the turret roof need have only one emergency exit (the commander's nacelle, say); just doing away with two hatches would enhance protection considerably. But even if the gunner must have an optical sight – as was necessary when the Mark 2 was designed – there is no reason why he should have his head above hull roof level; and, for Europe at least, the requirement for all-weather round-the-clock performance dictates the best optronic system available. So having the gunner in the turret appears to be a surprising concession to tradition. With manual loading, the need for a standing loader has always dictated the turret height and shape. But Merkava's loader normally has just a controlling and monitoring role, loading manually only in emergency. There therefore seems no reason why he should not normally be seated sideways behind the gunner, and also below hull roof level. Sloping that side of the turret away at 45° would give optimum protection against the future threat envelope and should give him enough room for emergency working. This would leave the other side of the gun free for the commander, as in the *nacelle* concept. The payoff in these changes can only be found by detailed design. But in face of the top attack threat, it appears to be a much more promising approach than the flat-roofed low-profile turret (*Flachturm*) towards which many Western designers seem to be leaning at the moment.

The Heavy Tracked Family

After expending years of effort and vast sums of money to get their beloved Marder IFV, hailed as a world-beater, the *Panzergrenadiere* can now talk of nothing but *unscrambling* it. The Soviet Army too is moving away from multi-role vehicles (except in the Airborne Forces). By and large, the all-in-one war machine has not proved too successful even in the uniform fluid media; with the added complexity of ground, proposed *land battleships* have sunk without trace rather quickly – and, in one or two cases, literally! Certainly it seems clear that, cost and complexity apart, no one crew could cope with the entire anti-armour threat spectrum. This lends particular interest to a proposal put forward by Brigadier General Gerd Röhrs, then Commandant of the Federal German Army's Officer School, in the context of some fascinating published discussion on the mechanised infantry of the 20s. He suggested a platoon of an MBT/IFV pair as the inseparable tactical unit, within a battalion of six companies of three such platoons. In the face of the anti-armour threat, there seems no reasonable doubt that some such combination must become the forward manoeuvre element in the mechanised battle. The first question is rather whether two types of vehicle are any longer enough.

The second question is whether the *section IFV* concept is any longer sound. Even given the elementary state of mechanised infantry and their equipment in the Second World War, both German and Soviet tactical commanders tended to regard a troop carrier, especially an armoured one, as a more worthwhile target than a tank. Certainly that is so of today's IFVs under most circumstances. Quite apart from the growing cost and combat worth of the individual infantryman, the evolutionary trend in both softskinned and armoured personnel carriers has been towards a smaller dismountable element – platoon, two-section, section. It would thus seem entirely logical to restrict the load to the half-section or *fire team* of four on which most advanced armies have now standardised – rather than to spread a section between two vehicles, which may or may not be of the same type.

The purpose of this whole manoeuvre element, in offence and defence alike, is to allow the tank to exercise its capacity for offensive shock action. Now that top attack is available to deal with enemy tanks, use of the tank gun for defensive roles runs contrary to this purpose. At the same time the arguments that rage, notably in the Soviet and Israeli armies and now in the Federal German and Swedish, over whether the IFV should mount a cannon or a light (60 to 75 millimetre) gun suggest that there is a role for both. If one went to a trio of vehicles, a tank, a fire-team IFV(gun) and a fire-team IFV(cannon), one would have a tactical unit of three capable of fire and movement, a separate specialised vehicle for each group of roles, and the dismountable element spread over two vehicles. One would assume that the IFV(cannon) would have an *emergency* ATGW capability (as now), and some form of grenade launcher for smothering fire within mortar safety distance; and that one of the men in its turret would be the section commander.

Militarily there is little doubt that the IFV, whether of one type or two, should ideally have not just good mobility and protection, but *the same mobility and protection of the tank*. The Bundeswehr, for instance, is talking of a battle mass of 40 tons and more for Marder's successor. In *Mechanised Infantry* I demonstrated that, even in 70s terms and allowing for substantial redesign of the tank hull, commoning the tank and IFV would produce a significant saving in the combined real cost slice of the two systems. But the argument is a complex one, not easy to sustain in face of armour-infantry internecine strife and the then need for a medium tracked family.

Now there are four new factors. The Germans, and apparently the Soviets, have now managed to extend the limit of battle mass at which wheels can compete with tracks on armoured cross-country vehicles from 20 to 30 tons; this makes the argument for putting all tactical vehicles, bar the tank and the IFV(s), on wheels almost irresistible in terms of operating cost, scope of peacetime use, and political acceptability in low-intensity operations. If this happens, the IFV joins the tank as an *exception*. The threat – in particular top attack – makes it imperative that any vehicle required to operate with the tank and in much the same way should have the same protection. This argument is reinforced by the need for three complementary types of armament and their essential interdependence in the game of getting the tanks forward. And the Merkava layout offers the possibility of putting all three types of vehicle on a truly common hull, thus minimising system cost slice, optimising the logistic situation and simplifying training.

But all this is in the middle term at best. Sooner or later technological advance will face armies with some extremely uncomfortable changes. It will squeeze out the mechanised heavy manoeuvre force between airmechanised and indirect fire elements on the one hand, and light infantry, trained to operate at low density, on the other. Ultimately, whether or not this is ever acknowledged in so many words, it will lead to a role reversal of combat and combat support arms, with light (*fast force*) armour and light infantry operating in support of artillery and airmechanised formations.

Introducing Chapter 9

FOR many years there was but little change in the design of small arms and at the end of World War Two armies were still using weapons which had been designed in World War One. The manually operated bolt action rifle was to be seen everywhere and automatic personal weapons were issued, in the main, only to NCOs or to special forces. As automatic weapons became more readily available, there was a fear that the supply of personal ammunition would fail to keep pace with expenditure and the first self-loading rifles were limited to single shot action largely for this reason. However, it soon became apparent, particularly in close country, that men with single shot weapons were at a great disadvantage so that many more weapons now have the facility for fully automatic fire. Also, much more thought goes into the design of ammunition with the result that it is more effective and, being smaller in calibre, more can be carried. This important subject is admirably covered in the next chapter by an author who is second to none in his field.

9
Small Arms

EDWARD C EZELL MA PhD

EVER since the dawn of the nuclear age and strategies of massive retaliation and mutual assured destruction, military thinkers and defence planners have been writing obituaries for the individual infantryman. They have also raised serious questions about the utility of his basic weapons such as the rifle and the machine gun in any future conflicts. Numerous conventional ground conflicts since 1945 testify that these reports of the infantryman's obsolescence were premature. Individual soldiers equipped with contemporary small arms and provided with the proper training have had, and can be expected to continue to have, a significant impact on the outcome of both low intensity and larger scale conflicts.

Take for example the Falkland Islands War of 1982. That small but brisk conflict reminded military leaders around the globe, that in our *modern age* of electronic warfare, high technology weapons systems and nuclear stockpiles, the decisive battles and skirmishes of that Anglo-Argentine conflict were still won by relatively small groups of men who were equipped with little more than the infantry rifle, general purpose machine gun, and bayonet. These individual fighting men were successful in combat because they followed the age-old infantry tactical doctrine of *closing with the enemy and destroying him by fire and manoeuvre*.

Yet the men who carried the day have been, since World War Two, the poor relations of the military family. This is especially true when one considers the size of the budgets made available for developing and acquiring new infantry weapons, as compared to the money spent on more technologically sophisticated (and expensive) ground, air and seaborne weapons systems.

In recent times, as Colonel Harry G Summers, Jr (US Army retired) has pointed out, infantrymen are *"rarely held up as symbols of military prowess"* by national leaders. *"Rather, it has been those who fly planes, sail ships, maneuver tanks, manipulate exotic electronic equipment, and fight wars at a gentlemanly distance with cannons and missiles who supposedly represent war fighting ability in our modern age."* But as Colonel Summers also correctly noted, *". . . in the Falklands War, modern technology was useful in getting the infantry to the point of decision, and it was helpful in preparing their way and supporting their efforts [but] in the final analysis . . . it was the*

Weapons and Warfare

men who *'slogged' up to Port Stanley with rifle and pack"* who ultimately carried the day.[1]

These lessons have been reinforced by the experiences of other armed forces which have engaged in the localised conflicts of the past four decades. Likewise, the continuing Iran–Iraq war indicates that men equipped with small calibre weapons still are an essential element in modern combat situations, even those involving large concentrations of armoured fighting vehicles and masses of artillery weapons.

Thus, in any major future conflict between the East and the West, military planners should anticipate a continued significant role for the infantryman as infantryman on the battlefields of Europe. Therefore, it is apparent that prudent defence intellectuals need to appreciate the strengths and limitations of infantry weapons, and to understand the current technological trends that point toward the future shape of the infantryman's hardware.

After nearly a century of evolution, currently available kinetic energy infantry weapons represent a mature technology in which further advances are likely to provide only incremental improvements. Still better hardware is constantly sought. Since the end of the Second World War, the military users and the professional developers of small arms have sought to improve the weapons available to the infantry soldier. Although most major armies have gone through three families of small arms since World War Two (the wartime generation, the immediate post-war 7.62 millimetre generation, and the current 5.56 millimetre/5.45 millimetre generation), the users and developers have often approached the creation of new weapons from significantly different perspectives.[2] The infantry planners, thinking in terms of their operational needs on the battlefield have sought new ammunition/weapon systems that would provide improvements such as reduced weapon and ammunition weight, longer combat life expectancy (i.e., simplicity, ruggedness, reliability) and the like on the logistical side of the balance sheet, and greater firepower on the performance side.

Within the professional world of the research and development, emphasis generally has been given to the creation of mechanical systems that would provide improved probability of hitting targets and greater killing effectiveness once the target was hit. Most engineers have seen their task in specialised mechanical terms. As a result of their respective approaches to the problem, in nearly all nations there has been a general lack of continued, daily, frank interchange of ideas and concerns between the developers and the users.[3] Only recently within NATO, and the military establishments of some of its member states, has there been a trend toward closer cooperation between user and developer. Still there remains much to be done in building a closer working relationship between these two communities of professionals.

During the past forty years, there have developed some clearly discernible trends in the evolution of infantry weapons. First, there has been a reduction in the size and weight of infantry weapon cartridges, which has been accompanied by concomitant reductions in the size and weight of weapons. At the end of the Second World War, the major armies of the World employed infantry rifles and machine guns that fired *full power* cartridges ranging in calibre from 6.5 to 8 millimetre (0.256 to 0.33 calibre). These cartridges predated the 1914–1918 war, and many had their genesis in the latter two decades of the 19th century. Building on the precedent established by the Germans during the 1939–1945 conflict, the Soviets, British, Belgians, Americans and other nations embarked upon the development of new cartridges of *intermediate power* ranging in calibre from 7 to 7.62 millimetre (0.276 to 0.30).

A development programme established by the German Army's Field Services in 1934 had yielded an *intermediate power* 7.92 × 33 millimetre *Kurz* infantry weapon cartridge by 1942.[4] Although the standard rifle and machine gun cartridge, the 7.92 × 57 millimetre, had been used for forty years, studies conducted during the First World War had indicated that the power of the cartridge could be reduced and the cartridge case could be shortened without significantly affecting the combat effectiveness of the infantry rifle at ranges of engagement less than 400 metres. This realisation led to the 7.92 millimetre *Kurz*, which employed a lighter projectile, shorter case and reduced propellant charge. The new cartridge was less expensive, conservative of critical raw materials. Because of its lower recoil impulse it was easier to use in automatically firing weapons.

In 1942, the Germans introduced the first of several designs of inexpensively fabricated automatic weapons; the precursors of the current generation of assault rifles. These *Sturmgewehr* represented a watershed change in infantry small arms. The tactical advantages offered by these rapid firing *Sturmgewehr* and their 7.92 millimetre *Kurz* ammunition, when compared with either the lower power pistol calibre submachine guns or the higher power infantry rifles, were quickly grasped by arms designers the world over. Future small arms ammunition in Great Britain and the Soviet Union were especially affected by the *intermediate range* German ammunition.

As the transition from the full power weapons to intermediate power weapons began, it was the Soviets who were the first to take full tactical advantage of this new ammunition concept. In their first postwar generation of weapons, the Soviets introduced at the squad level both the *Avtomat Kalashnikova* (AK47) series of assault rifles and the *Ruchnoi Pulemet Degtyareva* (RPD) light machine gun chambered to fire their new Model 1943 *intermediate range* 7.62 × 39 millimetre cartridge. Their platoon/company support machine guns and their sniper rifles continued to use the Model 1891 7.62 × 54 millimetre rimmed ammunition. In order of succession, the Soviets fielded the *Ruchnoi Pulemet 46* company machine gun (RP46), and the *Pulemet Kalashnikova* (PK) ground guns, and the *Stankovyi Pulemet 43* (SG43 or Goryunov) and *Stankovyi Goryunov Modernizirovannyi* (SGM) vehicle machine guns.

All these weapons were tailored to a clearly enunciated fighting doctrine.

Weapons and Warfare

PLATE 9.1 Nearly 50 million Kalashnikov assault rifles have been manufactured since the late 1940s. Shown here are two Warsaw Pact variants of the 7.62 × 39 mm **Avtomat Kalashnikova**. Top, the **Hungarian AMD65**, and bottom, the **GDR Volksarmee** MPiKMS.

The Soviets projected the use of their small arms as part of ground forces in active support of the offensive assault by armoured forces. Improving upon their World War Two tactical concept, involving infantry as an element of a mechanised armoured assault, the Red Army substituted their high rate of fire 7.62 × 39 millimetre assault weapons for the pistol calibre 7.62 × 25 millimetre submachine guns they had so effectively utilised during the latter years of the 1939–1945 conflict. The Soviets generally planned to use their AKs at ranges less than 400 metres. When used in conjunction with the machine guns and other vehicle mounted weapons, the AKs and accompanying squad automatic weapons could be used to overwhelm defensive enemy positions with a virtual hail of fire. While the Soviets tacticians knew how they planned to use their infantry weapons, their NATO counterparts did not.

Because they lacked a clearly enunciated tactical doctrine for the employment of infantry weapons, the NATO armies did not fare as well in the development of their first round of infantry weapon rearmament after the war. In the West, the military research and development establishments, often urged on by the industrial organisations manufacturing weapons, drove the creation of new small arms. While the adoption and manufacture of new rifles and machine guns was a beneficial business for both commercial and government arms factories, this approach resulted in new weapon technology being

Small Arms

developed without a clear tactical understanding of the manner in which the hardware would be employed.

In the immediate post-1945 period, the Belgian and British arms design establishments got off to the right start with their respective development of 7 millimetre and 0.276/0.280/0.30 intermediate power cartridges. These cartridges would have been better suited to a modern assault rifle than was the cartridge ultimately standardised by the North Atlantic alliance partners in 1953. Unfortunately, neither British nor Belgian military planners developed a clear tactical doctrine for the employment of a new assault rifle. As a result, they ultimately agreed reluctantly to the adoption of the 7.62 × 51 millimetre NATO cartridge. That American sponsored design was old wine in a new bottle; a full power cartridge in a smaller package (7.62 × 51 millimetre vs the older 7.62 × 63 millimetre).

Largely due to its heavy recoil impulse, the adoption of the 7.62 millimetre NATO cartridge eliminated the possibility of fielding a true assault rifle. Instead the British, Belgians, Canadians and several other NATO armies traded their bolt action World War Two rifles for a second generation self-loading rifle; the Fabrique National *Fusil Automatic Léger* (also called the FAL, L1A1, C1, *Gewehr 1*, etc.). The Germans, Danes, Greeks, Norwegians, Portuguese, and Turks adopted the G3, an evolution of a World War Two Mauser design. A Spanish version, the CETME, was adopted by that nation. The United States standardised a product-improved M1 (Garand) rifle, which they dubbed M14. Most of the FALs and nearly all of the M14s were ultimately issued to NATO troops as single-shot self-loading rifles. The firer was not given the option of full automatic fire.

On the machine gun front, several NATO nations adopted the Fabrique National 7.32 millimetre *Mitrailleuse d'Appui General* (MAG), while the remainder (excluding the United States) adopted NATO calibre versions of the World War Two German MG42 (variously designed MG42/59, MG1, MG3 etc.). The United States developed its own general purpose machine gun, the M60, to fire the NATO cartridge. Whereas the other NATO armies used the MAG and MG42 type weapons for both ground and vehicular applications, the United States adopted its disastrous 7.62 millimetre NATO M73/M219 armour machine guns (now replaced by the MAG and M60 vehicle guns). The Canadians modified their 0.30 calibre Browning M1919A4 machine guns to 7.62 millimetre for vehicle use. All these support weapons will remain standard for the next decade or so.

In the heavy machine gun category, the 0.50 calibre (12.7 millimetre) guns, until very recently little new development had been undertaken. All the NATO armies continue to rely upon the aging, but reliable, 0.550 (12.7 × 99 millimetre) M2 Heavy Barrel (HB) Browning machine gun as a vehicle and infantry support weapon. Until 1979, large scale manufacture of the Browning M2 HB had not been undertaken since 1946. Since then the Saco Defense Systems Division of Maremont Corporation in the United States has renewed

Weapons and Warfare

PLATE 9.2 **The ground version of the Soviet 12.7 × 108 mm NSV heavy machine gun.** This weapon is also found mounted on the T72 and later models of Soviet tanks.

large scale production of that weapon, while the Fabrique National and Ramo Inc. have fabricated this weapon in lesser quantities.

For most of the post-1945 era, the Soviets and their Warsaw Pact allies have used two heavy calibre machine guns the 12.7 × 108 millimetre DShKM (*Degtyareva-Shpagina Krupnokalibernyi Modernizirovannyi*; an updated version of their 1938 gun used in World War Two) and the 1955 vintage 14.5 × 114 millimetre KPV (*Krupnokalibernyi Pulemet Vladiironva*). These weapons have been employed in a variety of roles: infantry support, vehicular mount and anti-aircraft. In the mid 1970s, the Soviets introduced a new 12.7 × 108 millimetre gun called the NSV (after its three designers G. I. Nikitin, Yu. M. Sokolov, and V. I. Volkov). To date this weapon has appeared in ground (infantry support) and tank mounted models. While it still fires the standard Soviet family of 12.7 millimetre ammunition, this weapon appears to be better adapted to modern production techniques. It is likely that this weapon will supplant the DShKM on all T72 and later tanks. One should expect to see it in use for several decades.

The smaller calibre rifle and machine gun inventories of the NATO armies would probably not have undergone much change had it not been for the application of the 5.56 millimetre ArmaLite AR-15 to the jungle warfare of America's conflict in Vietnam. This rifle was the brainchild of Eugene M. Stoner who had taken to heart the early 1950s US Army sponsored operational research studies of infantry weapons usage. Collectively gathered together under the project name *Salvo*, these studies set out to determine just how infantry weapons had been employed during the 1939–1945 war. With the start of the Korean conflict, the *Salvo* team expanded their studies to weapons usage in that war as well.

The *Salvo* inquiries indicated the obvious. They noted that it made little sense to develop weapons of any sort without first considering the tasks to which they were to be applied. Still, in the absence of clearly defined tactical doctrine for future combat, the data on historical usage was the best reasonable guide. One of the most important *Salvo* study findings related to the ranges of engagement involving troops equipped with small calibre weapons. Typical of the findings: "*Of 602 men questioned about the use of the M1 rifle in Korea, 87 percent said that at least 95 percent of all their firing was done at targets within a 300-yard range.*"[5] When even expert riflemen attempted to use the weapon at ranges greater than these, they found that terrain features intervened to prevent adequate target observation and hence, meaningful fire. Indeed, analysis indicated that most infantry kills with aimed shots were made at 100 yards or less. These revelations, coincided with World War Two experience, and suggested that new thinking was required for small arms design.

The random nature of inflicting target hits was the second major conclusion that evolved out of the *Salvo* studies. When targets were actually detected, the stress of combat and the movement of both the target and the firer made it extremely difficult to get an aimed shot at a specific target. If one was wedded to bullet firing weapons, then volume of fire seemed to be the best means of inflicting casualties.

Project *Salvo* seemed to point the way toward a shoulder fired weapon that would produce shotgun-like salvos of projectiles, while maintaining the long range lethality of rifle type bullets. Numerous attempts were made to evolve mechanisms that could launch several bullets with one trigger pull. There were duplex and triplex cartridges, each firing two or three bullets down the barrel. There were multiple barrel firing devices which launched several projectiles simultaneously. But of all of these experiments, the most promising approach technically seemed to be a small calibre rifle that fired at a very high cyclic rate. Enter Eugene M. Stoner and the AR-15 rifle.

The ArmaLite AR-15 was a 0.223 calibre (5.56 millimetre) weapon that fired a high velocity (965 metres per second) 3.56 gram (55 grain) projectile at a cyclic rate of about 850 shots per minute. This weapon could thus deliver large volumes of fire onto a given target area. The killing power[6] of the small bullet derived from its relative higher velocity. Recent studies of wound ballistics point out that projectiles striking key organs such as the brain, heart and liver are almost always fatal. The weight and velocity of the projectile make little difference. Vietnam era post-mortem examination of combat casualties indicated that soldiers struck in the trunk of the body or the extremities by the 0.223 (5.56 millimetre) projectiles suffered more serious wounds than those hit by 7.62 millimetre NATO or 7.62 × 39 millimetre Soviet projectiles. The difference in the wounds first was ascribed to the *higher* velocity of the 5.56 millimetre bullets. More recent research suggests that much of the *effectiveness* of the 5.56 millimetre M193 bullet results from its fragmenting once it enters the human body.[7]

Whatever the source of the improved performance of the 5.56 millimetre, the

PLATE 9.3 **The 5.56 × 45 mm NATO calibre Colt M16A2 rifle with the 40 mm M203 grenade launcher.** To date just over 8 million M16 rifles have been manufactured. Shown here is the latest in the series of rifles evolving from E. M. Stoner's AR-15 rifle.

fact that this power could emanate from a cartridge half the weight and size of the 7.62 millimetre NATO cartridge has had a significant impact upon the design of small arms. The United States Army, after considerable bureaucratic trauma, adopted the AR-15 as the M16A1 rifle in 1967. Since that time, a large number of nations have followed this precedent, with Singapore, the Philippines and South Korea undertaking the manufacture of the M16A1. Since the late 1960s, the arms factories of several other nations including Austria, Belgium, Germany, Israel, Italy and the United Kingdom have also developed 5.56 millimetre rifles. Five of these the Steyr AUG, the Fabrique Nationale FNC, the Heckler & Koch HK33, the Israeli Military Industries Galil, and the Beretta AR70/0.223 have been sold to the ground forces of other nations.

The international shift of Western oriented countrties to the 5.56 × 45 millimetre calibre has accelerated since the 1980 NATO adoption of the 4 gram (62 grain) Fabrique Nationale SS109 projectile as co-standard with the 7.62 millimetre cartridge. The 5.56 millimetre NATO projectile has longer range than the original US M193 bullet and it performs better against body armour. Its wounding effects remain to be fully assessed. The Soviet Union made the shift to a smaller calibre projectile when it introduced the 5.45 × 39 millimetre cartridge in 1974, for which they adapted their AKM (itself a 1959 improvement of the AK-47). Within the past two years, the ground forces of the German Democratic Republic have begun to acquire the 5.45 millimetre MPiKMS-74. The Poles appear to be just starting the conversion to 5.45 millimetre rifles.

Concurrent with the development of the 5.56 millimetre NATO and 5.45 millimetre Soviet cartridges, the NATO and Warsaw Pact armies began to experiment with companion machine guns. This led to the adoption of the Fabrique Nationale Minimi light machine gun as the 5.56 millimetre NATO M249 Squad Automatic Weapon by the US Armed Forces, and as the C9 by the Canadian Armed Forces. While there is still considerable debate within NATO as to the virtues of the 5.56 millimetre cartridge as a support fire

Small Arms

calibre, it is likely that other countries, such as the United Kingdom, will adopt a 5.56 millimetre NATO calibre squad support weapon. Still the 7.62 millimetre NATO machine guns enumerated above can be expected to remain in use for many years.

Within the Soviet bloc, the belt fed 7.62 × 39 millimetre RPD light machine gun had first supplanted by a long barrel, box magazine fed 7.62 × 39 millimetre PRK which was evolved from the AKM assault rifle. Simultaneously, with the adoption of the 5.45 millimetre AK-74, the Soviets introduced their 5.45 millimetre RPKS-74 squad support weapon. To date only Soviet RPKS-74s have been observed, but it is reasonable to expect the other Warsaw Pact countries to adopt this light machine gun version as they field 5.45 millimetre assault rifles.

What of the Future?

The future course of small arms developments is at best poorly defined. Most of the NATO armies are just now getting their conversion programmes to 5.56 millimetre weapons fully under way. Thus in the West there are only a few serious small calibre research and development projects. Since liquid propellants, directed energy, and magnetic propulsion are not likely to be adapted to infantry weapons in the near future, the emphasis remains on further improvements of weapons firing kinetic energy projectiles or exploding munitions. *Bundeswehr* technical developers are placing considerable emphasis on the perfection of their experimental 4.92 × 34 millimetre caseless cartridge *Gewehr 11* (G11), which they would like to field in the mid-1990s. There have been unconfirmed rumours of East European caseless weapon developments for the last decade.

PLATE 9.4 **An early version of the Heckler and Koch 4.92 mm Gewehr 11** which operates in salvo bursts as well as single shots and sustained fire modes. This weapon thus far is the most successful of several attempts to develop a caseless cartridge personal weapon. The *Bundeswehr* hopes to field a version of this weapon in the early 1990s.

Operating principle

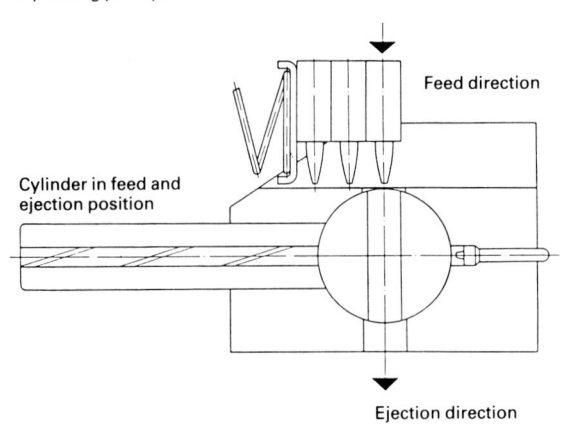

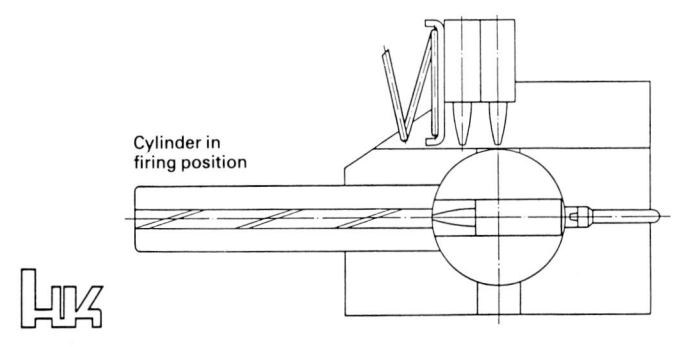

FIG 9.1 A schematic view of the Heckler and Koch 4.92 mm Gewehr 11 which illustrates the unique 'cylinder' breech mechanism designed to shoot a caseless cartridge.

In the United States, the Defense Department Joint Service Small Arms Program (JSSAP) is sponsoring an Advanced Combat Rifle (ACR) development project. Hecker & Koch, Inc. of the US has entered an Americanised version of the G11, while the AAI Corporation's caseless weapon has been terminated. At the end of September 1986, the JSSAP awarded five additional ACR development contracts: Colt Industries; ARES Inc. (E. M. Stoner); AAI Corporation; McDonnell-Douglas Helicopters; and Steyr-Daimler-Puch. It is far too early to predict the fate of any of these projects. Still, it is clear that it will not be easy to field a new weapon until the infantry user community can more clearly define the manner in which they wish to fight with such arms. In the United States there is a need for defining tactical doctrine.

At the beginning of 1986, the United States Army Infantry School issued a small arms development strategy document that challenged the *raison d'être* of the ACR. The Infantry School small arms staff argued, rather effectively, that we may be at the end of the line for fruitful advancements in conventional small arms designs. They noted that the current ACR programme weapon proposals is likely to produce few significant improvements in the probability of hitting enemy soldiers in the field. Modern rifles generally shoot well and true, but the basic fact of life remains that most soldiers do not aim their weapons properly when they pull the trigger. Fired from the hip or partially aimed, the rifle is, at best, a suppressive effect mechanism. It is not an effective killer. As a result, the Infantry School staff has suggested that the United States Army look to other technologies, such as improved grenade launchers that will use air bursting munitions. For example, a more sophisticated descendant of the shoulder firing grenade launchers used by the American and Soviet armies.

While their small arms strategy document has caused furore among the players in the American small arms development community, the Infantry School has clearly pointed up the central issue. Any arm needs to know how it will fight and against what enemies before it can launch a meaningful research and development programme for new weapons.

Recommendations

In the future the international infantry community needs to take a more active role in clearly stating requirements for new weapons. And in addition to taking such an active role, they need to participate more fully in the research, development, and acquisition (RD&A) process throughout all of its phases. Infantrymen have always taken pride in the fact that they spearhead the advance on the battlefield. In like manner, the infantry community needs to be the guide for the technical research and development (R&D) community. The men who use the guns need to tell those who develop them what they expect the weapons to accomplish and within what general physical parameters the infantry would like to have those weapon fall. Then the infantry community should cooperate and participate throughout the RD&A cycle until the next generation of weapons are available for distribution to its troops.

While all this sounds very simple and basic, historically it has not been the way the system has worked. Coordination between the using service (Infantry) and the technical service (Ordnance) has never been noteworthy. As noted earlier, the technical community generally has taken the lead in determining the basic specifications for infantry weapons. This has either been the result of the ordnance people having stolen the march on the infantry, or of the ordnance people having picked up the leadership role once it became obvious that the infantry community was not going to be timely in reacting to the possibilities offered by emerging technology. The lines of communication between the infantry and ordnance teams can always stand improvement. A few specifics will underscore the need for closer coordination between the infantry and the ordnance communities.

Weapons and Warfare

The infantry needs an arsenal of reliable weapons and ammunition, in quantities sufficient to sustain initial operations, available at all times so that its forces can react immediately to any crisis – from small scale deployment to full scale conflict. But upon examination of the historical record, it is apparent that few armies have entered a major conflict with the required number and types of standard rifles and machine guns. This fact has led to the repeated reliance upon substitute weapons and the need to acquire weapons after mobilisation. In future conflicts there is likely to be very little time to get organised and on the road. This zero lead-time at the start of any future conflict means that such a war will have to be fought with weapons and equipment already in place.

In the world of infantry weapons RD & A there is a constant tension between acquiring existing patterns of weapons and developing new ones. On the acquisition side of the coin, the infantry community needs that magic number of *sufficient* weapons to keep its troops equipped and to make up for field losses. On the development side of the coin, there is generally the desire to obtain *better* infantry equipment. Before 1945, world-wide the production of weapons took precedence over development. Since the end of World War Two, the emphasis in many countries has been placed upon R & D. But those priorities have been established by the Technical Community, with the concurrence of the Infantry.

Today, armies need to pursue a balanced programme of acquisition and R & D. Only the infantryman working in concert with his development organisation can guarantee the balance that is required. Take for example the American rifle scene, which involves two major programmes: the current M16A2 rifle acquisition programme and the current Advanced Combat Rifle R & D activity. The American Infantry needs the M16A2 in sufficient quantities to equip its regular and ready reserve troops. But the M16A2 rifle, like all of its predecessors, will not be the standard rifle forever. In fact, if things go as desired by the American development community, fielding of an Advanced Combat Rifle could begin in the same year as the last of the replacement complement of M16A2s are delivered.

Obviously, there is a potential conflict here between the existing standard and its possible replacement. Conflicts such as this are not necessarily bad, especially if properly managed. In fact they are an inevitable part of the RD & A process. The infantry community must be prepared to tell its ministerial superiors that, in some cases, it needs both such projects to be pursued as a top priority at the same time.

To convince the money providers to make funds available for both, the Infantry will need to be able to tell them just how they intend to fight with each type of weapon, rifle, machine gun, grenade launcher, vehicle killer and the like. That calls for clearly articulated doctrine and equally precise interrelated requirements statements.

By predicting the types of weapons required on the modern battlefield (mission are analyses and threat analyses), the manner in which they are likely to be used (doctrinal analyses), and an estimation of the numbers of weapons required to counter the threat, the Infantry serves not just itself. This makes life much easier for the technical community and the industrial community as well. Those communities then know the direction the RD & A should go, rather than trying to second guess that direction. And such clarity of purpose can lead to better weapons in being and still better ones in the development pipeline.

Years ago General Julian S. Hatcher, a career American Ordnance officer, noted in one of his publications that in the R & D business the *"best was the enemy of the good"*. By which he meant that the search for the ideal weapon often led users and developers to pass over the weapon most suitable at the moment. There is a corollary for Hatcher's law – *"The adequate is the enemy of the next"*. By that I mean that today's good weapon leads to complacency and a failure to look for its replacement. The Infantry user, the technical developer, and the industrial manufacturer must work together to insure that good weapons are always available for the infantryman, while working to guarantee that he will always have the next generation weapon as quickly as possible. That is a challenging undertaking, but it should be an enduring goal.

Notes

1. Harry G Summers, Jr., 'Ground Warfare Lessons,' In Bruce W Watson and Peter M Dunn, eds., *Military Lessons of the Falkland Islands War: Views from the United States* (Boulder, CO: Westview Press, 1984): 67–68.
2. As with all generalisations, this one has its exceptions. For example, the Federal Republic of Germany's *Bundeswehr* has used two of the three generations (7.92 × 57 millimetre World War Two calibre, 7.62 × 51 millimetre NATO calibre) but appears ready to forego adoption of the 5.56 × 45 millimetre NATO calibre and go directly to the 4.92 millimetre caseless type ammunition when it becomes available.
3. For more in depth studies supporting this argument see Edward C Ezell, *The Great Rifle Controversy: Search for the Ultimate Infantry Weapon from World War II through Vietnam and Beyond* (Harrisburg, PA: Stackpole Books, 1984), *The AK47 Story: Evolution of the Kalashnikov Weapons* (Harrisburg, PA: Stackpole Books, 1986).
4. In cartridge designations the first element denotes the bore diameter while the second indicates the length of the cartridge case by itself.
5. Operations Research Office, *Operational Requirements for an Infantry Weapon*, by Normal Hitchman. Technical Memorandum ORO-T-160 (Johns Hopkins University, 19 June 1952).
6. Terms such as killing power and lethality are very controversial. They defy scientific definition. Generally, '*killing power*' has been measured in terms of kinetic energy ($KE = 1/2\ MV^2$). What the light AR-15 bullet lacked in weight it made up in velocity. Recent research Colonel Martin L Fackler, MD of the US Army Medical Corps suggests that the wounding/killing function of bullets leaves much to be defined. See for example, M L Fackler, J S Surinchak and J A Malilowski, '*Wounding potential of the Russian AK-74 assault rifle,*' *The Journal of Trauma*, 24 (1984): 263–266 with bibliography.
7. M L Fackler, J S Surinchak, J A Malinowski, et al., '*Bullet fragmentation: A major cause of tissue disruption,*' *The Journal of Trauma*, 24 (1984): 35–39 with bibliography.

Introducing Chapter 10

IN two world wars Great Britain survived only by defeating the submarine menace. In any future global conflict that threat will, again, need to be overcome but anti-submarine warfare assumes an even greater urgency because the nuclear deterrents of both East and West depend in the main upon submarine launched intercontinental ballistic missiles. Add to this the characteristics of nuclear submarines, operating at considerable depths, silently, with no need to surface and capable of considerable speed, and the awesome nature of the problem is immediately apparent.

10

Anti-submarine and Mine Warfare

CAPTAN B R LONGWORTH RN AND
MAJOR GENERAL KEN PERKINS

ASW

ANTI-Submarine Warfare (ASW), by its very nature, is a secret war. The primary advantage of the submarine over surface forces lies in its exploitation of stealth or surprise. The success of the submarine has been dependent upon its ability to retain this advantage in spite of the advances in anti-submarine capability developed over the years.

Unlike all other forms of maritime warfare, there have only been two major ASW campaigns in history. Since the end of the Second World War there has been no war, large or small, in which ASW has played a significant part and in which the balance of capability between the submarine and its adversaries has been assessable, demonstrated or confirmed. In 1945, the submarine had been defeated primarily because it lost its inherent invisibility in the face of overwhelming ASW air power. In the ensuing forty years there have been enormous strides in both submarine capability and that of underwater sensors and weapons. Notwithstanding the lack of *hard kill* evidence, it is the intent of this chapter to examine the balance of ASW capability today and to assess both where we stand and what the future might offer.

To deal with the submarine it is necessary both to locate and to destroy it. The first requirement therefore is to find and identify the target and with the technical advances in nuclear submarine (SSN) design and general availability of long range weapons, both air flight and underwater, long range acoustic detection has become an essential ingredient of defensive ASW. Such detections are dependent upon the acoustic environment which is both complex and unpredictable. They are, in themselves, of little value unless detection can be followed by sufficiently reliable identification. But bottom mounted arrays, towed arrays, and even hull mounted equipment on both escorts and submarines can detect the target. When circumstances are favourable they do so with some assurance, when as all too often they are not, it can be a different

Weapons and Warfare

PLATE 10.1 **Tigerfish Torpedo.** A view of a decommissioned HMS Lowestoft, in use as a target ship, with her back broken by a Tigerfish heavyweight torpedo.
(Marconi Underwater Systems)

story. Detection then becomes uncertain or fleeting and subsequent classification at least unreliable and, at the worst, damagingly wrong. Underwater sound therefore, its sources and the variability of its propagation, dominates ASW sensor technology and hence the nature of the underwater battle.

Thus it is the environment which creates most of the problems and defines the opportunities for advancement in ASW. Whilst above water sensor and weapon performance can be accurately prescribed and mathematical models define capabilities as the sum of related probabilities, in underwater warfare we are faced with far higher levels of uncertainty.

Paradoxically, it is because water is such an excellent conductor of sound that difficulties are created. If, like radar in the atmosphere, sound simply travelled through the sea in straight lines to horizon distance, if its attenuation was accurately forecastable and its performance not degraded by all manner of environmental characteristics including temperature, density, depth, volume reverberation, own ship's motion, seabed conductivity, and reflections from seabed or surface, ambient noise levels and biological disturbance – life would be simpler. Acoustic propagation difficulties are caused not so much by the fact that sound propagation is variable, but because some changes may be predicted with confidence while many may not. The sea is a variable medium and small changes have major effects. So, in conditions which are apparently identical, small changes in the water structure of which you may not be aware, five, ten or more miles away, may radically affect detection capability.

Anti-submarine and Mine Warfare

There are sources other than sound which may yield information on a submarine's presence of which the best known is the airborne magnetic anomaly detector. Persistent wakes, temperature differences, changes in water chemical structure – all these effects occur after passage of any vessel surfaced or submerged, but even if they may give a detection opportunity in certain specialised circumstances, at present they do not seem to offer any possibility of providing a more reliable, secure or longer range capability than acoustics.

The best sensors are those which give nothing away and the main thrust of post-war development has been towards improving passive sonars.

Submarine Radiated Noise

All vessels, whether surface ships or submerged submarines, emit some noise, the main sources being internal machinery, propeller noise and flow noise past the hull. The conventional battery powered submarine at low speed can become almost silent by closing down virtually all machinery, except its battery powered electric motors. Only if forced to increase speed to close a target, or to snorkel and run diesels to recharge batteries, is there any significant sound output. The nuclear powered submarine, on the other hand, does not have that option, for so far it has proved necessary to circulate coolant through the reactor at all times. Sound associated with the reactor and associated auxiliary machinery may therefore form a major part of the acoustic signature of a nuclear submarine.

Submarines, nuclear or conventional, have two distinctive speed ranges which yield different acoustic characteristics. A low speed mode where, as far as possible, deliberate steps are made to reduce noise, but where machinery noise may still be significant, and a high speed regime, where operational requirements take priority and increased hull or propeller noise may make the submarine relatively easy to detect. Both machinery noise, which originates in the mechanical vibration of primarily rotating machinery and is coupled to the sea via the hull, and propeller noise, which is transmitted directly into the water, have a common feature. The noise emitted is a spectrum in which the original sources may be identified by lines at fundamental or harmonic frequencies; machinery line components may therefore permit identification of a particular type of submarine.

Sound Propagation

The lower the frequency of the noise emitted by the submarine target, the less it is attenuated by passage through the sea. It is the low frequency noise sources which yield the best long range detection opportunities.

The route by which radiated noise reaches a detector is dependent upon both the depth of water and its thermal structure. The principle propagation modes are the direct path (sometimes providing a surface duct), convergence

Weapons and Warfare

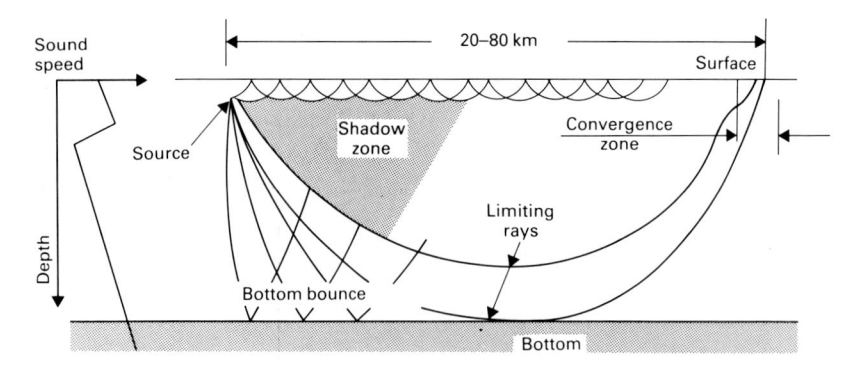

FIG 10.1 Sound propagation.

zone, bottom bounce and deep sound channels (see Figs 10.1 and 10.2). Whenever the water is sufficiently deep the sound waves which are refracted downwards by decreasing temperature are in turn refracted upwards when the water temperature becomes stable and the effects of increasing pressure cause the sound velocity to increase once more. As the sound approaches the surface it is focused together, with a consequent reduction in transmission loss. This process may be repeated but eventually the sound is dissipated into the deep sound channels. Submarine or surface ship passive systems, whether hull mounted or towed array, make use of the direct path and convergence zone modes.

If the depth of water is sufficient for the velocity of sound to reach, and then exceed that at the surface, the thermal structure creates a depressed sound channel with the point of minimum velocity acting as the axis of the channel. This situation occurs in almost all the deep ocean basins of the world; the deep sound channel therefore is a normal, not an exceptional, phenomena, and it is

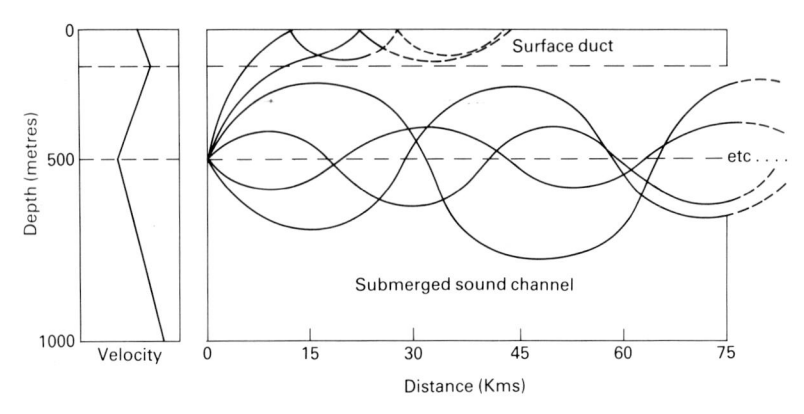

FIG 10.2 Sound propagation.

Anti-submarine and Mine Warfare

the deep sound channel which provides the propagation path most commonly exploited by undersea surveillance systems.

In shallow water these very long range effects disappear and additional features such as the type of seabed, the strength of tides and opacity of the water add to the variables which affect propagation. Shallow water has a deserved reputation for making ASW difficult – for both sensors and weapons – and at other than close range (sonobuoys for example) passive systems have very little part to play. There is little choice therefore other than to use active sonar for submarine detection – unsatisfactory as this may be for the target will always detect the sound pulses of the transmitting sonar at greater range than the transmitting vessel will detect the returning echoes.

Surface Ship and Submarine Sonar Limitations

The surface ship has never been a satisfactory platform from which to mount acoustic sensors. Passive sonars have been particularly ineffective, but active sonars are limited by temperature layers or sea state and restricted by the shallow fixed depth of the transducer. Some improvements have been effected by towing a transducer in a variable depth body, but size and usable power are inhibiting, and even the combination of a Variable Depth Source (VDS) and a hull mounted set may alleviate but cannot get round all degradation in sonar performance caused by the environment.

It is therefore necessary, and is indeed common practice, to assess the available data and to predict the range of each type of sonar set for the day. For the reasons discussed, this predicted range can be optimistic – sometimes by very large factors.

The main problem with active sonar, however, is not the range of detection but the uncertainty of making any detection at all. Unless previously alerted to the presence of a possible submarine, operators are notoriously bad at recognising submarine echoes or classifying non-sub contacts correctly. Current sonar development concentrates on improving the certainty of detection and correct classification by computer aiding rather than achieving increased range. As a further complication, sonar operators often find that when in contact with a submarine, that contact is subject to random fading, a feature which is probably caused by internal waves. The existence of these internal waves, a Russian discovery, is itself fairly recent and they are likely to be caused by the upward or downward momentum of small volumes of water. These oscillations propagate horizontally and they are observed as internal waves creating variable and largely unforeseeable temperature gradients.

It is not surprising therefore that the submarine which is a better sonar platform, uses passive sonar as its primary sensor. These sonars take the form of bow arrays or chin arrays, large horizontal arrays on the flanks of each submarine, or smaller arrays on the fin to cover the arcs. These passive systems give ranges which cover out to the first convergence zone but they have been

Weapons and Warfare

PLATE 10.2 **Submarine showing a bow-mounted sonar.** *(Marconi Underwater Systems)*

limited firstly because the submarine's self-noise interferes with detection and, secondly, the submarine hull configuration limits the size and shape of the hydrophone arrays that can be fitted. All these factors inhibit the sensitivity of the submarine sonar equipment.

The Towed Array

A break-through has, however, been achieved with the towed array. The towed sonar array, available for use by both submarines and surface ships, provides the most important advance in submarine-detection capability, since the post-war advent of medium-range active sonars.

Towed array sonar is a line of low frequency hydrophones mounted in a flexible neutrally buoyant tube which can be towed at a considerable distance from the towing vessel, well clear of the vessel's own noise sources. Arrays which are currently entirely passive in operation, may be up to several hundred metres in length depending upon the frequency coverage aimed for and the array gain required.

Nothing might seem easier than assembling a long string of hydrophones, enclosing them in a tube and towing them through water. But in reality towed array technology is both specialised and highly exacting. Great physical

Anti-submarine and Mine Warfare

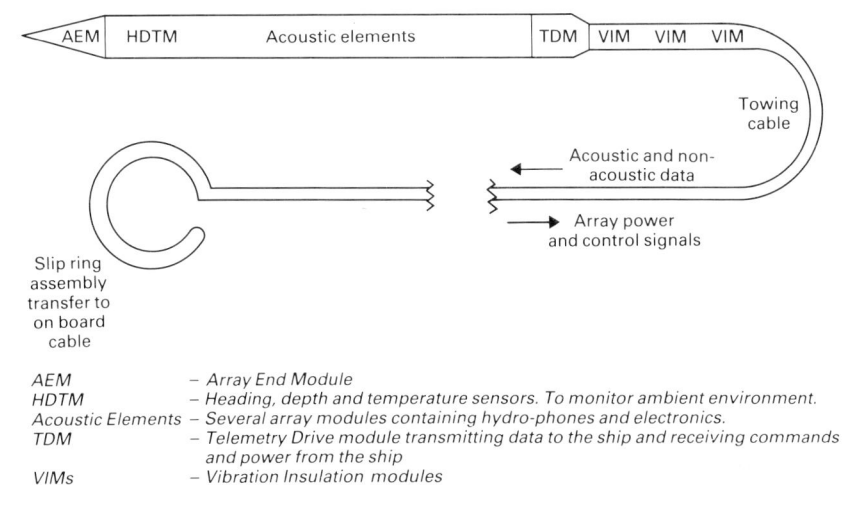

```
AEM | HDTM | Acoustic elements | TDM | VIM | VIM | VIM
                                                      Towing
                                                      cable
                                    Acoustic and non-
                                    acoustic data
                                    Array power
                                    and control signals
Slip ring
assembly
transfer to
on board
cable
```

AEM — Array End Module
HDTM — Heading, depth and temperature sensors. To monitor ambient environment.
Acoustic Elements — Several array modules containing hydro-phones and electronics.
TDM — Telemetry Drive module transmitting data to the ship and receiving commands and power from the ship
VIMs — Vibration Insulation modules

FIG 10.3 Towed Array.

strength is needed if the array is not to tear itself apart as the ship increases speed. Hydrophone and associated processor design calls for both rugged simplicity and sophisticated electronic complexity, flow noise has to be eliminated as far as possible, ship's noise or strumming of the towing cable must not interfere, the array must be stable and remain aligned at slow speed – and so on.

Depending upon configuration, they can fulfil three primary functions:

Self-protection
Tactical support
Area surveillance.

The towed array was first introduced into service as a submarine sensor, both to give passive cover in the blind arcs of the conformal bow sonar and to provide a low-frequency passive capability well clear of own ship noise. For a number of practical reasons, these arrays were relatively short and, in comparison with surface deployed systems, are likely to remain so.

The larger arrays, which can be more easily used by surface ships, offer both greater detection-ranges and high classification, and are well suited either to provide ASW protection in depth or to enhance the surveillance offered by fixed seabed systems.

Towed Array Performance

The performance of a towed array is more complex than that of conventional hull-mounted sonars, and imposes unique operational and tactical restrictions that must be fully understood if its performance is to be optimised. It is a complicated matter, the main elements of which are bearing accuracy, ambiguity, interference or masking, the variability of detection range, the resulting problems of investigating the contact and difficulty of determining range.

Bearing accuracy is dependent upon the array beam width and the stability of the array. A heading compass is fitted to each array, but when towed, maybe two miles astern of a slowly moving ship, some inaccuracies are inevitable. Beam-width accuracy is a function of the frequency, the length of the line array of hydrophones and the angle at which the sound is received at the array. Generally speaking, the lower the frequency and the greater the angle of incidence to the line of the array, the greater is the beam width. As the effective beam width increases, the ratio of array signal to noise decreases, thus reducing array performance, although this is hardly a primary factor in determining detection range. But, for practical purposes, in a modern array for frequencies over the range primarily covered, accuracy would vary from 2° on the beam to about 5° towards the bow or stern.

As the beam pattern is all-round, a target can lie either side of the array – thus producing a mirror image effect or *ambiguity* which has to be resolved either by the towing ship intentionally altering course or at close ranges from observation of target movement. Inevitably, these alterations of course take time for the plot to resolve target bearing, and even small alterations of course require time for the array to settle down on its new heading. The resolution of ambiguity can be time-consuming.

The detection ranges actually achieved are perhaps the most sensitive element in a sensitive subject. Detection range depends upon target radiated noise levels, frequency, sonar propagation paths, flow noise in the array, background noise or ambient noise in the sea, signal to noise ratios and the array gain. A towed array is a noise limited sonar susceptible to both background and flow noise. For this reason, detection ranges will also be dependent upon towing speed, the distance astern and depth at which the array is towed. Last but not least, performance will depend upon the background noise created by sea state, wind and rain.

Given this variability, detection performance cannot be discussed in simple terms. Indeed, it is usually quoted as a matter of relative probability rather than as a firm factor. But it is reasonable to suppose that, in good conditions and at optimum towing speeds, ranges in excess of 100 kilometres can be achieved to a high order of probability. At any specific time, and in the particular environmental conditions obtaining, a good assessment of detection ability can be made by careful analysis.

Detection at great range is all very well, but if a range of 100 kilometres is reasonably anticipated, a single ship may detect all contacts within some 25,000 square kilometres of ocean. Furthermore, in peace time, a large number of ships will inevitably be present, creating contacts, all of which need to be classified, checked for ambiguity, plotted and reported.

Anti-submarine and Mine Warfare

Resolution of the contact would be simpler if range were easily determined, but the resolution of the actual range of a contact is perhaps the most difficult problem facing a towed array frigate. Inherent bearing inaccuracy and the lack of bearing movement at the longer ranges reduce the effectiveness of traditional bearings-only analysis techniques. There is no simple way of telling whether the contact is by direct path, bottom bounce or first, second or even third convergence zone.

Perhaps the most restrictive aspect of towed array operations is that third party assistance is essential unless the contact is so close that the vessel's own active sonar can be employed. Rotary or fixed-wing aircraft are normally used but success is dependent upon range estimation which, as discussed before, may be inaccurate. The greater the detection range, the greater the uncertainty, but at least the time gained by making long range detection may give adequate opportunity to follow up and prosecute.

Towed array operations thus provide, on the one hand, the opportunity for long range detection of the enemy, but, on the other hand, their use entails a number of operational uncertainties which offer no simple solutions to the Command. They are in no way a lower cost substitute for a hull-mounted sonar. The two are complementary, to operate in different circumstances or in different deep or shallow water environments. But so great is the advance in detection opportunity which a towed array provides that an *ASW escort* hardly merits such a designation today unless an array is fitted.

Towed arrays are no universal panacea, but for the first time they offer a detection capability to the Fleet little less effective than that of the opposing submarines.

The Aircraft

The aircraft is, in many ways, the ideal ASW platform. Virtually immune from counter-attack by the submarine, it is able to deploy over and search very large areas of sea. The advances in signal processing and display which have made the towed array possible have contributed much to the increased effectiveness of airborne systems. The aircraft's main sensor, the sonobuoy, has been radically improved, both in making simple devices smaller and in providing buoys with directional capability and increased sensitivity. They remain, however, relatively short range devices and large numbers of buoys are needed to search large areas. However, if ranges are relatively short, the vagaries of long range propagation are avoided. The probablities of contact and correct classification are then higher than with many other sonars. If the maritime aircraft has some prior knowledge of the presence of a target in the search area, possibly from a fixed seabed surveillance system, then its effectiveness is immeasurably increased.

Once a target is located, the aircraft has the choice of refining the position passively or, more positively, by using an active buoy to pinpoint the target.

Weapons and Warfare

PLATE 10.3 **Sea King Helicopter with sonar dome.** *(Marconi Underwater Systems)*

However, the active buoy requires caution. Its use will immediately alert the submarine and permit evasion or possibly, at some future date, the launch of an anti-aircraft missile.

I have used the term aircraft indiscriminately to cover both the large shore based maritime patrol aircraft and the ship-borne helicopter. Both can carry similar sensor and weapon fits, but although the helicopter is restricted in terms of range, payload and endurance, as compared with the fixed wing aircraft, it enjoys the important advantage of being able to use an active dunking sonar – a device which, because of its random application, is most unsettling to a submarine. And dunking sonar is the one active system which offers exciting possibilities for the future.

Deep Ocean Surveillance

In simplistic terms, an ocean surveillance system is a fixed array of hydrophones laid on the seabed and connected to a receiving station by means of a submarine cable. To be effective these arrays need to be placed close to the axis of the deep ocean channels – that is 3,000 or 4,000 feet in the Atlantic.

The techniques by which these cables are laid are therefore those of the Cable Industry and the ships used are converted cable vessels. Special techniques have had to be developed, however, to lay the arrays which are heavy and extremely robust – they have to be, for the standard called for is to remain effective without any maintenance for a minimum of twenty-five years.

The ocean basins have many common features. For example, the continental shelves almost invariably end in steep cliffs which drop down to level plains. These may be interrupted by mountain ranges or by islands or seamounts, but these features permit the siting of the arrays at the optimum depth. There are few deep ocean areas which do not lend themselves to the effective siting of surveillance systems.

Detection Capability

As with the towed array, the detection capablity of any hydrophone array depends upon a complex relationship where range of detection varies with sound level, propagation loss, array gain and the recognition differential of the signal processing. In other words, the range achieved varies with the noise output of the source, attenuated as it spreads evenly through the ocean but concentrated by the underwater sound channel, and which has to be detected against the overall background noise of the sea.

The ambient or background noise is ever present but it is directional to a degree depending upon shipping concentrations or prevailing winds. Careful siting of the array can result in significant reductions of this background noise. A detailed hydrographic survey is essential if the best locations are to be found, both from the point of view of reduced ambient noise and physical ability to place the array on a particular slope or at a particular location. Mistakes are expensive and not easy to rectify.

SOSUS

The United States Navy's ASW Surveillance system SOSUS (Sound Surveillance System), covers much of the Atlantic and Pacific Oceans, but the location of arrays or the extent of coverage is a well kept secret.

Although nuclear power transformed the submarine offensive capability, the nuclear submarine was at first a relatively easy target for surveillance systems. It is not surprising that the sixties and early seventies saw a resurgence of interest in SOSUS and an expansion of the system. As Soviet nuclear submarines have become progressively quieter, it has become essential to improve the system to keep pace with submarine quietening, taking full advantage of technical advances in array design and data transfer over long distances, as well as the ability of the high capability digital computer to process the detailed harmonic analysis required at the shore stations.

Limitations of the Surveillance Systems

It is perhaps pertinent to recognise what deep surveillance systems do not do. Like towed arrrays, they provide only a bearing of a contact not a range,

range being obtained from long term target movement or, occasionally, cross fixing between different systems. They offer the possibility of attrition – they do not provide immediately processable contacts, for underwater propagation is enormously variable and differences over a few hours of plus or minus 6 to 9 decibels are not uncommon. At any one time particular probabilities of detection are offered which may not be high but, cumulatively, they add up to a significant figure.

You do not need to know where arrays are actually sited to make an assessment of their overall capability. Detection ranges may be measured in hundreds rather than in tens of miles, and it needs little imagination to estimate which areas of ocean are of priority interest. NATO happens to own the real estate along the track of Soviet submarine deployment routes so clearly these can be covered.

Surveillance arrays do not however provide *barriers* which pick off targets on the way through, for the focal areas where submarines may have to pass rarely offer good detection conditions. Because they are focal areas, ambient noise levels are high and difficult propagation conditions are almost invariably present. But when these arrays are used in association with other systems, submarine or airborne, it is unlikely that many Soviet submarines can run the gauntlet from the Northern Fleet bases to patrol areas in the Atlantic without their presence, if not their actual position at any moment, being known.

Overall ASW Detection Capability

Modern passive systems enable ASW to be played on a very wide stage indeed. ASW measures have historically been successful through a process of attrition, whereby a submarine is harassed at all stages of his attack. Modern ASW, if not significantly increasing the chances of detection at each opportunity, greatly increases the time at which the submarine is at risk, and hence the number of opportunities and the cumulative rate of attrition.

In the 1970s, a typical protective force might have included long range maritime patrol (LRMP) aircraft in close support at about thirty miles, helicopters dipping in mid-field, and surface escorts forming a close random screen at about five miles. Today the same LRMP aircraft, armed with far more effective sonobuoys, using processors no less capable than those of the towed array ships, are more likely to be at over one hundred miles. The towed array escorts therefore fill a new mid-field at about fifty miles, supported by helicopters to follow up their contacts, and a limited number of surface escorts still provide close defence against a torpedo-firing submarine which might penetrate the outer layer of protection. This defence may be further expanded by towed array submarines. With a total detection capacity extending to beyond two hundred miles radius, the problems of assessing and prosecuting contacts over this 125,000 square miles of ocean can be formidable.

This operation area is but part of the ocean covered by the deep surveillance

Anti-submarine and Mine Warfare

system. These are connected via an extensive satellite communication network, providing for the complete integration of underwater surveillance capability, whether by fixed systems, surface ship towed arrays or long range maritime patrol aircraft – real time ASW threat evaluation on a global scale.

Submarines will, of course, continue to get quieter through better design and as the submarine crews become more attuned to the dangers of noise emission. However, signal processing capability is improving in its turn as both array and processing technology develops. At present it appears that the one is keeping pace with the other, but quietening may eventually triumph. When this happens, long range passive detection may be a thing of the past. Just when and if this might happen will have a fundamental effect on the requirement for future sensors and the most appropriate platforms on which to deploy them, or indeed on the requirements for weapons to match sensor capability.

Weapons

All ASW Weapons are dependent upon the critical factor of initial submarine detection and classification, which determines the type of weapon needed. Unless very short range engagements (as typified by a World War Two mortar or aircraft depth charge attack) are considered, the slow data rate, the inaccuracies of sonar ranges and bearings and the lack of any ability to judge submarine depth, all demand a weapon which is itself capable of seeking out the target. And this is unlikely to change. The style of the delivery vehicle, the speed of reaction, the range at which an attack is practicable, all offer scope for improvement, but the fundamental nature of any terminal weapon is unlikely to be different. ASW is therefore dominated by the anti-submarine homing torpedo.

In an age when nations are encouraged to achieve standardisation in weapons but rarely do, one remarkable piece of standardisation has been achieved, more by accident than design. Almost without exception, submarine launched weapons are 21 inches or 533 millimetres in diameter and roughly the same length of 6 metres. This is both a remarkable achievement and an unusual constraint for it both circumscribes the performance obtainable from a weapon of these dimensions and similarly restricts the other types of weapons that might be deployed from the same launching tubes – Sub Harpoon or Tomahawk for example. Significantly the Soviet Navy has now introduced 26 inch weapons – perhaps others will follow.

The modern torpedo is therefore a compromise. Firstly, there is a balance between endurance, size of warhead and the weapons control equipment, for more of the one is only achieved at the loss of another; the maximum size is absolute. Secondly, whilst forty years ago the weapon was designed solely for use as an offensive weapon against surface ships, over the years the submarine has increasingly to regard the enemy submarine as its main adversary. The requirements for anti-surface ship and anti-submarine weapons are funda-

Weapons and Warfare

mentally different and the task of achieving a common weapon to do both tasks well is difficult.

At first sight, the surface ship target might appear to be a simple problem for there is no uncertainty as to depth, and determining the range, course and speed of the vessel is relatively easy. Selection of the firing range (at least for the SSN) can be at the behest of the submarine and the risk of counter detection can be minimised. Frequently, the submarine can control the firing position and the time of the attack, but these advantages only occur when the torpedo is itself sufficiently capable to localise its target towards the end of the firing run. Terminal homing against a surface ship presents difficulties to the torpedo designer for the weapon has to reject wake echoes, disregard noise makers deployed as countermeasures and remain effective in sea states where surface reflections can also create false echoes. These features have not been easy to include in a weapon optimised against a submarine target. With limited weapon stowage, individual weapons for individual targets are not an attractive alternative. The current tendency is to regard the anti-ship sub launched missile as the primary anti-ship weapon, but no submarine can be undefended against a counter-attacking escort at short range and the torpedo will always have to retain an anti-ship capability.

The Anti-submarine Weapon

The submarine versus submarine engagement is a far more complex affair and the different characteristics of the target call for differing homing techniques in the weapon. In any individual encounter there is a balance of advantage between the contenders, dependent upon the capability of the sonars fitted, the relative effectiveness of noise quietening and the submarine's speed through the water.

The over-riding aim is to remain undetected and to ensure that a weapon reaches the target without giving the target a chance to counter-attack. Using passive methods of detection alone has obvious disadvantages for detection is itself uncertain and variable, and the determination of range can be both time consuming and (unless the target is unwelcomely close) inaccurate.

The option of using an active transmission to determine accurate range might be foolhardy for it would almost certainly be intercepted and secrecy lost. In this cat and mouse game you may know in which direction lies the enemy, you are only likely to know his range with a level of accuracy that decreases with the square of the range, and you will not know his depth at all. To fire first is vital, What the submarine does not know, the weapon has to work out for itself.

To this end, the modern submarine launched anti-submarine torpedo has to meet a number of requirements which are at times mutually exclusive:

▷ it has to be fast enough to overtake and attack an evading target and yet be

Anti-submarine and Mine Warfare

quiet enough not to be detected itself. (Conventional wisdom is that a torpedo needs a speed advantage one and a half times that of its quarry.)
▷ It requires sufficient range and endurance to cover up for any inaccuracies in the submarine's estimate of where the target is.
▷ It has to be controllable with sufficient accuracy to place the torpedo into a position where its own sensors can determine the target's validity, position, aspect and depth.
▷ It must be able to distinguish between real and false targets and disregard counter-measures.
▷ The combustion products should not produce a detactable wake.
▷ It must be lethal.

The problems to be solved in meeting these criteria divide into these main areas: guidance, propulsion and homing, each involving separate technical disciplines but each being interdependent upon the other.

Guidance. This term covers the solution of the fire control problem, control of the torpedo until its own sensors are brought into play and the interface between the operator and the torpedo. Virtually all weapons use wire guidance to achieve this although the nature of the information that can be passed via the wire between submarine and weapon, and the means by which the wire is dispensed between the two, differ considerably in different torpedoes.

Wire guidance techniques rely upon the torpedo paying out wire as it speeds away whilst at the same time wire is paid off from a separate source within the submarine to compensate for submarine movement, thus ensuring that there is no strain on the very thin guidance wire. The currently favoured technique is to use a tube or hose pipe to keep the wire clear of the submarine as it pays out. A failure because the guidance wire parts is becoming increasingly rare in all weapons, although restrictions are imposed upon the firing submarine both in speed during launch and in its evasive manoeuvres after launch. Guidance ranges up to twenty miles are not uncommon.

For the future, fibre optics offer the option of an even thinner connection. Furthermore, they provide an enormous band width which will impose few restrictions on the data to be passed between torpedo and submarine. Future torpedo designers may well have the option of increasing the torpedo's self-reliance or of employing tighter control from the firing vessel, an option which may be attractive in a primarily anti-ship weapon.

Propulsion. Extremely high power outputs are required from a small engine and all the fuels and combustible products have to be carried within the torpedo. Until the forties, the conventional thermal engined weapon used high pressure air as the fuel oxidant, hardly an efficient method as 80% of the gas carried was inert nitrogen. Attempts to introduce more efficient oxidants had

Weapons and Warfare

a chequered history but the Japanese persevered with liquid oxygen and their Type 93 torpedo is still in service. High test peroxide was experimented with by Germany, tested disastrously by Britain in the fifties, toyed with by the United States in the Mark 16 weapon which remained in service until 1972, but was successfully tamed by Sweden, whose Type 61 weapon is still in service.

A more promising approach came with the mono propellant, a compound which contains its own oxygen and releases it to sustain combustion. The first successful application was Otto fuel, an oily, stable and effective fuel which was selected in the fifties and early sixties to power the United States Mark 46 lightweight and later the Mark 48 heavyweight torpedoes. Although Otto fuel offered a high energy density and hence higher speed and endurance, European nations persevered with the alternative of battery propulsion which, although generating less power, had two advantages. They were less noisy than the piston driven US engines and were in tune with an attack philosophy which relied upon stealth during the torpedoes' approach and secondly, their performance was independent of depth, where thermal engines had to contend with increasing back pressure. The overall speed disadvantage of the battery, however, is such that the threat imposed by the later submarine designs of the seventies has made conventional battery propulsion outmoded. Indeed the Otto fuel thermal engine too is limited for, without additional oxidant, much of the energy available in Otto fuel is wasted. For the future, three possibilities are open:

▷ the combination of Otto fuel with an oxidant to increase the releasable energy.
▷ The use of a closed cycle thermal engine which combines metallic lithium with sodium hexafluoride to generate very high temperatures, heating steam to drive a turbine.
▷ The use of advanced thermal batteries employing a variety of lithium derivations.

Although it appears likely that an advanced battery will finally emerge, with all the advantages that battery propulsion offers, a good deal of development is necessary before the conflicting demands of very high power outputs and safety can be reconciled.

To update the Mark 48 torpedo, the Americans were able to enhance mobile performance by increasing fuel stowage. The option of using a higher density fuel combination had to be rejected as the piston engine could accept neither the higher temperatures nor the corrosive combustion products of more dynamic fuel mixes. Starting somewhat later, and with a clean sheet of paper for Spearfish, the United Kingdom was able to use a mixture of Otto fuel and HAP (hydroxyl ammonium perchlorate) driving a Sundstrand turbine which offered the facility of quieter variable speed running and the generation of

Anti-submarine and Mine Warfare

sufficient power to drive the torpedo with the performance required to combat a 45 knot submarine.

Even higher power levels are produced by the closed cycle thermal engine, and the United States selection of this engine for the Mark 50 Advanced Lightweight Torpedo, due in service in 1990, is an important development, which is likely to find an application in their heavyweight weapons in later years.

Whatever propulsion method is selected and whatever form of guidance employed in the end, the torpedo has to act on its own and for this a comprehensive homing system is needed. The torpedo needs to be no less capable than a small warship with a highly effective sonar set installed in the nose, an 'action information organisation' to identify the target and generate the attack solution, and a control system to carry it out.

Homing. New generation torpedo sonars are certainly no less complex than an escort's active hull mounted set; FM pulses are required for high resolution, CW transmissions are needed for doppler discrimination and the rejection of false contacts in shallow water. The current sonar techniques of using fast fourier transforms for spectral analysis of pulse compression, and of employing a correlator to compare the received data with the transmitted signal to reject spurious returns, or of cross-correlation to intercept passive data in the presence of active returns, are as applicable to the torpedo as they are to other sonars. Indeed signal processing has to be more thoroughly carried out as there is no operator in the loop to assist in classification or target recognition.

Thus the torpedo needs to store and analyse this acoustic information and then, by detailed investigation of the echoes, their spatial characteristic and their movement, to differentiate between false contacts and the real target. It further needs to record this data and to be able to select a new target should the weapon be misled initially by false contacts, either deliberately released by the target or caused by wakes, surface or bottom reflections or even whales. The weapon has to adapt itself to the changing water conditions (which may be significantly different than at the firing point) and to the evasive movements of the target. All this calls for a computer suite of considerable flexibility and capacity.

Lastly, the torpedo has to be able to use this data to select the most effective point at which to strike, or if a surface ship is the target, to detonate below the keel where the most damage will result.

The Lightweight Torpedo

The submarine launched weapon is more complex and more expensive than its smaller brother, the air dropped weapon, but much of that complexity, cost and size is devoted to getting the weapon close to its target. In the case of the lightweight weapon, the delivery vehicle, whether aircraft, ship, helicopter, or

Weapons and Warfare

PLATE 10.4 **Lynx Helicopter with Stingray anti-submarine torpedo.** *(Marconi Underwater Systems)*

missile, performs that function, but once within homing range of the target, both weapons have a similar function. There are significant differences, however.

In the same way that nations have standardised for the most part on a size of 21 inch diameter for the submarine launched weapon, $12\frac{3}{4}$ inch diameter, $2\frac{1}{2}$ metres in length and an all up weight of about 260 kilograms seems to be a self-imposed standard for most lightweight weapons. Inevitably, the constraints on space and capacity which control the heavyweight's flexibility affect the lightweight weapon to a far greater extent. The search for more effective propulsion methods is therefore a dominating influence in their design.

Sea water batteries have just about reached the limit of their capability in Sting Ray as has that of the conventional thermal Otto fuel engine in the Mark 46 weapon. Power outputs approaching three times achieved levels in today's weapons are being called for, employing either the closed cycle engines or the lithium based batteries introduced earlier. Higher speed creates, in its turn, enormous demands on the *front end* capability of the weapon for the sonar transducers have to operate and the signal processing be effective under extremely adverse flow noise and generated noise conditions. Current lightweight weapons tend to be single speed weapons operating at the threshold of performance limitation, but their successors will inevitably demand variable speed to search in a quiet mode and only use higher capability in the closing

Anti-submarine and Mine Warfare

stages where the enhanced echo returns can compensate for the degradation in acoustic performance caused by higher speed.

Special Features of the Lightweight Torpedo

Perhaps the most critical element in the lightweight weapon is the warhead. Here the constraints of weapon size probably prevent a warhead of greater weight than 75 kilos ever being fitted – indeed present weapons carry smaller ones than that. Regrettably, a simple blast warhead of that size is simply not sufficient to rupture the hull of modern SSNs with their combination of inner hull strength and the stand off distance between outer and inner hulls. Just how much damage such a warhead might cause is a matter for conjecture and is a rather sensitive subject. The British Sting Ray torpedo, now entering service, the American Mark 50 Advanced Lightweight Weapon, the Italian A290S and the French Murenne will be fitted with a directed charge warhead designed to shoot a plug of molten metal through the pressure hull. To do this, the torpedo has both to strike the submarine in the right place and at the correct angle, orthogonal to the hull, to ensure penetration.

None of the above is easy to achieve. The torpedo has to be able to calculate the target position, course and speed, to determine its spatial extent and, by identification of its hull configuration, to determine the point of impact. The torpedo then has to be agile enough to follow correctly the predicted end of the run geometry to strike home. This cannot simply be done by fitting a directed charge warhead to an existing weapon for its effective delivery is an integral part of the weapon's total co-ordination capability – or that of its sonar and on board computer. But any lightweight weapon without the ability to deploy a shaped charge is clearly of marginal effectiveness.

Next, the lightweight torpedo has to be deliverable from fixed wing aircraft as a missile at relatively high speed, from helicopters at lower speeds or even when in the hover and also from manoeuvring surface ships. To be effective in the shallowest water in which enemy submarines can operate, the weapon has to recover from its water entry, pull out and commence its search in a very shallow depth of water. Diesel powered coastal submarines are fully able to operate in depths of 40 metres, possibly in as little as 30. This shallow water environment therefore imposes particular constraints on the lightweight weapon, both in its ability to be deployed and its capability to search and attack in very shallow water without either broaching the surface or suffering capture by the seabed.

Having no guidance wire, no instructions can be given to the torpedo once it is in the water. The weapon therefore has to be dropped as a round of ammunition, ideally being able to assess of its own accord the depth of water and hence the appropriate sonar transmissions and processing methods. Similarly, because no account can be taken of changes in submarine movement once the weapon has been dropped, it is essential that the torpedo is able to search out the column of water out to its maximum detection range with the minimum delay. The acoustic beam forming electronics must therefore allow for a wide range of combinations to be established automatically in response to the environment and altered as the engagement progresses.

Apart from these special requirements, all the acoustic and processing capabilities relevant to the heavyweight submarine launched weapon are required, but with considerably less space into which to package the necessary electronics, sensors and controls. For the future there are a number of areas where still further improvements will progressively be needed including:

▷ Greater operating depth to counter deeper diving targets.
▷ Enhanced speed to outpace succeeding classes of submarine in all conditions.
▷ Enhanced acoustic performance both to outwit future countermeasures and defeat further progress with anechoic coatings and noise reductions.
▷ Flexibility to adapt the weapon to future air flight missiles either ship or submarine launched.

Many of these capabilities are present in Sting Ray and are being included in the US Mark 50. Work is going ahead in Italy on the A290 weapon, in France with Murenne, and within the United Kingdom. As Sting Ray enters service, work is already in hand on the Mod 1 variant. For the first time a generation of weapons is emerging where software changes can be made to adapt to changing enemy tactics or countermeasures and these changes can be tested by advanced simulation. Further, a modular approach to the torpedo build can offer continuous development without the need for a completely new torpedo, thus avoiding the ten year process of feasibility, project definition and full development before a significant change in weapon capability can be achieved.

Today the torpedo has caught up in terms of complexity, versatility and capability with its cousin, the air flight guided weapon. The coming decade will see this process of change continuing at no less fast a pace. Perhaps, at last, the pendulum is swinging back in favour of the ASW defences and the submarine is becoming increasingly vulnerable to highly effective killing weapons.

The Future

Further surprises in submarine capability are no doubt in store. Those who thought that the SSN had already stretched the need for enhanced torpedo capability to the limits were surprised. Within the short space of ten years, anechoic coating to absorb torpedo homing transmissions, double hull structures to reduce damage, hitherto unbelievable diving depths and submarine speed thought unapproachable have all occurred. For the future, hard kill as well as more effective soft kill anti-torpedo jammers or decoys, must be anticipated, salvo firing may once again become the norm to ensure penetration of at least one weapon, and still further improvements in submarine performance and quietening are likely. Stealth and surprise will therefore become increasingly critical factors, and reduction in reaction time will be the most important single element in improving operational performance. The torpedo is but part of a total weapon system and that system must be considered as a whole in determining how best to proceed.

Overview

In this overall review of the ASW capability it has only been possible to highlight the significant trends and offer more detailed discussion of a few critical areas. Submarine warfare is dominated today by the passive detection systems which, from the inter-action of different sensors deployed by different platforms, offer a defence in depth which cumulatively provides the promise of a high level of attrition. This detection matrix, supported by the emergence of powerful homing weapons, will ensure a high kill probability. There are, of course, weaknesses. Contacts, once engaged, may be difficult to classify. Passive systems are probably enjoying their hey day and, as yet, long range active sensors are a pipe dream. Encouraging avenues of research are developing using bistatic projectors in association with large arrays, but they are far from being operational systems. Weapons are good and getting better, but for the most part they have been developed independently of the sensors which yielded their deployment opportunities. An optimum integrated approach which optimises ASW capability, whether from surface ships or submarines, is still in its infancy.

All ASW activities, whether sensors or weapons, are dominated by a difficult acoustic environment which, however much we are able to improve our understanding of it, cannot be tamed. Sonar detection will never have the certainty or the measureable consistency of radar. And yet, in 1987 ASW certainly stands more confidently and more assured than at any time in the past. The overall picture is not discouraging.

*   *   *   *

MINES

Although the underwater capabilities of the major powers devolve principally upon their submarine fleets, other activities beneath the surface play a considerable part. Mines in various forms can seriously impede the movement of naval and civilian vessels and the mere possibility that they may be present will, in war, necessitate the expenditure of resources and time upon countermeasures while, in peace time, the suspected presence of mines is likely to halt shipping completely. Furthermore, while the devices themselves may be extremely sophisticated, they can be positioned by the simplest of means, even

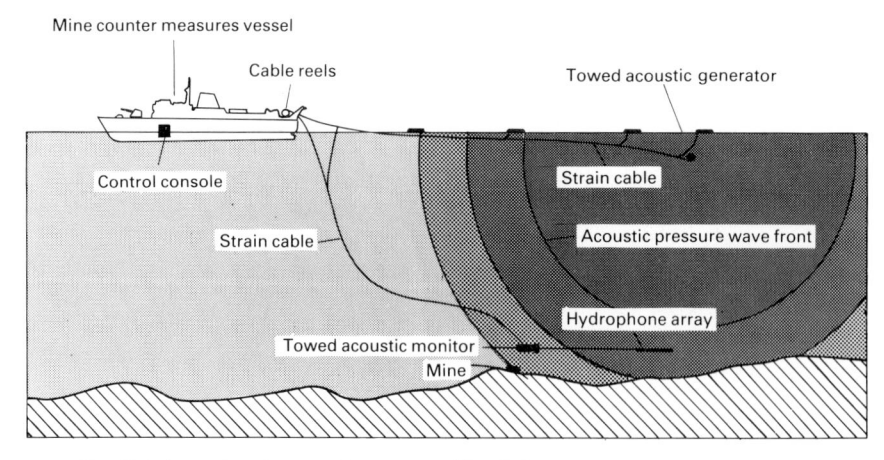

FIG 10.4 Acoustic minesweeping system. The Osbourne system now in service with the Royal Navy.

a fishing boat. Thus, mine warfare can exert strategic and tactical influence quite disproportionate to the resources employed.

Mines can be positioned on the seabed, called ground mines, or anchored and tethered so that they are buoyant near the surface. They can be triggered by a variety of means: by an increase in pressure resulting from the passage of a vessel nearby, by the magnetic effect of a ships hull, or acoustically. The activating mechanisms may be set to ignore the signatures of certain ships or, in an attempt to defeat mine countermeasures, only to respond after the passage of several potential targets. Mines can be modular in form permitting them to be configured by size of warhead and means of activation to the target in mind and the depth of water in which they are to be laid. In-built microprocessor controls ensure that the mines are not activated until the target is at the closest possible range to which its course will bring it, relative to the mine.

Countermeasures may, in essence, take one or two forms, sweeping or hunting. Sweeping involves disposing of a threat by activating the mines in a harmless manner while hunting is based upon locating all suspicious objects, investigating and, where the object proves to be a mine, destroying it. The diagram shows how a modern sweeping system works. The towed acoustic monitor moving ahead of the acoustic generator ensures that the latter produces the required seabed signature regardless of variations in the propagation conditions of the water. The configuration of the system is such that the separate pieces of equipment are planned to be at a reasonable distance from the mine when it is activated, a fact which, coupled to their resistance to damage, ensures that the system remains effective. Not all mines will be sensitive to the acoustic generator; they may be designed to be activated by

Anti-submarine and Mine Warfare

PLATE 10.5 **Limpet Mine.** *(British Aerospace)*

other means or to trigger only after they have been exposed to the correct acoustic signal several times. It is therefore necessary, depending upon intelligence concerning the threat, to hunt as well as sweep if a reasonable degree of security is to be assured. The mine hunter, which could be a ship, hovercraft or helicopter, deploys a specialised sonar which indicates the presence of unusual objects. These are then investigated, either by small underwater vehicles or divers and, when the object is found to be a threat, it is destroyed by an explosive charge.

Another device, more suited to sabotage than to the main stream of conventional war, is the limpet mine. This is designed to be attached to its target by a frogman and therefore limited in size to what a man can conveniently handle while swimming. Nevertheless, being directly attached to a ship's hull, where it is held in place magnetically or by suction, a relatively small amount of explosive can cause a great deal of damage.

Introducing Chapter 11

THE means of waging war are constantly evolving. Changes usually come about by evolution although the advent of nuclear war was an exception. Electronic warfare and all that it implies for command and control seems to be another as, quite apart from the threat of electronic warfare, the tactical conduct of operations is now at the mercy of immediate political direction from what has been called the 'President to fox-hole syndrome'. *Communications are such that a head of state or prime minister can now ring up the man at the very sharp end on the opposite side of the world, a temptation usually to be avoided but a facility to be properly harnessed. Command and control is a huge subject and the next chapter does exceptionally well to contain it within such a short space.*

11

Electronic Warfare: Command, Control Communications and Intelligence

AIR VICE MARSHAL P R MALLORIE CB AFC

THERE are several definitions of command and control. For some the phrase conjures up a picture of headquarters, communications and computers; others might first imagine the radar detection and control mechanisms of an air defence system and others might call to mind the organisation of headquarters and the flow of information, intelligence, planning and decisions essential for military operations. The picture will depend on the background and point of view of the observer. The complete picture of all the characteristics and activities which go to make up a command and control system is very large and rich in detail and could not be described properly in a single chapter. The approach adopted is to analyse the subject in an abstract way to outline answers to such questions as What is it? What does it do? What are the elements within it? How do the people involved perform and What equipment do they use? Then the major problems which new threats and new technical capabilities pose for commanders are examined and finally there is some speculation about the way ahead.

The picture is influenced by the point of view of the observer and is developed against a background of experience of a British serviceman and of the NATO command structure in what must be potentially the toughest environment anywhere for a command and control system. The threat posed by the Soviet political and military doctrine and their armed forces to the NATO nations is numerically and technically the greatest threat of force, both at the conventional and nuclear levels, that the world has ever seen. This threat includes a unique capability for chemical warfare. The Soviet military doctrine is strongly rooted in the offence and stresses the value of surprise and of confusing their enemies. In any attack by Soviet forces on NATO nations, the highest priority would be given to the seizure of nuclear weapons and the disruption of the allied and national command and control systems. The investment that any nation makes in providing military forces could be nullified if the command and control organisation could not withstand an attack sharply focused upon it. For NATO, in particular, it would be essential to maintain continuity of command and the momentum of operations to ensure a coherent defence by the numerically smaller and less ruthlessly trained allied forces. A robust command and control system is an essential factor in maintaining a credible deterrent.

The cost of deterrence is high and the cost of individual weapons and munitions is rising but the cost of providing command and control is rising at an even faster rate. Resources are constrained so there has to be some balance in the investment for defence between weapons and command and control systems. The interaction between weapons, military capabilities and command and control systems is extremely complicated. All that will be attempted here is to set a frame for the discussion of command and control and to add a perspective which may help towards finding that balance.

The Broad Picture

Two things are essential for the deliberate application of military power. First, the power must exist and, second there must be some means of control. For many years, the emphasis in military research and development has been on increasing the effect, accuracy and range of weapons. More recently, development of command and control systems has received greater attention. The command and control of modern weapons, and particularly nuclear weapons, has created new problems for commanders and their staffs. At the same time, new technologies can provide commanders with much more, and more up to date, information than used to be available. *Information* is used here and throughout this chapter in its broadest sense and includes intelligence about the enemy. The commander's task, however, is becoming more complicated by several factors; there is the need to handle and channel the increasing volume of information; the battlefield is expanding as the range of weapons increases; greater mobility, in particular the use of helicopters, also expands the battlefield and increases the tempo of operations; intense activity throughout the twenty-four hour day is both possible and probable as new sensors aid night and bad weather operations; there is a need to exploit the capabilities of new weapons which may impose heavier demands on the command and control system than their predecessors and, finally, electronic warfare, which has many direct consequences for command and control, adds a new dimension to all military operations. If that were not enough, headquarters, sensors and communications are more vulnerable than in the past to physical as well as to electronic attack. There are, in short, new threats, new capabilities and new challenges for command systems.

Recent discussion of command and control has emphasised the available

Electronic Warfare: Command, Control, Communications and Intelligence

PLATE 11.1 **The Fog of War.** In the top picture a smokescreen is effectively masking activity to the naked eye but not to a thermal imager through which an observer would see what is shown in the bottom photograph. *(Thorn EMI)*

Weapons and Warfare

technology. New equipment has provided commanders and staffs with new capabilities and is the seed corn of the industry which supplies it. The human side has had less emphasis. Here the rate of change is naturally much slower because new skills have to be learnt and comfortably familiar organisations and habits may have to adapt. However, in the end, the success of any command system depends on the leadership, drive and, above all, the judgement of the commander and the organisation and skill of his supporting staff. If there is a force multiplier it is in these human qualities. In exercising his judgement, a commander has to interpret the facts available to him in the light of his experience and of his knowledge of his own forces and the enemy. Judging the reaction of the enemy commander and anticipating his actions and reactions requires something more than a simple assessment of the available data. Increasingly sophisticated equipment within the command and control system can be used to assist commanders in the exercise of their judgement but cannot substitute for it. In any event, judgement is essential whenever the information available is incomplete or distorted. Distortion must be expected because, although new technologies assist in providing accurate and up to date information, they are also being used to confuse and mislead, by hiding weapons and installations and by presenting false information. It is up to commanders with the help of their staffs and command and control systems to pick their way through this fog and to avoid becoming the victims of surprise.

Purpose of Command and Control

The purpose of military command and control is to apply force at the time and place and in the quantity the commander chooses. If the commander controls adequate force, has made the right choice and if the command and control system works with adequate speed and precision, then the result he requires will be achieved with utmost economy of effort. There are therefore these three elements, adequate force, making the correct choice and adequate means of exercising command and control. If any one element is missing, the whole mechanism fails. Provision of adequate force is not the province of this chapter but must remain as the ever present backcloth to any consideration of a command system.

Control of Nuclear Forces

Nuclear forces pose an exceptional problem for command and control. There is no room for error or accident with nuclear weapons but, if they are to deter, they must be able to survive an attack and be capable of being launched after careful and deliberate political decision. Elimination of error requires layer upon layer of checks and verification of orders and a fail safe philosophy so that, if any check fails, there can be no firing. Survivability requires physical protection and concealment and numbers to ensure that there is a high chance of survival of a proportion of nuclear weapons. Finally, there must be survivable and secure means of communications between the launch crew and an equally survivable command authority. Command authority within the alliance requires a deliberate political decision. Such decisions would have to be taken at the highest level and in consultation with allies. Such consultations would take time, even if there were few alternatives to explore. Consultation would be made all the more difficult if the national political authorities were not themselves available and ready to take decisions. To ensure deterrence, weapons, the command system and the political authority must exist and be seen to be survivable.

Origins of Command and Control

The problems of command of nuclear forces illustrate in a stark way the political foundation of any system for the command and control of all military forces. Armed forces operate, at least in democratic nations, in accordance with political directives and constraints. Under this political direction a defence strategy is defined and forces provided with the capability, at least in theory, to support that strategy. In practice, in times of peace, when expenditure on defence is unpopular, the capabilities of the armed forces of the Western democracies have usually been below the level necessary to support the declared strategy at least in terms of conventional forces. The command and control system has therefore to be able to exploit to the full every single capability of the available armed forces. The components, strategy, capability and the command and control system, interact with one another (Fig 11.1). If inadequate forces are provided, the strategy would collapse if put to the test. In any event, if strategy or capability change, the command and control system usually needs adjustment. For example, the characteristics of a command system to support a flexible response strategy based on a conventional defence are rather different from those necessary to support a trip wire

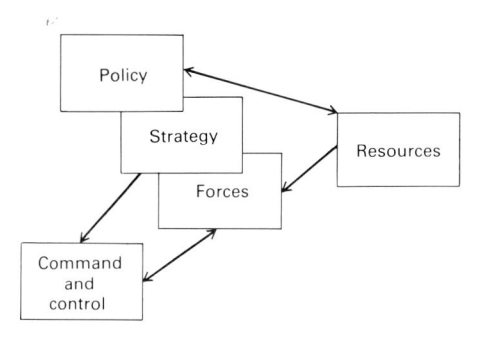

FIG 11.1 Command and control able to exploit full capacity of forces to implement strategy.

Weapons and Warfare

strategy based on a nuclear response to aggression. Again, if artillery weapons were to double or triple their range, the tactical doctrine for the employment of artillery, the requirements for target intelligence and the command system would all need to change to exploit the new capability.

Command and Control as a System

In engineering or physiological terms, a system is an arrangement whereby a control of some kind responds to a stimulus by initiating an action. The result of that action is felt by the control which may then modify or stop the action. A central heating system controlled by a thermostat is one classic example of a system, the human respiratory system is another. These are feed back systems where the effect is fed back to the control. The arrangements for the command and control of military forces can also be regarded as a system. In its most simple form there are two elements in a command and control system, a command element and an action unit. In response to some stimulus, the command element initiates some activity in the action unit. The result of that activity is made known to the commander who then decides what subsequent action is necessary to achieve his purpose and to respond to initiating stimulus (Fig 11.2). The connection between the command element and the action unit is through communications of some kind. Although it is incomplete and a gross simplification, this model can serve as a building block in describing a command and control system. It is incomplete because the command system is not entirely a reactive or feed back system; successful military operations require a large measure of planning and prediction. There is, in systems terms, feed forward of expectations as a result of planning and forecasting. Actions are controlled to fit plans and plans are modified where necessary to achieve the objectives. Sometimes the objectives themselves may need to be changed as events unfold. The model is also much more complicated because there is a hierarchy of commanders and action units and most commanders will control

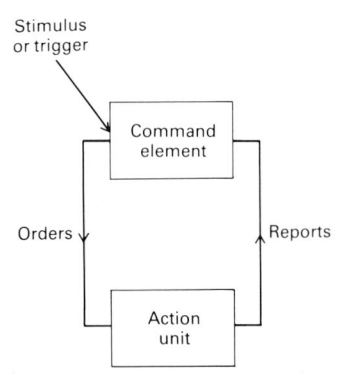

FIG 11.2 Basis of command and control system.

Electronic Warfare: Command, Control, Communications and Intelligence

a number of units. The action unit in the eyes of a senior commander may be the command element of a number of action units at a lower level. This pattern is repeated several times between the political authority, through the supreme military commander down to the serviceman firing his weapon.

A number of deductions may be made from the model just described. First, on survivability, the command element must be as survivable as the action units it controls or there would be a danger of undirected action; on the other hand, there should not be over investment in a command system at the expense of the combat capability or survivability of the units it controls; the right balance, which maximises the capability and effect of the available military forces, is hard to achieve. But in action some damage must be expected, therefore both the command element and the action unit must be able to function when both have been damaged to some extent. Second, on communications, the connection between the command element and the action unit is also liable to be damaged; indeed the communications may be the most fragile part of the system. It follows that the action should be able to continue when communications are interrupted. For action to continue it is essential that the lower formation should be fully aware of the plans and intentions of the higher commander and have the authority and initiative to support such plans with the minimum of direction. It appears that, in a robust command system, authority and hence decision, should normally be delegated to the lowest possible level.

For the system to work, there has to be some stimulus or trigger to initiate action. In practice, the triggers are the orders, plans and instructions from higher authority. Invariably, constraints are applied by such authorities including those at the controlling political level so, to complete the analogy, there is a safety catch as well as a trigger. Subject to the authority vested at any level within the command hierarchy, military action begins in response to some event. The control exercised and the action taken will follow a plan which will be the result of an intelligence assessment. In every case receipt of intelligence is essential for planning and the conduct of operations. The intelligence function, therefore, is as much an inherent part of a command and control system as communications.

Elements of the System

The elements of a command and control system are first the commander and his staff, or the human element; second their organisation and procedures, or their method of work; and, finally, the equipment they use (Fig 11.3). At every level of command these elements interact and, together, provide a picture in the commander's mind and should enable him to influence the battle through the timely direction of his forces. The level of decision within the system depends in part on the gravity of events and the size of the forces involved and in part on the speed which is required for effective action or reaction.

Weapons and Warfare

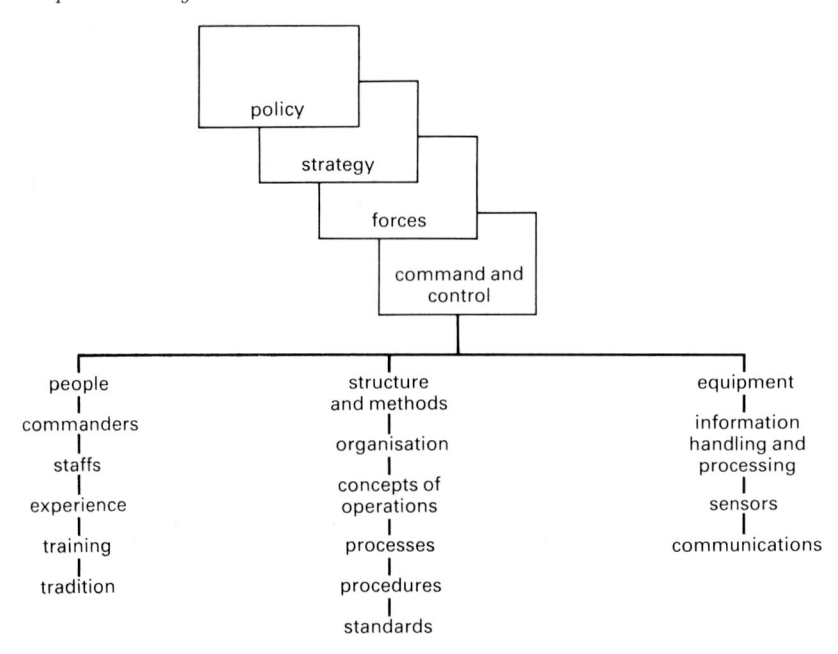

```
                    ┌─────────────┐
                    │   policy    │
                    │   ┌─────────┴───┐
                    │   │  strategy   │
                    └───┤   ┌─────────┴───┐
                        │   │   forces    │
                        └───┤   ┌─────────┴───┐
                            │   │ command and │
                            └───┤   control   │
                                └──────┬──────┘
        ┌──────────────────────────────┼──────────────────────────────┐
      people                       structure                       equipment
        |                         and methods                          |
   commanders                          |                         information
        |                          organisation                   handling and
      staffs                            |                          processing
        |                           concepts of                       |
    experience                      operations                      sensors
        |                               |                             |
     training                       processes                    communications
        |                               |
    tradition                       procedures
                                        |
                                    standards
```

Fig 11.3 The elements of a command and control system.

The Human Element

Ultimately, human judgement drives a command and control system. Successful commanders need an amalgam of intuition, perhaps luck, certainly confidence and above all judgement to decide which evidence to accept and which to reject. They also need the judgement and imagination to fill in where the evidence is weak or missing. This judgement, on which so much depends, must not fail even in the high stress of continuous day and night high intensity operations over a period of some days. The organisation and methods of the command and control system need to be designed to reduce this stress on the commander to a minimum. The military judgement which guides the system comes from personal qualities but depends on training and experience. Actual experience of combat is becoming scarce and has a declining relevance to the threat now posed by Soviet conventional military capabilities. There is certainly no experience among the allies of chemical warfare. The training is of three kinds. There is the basic cadet and weapons training which covers basic military doctrine. This is followed, after some practical experience in military units, by staff college courses for a proportion of officers including potential commanders. Staff colleges provide a deeper understanding of doctrine and of military planning. Training and experience are refreshed every year by annual manoeuvres and training exercises. Such exercises teach and

Electronic Warfare: Command, Control, Communications and Intelligence

practice the current concepts of operations and procedures and allow such practical experience of combat and command as is possible in peacetime. Finally, there are war games. These are of increasing value as they become more readily available and as computer simulation techniques become more powerful. Simulations, while free of the peacetime constraints affecting military exercises, are only as good as the assumptions on which they are based but they allow a wide range of assumptions, different tactics, real or potential military capabilities and perceptions of any threat to be tested.

The relationships between commanders and their subordinates and superiors in a command and control system are heavily influenced by their military social structure and traditions of command. These traditions differ between different nations, between different services and, for the British at least, to some degree between regiments and corps. The different training and traditions affect the delegation of authority and the degree to which initiative is expected and exercised within the system. These differences affect the degree of detail required in the information at different levels of command. Any command and control system has, therefore, to accommodate what could be called the human and social variables. This leads to consideration of the extent to which a command system should depend on battle drills and what scope is allowed for initiative. At one extreme there would be rigid battle drills and at the other complete freedom for individual initiative. Neither extreme is sensible and the balance in practice will depend on the traditions and training of the force, which will be different in different nations. In this respect, the battle drill approach of the Soviet forces, inherent in their political, social and military structure, may put them at a disadvantage in a confused battlefield in comparison to the Allies. Whatever approach is adopted, the complications of military operations and the need for coordination of different activities require concepts of operations to be specified by commanders, to be understood throughout the command and control system and to be practiced by the forces concerned. There is, unfortunately, no concept of command covering the whole command and control structure and which could guide the development of command and control systems. Such a concept would necessarily begin with some consideration of levels of authority.

Organisation – Levels of Authority

The different levels of authority within a command system may be labelled as political and strategic, operational (or grand tactical) and tactical. These levels may also be seen as layers of decreasing response times. Decisions on change of strategy taken at the highest level may take some time, perhaps months, to be realised simply because of the complications and time required to reorientate the forces concerned. Nevertheless, in an emergency, decisions taken at this highest level, for example on escalation or cease fire, will be quickly implemented. At the so called operational level, decisions are of a more immediate kind such as the deployment of sizable forces and the commitment of reserves. This *operational* level is more clearly defined in the Soviet command structure than it is in the forces of NATO nations. The operational level is a useful description and is used in this chapter to denote the level close to but at one remove from the immediate tactical battle. Control at this level is concerned with planning and support of the next engagement rather than with the immediate battle. Scarce and critical resources engaged in the immediate battle, however, may be directly controlled at the operational level. At the tactical level, immediate decisions are made and instant reaction and response may be essential for success when in direct contact with the enemy; but even at the tactical level commanders must plan ahead and deploy their forces, a process which takes time, to meet the attack or to exploit an advantage. In short, the stimuli and responses for command and control are different in timing and scale at each level of authority. The timing and response is also different for air, land and naval operations. For example, decisions on the employment of air power taken at a high level may very soon affect the tactical battle on land or at sea but, reflecting the time required for regrouping and redeployment, high level decisions on the deployment of land and naval power may not affect the battle for a considerable period.

Organisation – Crisis and War

Levels of authority change or at least concertina in times of tension and crisis. In periods of tension short of war high level authorities will need to take decisions on small but far from trivial matters on how to respond to events. There may be a need to demonstrate through increased readiness, mobilisation and the movement of forces such political will as is necessary to contain the situation and reduce the risk of conflict. In times of tension the time layers which distinguish strategic, operational and tactical operations in war do not exist and the political and strategic levels may well have to work in a tactical way. Crises also occur in war as when a strategy fails or starts to fail or when chemical or nuclear weapons are used by the enemy. Immediate changes of policy and strategy may be necessary, having an immediate effect on military operations. The command and control system has to have the flexibility to provide the necessary information and to facilitate the high level control necessary in times of tension and crisis.

Organisation – Structure and Procedures

The structural organisation of most command and control systems has evolved over many years and with different detail and different emphasis in different services and different countries. The creation of armies, navies and air forces reflects the different tenor, training, skills and equipment required for land, sea and air operations. Other major divisions could be made as in the

Electronic Warfare: Command, Control, Communications and Intelligence

Soviet Russian approach in which the strategic rocket and air defence forces are treated as separate services. The subdivisions of amphibious and airborne forces and of army and naval air arms show that there is no clear margin and much overlap between the operations in each element. Within individual services, the organisation is again broken down into different skills and functions and different levels of authority. A typical headquarters is organised into functional cells with the expertise and flow of information to deal with a specific function and to develop specific elements of plans. The whole is drawn together by planning and operational staffs. The higher the headquarters the wider the range of functions and the growing requirement to direct and coordinate different disciplines and capabilities. At higher levels this coordination crosses boundaries between services and, within an alliance, between national forces.

The coordination of activities involved in military operations requires procedures to simplify the processes of planning and controlling military force and to ensure rapid understanding of reports and orders throughout the organisation. These processes are illustrated in the diagram at Fig 11.4 (Coyle) reproduced by courtesy of the European Journal of the Operational Research. The diagram indicates the influence of one process on another and makes the important point that each process deals with a quantity of material and inevitably takes time. However fast the communications and flow of data may be, the production of plans and the other products of a headquarters takes considerable time. The processes will be speeded up if the formal procedures throughout the command system are designed to fit the processes. The many procedures stem from concepts of operations and support, which include the tactics and procedures defined in field manuals, reflect the organisation and tasks of the command system and the levels of authority. Procedures lead to standards; in modern forces hundreds of standards are necessary which would include, for example, standard formats for orders and reports and technical standards for communications and data. Where forces are dissimilar, as in an alliance, the procedures and standards are absolutely essential to ensure integrated operations. The effectiveness of a command and control system is influenced by procedures. Cumbersome procedures will slow down the responsiveness of the system; inadequate procedures and command and control is less effective. However, the load on communications is largely dictated by the procedures; it follows that both communications and procedures need to be developed as a single entity concerned with the distribution of essential information.

Equipment

The equipment within a command and control system (Fig 11.5) may be considered under three headings. First, there is the equipment used within headquarters; that is equipment used for the handling, processing and display

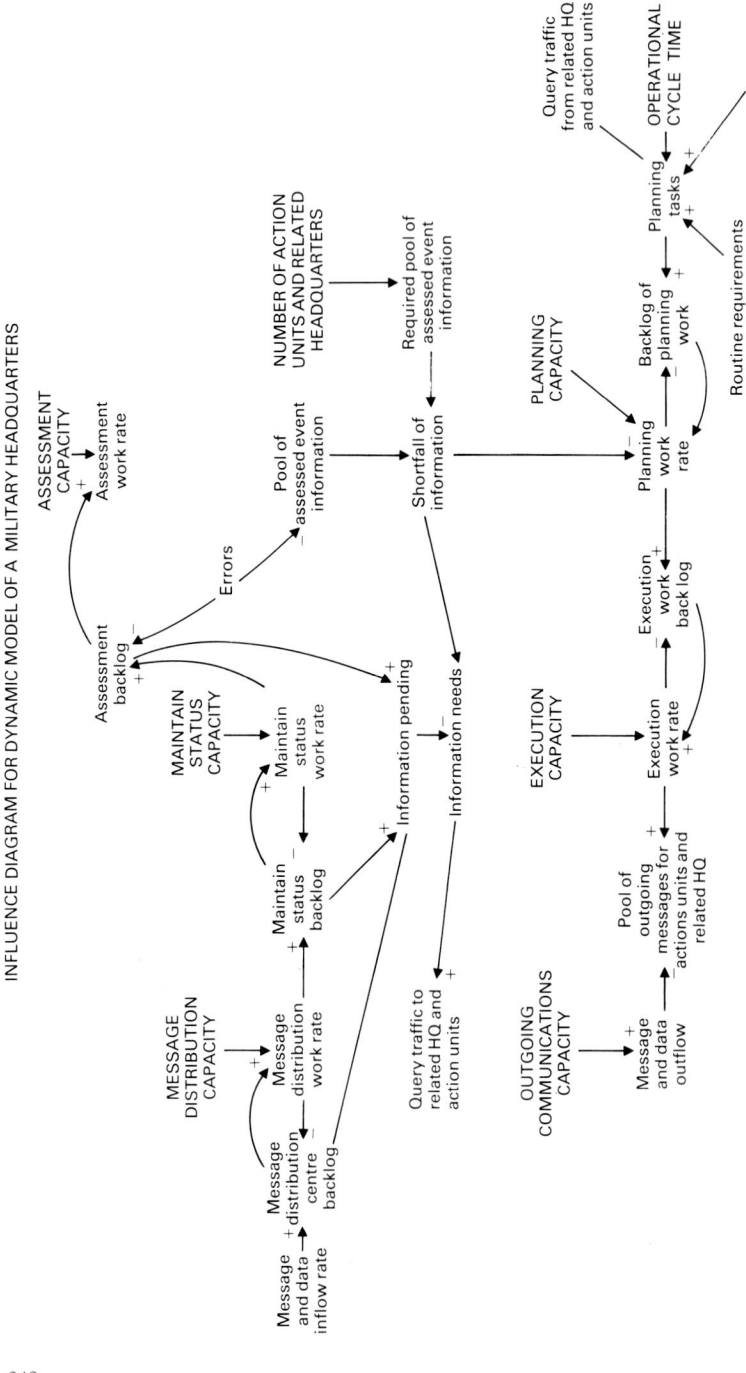

Fig. 11.4 Diagram showing Headquarters processes and their interaction. (Re-printed by kind permission of John Wiley and Sons Ltd from 'Management System Dynamics' and Dr R G Coyle.)

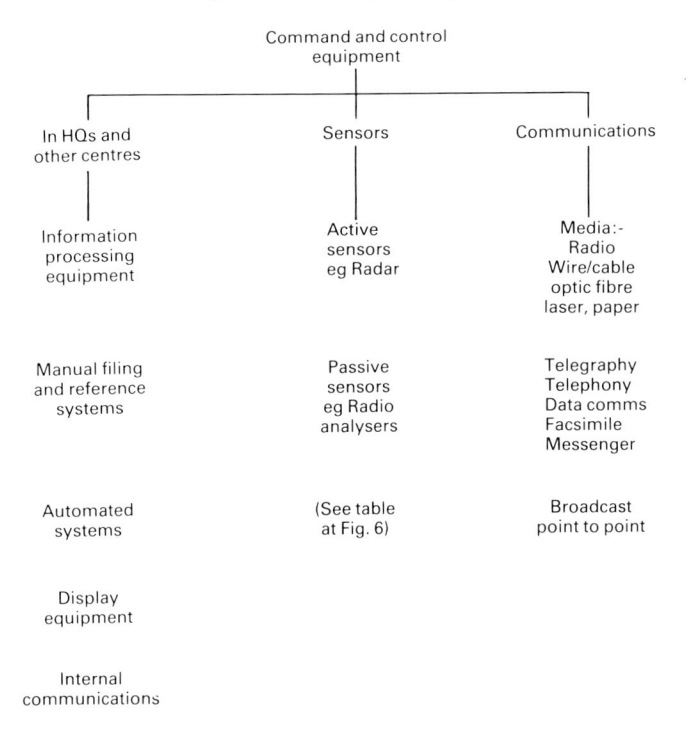

Electronic Warfare: Command, Control, Communications and Intelligence

```
                    Command and control
                         equipment
         ┌───────────────────┼───────────────────┐
   In HQs and             Sensors           Communications
  other centres
         │                    │                    │
   Information            Active                Media:-
   processing             sensors                Radio
   equipment              eg Radar              Wire/cable
                                                optic fibre
                                                laser, paper

   Manual filing          Passive              Telegraphy
   and reference          sensors              Telephony
     systems              eg Radio             Data comms
                          analysers            Facsimile
                                               Messenger

    Automated            (See table            Broadcast
     systems             at Fig. 6)          point to point

     Display
    equipment

     Internal
  communications
```

FIG 11.5 Command and control equipment.

---

1. Fig 11.4 shows the headquarters as a dynamic system. The processes are continuous and consideration of the diagram may start at any point. For the purpose of this explanatory note, start at the left '*Message and data inflow rate*'. Incoming messages create a backlog at the message distribution centre which is governed by the distribution work rate. As messages are distributed they add to the '*Maintain Status*' (ie the operational and supply state of own forces) backlog. At the same time messages and data add to the pool of '*information pending*' (information in this instance including intelligence and orders and instructions from higher authority) which, with the '*status*' information is waiting to be assessed. The rate of assessment is governed by staff capacity and if there is a shortfall of information query, traffic will be generated. If there is no shortfall or the shortfall is acceptable, there will be a command decision and the planning and execution tasks will begin.

2. Where the head of an arrow is marked + then an increase at the source of the arrow will result in an increase or a requirement for an increase at the head. Where the head of an arrow is marked − then an increase at the source of the arrow will result in a decrease at the head. Given capacities or observational data, the time necessary for a given headquarters to complete the processes of assessment, planning and execution may be shown for various conditions. For more information on this analytical method see 'Management System Dynamics' by Dr R G Coyle. (John Wiley & Sons Ltd)

Weapons and Warfare

of information. Second, there are the sensors on which intelligence so largely depends and which are increasingly essential for the control and direction of many types of engagement and operations, such as air defence, as well as for the self-protection of ships, aircraft and fighting vehicles. Incidentally, there are sensors for the control and guidance of missiles and, finally, there are the communications which are, in effect, the nervous system of command and control essential for the distribution of all kinds of information throughout the organisation.

Information Handling Equipment

Commanders need three main streams of information on which to base their decisions. They need information about their own forces such as their condition, their position, the supply situation, the support available and so on. The second stream of information is intelligence about the enemy; his condition, his position, his supply situation, the support available to him and the best possible assessment of his likely intentions. Finally, a commander needs to know about his operational environment; this information would include orders and instructions from higher authority and any political or military constraints as well as information about the weather, terrain and any other physical factors affecting operations. Taken as a whole, these three streams of information about own and enemy forces and the operational environment should be filtered so that they are related to the responsibilities and potential for action of the commander concerned; if some such filter is not applied, the sheer volume of information could delay the staff processes and overwhelm the system to the point where the functioning of the headquarters would be impaired.

Within a headquarters there is a need for some kind of equipment to assist the staff processes, particularly those involving the collation of information and intelligence and the production of the plans, orders and instructions which stem from command decisions. This equipment includes filing systems, displays, maps, briefing aids and internal communications. Much of the clerical work involved in the staff processes is being automated and as computer driven equipment increases in power, more powerful aids become possible. The automated equipment varies from the very large, fixed and costly installations down to desk top and portable computers. One effect of this speeding up and increasing accuracy of staff work is that the relationship between different staff cells is changing and there may be a need for different organisation, skills and training among the staff. Moreover, as large headquarters become more vulnerable and as information technology including communications improve, the possibility arises of some of the filtering and collation of information and intelligence being done elsewhere and of headquarters being dispersed for survival. Such external information processing

Electronic Warfare: Command, Control, Communications and Intelligence

already provides the weather forecasting on which vital operational decisions are taken.

Sensors

The second category of command and control equipment to be considered is sensors. As already mentioned, modern sensors are removing the problems of night operations and creating a twenty-four hour battlefield. Sensors have also become a primary source of information and intelligence of all kinds and in increasing amounts. Increasingly, command and control depends on the performance of the sensors which serve the system to provide strategic and tactical intelligence, information for the control of friendly forces and ultimately for the control and functioning of weapons. Air warfare in particular depends on sensors both in attack and defence and for the recovery and traffic control of aircraft. At the level of weapons, aiming and control sensors can now, and in some instances do, provide data which identifies and locates targets and guides weapons down to the point of impact. As sensor technology develops, the need for visual observation declines; unseen targets may be attacked and *fire and forget* weapons are becoming able to seek out and destroy their targets. Fighting the unseen in this way introduces new problems for command and control giving rise to a tendency for more detailed control to be exercised from higher levels or wherever the best intelligence is available.

Most sensors exploit the electro magnetic spectrum. This spectrum extends from very or extra low radio frequencies up through the frequencies used for radio and radar, through millimetric and sub millimetric used for some detectors and on to infra red, visible light, ultra violet and beyond. Another series of sensors exploits sound waves, including frequencies above and below normal human perception. To complete the picture, there are also sensors which detect magnetic anomalies in the earth's magnetic field and are used by the military to search in particular for submarines. Finally there are sensors which detect vibrations in the ground and can provide indications of vehicle movement; such sensors could, for example, be left behind during a withdrawal to give indications of enemy activity. Electro magnetic and audio sensors may operate in the active or passive mode. In the active mode, sensors derive information from the transmission of energy and then listening to the reflections while, in the passive mode, sensors listen for electro magnetic or audio noise from external sources which can then be analysed. Active sensors can be jammed by broadcasting noise on the appropriate frequency or confused by screening, in the way that reflective chaff and responders can produce radar returns which are intended to screen and hide returns from aircraft or possibly as a spoof to induce false impressions. Passive sensors may also be confused by the broadcast of electro magnetic noise and spurious sounds. Both active and passive sensors are vulnerable to physical attack; their vulnerability increases as their positions are revealed; all active sensors can be detected, although

Weapons and Warfare

some are harder to detect than others. By operating at all, such sensors reveal their position and become targets for homing weapons. However, technical measures give increasing protection to radio and radar transmitters. Among these measures are narrow beam techniques, which incidentally increase the range of the sensor by focussing the transmitted energy, and frequency hopping, where the transmitted signal changes frequency very rapidly over a broad frequency band and communicates to a companion receiver set to change frequency in precisely the same pattern. The energy required to jam the broad band becomes prohibitive and locating frequency hopping transmitters becomes more difficult. But the costs of such equipment are high and the frequency management problem may be exacerbated. Another protective technique is bi- or multi-static radar where the transmitter and receiver are at some distance from each other, effectively hiding at least part of the system. Jammers themselves, by radiating, become targets for passive sensors and homing weapons. However, both passive sensors and homing weapons may be fooled by decoy transmitters. Decoy transmitters and jamming, unless carefully controlled, may introduce additional difficulties into one's own operations. Sensors look for targets; means are developed to protect targets and to hide activity from sensors; these means include physical and electronic or audio attack on the sensors; means are then developed to protect the sensors. This roundabout of action, counter action and counter counter action is illustrated in the table of sensor types, targets and vulnerability at Fig 11.6 and is the essence of electronic warfare. Success very largely depends on the level of technology and consequent performance of the available equipment. Tactics need to be adjusted to fit the capability of the equipment and the threat. It follows that the provision and operation of sensors should always be considered in the whole frame of electronic warfare which is considered later.

Communications

The next category of equipment is communications. Military command and control is completely dependent on communications. As military operations have become more complicated and as radios have become lighter and more efficient, the sheer quantity of communications has grown at an almost explosive rate. Yet it is common experience for military exercises to be hampered to some extent by communications bottlenecks and delays. This may in part be due to the artificialities of exercises but there are dangers of both communications and information overloading headquarters' staffs. In such a condition some information may be lost or ignored and there is a consequent tendency for headquarters at all levels to grow in size and thus to become more vulnerable to attack. There is an additional effect because if information is lost, either in the headquarters or through communications delays, the staffs concerned start to generate query traffic which further overloads the system and increases delays. The situation is being eased by the introduction of

Part 1 – Active sensors

Fig 11.6. *Sensors, sensor targets and their respective vulnerabilities.*

Sensor	Targets	Measures to reduce target vulnerability	Sensor vulnerability	Measures to reduce sensor vulnerability	Remarks
Radar surface based land or sea	Aircraft Missiles Arty and mortar shells Vehicles Personnel	Tactical measures[1] Reduce reflections Decoys[2] Saturation[3] Jamming ECM screen eg chaff	Physical attack Radiation homing weapons[4] Electronic measures including jamming EMP	Physical defence Mobility, redundancy Decoy, frequency hop EECM design, narrow beam, networking Bi/multi static operation[5] Short burst	Surface based radar includes missile guidance and gun aiming systems eg beam riders and LL air defence systems
Radar airborne – target seeker in aircraft, RPV or missiles	Aircraft – incl low lev, ships snorting subs, missiles, incl cruise, vehicle movement, area recce	Shelter by terrain Reduce reflection Decoy, ECM screen Jamming, attack comms, Tac measures to confuse C2	Physical attack Rad homing wps Jamming of radar Jam comms to confuse C2	Physical defence ECCM design eg frequency hop/ agility, narrow beam, short burst operation	
Radar airborne self protection	Aircraft and missiles	Reduce reflections Decoy, screen Disrupt C2 comms	As above	Physical defence ECCM measures eg frequency agility	
Over the horizon radar	Aircraft, ships, low lev missiles	Reduce reflections Decoy	Physical attack, homing weapons Jamming	Frequency agility (limited)	
Sonic	Submarines and ships	Tactical measures (Temp layers etc)	Physical attack (simplified by sonic x-mission)	Physical defence remote x-mitters and data links (sonobuoys)	
Laser markers	Mainly ground targets eg tanks	Hide, decoy, reduce reflections	Detectable at target	Minimise illumination	
Satellite radar	Strategic recce fixed installations	Concealment	Asat weapons ECM, EMP	ECCM design EMPP engineering	

Continued

FIG. 11.6 continued
Part 2 – Passive sensors

Sensor	Targets	Measures to reduce target vulnerability	Sensor vulnerability	Measures to reduce sensor vulnerability	Remarks
Radar receiver/analyser (search radar)	Radar transmissions	Frequency hopping Decoy x-missions	Vul to decoys May not detect hop Random PRF	ECCM design – inbuilt threat library	Product – targets & ELINT
Radar receiver/analyser (missile guidance)	Radar X-mitter (attack warning)	ECCM design – Freq ncy hop, decoy X-missions	As above	As above	Product is tac warning mainly for a/c & ships
Wide spectrum radio receiver/analyser	Any emission in frequency range	Do not emit. Use narrow beam point to point Operate decoys. Screen high voltage equipt Encrypt vs comint	Vulnerable to deception, noise and ECCM	Improve technical performance. Build in intel library. Plan to exploit operational situation	Product is comint other intel and target data
Infra red	Any heat source – missile launch & in flight. Aircraft, vehicles, generators etc	Reduce heat, decoy conceal activity among other heat sources	Vulnerable to decoy eg heat flares to confuse IR missile guidance. Performance affected by weather	Combine with other sensors. Improve technical performance	Product is intel esp tac intel, targeting & missile guidance & warning
Photography	Strategic to tactical targets	Camouflage & decoys	Vulnerable to camouflage & decoys Performance affected by weather	Improve sensitivity selective use of spectrum (IR & UV) Computer enhancement	
Television	Tactical targets Security surveillance Space systems	As for photography	As for photography. Good low light performance	Spectrum techniques Computer enhancement	Recce use needs active data link Adaptable for wps guidance

Sound	Submarines and ships	Quiet techniques incl low speeds Tactical measures Decoys	Vulnerable to decoys and noise reduction	Improve equipment eg fixed & towed arrays, multi depth sensors	Products include identification, weapons homing & detonation
Sound and/or vibration (incl leave behind sensors)	Vehicle or human movement	Deliberate movement to provide misleading response	Needs means to transmit data – subject to comms vulnerability	Burst transmission possible to reduce comms vulnerability	
Magnetic anomaly	Submerged submarines	Lower magnetic effect – titanium hull	Needs carriage by low slow aircraft which are vulnerable	Physical defence of carrier	

Notes

1. Tactical measures to reduce target vulnerability applies to all targets.
2. Decoys may be used in most cases to reduce target vulnerability.
3. Saturation of sensors applies to all sensors, making analysis more difficult.
4. Degree of vulnerability to EMP, electronic measures and homing weapons depends on design.
5. Bi or multi static uses transmitters and receivers in different locations.
6. Short burst operation reduces vulnerability particularly when followed by movement.

Weapons and Warfare

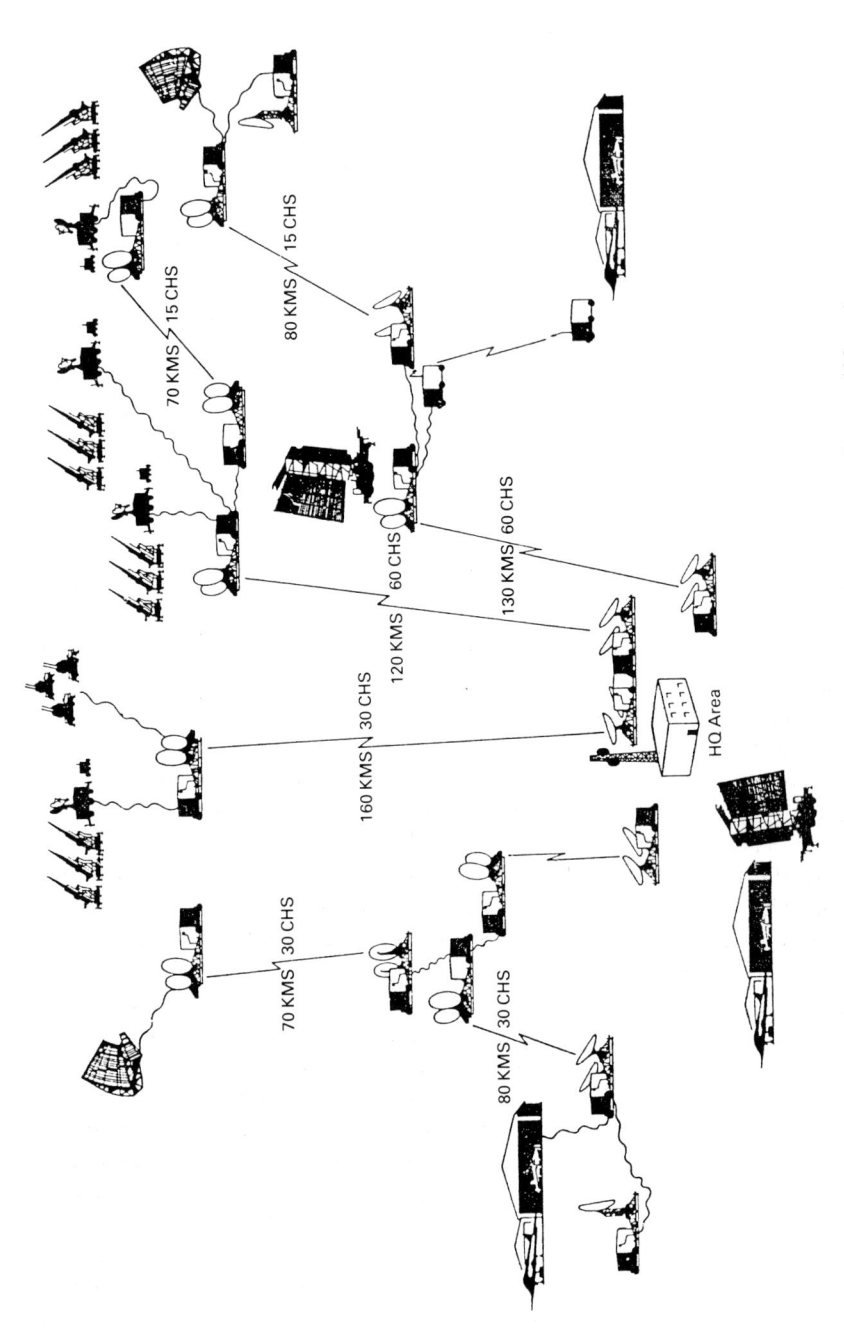

Fig. 11.6 Air defence communications. A typical troposcatter layout. (*Marconi Company Ltd.*)

Electronic Warfare: Command, Control, Communications and Intelligence

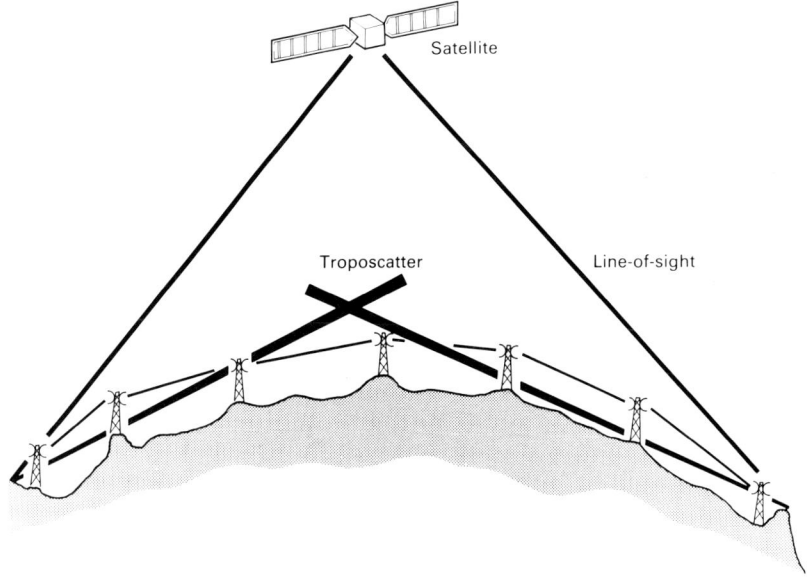

FIG 11.8 Microwave. An illustration of three basic systems.

computer-to-computer data exchange in which tables of data are amended automatically; with such data exchange systems, widely separated staffs can be confident that they are working from the same and most reliable data available. This speeds up planning and simplifies the task of coordination.

Radio traffic is a major source of intelligence for the enemy, even if encrypted. Whether or not communications are encrypted, headquarters and communications nodes generate identifiable signatures and indicate the position of the transmitters, if not of the headquarters or node. Unencrypted traffic, like much of the older generation tactical voice communications, provides even more intelligence. Individual transmitters can be located and both the location and pattern of traffic give clues to the activity being supported. For these reasons, the communications system can become the Achilles' heel of command and control and requires particular care in design and control in use. Radio communications have to operate in spite of enemy electronic warfare. Jamming, although not the only threat from electronic warfare, will reduce the range of signals, slow down the transmission rate and increase the number of relays required. This means that command and control systems and procedures need to be designed for a communications system which is likely to be severely degraded. Fortunately anti-jamming design and operation, such as frequency hopping already described, provides a partial solution for the time being by increasing the difficulties of location and overcomes the problems of being jammed by the current generation of jammers. However, the problem is not entirely solved because it is becoming

Weapons and Warfare

PLATE 11.2 **Large Troposcatter dishes, Hong Kong.** *(Marconi Company)*

PLATE 11.3 **Portable Troposcatter Aerial.** *(Marconi Company)*

feasible to produce jammers which will follow a frequency hopper. Another technical solution is in the development of fibre optic cables for military communications including tactical communications. Fibre optic cables are lightweight, high capacity and do not radiate and therefore cannot be picked up by any sensor. Fibre optics are not a complete answer to the problems of combat communications because of the obvious difficulties of laying cables however small they may be, and there are considerable problems in covering long distances unless the cables have been laid down beforehand and are engineered in a survivable way; this implies a network which could function even if some links are destroyed. For long distances, satellite communications have great advantages and are increasingly being used. As satellite receiver dishes are coming down to man pack size, tactical communications through satellites is becoming possible although costly in comparison with terrestrial systems. However, satellites are not invulnerable to attack. The Soviet Union has tested anti-satellite weapons and satellites can be jammed. For military use they need anti-jamming characteristics incorporated in their design. All communications and computers, unless specially protected, are vulnerable to the electro magnetic pulse generated by nuclear explosions. A feasible tactic would be to explode a nuclear bomb well outside the atmosphere to cause little or no damage except to disrupt communications and destroy data in unprotected computers.

In summary, communications are the essential nervous system in the body of command and control. But they are, like sensors, at risk from both physical and electronic attack. Electronic warfare can be seen as a war between command and control systems in which each side seeks to disrupt or destroy the other's communications and sources of intelligence. Any examination of command and control would be incomplete without some consideration of electronic warfare.

Electronic Warfare

Electronic warfare, or the exploitation of the electro magnetic spectrum for military purposes, presents new challenges for command and control. Much of the technology is new and development is rapid. The principles of war do not change but electronic warfare gives a new dimension to the principles of security, surprise and cooperation. Electronic warfare is already a crucial element in air operations; without protective electronic warfare equipment and, possibly, special electronic escort aircraft, aircraft are extremely vulnerable to surface-to-air or air-to-air missiles. Much of the expenditure, as much as 80% in the case of the United States, according to an *Aviation Week* and *Space Technology* report, is for electronic warfare systems for aircraft. Costs are rising and will inevitably influence defence budgets and hence the size and structure of national armed forces in the future.

Weapons and Warfare

PLATE 11.4 **AWACS.** One of the E-3 airborne warning control system aircraft destined for Saudi Arabia. The aircraft travel in US Air Force markings to the Kingdom where they are re-painted in Royal Saudi Air Force colours on arrival.
(Boeing Aerospace Company)

The sensors involved in electronic warfare have already been described. The table at Fig 11.6 illustrated the methods of attack on the sensors and the consequent protective measures. The threat to communications and some of the consequent protective measures have been described in the section on communications. Fig 11.9 gives a simplified outline of the activities encompassed by electronic warfare and the implications for command and control. The outline divides electronic warfare into three divisions, intelligence gathering, defensive action and offensive action. Many other such arbitrary divisions are equally possible and the table could be rearranged, for example, into sections dealing with intelligence gathering, intelligence denial, target acquisition and target protection. From the point of view of command and control systems, however, the division adopted illustrates the activities in what might be termed the battle between command systems. In each division the activities are separated between active and passive sensors. But the battle between command and control systems, sometimes called the counter C3 campaign, involves more than just the electronic element and includes all means of deception and disruption of the enemy system while preserving one's own. In this battle electronic and physical attack, decoy equipment, spoof movement and the generation of false and mis-information all need to be coordinated for maximum effect. This need adds to the complications of planning and to delay in producing fully coordinated plans.

Electronic Warfare: Command, Control, Communications and Intelligence

PLATE 11.5 **Satellite Reconnaissance.** A computer enhanced satellite photograph showing a 75 thousand ton nuclear aircraft carrier under construction in the Nikolaiev 444 yard on the Black Sea. *(Associated Press)*

Electronic surveillance and reconnaissance has grown to be the major source of intelligence and is certainly the most timely. But it must be remembered that there are many other ingredients in the complete intelligence picture on which commanders depend. These other ingredients include combat reports and photographic reconnaissance although, increasingly, photographs are electronically processed and transmitted. At the level of target identification and location more and more electronic equipment is becoming available.

It is necessary to divert for a moment to consider the implications of electronic development and electronic warfare on weapons and on the close combat end of the command and control structure. Target identification and location equipment includes laser markers, operated by spotters and controllers to enable weapons to home onto indicated targets, and a very wide range of seekers, guidance systems, range finders, position finders and designators and identification devices. Many of these devices increase the range at which targets are engaged. Self contained weapons with navigation, seeker and guidance systems are already in service. These include all medium and long range nuclear weapons, virtually all air-to-surface, surface-to-surface and submarine launched anti-shipping weapons, and numbers of air-to-air and ground-to-air missiles. In addition, anti-tank missiles are coming into this category after a generation of visually guided weapons. There is also a range of electronic radiation homing missiles of particular significance for command and control because they can remove sources of intelligence and seriously damage communications, as well as disrupt the means of weapon control. Many of these weapons can be fired from well beyond visual range, which introduces at least two major problems for command systems. The first of these is the problem of timely target identification and the second is problem of weapons control and the level of command. Target identification, including the particular problem of the identification of hostile and friendly aircraft in a crowded sky or, for local air defences, at very low level, is a long standing technical problem which requires solution through some application of electronics, possibly including advanced information technology.

The problem of weapons control and the level at which control is exercised is central to command and control and is an example of where a command system has to adapt to exploit new capabilities. In brief, each level of command in the land battle has an area of influence where its weapons can reach and influence events and an area of interest stretching beyond the range of these weapons. The area of interest for a particular level of command needs to be covered by intelligence so that the commander concerned can gauge enemy capabilities and intentions and prepare for the use of appropriate weapons in the area of influence. However, long range weapons expand the areas of influence and interest. The scarce and expensive weapons tend to be controlled at higher levels of command. But the longer range weapons may have a very close coupled effect on the tactical battle. Thus higher headquarters may become more and more closely involved in the tactical battle as more of these weapons become available. In any event, many reconnaissance and electronic warfare assets, essential both for the tactical battle and for the control of the longer range weapons, are likely to be in very short supply and will need to be directed to the most critical areas. Again, the higher level headquarters may be obliged to become involved in minute-to-minute decisions affecting the tactical battle. This effect of electronic warfare and the increasing application of electronics to weapons means that the levels of authority will need examination and probably adjustment, particularly for land forces.

The problems for air forces is different, simply because air forces have centralised high level command and decentralised, relatively low level, responsibility and authority for the detailed planning and execution of air operations. In passing, it must be noted that this classic structure for the direction of air power depends completely on a survivable command, control and communications structure, something which is becoming increasingly difficult and expensive to ensure. At sea, tactical command vested in the task force commander afloat is affected by the increasing lethality of anti-ship weapons and by the rapid expansion of his area of interest to cover the air, surface and underwater spaces from which such weapons may be launched. The strategic and operational command and control of maritime forces is exercised from headquarters ashore where air support of maritime operations from land based air force is planned. Integration of such air support, vital to give the tactical commander the long range surveillance and intelligence he needs, places a heavy load on communications and increases the vulnerability of such operations to electronic warfare.

Major problems

The major problems with command and control systems may be summarised under three headings; the control and exploitation of information, survivability of command and management of the command and control system. An associated and pervasive problem lies in the procurement and costs of the systems.

Control and Exploitation of Information

Information, as the word is used here, which includes intelligence, is not the same as data. A dictionary definition of information is *communication of instructive knowledge* (OED) and *inform* has a sense of putting into shape or form. The command and control process requires the gathering of raw facts or data and a transformation of data into useful information on which commanders may take their decisions, develop plans and issue orders and instructions. Following the collection of the data and the assembly of it in an ordered and collated form, it is assessed and related to other information so that a picture is built up of the relevance of the data within a frame of reference; at this point it could be regarded as information. In a command and control system, the frame of reference will include the intentions and plans of the commander and the operational constraints. As modern systems provide more and more data at all levels, control mechanisms are necessary to prevent a flood of data overloading the capacity of the staff and commander to make sense of it. Data has to be turned into assessed information or *instructive knowledge* as early as possible within the command and control process, both to reduce the volumes of data and to help consistency of assessment throughout the system. However, one of the dilemmas in developing command and control systems is that sensors provide large streams of data, frequently much of it is redundant, but all of which may need to be examined and assessed to discover the required information. Comparison of the output of different sensors, again within a frame of reference, may produce additional information or be able to provide required information to several different users. This *fusion* process is extremely complicated and requires advanced computer techniques as well as large and expert staffs. The exploitation of information which exists within the system creates a very heavy demand for communications, with all the attendant risks already described.

Survivability

As already explained, it is essential to maintain the coherence and momentum of military operations, particularly where relatively small defence forces face a numerically stronger and well equipped aggressor. Maintaining coherence of operations implies continuity of command. However commanders, staffs and the whole command and control system are prime targets. Never before has the command system been at such risk; because of the nature of the threat, this high risk applies, in particular, to the NATO command structure. If NATO were to be attacked, the command and control system, its communications and intelligence systems and sensors would certainly be attacked and some damage should be expected. There are three major approaches to ensure survivability of command. First, there is physical protection and defence; second, there is concealment and dispersal, so that the system presents a very difficult target; and third, there are measures of organisation and procedures to ensure that, whatever damage is sustained, effective command and control can be exercised without loss of operational momentum from somewhere within the surviving elements.

Physical protection is necessary against sabotage, *coup de main* operations and conventional or chemical attack. In the main, the approach to obtain such physical protection for higher level headquarters has been to construct bunkers and to organise local air defences and security forces. Such bunkers, with hardened communications, could withstand a considerable conventional attack. But the possibility of a new generation of conventionally armed ballistic missiles poses a new threat. However, such headquarters have certain advantages. Large staffs can be housed, they can be protected against chemical attack, computer systems able to handle very large amounts of intelligence and a very large planning load can be available and both computers and communications can be protected against the electro magnetic pulse from nuclear detonations in space or at some distance. Such headquarters are ideal for crisis management short of war and for conventional war up to a critical level provided, of course, that they are not overrun. Lower level headquarters depend on concealment, movement and some redundancy for survivability. In the field, such headquarters are probably as survivable as the units they control.

At some point however, the weight of attack or the risk of a nuclear attack would lead to the normally fixed and permanent headquarters changing to a concealed, probably mobile and possibly dispersed headquarters which could be expected to survive even if some part of it was destroyed. In such a configuration the headquarters depicted would resemble a tactical headquarters which has to be mobile to be with the units it controls in a mobile battle. The mobile higher level headquarters has necessarily to be small to make concealment feasible and has therefore to operate with a very small staff. At the stage of combat which would force such a headquarters to become mobile, much authority would have been delegated and, to some extent, the task of the staff would be simplified. To increase survivability, this staff needs to be trained in more than one expertise and be able to fulfil more than one staff function. The communications for a dispersed and mobile headquarters will be limited and should be restricted to essential information related to the circumstances. How that is to be achieved is a problem which has yet to be solved.

The next level in the survival of a command system is through a procedure which passes the responsibility and authority of a commander whose headquarters can no longer exercise command to another, in another headquarters. This succession of command requires that the necessary information and intelligence is available in the successor headquarters and again produces a crucial problem for communications. However, succession of command is a last ditch procedure and implies a situation where such authority would have been delegated down to the tactical level. In such a situation, if coherent operations are to be maintained, it is important that the plans and intentions of the command concerned are known to the successor command as well as to the subordinate units.

Management of the Command and Control System

Management of the command and control system and of its development is complicated because the system is pervasive throughout the military organisation; it cannot be separated and treated in isolation. Any change or deficiency in one part is liable to affect the rest of the system and will have implications for the employment of the forces concerned. However, the command and control system has been built up from a number of separated functions such as communications, information and intelligence systems, air defence ground environment, air control systems and so on. Under the guidance of those responsible for each of the functions, considerable and far reaching improvements have been made in the performance and effectiveness of each individual function. For example, over the last decade, communications have been much improved throughout the command and control systems of all NATO nations. Similar statements may be made about the equipment in command and control information systems, air command and control systems and about many of the procedures involved. However, there has been relatively little change in the pattern of training. Improvements in one part of a system do not necessarily improve the performance or effectiveness of the complete system. For example, increasing the quantity of information in a headquarters through, say, better communications, will have no effect and may even slow down staff processes unless there is a commensurate improvement in the ability of the staff to deal with the increase. There is therefore a need both to develop and manage a command and control system as a single entity. In most instances such an approach would cut across the current organisation and responsibilities. In other words, the concept of a command and control system as a single entity has implications which are probably difficult to accept from the point of view of human relationships and organisation but such a concept

Weapons and Warfare

is necessary if new technical capabilities are to be absorbed and new threats are to be countered.

Costs

Command and control of military forces begins at the national political level but where it ends and where precisely the margins lie is more difficult to define. Is, for example, an airborne early warning aircraft part of an air defence weapons system or part of the command and control structure? The function of command and control is pervasive throughout all military activity and for this reason it has always been difficult to assess the costs. Most of the available estimates concentrate on the equipment costs and ignore the personnel and the not inconsiderable training cost. However, a recent Frost and Sullivan Inc report quoted in *Signal* (The Journal of the Armed Forces Communications and Electronics Association), the percentage of Western European defence expenditure devoted to command, control, communications, intelligence and electronic warfare equipment is 1.8% and is estimated to rise to 2.8% by 1991. In US dollars that is a rise from $1.17 billion to $2.86 billion in 1991. The average European rate of growth in this sector is about 10% per annum although the United Kingdom is expected to increase expenditure by about 12% per annum. For comparison, the 1986 US Department of Defense request for command, control and communications was for $22.1 billion, which included $3.9 billion for personnel costs. The request for intelligence was classified but the total command, control, communications and intelligence was estimated by *Signal* to be $40.6 billion or about 13% of the total defence budget. Any comparison between the United States and Western Europe must be treated with caution as the United States has a very large investment in strategic nuclear command and control systems and in satellite communications and intelligence systems; the United States also has a worldwide command network covering forces in the Pacific, Japan, Korea and the Philippines. Looking at electronic warfare equipment separately, the Western European expenditure is expected to grow from $188 million to $314 million per annum between 1986 and 1991 (*Signal*) while US suppliers expect to deliver $4–5 billion of airborne and ship/surface electronic warfare equipment in 1986 (*Aviation Week*). For the United States it is estimated that about 80% of the expenditure on electronic warfare equipment is for combat aircraft (*Aviation Week*). It may be assumed that the European expenditure is in roughly the same proportion. However, the scale is quite different in America where, again quoting the *Aviation Week* report, the fit of electronic warfare equipment in the B1B bomber costs $20 million per aircraft [1986] and the integrated electronic warfare system for next generation aircraft is being developed with a cost target of between $1.8 and 2.8 million per aircraft.

Figures must be treated with caution but the broad conclusion may be drawn that, to ensure the effectiveness of the armed forces in the decades ahead, there

Fig 11.9. *Command and control implications of electronic warfare.*

Major EW activity	Supporting activity	Sensor category	Activity	Example equipment	Technical concern	Command and control implications
Intelligence gathering	Strategic & operational surveillance & recce	Active	Surveillance by radar (fixed, mobile, airborne, shipborne and space)	BMEWS, satellite	Rapidity and accuracy of threat analysis	Overriding necessity for rapid intelligence at all levels. Need for accuracy and secure distribution
		Passive	Photo & IR, air & space recce, ELINT, COMINT Inten & data correlation	Recce pods	Method for intel correlation (fusion) & integration of output	Need to avoid or minimise all electro-magnetic emissions
	Tactical surv & recce & target ident & location	Active	Surface and airborne radars Movement detection Target ident & illumination Weapons guidance & homing	AEW ADGE sensors Laser markers	Sensor discrimination, sensitivity & range Target identification	Increasing complexity of operational plans to include EW and to direct EW and recce assets. Need for rapid planning aids
		Passive	ELINT, COMINT, signal analysis, Photo & IR recce, intelligence correlation	LOCE — BICES	Signal processing and pattern analysis Communications systems	Need to exploit all intel sources for tactical battle and for target data. Requires correlation/fusion & rapid distribution to weapons level – has implications for command and control procedures
Defensive action	Target protection	Active	Jamming, screening, false echoing, Decoys Radar search for a/c and missiles	EW fit & pods eg Zeus EW escorts	Survivability of sensors and platforms Development of stealth technology	Expansion of battlefield, increasing capability to attack targets beyond visual range. Possibility of remote control and change of target data in flight
		Passive	Tactical measures Warning receivers Stealth		Development of automatic detection/response systems and aids for	Increased need for deception planning and action to support operations

Continued

FIG. 11.9 continued

Major EW activity	Supporting activity	Sensor category	Activity	Example equipment	Technical concern	Command and control implications
Defensive action	Sensor protection	Active	Frequency hop/agility Bi/multi static operation Narrow beam/sweep. Burst open		active/passive mode switching Signal processing and analysis methods and equipment	Increased tempo of operations, day and night, reduced time between target identification and attack growing importance of concealment from sensors
		Passive	Physical incl IR concealment Reduce transmission Movement eg mobile radar		Development of non radiating comms eg fibre optics	Need for rapid trend analysis to assist strategic, operational and tactical command decisions
Offensive action	Denial of intelligence	Active	Jamming. Screening (Chaff) False echoes, Decoys Corruption of enemy data Create electronic noise		Development of improved & disposable jammers & responders Decoy & responder design	
		Passive	Tactical measures Radio/radar silence Reduce radiation & heat Use electronic background		Provision of cool equipt & generators	
	Deceptive action	Active	False echoes & responses Decoys, inject false intel Spoof activities		Development of improved 'intelligent' radiation seeker weapons	
		Passive	Hide among radiating and heat sources		Improved active missile guidance systems	

Electronic Warfare: Command, Control, Communications and Intelligence

is for the Western European nations some catching up to be done and that for a period an increasing proportion of the defence expenditure should be devoted to command and control, communications, intelligence and electronic warfare. Allowing that the United States' 13% includes large elements for their strategic nuclear forces and world wide commitments, the equivalent figure for a nation such as the United Kingdom could be expected to be about 5 to 7% depending on how systems are defined and what is included.

Conclusion – Putting the Jigsaw Together

There are many pieces in a command and control system. It begins with national policy and strategy and extends down to where weapons are fired and military power is exerted. It includes the commanders and their staffs, their methods of working, the procedures they use, their need for information and intelligence and their equipment. The equipment may be considered as the equipment within headquarters, the sensors on which so much intelligence, target data, control systems and weapons depend and, of course, communications. As the command and control system is dependent on sensors and communications, it is inextricably involved in electronic warfare and in protection against electronic attack. It is difficult to envisage all these different items and aspects being contained within a single system. In practice, many of the items are developed, organised and controlled separately although there are marked interactions. The technology involved, however, is developing in a way which creates new links within the system, crosses organisational divisions and influences staff processes and the command and control procedures. Not many attempts have been made to examine command and control as a whole, even without the added complication of the inclusion of the human relationships, capabilities and behaviour which represents a pervasive element throughout the system.

One view of the command and control system as a whole, with the exclusion of the behavioural factors, is reproduced, by courtesy of the Marconi Command and Control Systems company, in Fig 11.10. This diagram shows notional links between the gathering of sensor data and intelligence, the processing of that data through the battle management element of command and control, down to the firing of weapons. The diagram shows sensors and reconnaissance feeding intelligence and identification data into a data analysis and correlation process. In practice, this process is widely scattered throughout the system and produces two products. The first is strategic and operational intelligence and the second is target information. There is not always a clear division between the two as, for example, much of the intelligence on distant targets serves both purposes. Both streams serve the command and control structure and the diagram shows the steps of planning, resource control and target engagement. The diagram also shows two imaginary boxes, one labelled sensor, reconnaissance and electronic warfare management, and

Weapons and Warfare

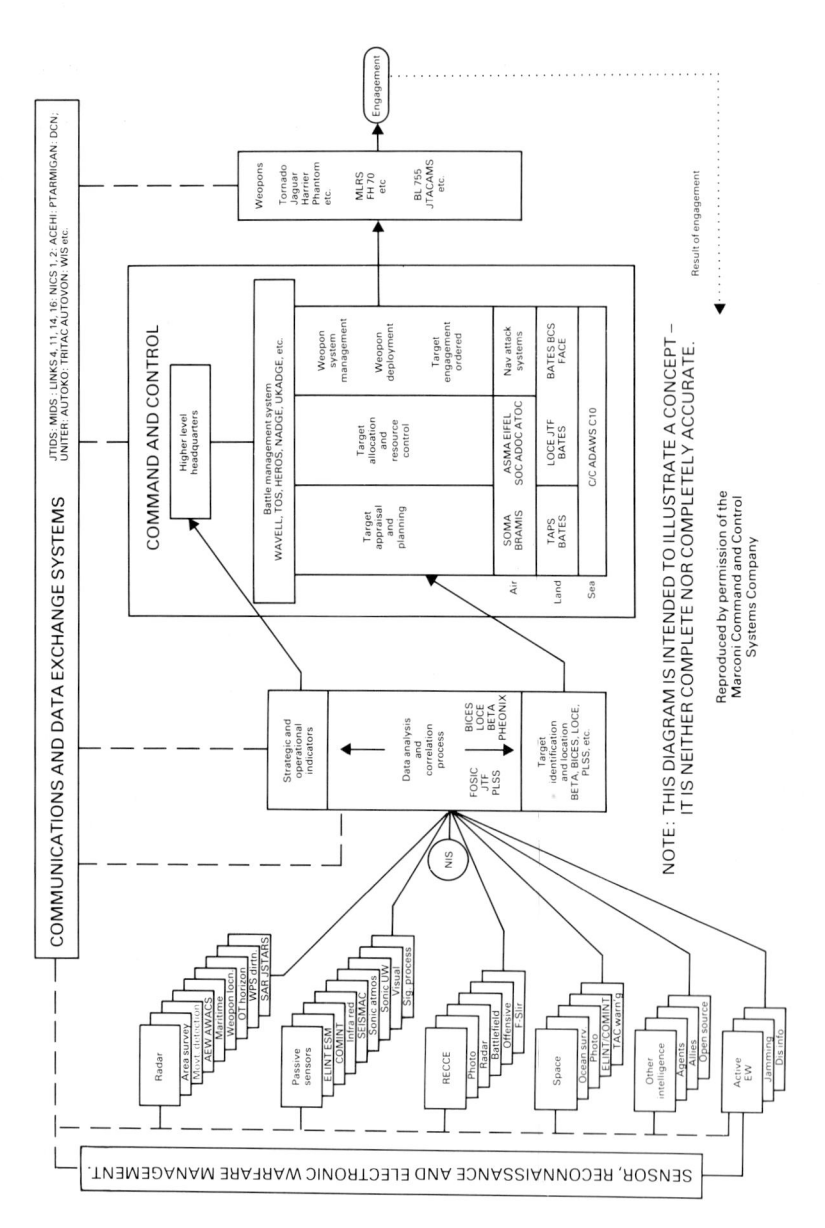

Fig 11.10 Weapons, sensors and the command system. (*Marconi Command and Control Systems Journal.*)

Electronic Warfare: Command, Control, Communications and Intelligence

the other communications and data exchange systems. Many of the items in each box are separately managed and may be incompatible but that is hardly surprising because, at least in the NATO context, they cover different national systems, and widely different purposes. For a common defence, however, there needs to be a degree of integration and mutual support. At least there needs to be a common conceptual framework to guide the fundamental choices which will have to be made in the future as more experience is gained in the use of both sensor and information technology and as such technology develops. For example, investment in research and development of the distant sensors might so improve their performance that it could become possible to reduce the complexity and cost of weapons. More weapons might be afforded but control could depend on the management of the sensors with obvious repercussions for the command and control system. Such a possibility once again underlines the need for command and control systems to be developed as a whole and in concert with the capability of the forces under command.

Looking Ahead

In the past ten years there have been very rapid developments in the technology of information handling, in the extraction of information from sensors and in the ability to distribute data and information. At the same time, the costs of computing have fallen dramatically. However, command and control systems have developed rather more slowly in their ability to exploit the developing technology. As already explained, this is partly because the human organisation and relationships are relatively slow to accept change. The squeeze on resources for defence also tends to slow down the development of command and control systems because weapons and weapons systems, tanks, ships and aircraft attract higher priorities for sound political and industrial reasons. For the future, the rate of change in the technologies serving command and control is likely to accelerate as advanced computer capabilities become more generally available. Machines such as array processors and transputers and techniques such as logic processing are bound to bring a different order in the information and intelligence services available to commanders and in the ability of headquarters to assess possibilities for action. The ability to develop plans and to manage resources must also be expected to leap ahead and to affect the operation of headquarters and tactical concepts of operations.

The battlefield is equally likely to be affected and it is not unreasonable to speculate that sensors and intelligence systems will exist which will mean that no movement of vehicles and, at shorter ranges, of people would go undetected. Weapons with very much improved accuracy and discrimination will also be available. The effect of all these developments would be that the advantage would be to those who had the capability in electronic warfare to neutralise the opposing sensors and communications. There are far reaching implications for command and control in these changes, affecting both the battlefield and the command and control system itself. Probably the most urgent need is to analyse the factors in much greater depth than is possible here and to begin the training which will be necessary to take advantage of the capabilities which are on the horizon or at least to diminish the threat.

Conclusion

Military command structures and headquarters organisations tend to change slowly in times of peace and rapidly in times of war. The present need is to maintain deterrence over coming decades as the technology of weapons, intelligence and information handling is undergoing rapid change. The essential need is to preserve deterrence into the future in the face of a growing Soviet military capability which at some point they might be tempted to use. If there were to be an attempt, current Soviet doctrine indicates that there would be an immediate and intense conventional war possibly including the use of chemical weapons. Such an attack would focus on the command and control system. A range of technical solutions are available as possibilities to safeguard parts of the command system. There is no doubt that communications and computers can be made more survivable and that more competent electronic devices can be developed. However, survival of a hard pressed defence also requires commanders and staffs with extraordinary mental stamina and endurance to cope with high stress and the flexibility to deal with very rapidly changing circumstances. These factors and the development of small dispersed headquarters, combined with an ability to switch command from one commander to another, while maintaining the momentum of operations, requires specialised and intensive training and the exploitation of very advanced information handling techniques. The skills and techniques now necessary and those which may be expected in the relatively near future require new expertise within the military. In the end, commanders must be given the support and information necessary for them to exercise their judgement and to control and influence operations. The complete system has to be, and be seen to be, robust enough to withstand the attack which could be made upon it otherwise the command and control system may erode rather than contribute to deterrence.

Introducing Chapter 12

THE most difficult question facing most defence planners concerned with policy is how to afford all that seems necessary. In the next chapter the author, with wide experience both as a purchaser and a vendor, looks at the factors involved and the options open.

12

Cost Affordable Defence

MAJOR GENERAL KEN PERKINS CB MBE DFC

It is not surprising, given the increasing sophistication described in the preceding chapters, that the escalating cost of military equipment outstrips inflation and more and more money buys less and less defence. Although each succeeding generation of equipment has a greater performance than its predecessor, the opposition is also more sophisticated so that seldom does increased capability result in economy of resources. Thus, a major preoccupation of those concerned with the higher direction of national strategy is containing costs within available budgets. Solutions, if there are any, will vary with the strategic situation and industrial capacity of the countries concerned but, for a given amount of money, all are subject to the same constraints: quality and quantity, source of supply, and procurement procedures.

Undoubtedly, defence costs have suffered from what has been called the gold-plating of equipment which arises either as a result of ambitious initial specifications or because, as projects proceed, someone decides that additional capabilities are needed or can be usefully provided. In the case of afterthoughts there is a double penalty as extra costs will arise, not only from increased capability but also from expense incurred by the delay which is inevitable when a project is modified once it is underway. The last few per cent in capability accounts for a great deal more than that proportion of the total cost and can usually be dispensed with unless crucial to survival in battle. An example springs to mind from many years ago: the contrast between the anti-tank guns which Britain deployed at the beginning of World War Two and at the end. At the beginning was the two pounder, a beautifully machined weapon which might be described in modern parlance as *user friendly* except that its shot failed to penetrate the enemy armour then in service. At the end was the seventeen pounder, conceived and produced in a hurry, treating its operators none too kindly but drilling holes unerringly through the best armour plate.

Defence planners also have options concerning the mix of weapons and, while specific situations will require a minimum of equipment for effective defence, it may be possible to achieve a satisfactory answer by employing a small amount of the highest quality together with a larger quantity of adequate but lesser quality. Thus, there are many countries who might employ a few Tornado air defence aircraft in conjunction with larger numbers of air superiority fighters such as the F5. The Tornado in addition to coping with a threat at well beyond visual range could, by means of its data links, provide early warning and direction which would enable more effective use to be made of the other aircraft. The Tornado would in effect be a force multiplier.

Defence planners may also save money by restricting the use to which equipment is put in peacetime; limiting the amount of training will reduce through life costs by reducing the frequency of replacement in addition to saving money on maintenance and fuel. However, sophisticated equipment requires its operators to be in good practice and although simulators often enable a good deal of practice to be obtained at a lesser cost, they cannot substitute for practice on the real thing. Scrimping on maintenance and training is a slippery slope, witness the rusting equipment and ill-disciplined forces in various parts of the Third World.

Aircraft, tanks and ships are but platforms for the weapons they carry and one frequent means of economy is a reduction in the amount of munitions stockpiled for war. This could turn out to be false and dangerous economy indeed, as in the event of a prolonged war it is unlikely that industry could gear itself for additional production before the supplies in hand were exhausted. However, if deterrence is the major plank in a strategy it is better to economise in the munitions which are stored out of sight than in the equipment which is visible on exercises and parades. There is also no doubt that given the choice, admirals, generals and air marshals will put priority on the visible elements of their command so that economies tend to fall automatically upon weapons rather than platforms.

Having exercised all available options concerning quality and quantity, the next step open to the defence planner in search of reduced costs concerns the procurement procedures themselves. Where the capability exists to manufacture at home, a country has the choice of acquiring equipment to its own detailed specification or buying from a foreign shelf something which approximates to the requirement. Purchasing off the shelf will usually be the least expensive option because the research and development involved will have already been paid for while, in the event of a long production run, the cost per unit of equipment will have been reduced. There may be several equipments available which fill the bill, in which case competitive tendering is likely to result in the best bargain. However, those countries which seek to maintain a widely based defence industry, either for strategic or economic reasons, will wish to buy at home and here there are varying approaches.

Attitudes towards the balance of home and worldwide sales are epitomised by the contrast in the British and French approaches to the issues involved. British specifications are invariably written with the British Armed Forces firmly in mind and, although they are looked at with a view to their attractions for the overseas market, specifications take but little account of this. The

Cost Affordable Defence

French, on the other hand, tend to build equipment with world markets firmly in view and the French Armed Forces are required to accept the result. As a result it tends to be less expensive on account of a slightly lower degree of sophistication whilst success in selling abroad creates longer production runs which further lower costs. Thus, although the French Armed Forces have accepted aircraft and tanks which are not entirely suited to their needs in Europe, their equipment costs are more manageable. Examples abound which illustrate the French practice. The most recent one, at the time of writing, is their unwillingness to participate in the future European fighter aircraft on account of its lack of export potential and going their own way with the aircraft they have called Rafale. America is in a different category to both Britain and France in that its own internal market will permit long production runs which enables it to build to the higher NATO specifications (which France does not have to bother about) and yet be able to compete worldwide, in terms of costs, with the French.

A further choice concerns the manner in which industry is organised. There are the alternatives of encouraging competition in the hope that this will result in lower prices, or rationalising industry so as to remove that element of waste inherent in competition: the design, and research and development involved in the projects that never reach production. Earlier British governments, of whatever political view, favoured rationalisation; hence large companies appeared with virtual monopolies, such as British Aerospace and the Royal Ordnance factories. Subsequently, the tendency has been towards competition, including that introduced from abroad. It has undoubtedly resulted in reduced prices and, in addition, given the government political leverage over matters not directly related to the price and quality of product, such as employment in depressed areas. However, industrial success requires lengthy production runs and competition, in the end, tends to leave only one or two firms in each major field. We see this clearly in America.

International collaboration is another option open to defence planners in their endeavours to contain costs and the Tornado, a most successful example of this, is likely to be the forerunner of similar projects. Three countries, Britain, Germany and Italy, none of whom would have been able to afford to build such an aircraft individually, jointly agreed its specification and provided the technical and financial resources required to produce what is probably, in the late 1980s, the finest interdiction and air defence aircraft now flying. Collaboration is by no means a soft option. It is not easy, in the first instance, to agree the specification as the different armed forces are likely to have different requirements; and there will be complicated matters of work and profit sharing to be agreed. Discussion, compromise and agreement entail delay and cost, but Tornado has demonstrated that collaboration makes economic sense.

Care in defining specifications, industrial competition, buying off the shelf, and international collaboration all have their part to play in managing defence

Weapons and Warfare

costs. More difficult choices arise from the wish to maintain a defence industry without an adequate sized captive market such as America has, and here are some difficult decisions. Is there a need, strategically, to be self sufficient in all aspects? If not, and it is decided to rely on off the shelf purchases from abroad for a particular sector, will the resulting loss of technology be felt in other sectors at home? As defence is now principally concerned with deterrence, what is the best balance between quality and quantity? And finally, the fundamental question which tends to be obscured by emotion, prejudice and wrongly interpreted history, what are the national interests at stake?